METEOROLOGY AND CLIMATOL(
FOR SIXTH FORMS
AND BEYOND

SOME BROKEN CUMULUS WITH A 'MACKEREL SKY' OF CIRROCUMULUS ABOVE

Crown copyright reserved

Fr.

Meteorology and Climatology
for Sixth Forms
and beyond

By

ERNEST S. GATES D.F.C. M.A. F.R.G.S.

FOURTH EDITION REVISED, ENLARGED, AND METRICATED

Nelson

Thomas Nelson and Sons Ltd
Nelson House   Mayfield Road
Walton-on-Thames   Surrey
KT12 5PL   UK

51 York Place
Edinburgh
EH1 3JD   UK

Thomas Nelson (Hong Kong) Ltd
Toppan Building 10/F
22A Westlands Road
Quarry Bay   Hong Kong

Distributed in Australia by

Thomas Nelson Australia
480 La Trobe Street
Melbourne   Victoria 3000
and in Sydney, Brisbane, Adelaide and Perth

© Ernest S. Gates 1961, 1963, 1965, 1972
First published by Harrap Ltd 1961, 1963, 1965, 1972
Reprinted 1962
Second Edition, Revised and Enlarged, 1963
Third Edition, Revised and Enlarged, 1965
Reprinted: 1966; 1968
Fourth Edition, Revised, Enlarged, and Metricated, 1972
Reprinted: 1974; 1975; 1977
Reprinted: with amendments, 1978
Reprinted: 1979; 1980; 1982

Published by Harrap Limited under ISBN 0-245-52869-5
Ninth impression of this edition published by Thomas Nelson and Sons Ltd 1984
ISBN 0-17-444239-4
NPN 9 8 7
Printed in Hong Kong

PREFACE

METEOROLOGY is often a neglected subject, and many geography teachers tend to relegate the study of this science to a minor part in the syllabus. Fundamental geographers readily appreciate the value of studying the physical characteristics of an environment before examining the ways in which man adapts himself to, or is controlled by, his surroundings, but they often accept climates and their effects with very little understanding of the physical science involved. Yet most of them would agree that meteorology, besides being a basic physical geographical study, is essentially practical and, as such, excites the interest of young students.

In this book the author has set out to develop that interest. An attempt has been made to convey the physics of meteorology to geographical students in a non-technical and non-scientific language and to stimulate their eagerness to go beyond the classroom and to carry out some practical studies in the subject. However, notice has also been taken of the requirements of certain examinations in geography. Thus, the book is intended to supply two needs. First, it explains simply and concisely the basic principles of meteorology and climatology; second, it equips students with all the information necessary for answering the questions on these subjects which are to be found in many geography papers of examination boards for the General Certificate of Education. A useful collection of typical questions (which will provide the geography teacher with a comprehensive selection of essay topics) is therefore included at the end of the book.

A short bibliography lists those works which will enable students most satisfactorily to enlarge their knowledge of the material presented in this book. The extent of the author's indebtedness for information is such that it would be impossible to make specific acknowledgments, but recognition must be made here of the way in which he was able to draw freely upon the works and publications of the Meteorological Office, and grateful thanks are extended to its Director-General for permission to use Crown Copyright photographs.

E. S. GATES

March 1960

NOTE TO THE SECOND EDITION

THE reprinting of this book allows me to make useful alterations to the text and certain diagrams, to enlarge the bibliography, and to correct errors to which critics have drawn my attention. Additional appendices have been included: temperature and linear conversion tables have been listed, and it has been possible to tabulate climatic statistics for many stations throughout the world. For ease of reference the stations are tabulated alphabetically by continents, and, in conformity with new procedures, the figures are given in Centigrade and millimetres instead of in Fahrenheit and inches.

E. S. G.

CRANWELL
Spring 1963

NOTE TO THE THIRD EDITION

ANOTHER reprinting of the text has once again permitted me to fulfil the requests and suggestions of helpful critics. In addition to correcting certain statistical errors, I have added several new sections and completely rewritten the final chapter. New theories about thunder-cloud formation have been described, a detailed section on tropical revolving storms has been included in Chapter 10, and reference has been made to the study of microclimatology. The influences of climate on organic life and everyday activities justify greater prominence in any book on climatology, and therefore I have largely remoulded Chapter 20 to consider more fully the implications of climate and life.

Spring 1965   E. S. G.

NOTE TO THE FOURTH EDITION

THE rapid progress in space technology during the past few years, and the successful development of satellites for meteorological and atmospheric investigation, has made it necessary to revise certain sections of the text and to include a completely new chapter (Chapter 13) on weather observation from space. Several extra diagrams and photographs have been incorporated to support the new text, and a new Appendix lists some of the weather satellites so far launched by the Americans and Russians. All units have been rationalized according to the Système International d'Unités.

Spring 1972   E. S. G.

CONTENTS

Part One

METEOROLOGY

CHAPTER   PAGE

1. What is Weather?   15
2. The Atmosphere   26
3. The Temperature of the Atmosphere   36
4. Atmospheric Pressure and its Relation to Winds   53
5. Water Vapour in the Atmosphere   68
6. Clouds and Cloud Formation   74
7. The Principle of Fog Formation   91
8. Thunderstorms and Optical Effects   96
9. Ice in the Atmosphere   105
10. Air Masses and their Characteristics   108
11. The Meteorology of the Upper Atmosphere   130
12. Weather Forecasting and Weather Maps   136
13. Weather Watchers in Space   146

APPENDICES

I. Summary of Cloud Characteristics   165
II. Properties of Main Air Masses around Great Britain   166
III. Summary of Frontal Characteristics   167
IV. Summary of Fog Characteristics   168
V. Short Glossary of Meteorological Terms   169
VI. Description of Code Figures for Present Weather   172
VII. Weather Satellites launched up to July 1975   174

Part Two

CLIMATOLOGY

14. General Atmospheric Circulation and its Relation to World Climates   176
15. The Classification of World Climates   191
16. The Tropical Rain Climates   196
17. The Desert Climates   207
18. The Temperate Climates   212
19. Polar and Mountain Climates   220
20. Weather, Climate, and Life   226
21. Climatic Changes   241

CONTENTS

APPENDICES

	PAGE
I. Specimen Questions on Meteorology and Climatology	251
II. Metric Data Conversion Tables	255
III. Climatic Data for Selected Stations throughout the World	257
BIBLIOGRAPHY	289
INDEX	291

ILLUSTRATIONS

PLATES IN HALF-TONE

PLATE   PAGE

Some broken cumulus with a 'mackerel sky' of cirrocumulus above   *frontispiece*

I. A layer of stratocumulus, with cumulus building up within it   87

II. An altocumulus layer seen from 7500 metres   88

III. A layer of stratocumulus at 450 metres   88

IV. Fair-weather cumulus   99

V. A large cumulonimbus cloud showing the anvil cirrus   99

VI. Altocumulus castellatus from above   100

VII. An extensive layer of altocumulus   125

VIII. Cirrocumulus and high altocumulus   126

IX. ESSA 7 satellite   151

X. Sandstorm across the Sahara   152

XI. Track of Hurricane Camille, August 1969   157

XII. A cyclonic storm near Hawaii from Apollo 9   158

XIII. American weather from ESSA satellite, 22 October 1968   161

MAPS AND DIAGRAMS

FIGURE   PAGE

1. The mercury barometer   17

2. The aneroid barometer   18

3. The mercury thermometer   19

4. Maximum thermometers   19

5. The minimum thermometer   20

6. Dry- and wet-bulb thermometers   21

7. The standard rain-gauge   23

8. A sunshine recorder   24

9. The zones of the atmosphere   29

10. How molecules of air control atmospheric pressure   32

11. Atmospheric-pressure patterns   34

12. A high-pressure system   34

13. A low-pressure system   34

14. A secondary depression   35

15. A trough of low pressure   35

16. A ridge of high pressure   35

17. A col   35

18. Solar radiation and the atmosphere   37

19. The methods by which air is heated   38

FIGURE PAGE

20. The distribution of upper-air temperatures 40
21. A graph to illustrate the adiabatic cooling of rising air 42
22. A graph to illustrate a temperature inversion 43
23. World distribution of isotherms in January (in ° C) 44–45
24. World distribution of isotherms in July (in ° C) 46–47
25. Temperature anomalies in January (in ° C) 48–49
26. Temperature anomalies in July (in ° C) 50–51
27. A geostrophic wind scale 55
28. The world distribution of pressure and winds in January 56–57
29. The world distribution of pressure and winds in July 58–59
30. Sea breezes 61
31. Land breezes 61
32. Anabatic winds 62
33. Katabatic winds 62
34. The föhn wind 63
35. Pressure differences in the upper atmosphere 64
36. Upper-level isobars, resulting from pressure differences 65
37. Resultant wind produced by resolving the Thermal and Isobaric wind at 600 metres 65
38. Graph showing moisture content plotted against temperature in the air 71
39. Turbulence cloud 74
40. Orographic cloud 75
41. Convection cloud 75
42. Frontal cloud 76
43. A comparison between stable and unstable air conditions 78
44. Principle of cloud formation 79
45. Graph showing how cloud heights, types, and thickness may be calculated 80
46. A reproduction of a tephigram 81
47. A comparison between graphs. One shows unstable conditions, the other illustrates stable conditions 82
48. Graph to illustrate the effect of the föhn wind 84
49. (a) Convection cloud forming as a result of heating from the surface 86
    (b) Convection cloud forming where air moves from high to low latitudes 86
50. Radiation fog 92
51. Advection fog 93
52. Stages in the development of the thunder cell 98
53. Summer-heat thunderstorms over N.W. Europe 101
54. The physics of rainbows 103
55. The mirage 104
56. A diagram to show the difference between a warm and cold front 108
57. Polar maritime air over Britain 110

FIGURE   PAGE

58. Polar continental air over Britain — 110
59. Tropical continental air over Britain — 111
60. Tropical maritime air over Britain — 111
61. The position of the polar front in the North Atlantic—winter and summer — 112
62. The position of the intertropical front—January — 113
63. The position of the intertropical front—July — 113
64. The growth of a polar frontal depression — 115
65. A typical polar frontal depression and the rain belts associated with it — 116
66. A cross-section through a depression — 117
67. Sections through warm fronts — 118
68. Sections through cold fronts — 119
69. The two forms which occlusions may take — 120
70. A cross-section of the intertropical front — 122–123
71. The regions and tracks of tropical storms — 124
72. The paths of tropical storms in the West Indies and the South China Seas — 128
73. The structure of a hurricane — 129
74. A contour chart for 300 millibars, showing a jet stream — 132
75. Jet streams near fronts — 133
76. A vertical cross-section of a jet stream — 134
77. An example of a synoptic chart — 138
78. Code figures and symbols for various weather elements — 140
79. List of present weather symbols — 142
80. The Station Model — 143
81. Station model for illustrated code groups — 144
82. Wind-speed symbols on wind arrow — 144
83. Space-oriented TIROS satellite — 148
84. "Cartwheel" TIROS satellite — 149
85. NIMBUS satellite with sun-oriented paddles carrying solar cells — 150
86. ITOS I – schematic diagram — 156
87. Geo-stationary Operational Environmental Satellite—GOES I—to be placed near the equator at 100° W — 160
88. Synoptic chart of American weather for 22 October 1968 — 162
89. Distribution of winds and general atmospheric circulation on a non-rotating earth of uniform surface — 177
90. Distribution of pressures and winds on a rotating earth of uniform surface — 177
91. Layout of pressures and winds on a non-homogeneous earth's surface — 180
92. Duration of frost-free periods — 182
93. Cross-section from Pole to Pole showing Horse Latitudes and Doldrums — 183
94. The distribution of annual world rainfall — 185
95. Seasonal distribution of rainfall — 186

FIGURE   PAGE

 96. The ocean currents of the world   189

 97. A simplified version of Köppen's classification of world climates   192

 98. A simplified distribution of world climates   194

 99. The annual distribution of rainfall in tropical latitudes   197

100. Equatorial conditions at Douala, Cameroons   198

101. Equatorial conditions at Manáus, Brazil   198

102. Equatorial conditions at Pontianak, Java   200

103. Tropical climate of Saigon, South Viet Nam   200

104. Tropical climate at Bathurst, Gambia   202

105. Tropical climate at Darwin, Australia   202

106. The north-east monsoon   203

107. The south-west monsoon   203

108. The tropical monsoon at Bombay, India   204

109. The temperate monsoon at Tokyo, Japan   204

110. The warm east-coast climate of New Orleans, Louisiana   205

111. The low-latitude desert station of In Salah, Algeria   209

112. The low-latitude desert and western littoral station of Port Nolloth, South Africa   209

113. The mid-latitude desert climate of Astrakhan, U.S.S.R.   210

114. The Mediterranean climate of Rome, Italy   214

115. The West European conditions of Vancouver, British Columbia   214

116. The cold temperate climate of Whitehorse, Yukon   217

117. The cool east-coast conditions of Boston, Massachusetts   217

118. The continental climate of Edmonton, Alberta   218

119. The Tundra climate: Spitsbergen   222

120. Ice-cap climate: McMurdo Sound, Antarctica   222

121. Illustration to show how vegetation, and hence climate, changes as elevation increases on a tropical mountain   224

122. Illustration to show how vegetation, and hence climate, changes as elevation increases on a temperate mountain   225

123. Map to show distribution of natural vegetation   232

124. Soil profiles of a podsol and chernozem   233

125. The world distribution of soils   234

TABLES

TABLE		PAGE
1.	Barometric pressure conversion table	19
2.	The relation between compass points and degrees from true north	22
3.	The Beaufort Scale of Wind Force	22
4.	The percentage composition of dry air	27
5.	The International Standard Atmosphere	31
6.	Height difference in feet corresponding with a fall in pressure of one millibar	33
7.	The insolation received at the limit of the atmosphere	36
8.	Temperature at the earth's surface, assuming that there is no atmosphere	37
9.	The values of the moisture content at saturation for given temperatures	69
10.	Temperature as a controlling factor in relative humidities	70
11.	The size of water droplets and their terminal velocities	73
12.	Falls in temperature for adiabatic pressure changes	77
13.	A cloud classification table	89
14.	Height of the Tropopause in various latitudes	131
15.	Temperature contrasts for stations on east and west coasts in similar tropical and sub-tropical latitudes	188
16.	Variations in rainfall amounts at desert stations	208
17.	The intensity of insolation at different elevations of the sun	221
18.	Calculated insolation reaching the earth	221
19.	The geological time scale	242–243
20.	The correlation of climates and the cultures of man from Pleistocene times	248–249
21.	Climatic fluctuations in Britain during the historic period	250

PART ONE

Meteorology

Chapter 1

WHAT IS WEATHER?

A DEFINITION OF WEATHER

IT is probably true to say that the easiest introductory conversation for the average Briton concerns the past, present, or future conditions of the atmosphere. His barber, while tucking a cover into his collar, comments on the changeability of these conditions; his grocer or baker passes the time of day with a criticism of the conditions, and perhaps expresses a hope for a fine weekend for the local soccer fixtures; and he himself may earnestly desire a sunny Saturday afternoon in order that he will not require a raincoat while watching the village cricket match. Almost daily we are conscious of our concern for the atmospheric conditions and their vagaries, and we investigate the newspaper, or tune into the B.B.C. at the relevant times, in order to ascertain what qualified observers can tell us about these changes and what are the prospects for the coming few hours.

At a few minutes to eight each morning a B.B.C. announcer utters his well-known remark, "Here is the weather forecast for the next twelve hours," and then follows a description of the present atmospheric conditions for given areas, together with predictions for the remainder of that particular day. Following the main television news on B.B.C. 1 at 5.40 p.m. each evening a qualified meteorologist explains the current weather as displayed on a map. Then he presents the details of a second chart showing the conditions that he forecasts for the British Isles during the next day. The weather is of immediate concern to us all, and whether it be the housewife troubled with the weekly wash, the fisherman with his daily voyage to the lobster-pots, or the schoolboy and his concern for afternoon games, every one of us at some time feels the need for knowing something of the probable conditions of the atmosphere. Always we turn to the trained meteorologist, who makes a special study of the sum total of these atmospheric conditions, and we rely upon his skilled interpretation of them and upon his estimation of the future conditions. But the weather is available for anyone to study, and this book attempts to explain simply the world's atmosphere and its conditions, and to initiate the reader into the science of weather forecasting.

'Weather' has been described as the sum total of the atmospheric conditions for any place for a short period of time. The elements thus comprised under weather include atmospheric temperatures, pressures, winds, humidity, and precipitation. These and the other elements must be recorded by means of certain instruments or observations so that they may be made available for analysis, and thus allow the meteorologist to predict future conditions of the weather.

The Elements of Weather

The meteorologist attempts to obtain as much factual information about atmospheric elements as possible, and, while some facts are of greater importance than others, they all contribute something towards his picture of the weather. The following list indicates those conditions of the atmosphere which are recorded by the meteorologist, so producing for him an exact vision of the present weather for any given place:

1. Atmospheric pressure and its tendency.
2. Air temperature.
3. Maximum, minimum, and grass minimum temperatures.
4. Relative humidity.
5. Wind direction and speed.
6. Cloud types and amounts.
7. Visibility.
8. Weather characteristics (past and present).
9. The state of the ground.
10. Precipitation.
11. Sunshine.

Where possible the meteorologist makes observations of upper-air characteristics— that is, winds and air temperatures.

The Recording Apparatus used by the Meteorologist

Many of the weather elements to be observed can be examined visually. Cloud types and their amounts may be assessed by simply observing the heavens, visibility can be judged by reference to known landmarks, and weather characteristics can be observed directly. Pressure, temperatures, humidity, and rainfall must be recorded by means of instruments, and a short outline of the features of the main recording apparatus will now be given.

The Measurement of Pressure

A full discussion of the importance of atmospheric pressure and its relation to winds will be given in Chapters 2 and 4. In order to appreciate the methods of measurement it is adequate to assume that the atmosphere is a fluid, and may be looked upon as an ocean of air surrounding the earth. This exerts a pressure due to the head of air in the same way as water exerts a pressure caused by the weight of fluid above. Atmospheric pressure is measured by balancing it against a column of mercury. The principle may be comprehended from the experiment shown in Fig. 1. A glass tube about one metre long and closed at one end is completely filled with mercury. The open end is closed, and the tube immersed in a bath of mercury. When the end of the tube is opened below the surface of the mercury in the bowl and the tube is held vertically, the upper level of the mercury in the tube will adjust itself until its height is about 760 mm above the level in the bowl. The space above the mercury in the tube is a vacuum, and the column is supported by the air-pressure outside. The height of this mercury column is therefore a measure of the air-pressure.

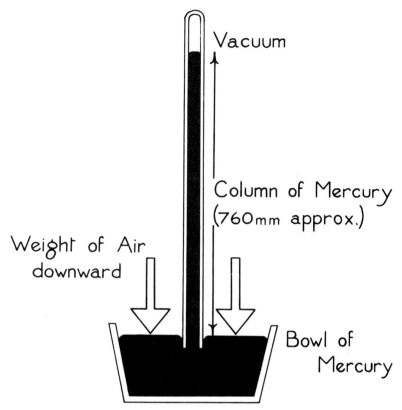

Vacuum

Column of Mercury
(760mm approx.)

Weight of Air
downward

Bowl of
Mercury

Weight of mercury column is same as weight of a
column of air having same cross-sectional area as
glass tube.

Average pressure - 100 kN/m²

FIG. 1. THE MERCURY BAROMETER

The pressure-recording instrument is called a 'barometer,' and the mercury type is the one usually employed for accurate measurement. With this instrument, however, it is not possible to examine changes in atmospheric pressure as they occur, and the aneroid barometer and barograph (Fig. 2) are used for this purpose. The apparatus consists of an airtight metal box which is almost exhausted of air. The box responds to changes in pressure by expanding when the pressure falls and collapsing slightly when the pressure increases. These movements are geared in such a way that they are communicated to a pointer on a dial, or to a pen which draws a trace on a chart mounted on a revolving drum. All variations in pressure during any period are traced on the chart, and from these recordings it is possible to examine the barometric tendency—that is, the change in pressure which has taken place during the preceding hours. The nature of the change, known as the 'characteristic,' may be recorded as "steady," "rising," or "falling."

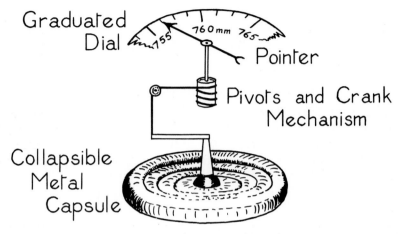

FIG. 2. THE ANEROID BAROMETER

Units for Pressure-measurement. The unit used for measuring air-pressure was derived from the mercury barometer, and the length of the column of mercury was measured either in inches or millimetres. The weight of the column of mercury exactly balances the weight of the column of air, and, as the weight of the mercury column will depend upon density and the force of gravity, no precise meaning can be given to a pressure expressed as 760 mm, because both factors are variables. Density depends upon temperature, while the force of gravity varies all over the earth's surface. For scientific accuracy, the 'millibar' has been adopted as a unit of pressure. To the scientist, pressure is force per unit area. The basic unit of force is the 'dyne'—that is, the force required to produce an acceleration of one centimetre per second per second in a mass of one gramme. The force of gravity acting upon one gramme is 981 dynes. The natural unit of pressure is therefore one dyne per square centimetre. This is too small for convenience when measuring atmospheric pressure, and so the 'bar' is used, since it contains one million dynes per square centimetre and is approximately the average sea-level pressure. The millibar—or, a thousand dynes per square centimetre—is the unit commonly used; it is a scientific measurement and is quite independent of variable factors, such as density and the force of gravity. Table 1 shows the relationship between barometric pressure in millimetres with those recorded in millibars.

$$1000 \text{ millibars} = 750 \cdot 1 \text{ millimetres}$$

Note The International System of Units uses the 'newton' as the coherent unit of force. One newton is the force required to produce an acceleration of one metre per second per second in a mass of one kilogramme. Meteorologists continue to use the millibar as the basic unit of atmospheric pressure.

$$1 \text{ millibar} = 10^2 \text{ N/m}^2$$

TABLE 1.—BAROMETRIC PRESSURE CONVERSION TABLE

Mm	Mb	Mm	Mb	Mm	Mb
710	947	735	981	760	1014
715	954	740	987	765	1021
720	961	745	994	770	1027
725	967	750	1001	775	1034
730	974	755	1007	780	1041

The Measurement of Temperature

The usual type of recording instrument is the 'mercury-in-glass' pattern of thermometer (Fig. 3). Changes of temperature are registered by changes in the length of a mercury thread in a glass capillary tube. An increase in the temperature causes expansion of the mercury up the tube, while a decrease in temperature brings about a contraction of the mercury thread down the tube.

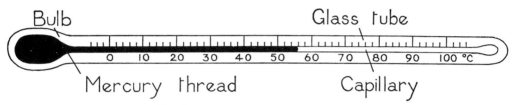

FIG. 3. THE MERCURY THERMOMETER

Maximum temperatures can be recorded by a thermometer in which the mercury thread pushes along the capillary tube a small metal index which remains at the highest temperature attained. Another type of maximum thermometer contains a constriction near the bulb. As the temperature rises the mercury is forced past the

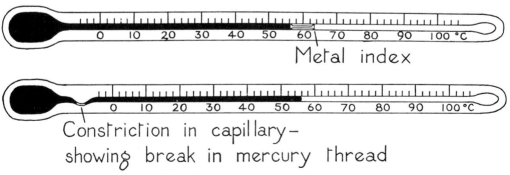

FIG. 4. MAXIMUM THERMOMETERS

constriction, but as it falls the thread breaks at the constriction, and the thermometer continues to show the highest temperature attained. (See Fig. 4.)

Minimum thermometers are usually of the 'spirit-in-glass' pattern (Fig. 5), where a small metal index is suspended inside the column of spirit. As the temperature falls, and the alcohol thread moves backward along the tube, the index is dragged towards the bulb by the meniscus—that is, the curved upper surface of the liquid in the tube. The surface tension is sufficient to prevent the break-through of the meniscus

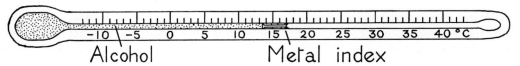

Alcohol   Metal index

FIG. 5. THE MINIMUM THERMOMETER

by the index, and when the temperature increases again the index remains at the lowest position attained.

Maximum and minimum thermometers must be set after each reading. The types of thermometer containing metal indices can readily be reset by means of a magnet, and each index can be drawn along the capillary tube. With the constriction type of thermometer the broken column of mercury is made to rejoin the main column by a vigorous shaking of the instrument.

Ordinary 'mercury-in-glass' thermometers do not provide a continuous record of temperature; for this purpose a thermograph is needed. This instrument employs the bimetallic-strip principle. The differential expansion of two metals with variations in temperature causes the metal strip to bend. The movement of the strip is conveyed by means of a lever-and-crank mechanism to a recording pen.

Scales of Temperature. Temperature may be expressed in degrees on one of the following scales:

Celsius (° *C*). The freezing- and boiling-points of water are conveniently defined as 0° and 100° respectively. This scale has been adopted internationally for the scientific recording of temperature, and it is used by all meteorological organizations outside the U.S.A. and Eire.

Fahrenheit (° *F*). On this scale the freezing-point of water is 32° and the boiling-point 212°. Until 1962 this scale was used for meteorological reports in Britain.

Réaumur (° *R*). The freezing-point of water is registered at 0°, and the boiling-point at 80°. Certain Continental countries use this scale, but it is never used in meteorology.

Kelvin (° *K*). This is purely a scientific scale on which the degree is of the same size as the Celsius degree, but the zero is taken to be —273° C. The freezing-point of water is therefore 273 K and the boiling-point 373 K.

The rules for the conversion of temperature scales should be noted:

1. To convert Celsius to Fahrenheit, multiply by $\frac{9}{5}$ and then add 32.
2. To convert Fahrenheit to Celsius, subtract 32 and then multiply by $\frac{5}{9}$.

Temperature Observations. Numerous recordings are made for meteorological purposes, but the following are the ones usually made when recording the temperatures at stations:

1. The ordinary air, or 'dry-bulb' temperature.
2. The 'wet-bulb' temperature. This is used in humidity determination.

3. The day maximum and minimum temperatures.
4. The minimum night temperature near the ground—the 'grass minimum.'

The Measurement of Humidity

Water vapour in the atmosphere will be considered in greater detail in Chapter 5. Though self-recording instruments are available, it is usual, for accurate meteorological records, to assess the amount of water vapour in the air indirectly. The type of instrument normally used is the wet- and dry-bulb hygrometer, known as the psychrometer. The apparatus consists essentially of two thermometers (Fig. 6). One

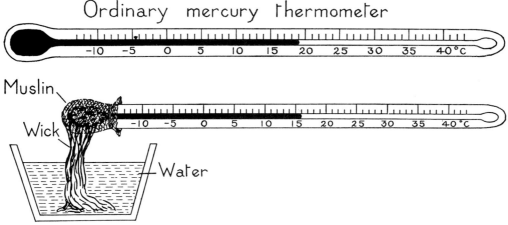

FIG. 6. DRY- AND WET-BULB THERMOMETERS

is an ordinary mercury thermometer, which gives the direct reading of the air-temperature; the other is also an ordinary mercury thermometer, but its bulb is covered with a single layer of thin muslin, which is kept moist by means of a wick, whose end is immersed in a small container of water.

The instrument depends upon evaporation and the consequent cooling effect upon the wet bulb. When the air is dry evaporation from the muslin will cause considerable cooling, and the wet-bulb thermometer will read lower than the dry-bulb part of the instrument. The relationship between humidity and the wet- and dry-bulb temperatures is complicated, and will be examined more closely in Chapter 5. It is sufficient to state here that the humidity value can be calculated by reference to tables, once the two thermometer readings have been registered.

The Measurement of Wind Speed and Wind Direction

Wind is simply air in motion, and it must be expressed in terms of both speed and direction. The direction is always given as that from which the wind is blowing, and may be expressed in points of the compass or in degrees from true north. The relationship between compass points and degrees is shown in Table 2.

The speed of the wind is given in any convenient unit. In those countries adopting the Système International d'Unités (SI Units) the unit of speed is the metre per second. In air and sea navigation at present the knot, or the sea mile per hour, will continue to be used.

TABLE 2.—THE RELATIONSHIP BETWEEN COMPASS POINTS AND DEGREES FROM TRUE NORTH

Compass points	N.	N.N.E.	N.E.	E.N.E.	E.	E.S.E.	S.E.	S.S.E.
Degrees	000	022½	045	067½	090	112½	135	157½

Compass points	S.	S.S.W.	S.W.	W.S.W.	W.	W.N.W.	N.W.	N.N.W.
Degrees	180	202½	225	247½	270	292½	315	337½

N.B. Only the sixteen important compass points have been listed.

The simplest instrument for measuring the direction of the wind is the weather-vane. Even the meteorological instrument is but a refinement of this: electrical apparatus has been attached to the weather-vane, and the wind direction is indicated on a dial in the meteorological office. Wind speeds can be estimated by using a numerical scale, devised originally by one Admiral Beaufort and named after him. This scale (see Table 3) ranges from 0 to 12, each number corresponding with a term which describes wind effects upon ships and land features.

TABLE 3.—THE BEAUFORT SCALE OF WIND FORCE

BEAUFORT NUMBER	DESCRIPTIVE TITLE	EFFECT ON LAND FEATURES	RANGES OF SPEED, IN M/S
0	Calm	Smoke rises vertically	Less than 0·3
1	Light air	Direction shown by smoke but not wind-vanes	0·3–1·5
2	Light breeze	Wind felt on face; leaves rustle; vane moved	1·6–3·3
3	Gentle breeze	Leaves and twigs in constant motion	3·4–5·4
4	Moderate breeze	Raises dust and paper; small branches moved	5·5–7·9
5	Fresh breeze	Small trees begin to sway	8·0–10·7
6	Strong breeze	Large branches in motion; whistling in telephone-wires	10·8–13·8
7	Moderate gale	Whole trees in motion	13·9–17·1
8	Fresh gale	Breaks twigs off trees	17·2–20·7
9	Strong gale	Slight structural damage to roofs, etc.	20·8–24·4
10	Whole gale	Trees uprooted; considerable structural damage	24·5–28·4
11	Storm	Widespread damage	28·5–33·5
12	Hurricane	—	Above 33·5

Instruments for measuring wind speeds are called anemometers. They are based upon the windmill principle, the speed of rotation of blades or cups being related directly to the speed of the wind. Refinements have now been incorporated, and speeds can be read off from dials attached to the anemometer, or, by the use of electrical contacts, remote readings can be registered in the meteorological office, so overcoming the difficult task of counting revolutions of the cups or reading dials at great distances. Upper winds are more difficult to record; the examination of cloud movements and the study of the behaviour of balloons are the two most important methods used in meteorology. In recent years radar devices have been evolved for the tracking of balloons, and wind speeds and wind directions can be ascertained for heights up to 15 kilometres.

The Measurement of Rainfall

The rain-gauge is essentially a funnel of standard diameter which collects the rain falling into it (Fig. 7). The rainwater collected is poured into a measuring cylinder

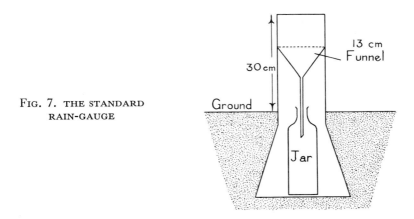

FIG. 7. THE STANDARD
RAIN-GAUGE

graduated to read millimetres of rainfall. The meteorological standards for the gauge are as follows:

1. The diameter of the funnel is 13 centimetres.
2. The height of the funnel above ground-level is 30 centimetres.

More elaborate instruments are now in use, and self-recording apparatus enables a more informative register of rainfall to be kept.

Any hail, sleet, or snow should be melted before measurement of precipitation amounts is made. As a rough approximation, 30 cm of snow is equal to 30 mm of rain; but the density of snow will vary, and consequently the figure quoted will also change.

The Measurement of Sunshine

Bright sunshine is recorded by means of the Campbell–Stokes apparatus (Fig. 8). A spherical glass lens concentrates the rays of the sun upon a card, and a trace is burnt into the paper as the sun moves across the sky; if the sun shines intermittently the line trace is broken, and the combined lengths of all the sections of the trace give a direct measure of the duration of sunshine.

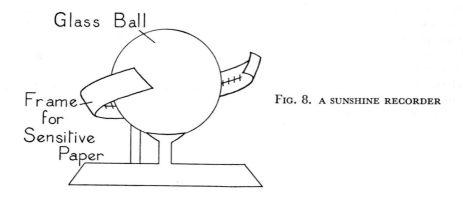

FIG. 8. A SUNSHINE RECORDER

THE WEATHER FORECAST

The instruments and records mentioned in the previous section enable the meteorologist to examine the immediate present and past weather conditions. Nevertheless, his aim is to produce a prediction of future conditions, and we must ask ourselves how he can assess future weather from the examination of past and present conditions.

At five minutes to eight on Tuesday, the 27th April, 1971, a qualified meteorologist issued the daily weather forecast on the B.B.C. Radio 4 programme along the following lines:

The general situation was described. Pressure was rising steadily and a ridge of high pressure extended from the north-west towards south and west Britain. Weak disturbances were affecting the northern and eastern areas. In Scotland the day would be cloudy in the north and east, but bright in the south and west. Showers of rain, sleet, or even snow could be expected, especially over the mountains. Wales would have a dry, sunny day with isolated snow showers over the high ground. In England the patchy mist in the central Midlands and eastern counties would disperse to give a dry and mainly sunny day. In the south and west of England there would be long sunny periods. The temperatures would be below average everywhere, and it would continue to be cold with frost at night.

Long experience has enabled the meteorologist to produce this forecast; he has been examining the weather conditions for the British Isles over a number of years, and, together with his appreciation of the physical and scientific principles relating to the atmosphere, these facts enable him to predict the future developments of the weather situation. An examination of the past weather will naturally depend upon the experiences of the meteorologist, and it is unlikely that the young student of the subject will have much practical knowledge. It is, however, possible for him to obtain an understanding of the scientific problems involved; he can familiarize himself with the terms used in forecasting and with the jargon employed by the meteorologist.

The surface of the earth and the surrounding atmosphere are the laboratory of the meteorologist, and it is here that nature continually performs experiments well beyond the scope of humans. But fundamentally these experiments are similar to those carried out by the physicist, and if we can obtain a thorough understanding of the principles of physics we lay the foundations upon which to build our knowledge of the atmosphere. The observations taken by the meteorologist can be explained by the physicist, and it is hoped that the following chapters will enable the student of meteorology to understand more about the atmosphere that surrounds him and to assimilate the facts which are important to him, while at the same time appreciating the underlying scientific principles.

Chapter 2

THE ATMOSPHERE

THE CONSTITUENTS OF THE ATMOSPHERE

THE atmosphere may be divided into two main groups of constituents:

1. Permanent constituents:
   - (*a*) Nitrogen—78 per cent. by volume.
   - (*b*) Oxygen—21 per cent. by volume.
   - (*c*) Inert gases—1 per cent. by volume.

2. Variable constituents:
   - (*a*) Solid.
   - (*b*) Liquid.
   - (*c*) Gaseous.

The solid constituents may consist of a variety of particles, but in the main they are composed of dust, smoke, salt, or volcanic ash. Dust may get into the atmosphere from the earth's deserts and arid areas, and samples of air may contain as many as 100 000 particles per cubic centimetre. Volcanic dust gets into the upper atmosphere as a result of explosions and eruptions, and its consequent effects may last several years. For example, brilliant sunsets were recorded for some years after the Krakatoa eruption of 1883. Salt in the atmosphere is the result of the evaporation of sea spray. Smoke is by far the most important solid content of the earth's atmosphere. Britain and its great industrial areas afford practical proof of this solid content. Theoretically, Manchester should receive an annual amount of sun of 1400 hours. In practice, however, despite the Clean Air Acts, the city receives about 1000 hours annually, and this is in the main relatively weak.

The solid particles of the atmosphere produce varieties of optical effects, and the transparency of the atmosphere depends upon these minute specks of solid material. The short waves of light from the sun are scattered by the particles, and, if the particles are large enough, there is total reflection of light, and the sky appears milky in colour instead of blue. When the sun is at a low angle both short and long waves are scattered, and the colour of the sky is influenced only by the red waves, so producing the colours associated with sunsets. At very great heights, where the dust content is small, the blue colour is very much intensified and may even have a violet hue.

The only liquid likely to be present in the earth's atmosphere is water, which is usually in liquid form when condensed from water vapour. Of the variable gaseous constituents water vapour is the most important. Nowhere in the world is the atmosphere completely dry, and even in the Sahara Desert there is a small percentage of water vapour present in the air. The water constituent of the atmosphere is confined to the troposphere—that is, to the first 11 kilometres at the Poles and the first 16 kilometres at the equator.

TABLE 4.—THE PERCENTAGE COMPOSITION OF DRY AIR

Gas	By Volume	By Weight
Nitrogen	78·03	75·48
Oxygen	20·99	23·18
Argon	0·94	1·29
Carbon dioxide	0·03	0·045
Hydrogen		
Neon		
Helium	Traces only, being less than 0·001 per cent.	
Krypton		
Xenon		

The proportions of the gases of which dry air is composed (see Table 4) do not concern the meteorologist, and he may assume that dry air is a uniform gas, obeying the same physical laws as any other gas. The only difference is that air is mixed in varying proportions with another gas, water vapour, the presence of which greatly affects the behaviour of the atmosphere as a whole.

The atmosphere has no clear-cut upper limit; it gradually decreases in density, and in the highest levels becomes extremely tenuous. Before the introduction of rockets and space satellites the methods used to study the earth's atmosphere were indirect and limited in scope. After more than 20 years of space research considerable descriptive evidence of the atmosphere is now available. Man has long been aware that there is still sufficient air at great altitudes to obstruct the movement of meteors. By friction due to the meteor passing through atmospheric gases, sufficient heat is generated to make the solid visible as a white-hot shooting star.

In recent years this has been of more direct concern to astronauts returning to earth. The space vehicle, re-entering the denser layers of the atmosphere and being subjected to forces eight times that of gravity, has to dissipate both its kinetic and potential energy. This energy appears as thermal energy, and the air surrounding the space capsule is heated considerably, some of this heat being transferred to the vehicle's surface. To protect the personnel inside the American Apollo spacecraft a thermal shield (constructed of a mixture of asbestos, fibre-glass, and nylon) is attached to the forward portion of the craft. On entering the denser atmospheric layers at about 80 kilometres altitude, the heat shield reaches 1650° C from the frictional effects of the air particles. The shock wave only a couple of metres from the astronauts' backs incandesces with a temperature of 28 000° C, nearly five times that of the sun's surface.

The meteorologist takes the entire atmosphere as being within his field, but for practical purposes he tends to concentrate upon the first 13 or 14 kilometres, which contain more than 85 per cent of the air. Nevertheless, space research has presented him with considerable amounts of important scientific information about the atmosphere at much greater altitudes. Today the meteorologist is aware that what is happening in the space environment immediately surrounding the earth materially affects the lower levels of the atmosphere. Consequently, he is becoming more and more interested in the data supplied regularly by weather satellites. See Chapter 13.

THE HOMOSPHERE

As long as the permanent constituents—nitrogen, oxygen, and inert gases—are maintained in the same proportions by circulation, the atmosphere is known as the *homosphere*. Up to a height of 80 kilometres the mixing of the gases is perfect. In the homosphere three different regions exist, each separated by a boundary zone:

1. The lowest section, called the 'troposphere'.
2. A boundary zone, named the 'tropopause'.
3. A second region, called the 'stratosphere'.
4. A further boundary zone, the 'stratopause'.
5. The third layer, called the 'mesosphere'.

The Troposphere. This was a term invented by Teisserenc de Bort for the lower layer of the atmosphere, and applies to the region in which the meteorologists are continually searching to make their daily forecasts. Here temperature falls with increasing height, sometimes as low as −80° C around the equator, up to a certain altitude. It is that zone in which all the water present in the atmosphere is located. At the Poles the thickness of the layer is about nine and a half kilometres, at temperate latitudes (50°) it extends from the surface for a distance of about 11 kilometres, and at the tropics the zone may be some 15 or 16 kilometres thick.

The Tropopause. This is the name given by Sir Napier Shaw to the upper limit of the atmosphere where the troposphere borders the stratosphere.

The Stratosphere. This is an outer layer of the atmosphere in which no convection occurs. After the tropopause the temperature no longer falls and, in the stratosphere, actually increases with height from −80° C to about 0° C. The mean maximum temperature is reached at about 48 kilometres, which marks the stratopause. This rise in temperature is essentially due to the absorption of the ultra-violet radiation from the sun by a minor atmospheric constituent, ozone.

The Mesosphere. After the stratopause the temperature again falls within a thirty-kilometre vertical layer called the mesosphere. Exceedingly low values, −75° C to −100° C, and sometimes −120° C, are recorded.

THE HETEROSPHERE

Beyond the mesopause is the *heterosphere*, at heights above 80 kilometres, where atmospheric conditions change radically. The beginning of the heterosphere is marked by a change in composition, due both to the effect of gravity on the gaseous particles and to the progressive conversion of the molecules of oxygen into single atoms by ultra-violet radiation. This molecular dissociation occurs during normal daylight, but is followed in the darkness of night by a recombination of the oxygen atoms below 80–100 kilometres. The ensuing chemical action results in a phosphorescence which can be identified with the luminosity of the night sky.

Atomic oxygen and nitrogen become more abundant at heights above 100–115 kilometres, therefore, and cover a region extending in altitude over several hundred kilometres. At the outer limit of the heterosphere (500 kilometres) the light elements, hydrogen and helium, become the principal constituents.

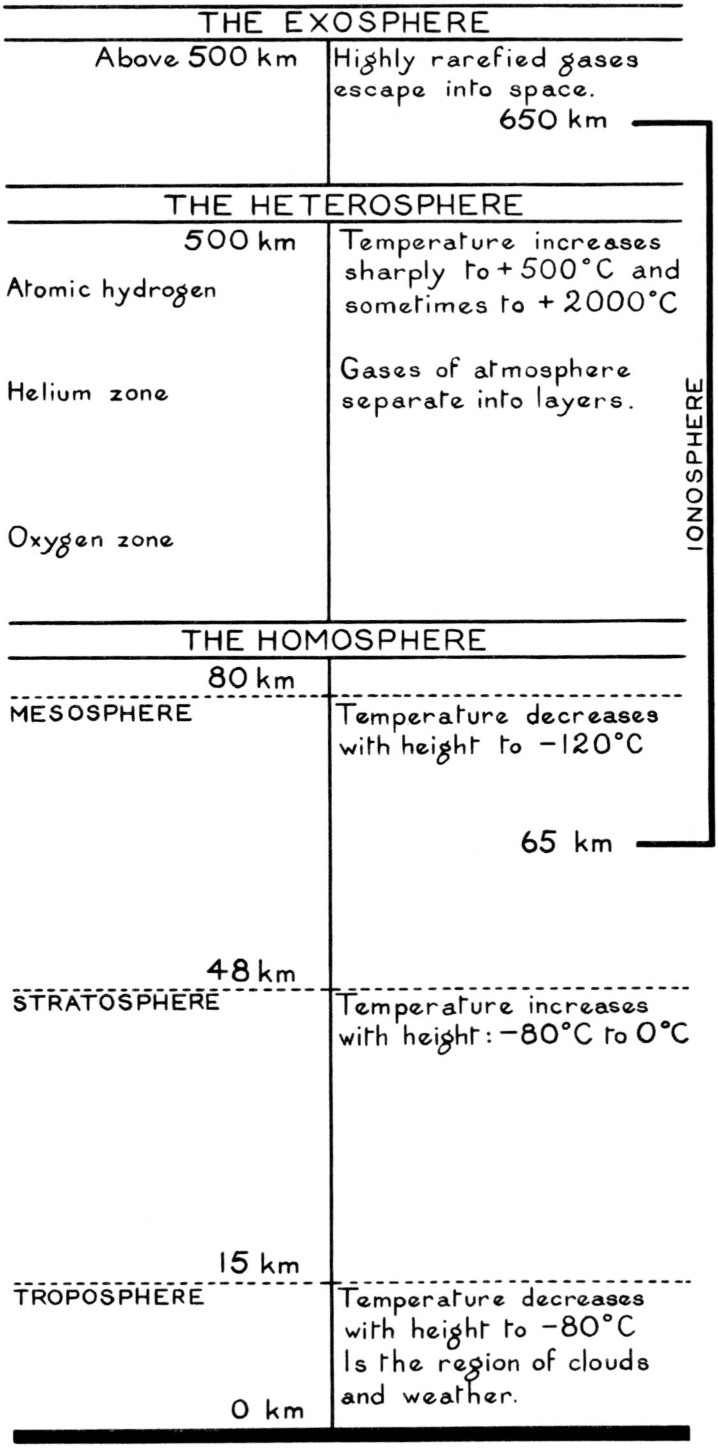

THE EXOSPHERE

| Above 500 km | Highly rarefied gases escape into space. |
| | 650 km |

THE HETEROSPHERE

500 km	Temperature increases sharply to +500°C and sometimes to +2000°C
Atomic hydrogen	
Helium zone	Gases of atmosphere separate into layers.
Oxygen zone	

IONOSPHERE

THE HOMOSPHERE

80 km	
MESOSPHERE	Temperature decreases with height to −120°C
	65 km
48 km	
STRATOSPHERE	Temperature increases with height: −80°C to 0°C
15 km	
TROPOSPHERE	Temperature decreases with height to −80°C Is the region of clouds and weather.
0 km	

FIG. 9. THE ZONES OF THE ATMOSPHERE

Beyond this point the density is so low that collision between atoms of hydrogen and helium are rare and the mean free path velocity is such that many atoms reach the escape velocity (10·94 kilometres per second). They are freed from the earth's gravity and are lost to interplanetary space. This outer region of the atmosphere is consequently termed the *exosphere*. The escape determines the atmospheric balance in concentration of hydrogen and helium which are being produced continually within the earth environment: hydrogen by the disintegration of methane and water vapour in the lower levels of the atmosphere, and helium by the decomposition of uranium in the earth's crust.

The thermal conditions in the heterosphere are different from those to be found in the homosphere. Absorption of solar ultra-violet radiation on wavelengths less than 0·1 micrometre (a micrometre is one-millionth of a metre) results in considerable heating of the upper atmosphere. Temperature rises sharply to 500° C, and during periods of maximum solar activity (as in 1957) may even reach 2000° C.

In conclusion, therefore, it may be said that the earth's atmosphere, including the ionized zones, extends for at least 40 000 kilometres above the surface. At such levels there are still some five or six hydrogen atoms in every cubic centimetre. Beyond this, in interplanetary space, there are rapidly moving particles, chiefly protons derived from the solar wind, which are trapped by the earth's magnetic field. Thus one might say that the final sphere indirectly concerned with the atmosphere is the earth's magnetosphere. The interactions between the captured protons of the solar wind and the ionized particles of the heterosphere may well play a leading part in conditioning events in the homosphere. This is certainly a line of research now being followed by the latest weather satellites.

The General Law of Gases applied to the Atmosphere

Since the dry air of the atmosphere may be regarded as a uniform gas, it must inevitably obey the law common to all gases, connecting pressure, temperature, and density. Changes in any of these three quantities directly affects meteorology, and the General Law of Gases is therefore the foundation upon which the theory of meteorology rests.

If the pressure of any gas is p, its density d, and its absolute temperature T the gas law states:

$$p = RTd$$

where R is a constant the value of which depends on the gas concerned.

A gas is composed of a large number of molecules which are in irregular and constant motion; the effects of the impacts of the individual molecules produce the pressure of the gas upon given surfaces. The pressure of a gas therefore depends upon the number of particles, their weight, and the speed at which they are moving. The number and mass of the molecules define the density of the gas; therefore the pressure is directly proportional to the density. The speed of movement of the particles depends upon temperature; the higher the temperature, then, the faster will the molecules travel. At absolute zero (−273° C) the molecules would be at rest, and the pressure of the gas would be nothing.

This law can be applied to the atmosphere. If the temperature of the atmosphere remains unchanged the pressure will be proportional to the density. Similarly, if the pressure remains unchanged, a rise in temperature of the atmosphere will result in a proportionate decrease in density. The presence of water vapour does complicate the problem, but the correction is small.

THE PRESSURE OF THE ATMOSPHERE

The pressure of the atmosphere is the effect of the motion of the individual molecules, and since the molecules move in all directions the pressure will be

TABLE 5.—THE INTERNATIONAL STANDARD ATMOSPHERE

HEIGHT (km)	TEMPERATURE (° C)	RELATIVE PRESSURE (760 mm at sea-level	DENSITY, AS A PERCENTAGE OF SURFACE DENSITY
0	15	1	100
1	8·5	0·89	90·7
2	2·0	0·73	82·2
3	−4·5	0·69	74·4
4	−11·0	0·61	66·9
5	−17·5	0·54	60·1
6	−24·0	0·46	53·9
7	−30·5	0·41	48·2
8	−37·0	0·35	42·9
9	−43·5	0·30	38·1
10	−50·0	0·26	33·7
11	−56·5	0·22	29·7

exerted in all directions. But if a column of air is considered the pressure of the atmosphere is given by the weight of air within that column extending upward throughout the entire atmosphere. The recording of the pressure has been considered already, and the height of the mercury column in a barometer bears a direct relationship to the weight of air in a column of the same cross-sectional area.

It has already been stated that the pressure of the atmosphere is proportional to the density, and density is controlled by temperature. Consequently the average pressure at any height in the atmosphere varies with the temperature. By international agreement, however, a Standard Atmosphere has been evolved (Table 5). This assumes a mean sea-level pressure of 760 mm at 15° C and a lapse rate of 6·5° C/km.

It will be apparent that, in a column of air, there will be less molecules exerting a pressure as height increases (see Fig. 10). The fall-off in pressure with height depends on temperature, but the approximate figure for the decrease in pressure near the earth's surface is one millibar in every nine metres (see Table 6). More accurately, the difference in height corresponding to a change in pressure of one millibar can be calculated for any value of temperature or pressure from the following formula:

$$\text{Height difference in metres for millibar pressure change} = \frac{29\cdot 25 \times T}{p}$$

where T is the thermodynamic temperature and p is the pressure.

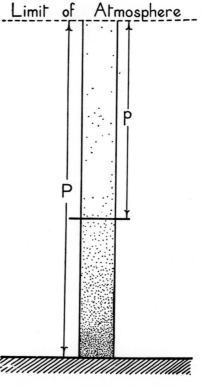

FIG. 10. HOW MOLECULES OF AIR CONTROL
ATMOSPHERIC PRESSURE

P is the pressure resulting from weight of molecules
in whole column.

p is the pressure resulting from weight of molecules
in upper portion of the column of air.

Observation stations for recording atmospheric pressure are not necessarily at the same altitude, and therefore it is essential to reduce all readings to a common level if comparisons of pressures are to be made and if pressure maps are to be drawn. Usually sea-level is chosen as the standard, and the corrected pressure is really only a hypothetical value. To obtain the corrected reading requires the addition of the weight of the air column between station-level and sea-level; but this has no evident meaning, because the space consists of solid ground. An estimate is made of what the pressure would be if the land were removed and the space filled with air. For altitudes up to three hundred metres reasonable corrections may be made, but after that reduction to sea-level becomes unreliable.

The Altimeter. The construction and operation of the aneroid barometer have already been mentioned (p. 17); in this instrument the atmospheric pressure exerts itself upon a collapsible metal capsule, and the movements are transferred to a dial or drum. A close relationship exists between pressure and height, and an aircraft

TABLE 6.—HEIGHT DIFFERENCE IN METRES CORRESPONDING WITH A FALL IN PRESSURE OF ONE MB

TEMPERATURE		PRESSURE, IN MB									
° C	° K	1050	1000	950	900	800	700	600	500	400	300
		m	m	m	m	m	m	m	m	m	m
40	313	8·7	9·1	9·6	10·2	11·5	13·1	15·3	18·3	22·9	30·5
10	283	7·9	8·2	8·8	9·1	10·4	11·9	13·7	16·4	20·7	27·4
0	273	7·6	8·0	8·4	8·9	10·0	11·4	13·3	16·0	20·0	26·6
—20	253	7·0	7·4	7·8	8·2	9·2	10·6	12·3	14·8	18·5	24·7

altimeter is a simple form of aneroid barometer in which the scale is graduated in linear units instead of millibars. As an aircraft increases its altitude there will be a corresponding decrease in the atmospheric pressure, and the appropriate expansion of the metal capsule, geared to a needle, registers as an increase in height.

Atmospheric-pressure Variations and Pressure Distributions. The pressure of the atmosphere is usually recorded by many observation stations situated over a very wide area, and all the readings are converted to sea-level. If the readings are registered on a map of the area concerned it will be possible to link up those stations having the same pressure. A line joining places which have the same mean sea-level pressure is called an 'isobar.' Isobars are usually drawn at intervals of two or four millibars, according to the scale of the chart, and from the completed lines (which are always simple curves or closed circuits) definite pressure patterns can be recognized. Experience shows that the configurations of isobars may be very complex, but they fall into a number of types:

1. High-pressure area, or 'anticyclone' (H in Fig. 11).
2. Low-pressure area, depression or 'cyclone' (L in Fig. 11).
3. Secondary depression (S in Fig. 11).
4. Trough of low pressure (T in Fig. 11).
5. Ridge of high pressure (R in Fig. 11).
6. Col (C in Fig. 11).

High-pressure Area, or Anticyclone (Fig. 12). A region of the atmosphere in which the barometric pressure is high relative to the surroundings is known as an 'anticyclone.' It is indicated by more or less circular isobars, with the highest pressure at the centre. In the high-pressure region in the Northern Hemisphere the wind circulation is clockwise, and the weather is of the settled type. In the Southern Hemisphere the wind-circulation is anticlockwise.

Low-pressure Area, or Cyclone (Fig. 13). A region of low pressure is known as a 'cyclone'—or usually in temperate latitudes as a 'depression,' leaving the term 'cyclone' to refer to tropical storms. Essentially, the cyclone and depression are alike. The isobars are closed circuits, and, in the Northern Hemisphere, the winds circulate anticlockwise; in the Southern Hemisphere the movement is clockwise. The isobars are closely spaced, and consequently the winds are stronger than those associated with the anticyclone.

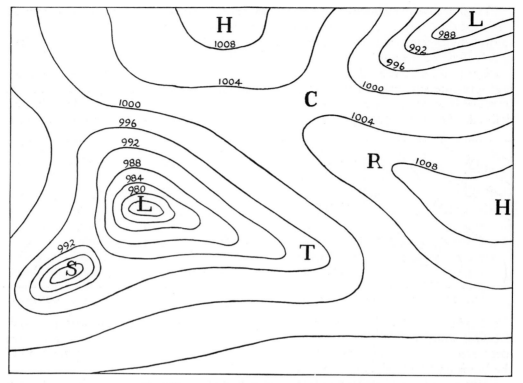

FIG. 11. ATMOSPHERIC-PRESSURE PATTERNS

Secondary Depression (Fig. 14). Isobars around a depression are not always symmetrical, and may be distorted in such a manner that a small, localized low-pressure system exists within the boundaries of a primary low-pressure area. A small low-pressure region of this type is called a 'secondary depression.' The secondary usually travels with the main system, and rotates anticlockwise with the wind-circulation within the primary low.

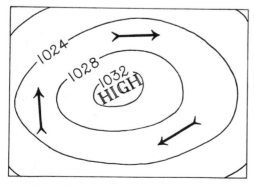

FIG. 12. A HIGH-PRESSURE SYSTEM

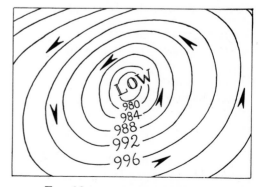

FIG. 13. A LOW-PRESSURE SYSTEM

Trough of Low Pressure (Fig. 15). The isobars of a main depression may become so distorted that they form a V-shape and extend outward from the low in any direction, so that the pressure is lower at the open end of the V. The region may be described as a 'valley' or 'trough' of low pressure.

Ridge of High Pressure (Fig. 16). This is an extension of the isobars of an ordinary high-pressure system, and their pattern is similar to that of the trough. The higher pressure is located towards the open end of the V, which tends to be less sharply defined. The terms 'wedge,' or 'tongue,' of high pressure are sometimes used also.

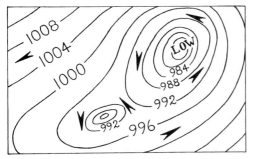

FIG. 14. A SECONDARY DEPRESSION

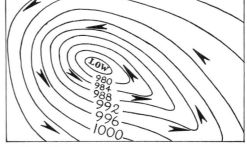

FIG. 15. A TROUGH OF LOW PRESSURE

Col (Fig. 17). This is a neutral area of pressure between two high- and two low-pressure systems which are arranged alternately. The wind circulations are associated with the neighbouring pressure areas, and, in view of the juxtaposition of the highs and lows, the air movements are light.

From a study of successive isobar systems it may be seen how their shape changes continuously; depressions are said to deepen and intensify, or fill up; anticyclones build up or intensify, or they may collapse.

Pressure has already been described as the weight of a column of air above the ground, and therefore differences of pressure imply that the quantity of air within the column varies from time to time and also from place to place. Air is transferred from one place to another through the medium of wind, and any discussion of pressure naturally involves the analysis of atmospheric motion. This relationship between atmospheric pressure and winds will be considered at greater length in Chapter 4, after due thought has been given to the temperature of the atmosphere.

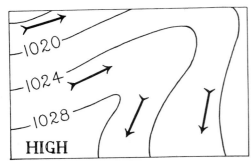

FIG. 16. A RIDGE OF HIGH PRESSURE

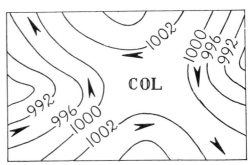

FIG. 17. A COL

Chapter 3

THE TEMPERATURE OF THE ATMOSPHERE

SOLAR RADIATION, OR INSOLATION

THE sun is the sole source of heat for the earth's atmosphere. From the sun, whose diameter is more than a hundred times that of the earth and whose surface is believed to have a temperature of about 6000° C, there streams an immense quantity of radiant energy. Although only a small fraction of the energy emitted from the sun reaches the earth, all life on the planet owes its existence to this radiation.

The radiant energy which is received from the sun, and which is transmitted in the form of short waves (1/250 to 1/7000 millimetre in length), is called the solar radiation, or 'insolation.' Less than one-fifth of the solar radiation can be perceived as light: the rest is made up of waves (ultra-violet and infra-red) which cannot be seen. The average intensity of the sun's radiation varies with the time of day and the day of the year, largely as a result of the variations in the inclination of the earth's axis towards the sun as the planet moves along its orbit throughout the year. As a consequence of this change in inclination the length of daylight varies, and the angle at which the sun's rays strike the earth's surface changes throughout the seasons. In addition, the distance of the earth from the sun varies from month to month. All these factors are responsible for the variation in the amount of insolation received by the earth. Table 7 indicates the insolation received at different latitudes for the months of December, March, June, and September. The figures take into account the angle of incidence and length of day, and the values do show that the distance of the sun from the earth does affect the insolation received—note the values for December and June at the North and South Poles.

TABLE 7.—INSOLATION RECEIVED AT THE LIMIT OF THE ATMOSPHERE, IN KWH PER DAM^2

MONTH	EQUATOR	20° N.	40° N.	60° N.	N. POLE	S. POLE
December	977	702	371	58	0	1331
March	1038	980	805	532	30	0
June	915	1085	1150	1135	1249	0
September	1023	972	805	541	20	0

Assuming that the earth had no atmosphere, which materially alters the amount of solar radiation reaching the surface, the temperature at the earth's surface would be as shown in Table 8. But, as a result of the atmosphere's presence, the insolation, on arrival at the upper limits of the air layer, passes through a complicated series of events. A great deal of radiation is reflected back into space from the clouds and other light surfaces.

Slightly over $\frac{4}{10}$ of the radiation received from the sun is reflected back again. This reflective power is known as the earth's 'albedo' and has a value of 0·43. Consequently some 57 per cent. of the insolation passes through the atmosphere at all angles. Some is absorbed by the air. (The degree of absorption increases in geometrical progression as the length of the path increases in arithmetical progression. This goes some way to explain the existence of the cold polar regions, where

LATITUDE	WARMEST MONTH	COLDEST MONTH	ANNUAL MEAN
	° C	° C	° C
0°	61·4	13·3	16·7
10°	61·4	10·0	16·1
20°	70	2·2	13·9
30°	74	— 8·9	10·0
40°	75	— 12·2	3·9
50°	75	— 42·8	— 4·4
60°	75·8	— 75	—17·2
70°	76·1	—169·4	—41·7
80°	80	—169·4	—62·8
90°	82·2	—169·4	—76·1

the length of the path of the incoming solar radiation is very long.) The absorption depends upon the transparency of the atmosphere: on a clear day about 90 per cent. of the sun's rays reach the earth when the sun is vertical. With a thick fog and a low sun, the radiation received is negligible. Thus it is obvious that the amount of insolation received at the surface of the earth depends upon the water and solid

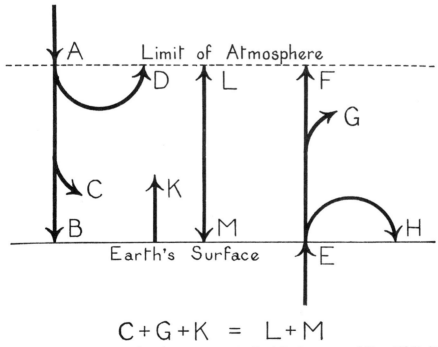

$$C + G + K = L + M$$

A: Incoming Radiation $30\cdot14 \times 10^6$ J/m²/day.
B: Effective Radiation $12\cdot56 \times 10^6$ J/m²/day.
C: Radn. absorbed by air.
D: Radn. reflected back.
E: Outgoing Earth Radiation $20\cdot93 \times 10^6$ J/m²/day.
F: Earth Radn. to space $3\cdot35 \times 10^6$ J/m²/day.
G: Radn. absorbed by air.
H: Radn. reflected back.
K: Heat lost by conduction and convection.
L: Heat radiated by air to space.
M: Heat radiated by air to earth.

FIG. 18. SOLAR RADIATION AND THE ATMOSPHERE

particles present in the atmosphere; water droplets are the most important obstacle to radiation, either to or from the earth.

The varying angle at which the sun's rays strike the earth's surface is also important in controlling the intensity of insolation. The effect of this angle is best seen in the daily movement of the sun across the sky. At noon the intensity of solar radiation is greatest, but in the early morning or evening when the sun is at a low angle the amount of insolation is small. This principle has a much wider application with respect to latitude and the seasons. The oblique rays of a low-angle sun in high latitudes are spread over a greater surface area than are high-angle rays in low latitudes and, as a result, produce less heating per unit area.

It may be seen from Fig. 18 that the atmosphere is heated by radiation from the

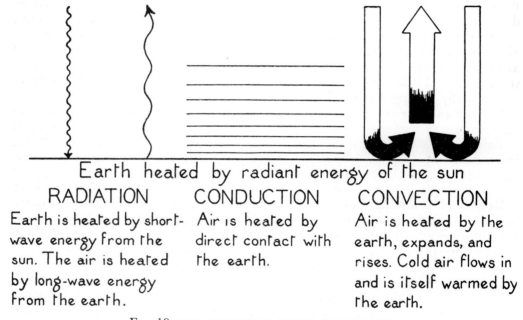

Earth heated by radiant energy of the sun

RADIATION | CONDUCTION | CONVECTION

Earth is heated by short-wave energy from the sun. The air is heated by long-wave energy from the earth.

Air is heated by direct contact with the earth.

Air is heated by the earth, expands, and rises. Cold air flows in and is itself warmed by the earth.

FIG. 19. THE METHODS BY WHICH AIR IS HEATED

earth's surface, which retransmits the sun's radiation in the form of long, or heat-, waves. Consequently the temperature of the atmosphere will vary with height above the earth's surface. In the troposphere temperature decreases with height, an approximate figure being 0·6° C per 100 metres. Since this is the zone containing most of the air and almost all the water vapour, it is here that absorption of the insolation is greatest. Beyond the boundary of this layer (sixteen kilometres at the equator and nine and a half kilometres at the Poles)—that is, beyond the tropopause—is the stratosphere. The troposphere is therefore that part of the atmosphere which contains all the elements of weather.

Air, like all other substances, may be heated in three ways: by radiation, convection, and conduction (Fig. 19). Radiation is simply the direct heating of a body by the transmission of heat-waves. The long waves from the earth's surface heat the air in close proximity to the ground. Convection currents are upward movements of warm air which, because it is at a higher temperature than its surroundings, is less dense, and lighter, and therefore tends to rise. Air may also be heated directly in the daytime by contact with the earth's surface.

Since the air tends to be heated in these three ways, the air near the surface on the whole attains the same temperature as the ground with which it is in contact. The ground temperature, however, depends upon the amount of solar radiation reaching the earth's surface and upon the character of the surface which is receiving that radiation. Land and water do not absorb or transmit heat at the same rate, and, although the greatest contrasts are between land and water surfaces, there are even no fixed values for the land regions, since there are great varieties in those surfaces, such as snow cover, vegetation, and soil colours. The most striking differences between land and water areas may be summarized under the headings:

Specific Heat. It requires about five times as much heat to raise the temperature of a given volume of water by a certain amount as it does to raise the temperature of a similar volume of dry earth. This relationship is known as the 'specific heat' of substances, and it follows that the specific heat of water is higher than that of land, consequently causing water to heat and cool more slowly.

Reflection. The colour of surfaces plays an important part in the power of those surfaces to reflect solar radiation. Water's reflecting power is not as great as might be imagined, and it is calculated that only 15 per cent. of the insolation is reflected from water surfaces. Land surfaces appear to have a greater reflecting power: snow surfaces reflect 70–90 per cent. of the sunlight; rocks reflect 12–15 per cent.; grass reflects as much as 30 per cent.; and forest areas reflect anything up to 20 per cent.

Degree of Transmission. Owing to the relative transparency of the oceans, the incoming radiation penetrates to considerable depths, and consequently the energy is more widely distributed than on land. Conversely, the opaque nature of the land surface results in the more rapid heating of a comparatively shallow layer.

Movement. The effect of movement in the waters of the oceans is to distribute the sun's energy more widely. Hence, although the process of heating is slower, it affects a much greater mass than is the case with land areas, and consequently when a water surface begins to cool vertical convectional currents are set up. The cooler, heavier layers sink and are replaced by warmer water. The whole water mass must inevitably be cooled. As a result the mass of water imparts its heat to the surrounding air, and the supply of heat is maintained for a long period of time.

Land tends to be heated daily to depths of about one metre, while annually the temperature varies down to a depth of approximately 15 metres. In water the daily temperature changes are felt to depths of six metres, but the annual variations may exist to 150 metres, and in some cases down to 600 metres.

It is evident from the above information that, with the same amount of solar radiation falling upon a land and a sea surface, the former will reach a higher temperature more quickly than the water surface. Conversely, a land surface also cools more rapidly. Climates of continental areas will therefore be characterized by large diurnal (daily) and seasonal changes of temperature. On the other hand maritime areas will be moderated by the effects of the oceans.

The Vertical and Horizontal Distribution
of Air Temperature

The Vertical Distribution of Temperature. We have already examined the methods by which the atmosphere is heated, and have noticed that radiation from the earth's surface is the fundamental source of heat. Experimental observation of air temperature at different altitudes has verified the assumption that air temperature decreases as the height increases. Under normal conditions, while the rate of

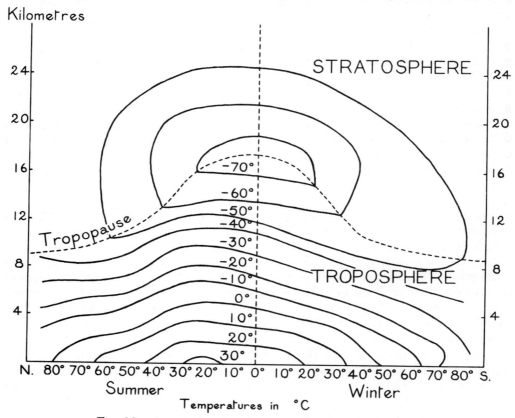

Fig. 20. THE DISTRIBUTION OF UPPER-AIR TEMPERATURES

decrease is not uniform, the average is about 1·8° C per three hundred metres. This is called the 'lapse rate'; the steeper the lapse rate the more rapid the decrease in temperature. The average distribution of upper air temperatures is shown in Fig. 20. This diagram represents a vertical section along a line of longitude from the North to the South Pole; it is to some extent theoretical, since the effects of oceans and continents have been eliminated. The rate of temperature decrease naturally varies from place to place and from one part of the year to the next, and by means of temperature observations made during balloon or aircraft ascent the 'environmental lapse rate' may be obtained and graphically recorded.

The fact that temperature is almost uniform in the lower levels of the stratosphere substantiates the theory that heat is transmitted upward by radiation, but within the troposphere the observed lapse rates are insufficient to produce the necessary outflow of heat. The fundamental reason for the failure of the radiation theory to explain the temperature distribution in the troposphere lies in the fact that when the lapse rate reaches high proportions the air becomes mobile, convection currents arise, and heat is carried upward by the moving air more rapidly than by radiation. It is therefore necessary to examine the process of convection and consider the properties of gases which are allowed to expand or be compressed—as is the case with air, which moves vertically.

It is a property of all gases that when they are compressed the temperature rises, and when they are allowed to expand the temperature decreases. To compress a gas requires energy, and, in accordance with the law of conservation of energy, the energy is not lost but is transferred to the gas, so raising the temperature. Similarly, on expansion a gas loses some energy, with the result that the temperature of the gas decreases. These changes of temperature are said to be 'adiabatic'; expansion and compression in the atmosphere occur when the air moves to a region with different pressure. Changes of pressure occur when air rises or falls, the amount of change being about 3 per cent. per 300 metres of height. The relation between temperature and pressure changes can be expressed by the following formula:

$$\log T - \log T_0 = 0 \cdot 288(\log p - \log p_0)$$

where T_0 and p_0 are the initial absolute temperature and pressure and T the new temperature when the pressure has changed to p. Simple application of the formula will show that temperature changes are large for small changes in pressure.

Dry air, when forced to rise, will expand and cool at a rate of 3° C per three hundred metres. This is known as the 'dry adiabatic lapse rate,' and is the rate at which rising dry air cools or subsiding dry air warms when no heat is transferred from other surrounding sources. If the environmental lapse rate for a section of the atmosphere was 2·5° C in three hundred metres, and a portion of that air were made to rise, after three hundred metres the temperature of that dry air would be reduced by 3° C. The portion of air would be 0·5° C cooler than the surrounding air at the same level. As it is cooler it is heavier and will tend to sink again. Such an atmospheric condition is said to be 'stable', and any rising air tends to return to its original state. Should the environmental lapse rate be greater than 3° C per 300 metres—should it be, for example, 3·5° C—air forced upward would be 0·5° C warmer than its surroundings and, being lighter, would tend to rise farther. The original portion of air would continue to rise as long as the environmental lapse rate remained greater than the dry adiabatic lapse rate. The atmosphere, under these conditions, is said to 'unstable,' and any rising air tends to continue to rise, so forming rapid, vertical up-currents.

When the surface of the earth is heated by the sun the air in contact with the ground becomes heated by conduction, the lapse rate near the surface passes the dry adiabatic rate, and vigorous convection currents transfer the heat upward. It is by this means that a vast proportion of the heat of the surface layers is transferred through the troposphere. But the process is much complicated when, on cooling adiabatically, the air reaches a temperature at which any moisture present condenses out.

When water is made to change its state from liquid to vapour large amounts of heat must be supplied. To change boiling water into steam requires five times as much heat as is required to bring the same amount of ice-cold water to the boil. During the process of boiling the temperature remains constant, and therefore the heat required to change the water into vapour is stored up. The heat is 'latent heat' and can be released only on condensation of the vapour back to liquid again. In the atmosphere liquid water becomes changed into vapour by the ordinary process of evaporation, and the same amount of latent heat must be provided. When air containing water vapour is cooled by ascent to the temperature at which the water would condense into liquid, heat is liberated which tends to raise the temperature of the upper air. Wet air rising vertically will try to cool at the adiabatic lapse rate of 3° C per three hundred metres, but, as the cooling causes condensation, latent heat will be liberated which will reduce the rate of cooling. The lapse rate will therefore be less than 3° C. The rate of decrease of temperature in ascending saturated air is known as the 'saturated adiabatic lapse rate,' and for lower levels of the troposphere in temperate latitudes is of the order of 1·5° C per three hundred metres. The value is not constant and depends on the amount of moisture condensed. Cold air can contain less moisture than warm air, and so the latent heat released in cold air will be less than that released in warm air. Thus, as temperature decreases, the saturated adiabatic lapse rate approaches the value of the dry adiabatic lapse rate. A portion of saturated air made to rise is 'stable' if the environmental lapse rate is less than the saturated adiabatic lapse rate and 'unstable' if the environmental lapse rate is greater than the saturated adiabatic lapse rate. (See Fig. 21.)

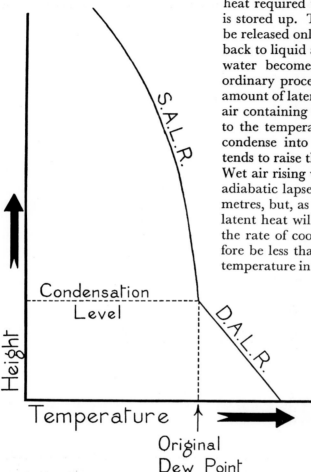

FIG. 21. A GRAPH TO ILLUSTRATE ADIABATIC COOLING OF RISING AIR (S.A.L.R. = SATURATED ADIABATIC LAPSE RATE; D.A.L.R. = DRY ADIABATIC LAPSE RATE)

Original dew point is the temperature to which the air must be cooled such that any water vapour present will be condensed.

Although the normal-temperature lapse rate shows a decrease as height increases in the troposphere, the situation will frequently occur where the lower layers are cooler than the air at higher altitudes. With the coldest air in close proximity to the ground, the normal lapse rate is reversed: a 'temperature inversion' is said to exist. This condition is produced by the rapid cooling of the earth's surface, usually by night radiation, and this cooling is transferred to the layers of air immediately adjacent to the ground. Other methods of producing inversions will be discussed in the chapters dealing with fog and weather forecasting.

The main feature of an inversion is the marked stability of the air. Convection currents cannot develop readily, and only minor mixing of air layers is possible. Temperature inversions are not always confined to the surface layers, nor are they always the result of radiation cooling, but in essence their characteristics are the same, and the environmental lapse rate may take on the sort of form shown in Fig. 22.

The Horizontal Distribution of Temperature. The main features of surface air temperatures over the earth are largely decided by latitude, temperatures decreasing gradually from the equatorial to polar regions. These distributions, however, are largely modified by the position of land and sea surfaces and the seasonal changes in the sun's position relative to those surfaces.

Surface air temperatures can be shown on a map by a series of lines called 'iso-

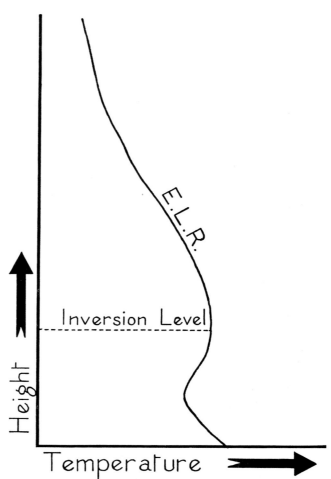

FIG. 22. A GRAPH TO ILLUSTRATE A TEMPERATURE INVERSION (E.L.R. = ENVIRONMENTAL LAPSE RATE)

therms.' An isotherm is simply a line joining places having the same mean sea-level temperature. The mean isotherms for January and July are shown in Figs. 23 and 24. These two maps do indicate the extremes of winter and summer, and the distribution at other seasons is approximately intermediate between the January and July patterns. From a comparison of the two maps it may be seen that there is a marked latitudinal shifting of the isotherms between January and July, following the latitudinal movement of the sun's rays and insolation belts. The movements of

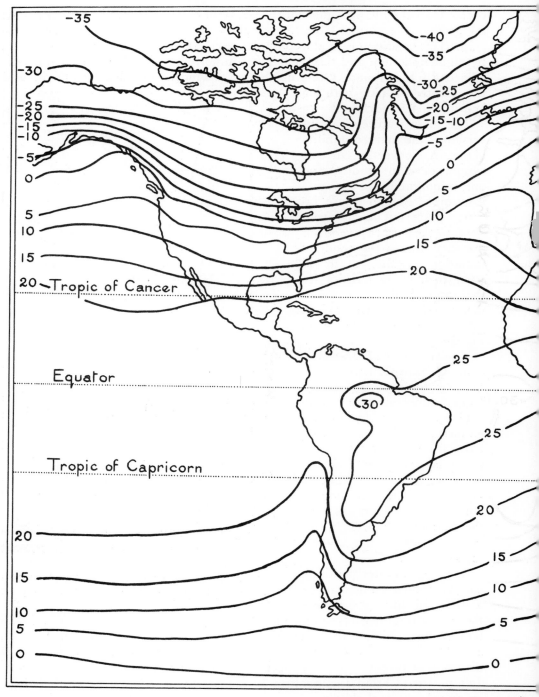

FIG. 23. WORLD DISTRIBUTION OF ISOT[
To convert degrees Fahrenheit to d

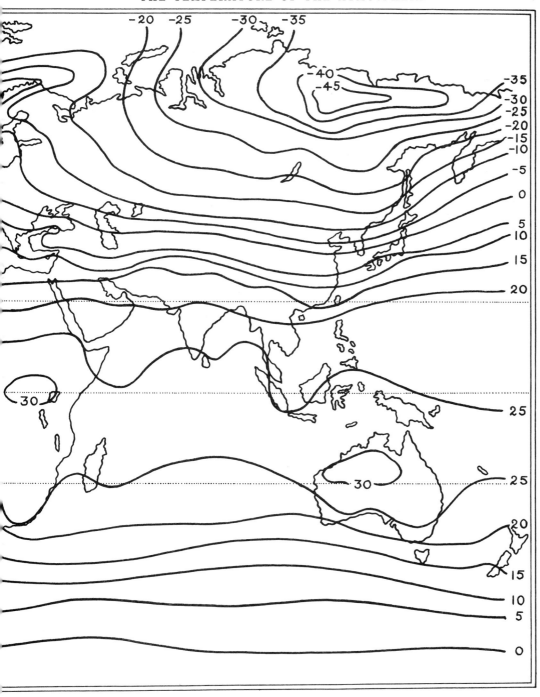

ubtract 32 and multiply by $\frac{5}{9}$.

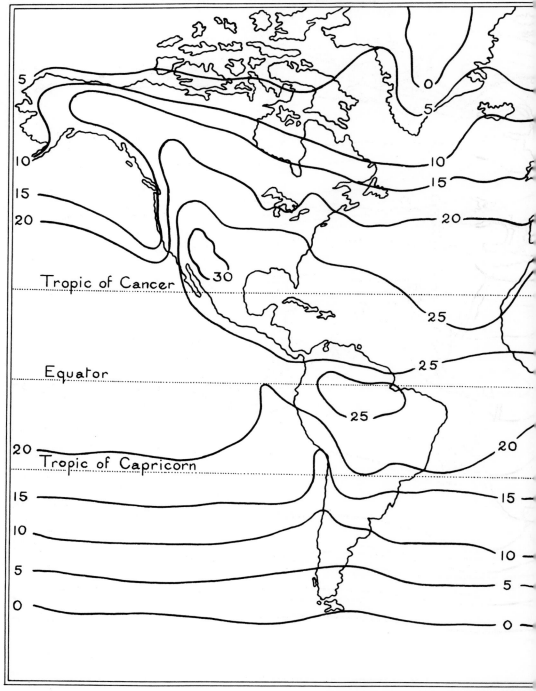

FIG. 24. WORLD DISTRIBUTION OF ISOT
To convert degrees Fahrenheit to

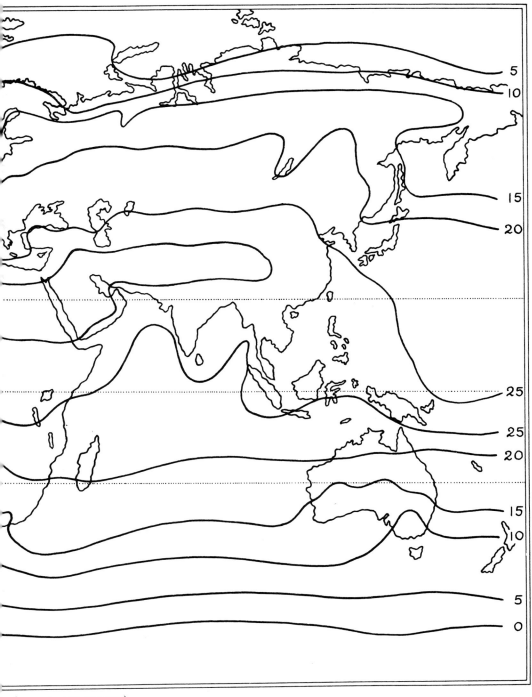

5
10

15

20

25

25
20

15
10

5

0

Y (IN DEGREES CELSIUS)
subtract 32 and multiply by $\frac{5}{9}$.

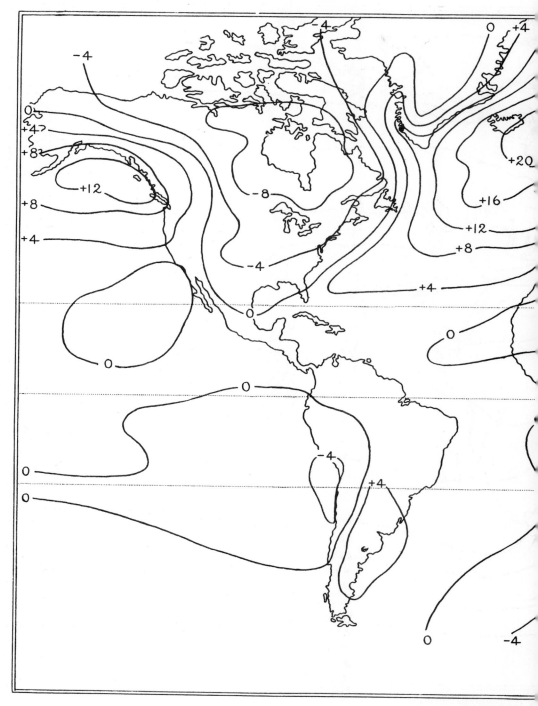

FIG. 25. TEMPERATURE ANOMAI
To convert degrees Celsius to

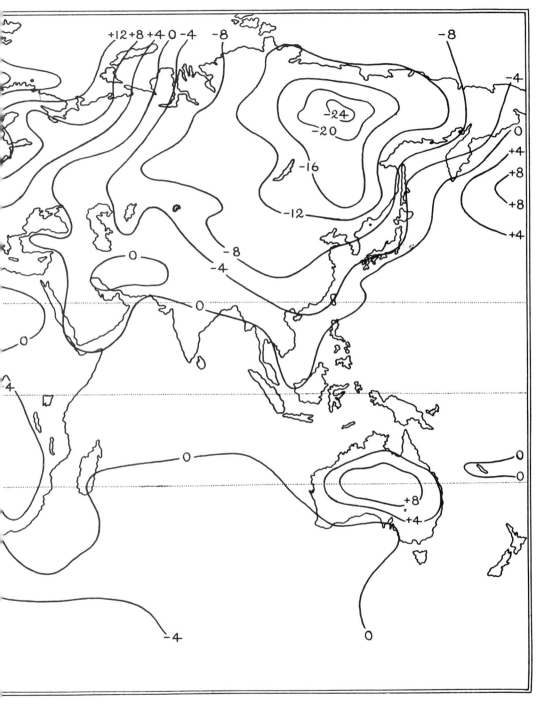

NUARY (IN DEGREES CELSIUS)

hrenheit multiply by $\frac{9}{5}$ and then add 32.

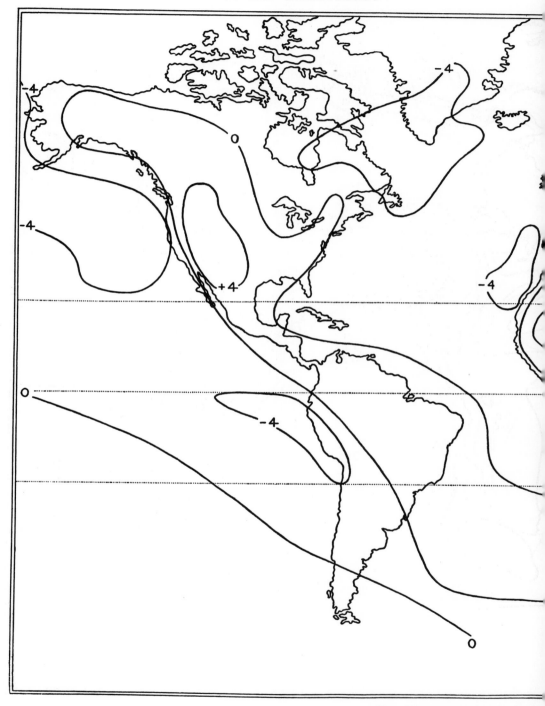

FIG. 26. TEMPERATURE ANOMA
To convert degrees Celsius to de

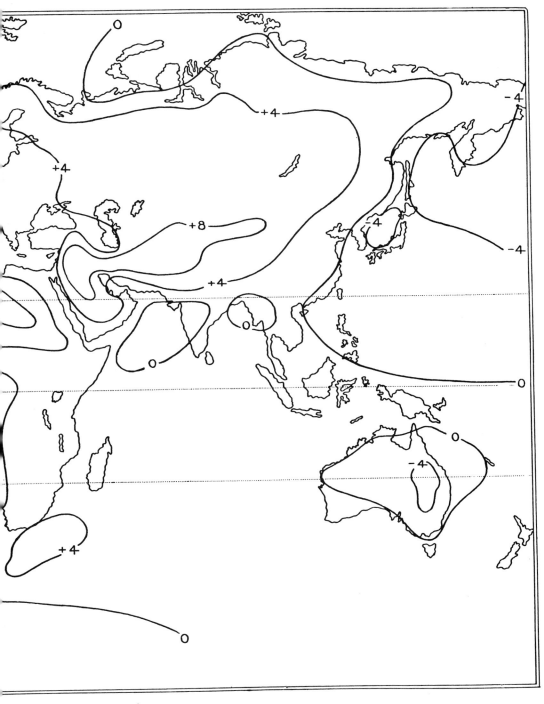

JULY (IN DEGREES CELSIUS)
enheit multiply by $\frac{9}{5}$ and then add 32.

the isotherms are much larger over the continents than over the oceans. The highest temperatures on both the January and July maps are situated over land areas, while the lowest temperatures in January are located over Asia and North America, the largest land-masses in middle and higher latitudes. Further, the January isotherms bend sharply equatorward over the continents and Poleward over the oceans. In July the opposite conditions are prevalent. No obvious seasonal contrasts can be distinguished south of the equator, because there are no large continents in the mid-latitudes.

Analysis of these two isotherm maps enables temperature ranges to be compiled for certain places on the earth's surface. The annual range of temperature is simply the difference between the average temperatures of the warmest and coldest months. The ranges are always small near the equator, where insolation does not vary greatly, and also over water surfaces. The largest annual ranges are to be found over the continents in the Northern Hemisphere.

The temperature distribution as illustrated by isothermal maps is the direct result of the balance between incoming solar radiation and outgoing earth radiation. This balance is controlled by the unequal heating and cooling of land and water surfaces, prevailing winds, and ocean movements. It is possible to separate these two radiation controls by determining the mean temperature of the parallels of latitude and by ascertaining the difference between the observed mean temperatures of localities and the mean temperatures of their parallels. This difference between the mean temperature of the place and that of its parallel is known as the 'thermal anomaly.' The anomaly merely represents the amount of deviation from the normal caused by the various earth controls. Lines can be drawn on world outline maps joining up places of equal thermal anomaly, and an 'isanomalous map' will thus be created. (See Figs. 25, 26.)

It should be clear that the greatest thermal anomalies are situated in the Northern Hemisphere, where the extensive land-masses are located in the mid-latitudes. In the Southern Hemisphere, where there is a much more homogeneous surface, thermal anomalies are less obvious.

Where the observed mean temperature is higher than that of the parallel a positive anomaly is said to exist, and where the observed mean temperature is lower than that of the parallel a negative anomaly is said to prevail. On the January map positive anomalies are found over the oceans in the Northern Hemisphere and over the small land-masses in the Southern Hemisphere. Negative anomalies are located over Northern land-masses and to some lesser degree over the Southern oceans. The greatest positive anomalies are found along the eastern sides of the mid-latitude oceans, where warm ocean waters are flowing. The Norwegian coast has the largest recorded positive anomaly, the temperature at 63° N. being 7·8° C too warm for its latitude in January. The largest negative anomaly exists in north-east Siberia, which is 7·8° C colder than the average for its latitude. In July the situation is reversed: in the Northern Hemisphere the continents have the positive anomalies, while the oceans have negative ones.

Chapter 4

ATMOSPHERIC PRESSURE AND ITS RELATION TO WINDS

WIND has already been defined as air in motion. This description and the invention of the wind-vane go back to pre-Christian times. The Greeks recognized that different weather types were associated with winds from different directions, and the Tower of the Winds at Athens represents the winds and their appropriate characters. It is true that, compared with temperature and rainfall, winds are relatively insignificant as elements of weather and climate. Nevertheless, they may be regarded as controllers of temperature and precipitation, and, apart from maintaining a balance of heat in the atmosphere, they do transport water vapour from the oceans to the lands where condensation occurs and rain falls. Rainfall distribution is closely associated with wind systems, and now that the elements of temperature and pressure in the atmosphere have been discussed, it is logical to consider the relationship of these to winds.

The primary cause of wind can be attributed to differences between solar and terrestrial radiation. These differences create temperature irregularities which produce convection currents. A column of air one square centimetre in cross-sectional area which extends from sea-level to the upper limits of the atmosphere weighs approximately 1034 g. This weight of air is balanced by a column of mercury (see Fig. 1) 760 mm tall and having the same cross-section. This value is accepted as a normal atmosphere at 45° N. or S.

It has been stated previously that atmospheric pressure, temperature, and density are all related. Changes in temperature produce changes in air density which set up movements resulting in differences in air-pressure. Over a warm area air becomes heated, expands, and overspills to adjacent regions in which the temperatures are lower. The obvious result is that the weight of air is reduced in the warm region and increased in the adjacent cooler ones. A general statement may now be made: high temperatures tend to produce low sea-level pressures; low temperatures produce high sea-level pressures.

Wind is therefore caused by differences in air density, resulting in horizontal differences in air-pressure. This rate and direction of change of pressure can be indicated by the isobaric lines on a chart and are referred to as the 'pressure gradient.' It is this gradient which indicates the velocity and general direction of air movements; the gradient can therefore be defined as the decrease in pressure per unit distance in the direction in which the pressure decreases most rapidly.

The direction of air flow is from areas of high to areas of low pressure—that is, down the barometric slope. This can be shown by a line drawn at right angles to the isobars. The rate of flow, or wind velocity, is indicated by the steepness of the pressure gradient or the rate of pressure change. Where the gradient is steep air flow is rapid; where there is a shallow gradient the air flow is weak.

It follows, then, that if a small portion of the atmosphere is stationary it will commence to move only if the forces acting upon it are out of balance. The only forces which can act are the pressure exerted by the surrounding air and the force of gravity. Since gravity is a force which acts vertically downward it cannot itself produce wind. The only effective forces are those due to the horizontal differences in air-pressure, and it would appear that any portion of air will tend to move from regions of high to regions of low pressure—that is, at right angles to the isobars. All observations, however, indicate that winds tend rather to move parallel with the isobars, and some brief explanation is therefore necessary.

Once any mass has been set in motion it will, according to Newton's Law, move indefinitely in the same straight line until some other external force acts upon it. Gravity acts upon any body moving over the earth's surface. In addition, however, a body comes under the influence of the motion of the earth around its axis. This acceleration due to the rotation of the earth is termed 'geostrophic,' and it results in a body having a relative acceleration to the right or left of its original path, according to the hemisphere in which it is situated. According to Ferrel's Law, "a body, freely moving in the Northern Hemisphere, will be deflected to the right, and in the Southern Hemisphere will be deflected to the left."

Air will flow as a steady wind only when the two accelerations balance—that is, when the pressure gradient and geostrophic force balance one another. When the two forces balance they must act in opposite directions. As the rotation effect is always at right angles to the air flow it is clear that the wind must blow along the isobars with the low pressure to the left in the Northern Hemisphere. When the isobars are close together the pressure gradient is large, and the effect of the earth's geostrophic force must also be large in the same proportion. Consequently the wind must blow more strongly. The wider the isobar spacing, the smaller will be the forces acting, and the wind strengths will be correspondingly less.

It is evident, therefore, that there is a definite relationship between the isobars and the wind direction. This relationship is conveniently stated in Buys–Ballot's Law:

"If an observer stands with his back to the wind, then the lower pressure is situated on his left in the Northern Hemisphere and on his right in the Southern Hemisphere."

It becomes mathematically possible to calculate these geostrophic winds, and it is comparatively easy to produce geostrophic wind scales for assessing wind speeds on charts of known scale and latitudes. Although the mathematics behind the scale are somewhat advanced, the results may be stated here.

For wind moving with a velocity V in the Northern Hemisphere the acceleration to the right may be given by

$$2w \sin \theta . V$$

where w is the angular velocity of the earth and θ is the latitude.

If the pressure gradient is G the acceleration will be given by G/p, where p is the air density. Hence for balance of forces

$$2w \sin \theta . V = G/p$$
$$\text{i.e., } V = \frac{1}{2w \sin \theta . p} . G$$

The velocity is directly proportional to the gradient, or inversely proportional to the distance apart of the isobars. The geostrophic wind scale can be prepared to indicate the velocity of the wind according to this formula. In any one latitude the speed depends upon the distance apart of the isobars. Obviously the distances apart

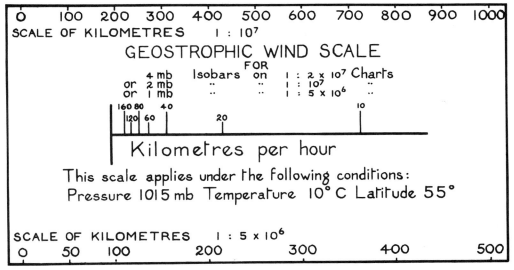

FIG. 27. A GEOSTROPHIC WIND SCALE

Percentage corrections are usually shown on the scale to compensate for differences in pressure, temperature, and latitude.

Corrections for the above scale are: for an increase of 10 mb pressure subtract 10 per cent. from velocity; for an increase of 5·5° C add 2 per cent. From latitude 55° to 65° subtract 1 per cent. for each degree above 55°. From latitude 55° to 45° add 1 per cent. for each degree below 55°.

of the gradations on the scale depend upon the scale of the chart in use and also on the interval of pressure between consecutive isobars. (Fig. 27 shows such a scale.)

WINDS NEAR THE EARTH'S SURFACE

The details explained above refer primarily to winds above six hundred metres. Air moving along the earth's surface continually strikes against obstacles which cause eddies and turbulence. Energy is lost by friction, and some of the momentum of the air is dissipated. The result is a loss in the geostrophic force. The latter now will not balance the gradient force, and the wind will, at the surface, blow somewhat across the isobars. The angle at which the surface winds cut the isobars depends upon the local surface conditions. Over the sea, where the friction is small, the reduction in velocity—and hence in the inflow across the isobars—is small; over wooded and built-up areas the loss of momentum is large, and consequently the effect is also large. A surface wind is therefore never steady; it is always gusty and veering, and backing and lulling. The surface wind velocity over the sea is inclined at approximately 15° towards the low-pressure area and is two-thirds of the wind speed at six hundred metres; over land the wind at the surface is inclined at 25°–30° towards the low and is half of the six hundred metre wind velocity.

It has already been stated that winds which are above six hundred metres and away from frictional effects are determined by the pressure gradients and the rotation of

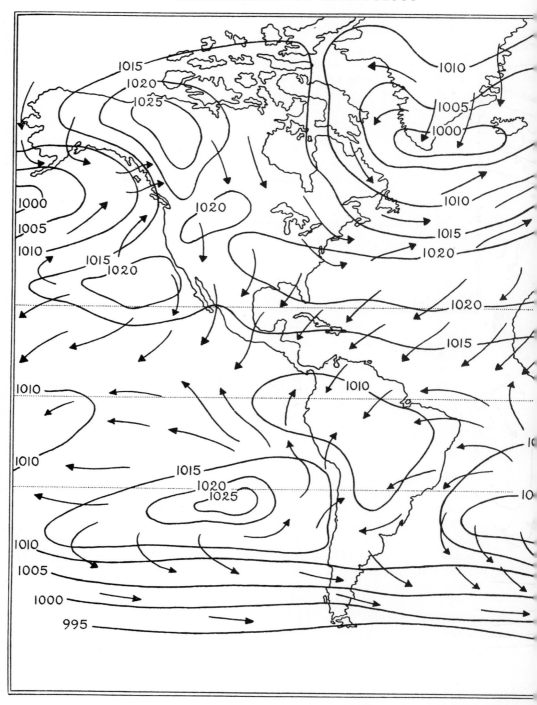

FIG. 28. WORLD PRESSURE AND WIND DISTRIB

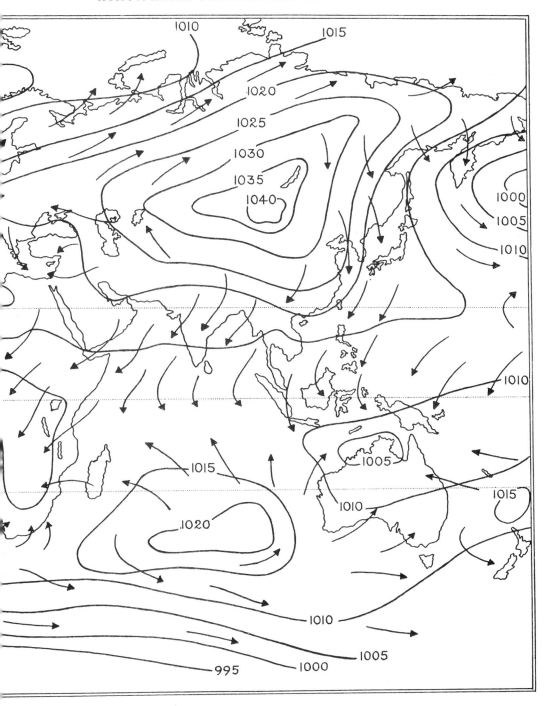

1010
1015
1020
1025
1030
1035
1040
1000
1005
1010
1010
1005
1010
1015
1015
1020
1010
1005
1000
995

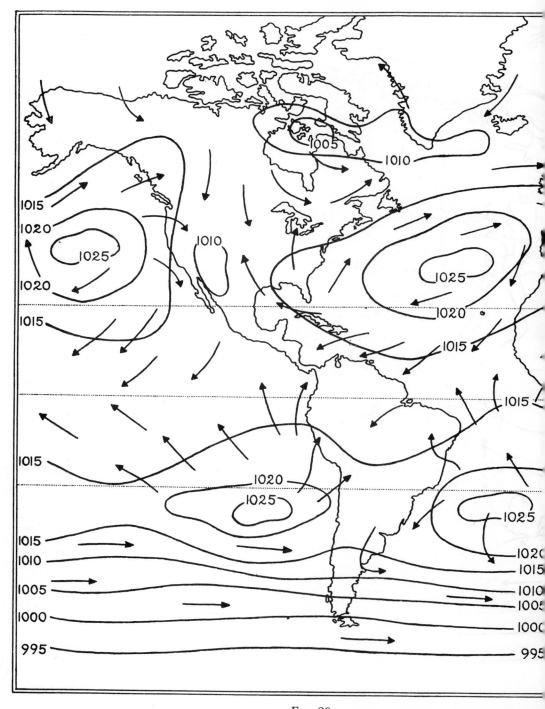

FIG. 29. WORLD PRESSURE AND WIND DISTRIBU

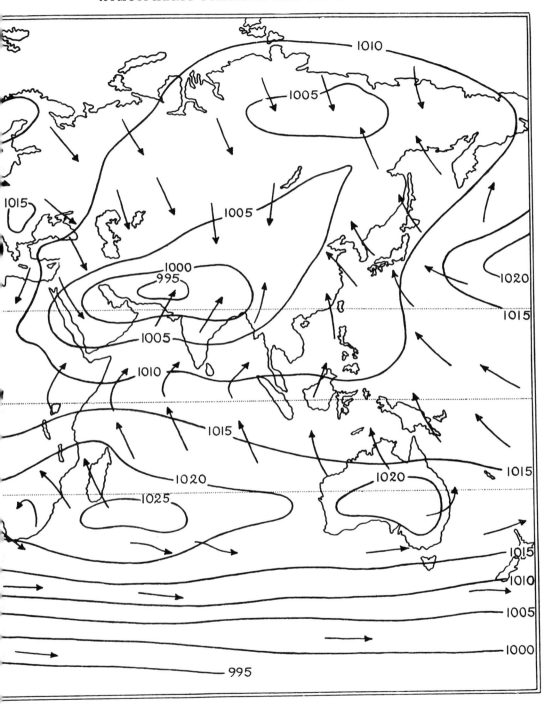

JULY (PRESSURE IN MILLIBARS)

the earth. One may obtain a good estimation of the prevailing wind and its geo-strophic force by an examination of the sea-level isobars (see Fig. 77). It should, of course, be remembered that an allowance must be made for friction near the surface, which will give reduced velocities and a deflection towards the lower pressures.

Figs. 28 and 29 show the world distribution of pressures and winds in January and July respectively.

There are, naturally enough, irregular variations in the mean winds. In regions of varying pressures there may be no well-defined wind speeds and directions, and although these variations follow a marked pattern according to the pressure patterns and their behaviour, they may provide many phenomena of weather. The small-scale variations in wind are generally referred to as turbulence, or gustiness. Gusti-ness may be due to

1. The mechanical effect of irregularities in the ground.
2. Thermal effects due to variations in ground heating.

The latter type of turbulence varies with the time of the day and the consequent variations in surface temperatures. Normally thermal currents are greatest during the daytime, reaching their maximum during the early afternoon. At night the air over a land surface tends to cool, and thermal currents die away. Where there is little diurnal variation of temperature there will be little turbulence. The effects of thermal heating and the resulting instability will be considered in the chapter on cloud formation.

SEA AND LAND BREEZES

Diurnal variations in winds are only to be expected when thermal currents develop by day and disappear at night. In coastal areas large daily wind changes are an important factor of climate. The wind is off the sea in the daytime; air is flowing from a region of relatively high pressure to a region of low pressure over the land. The condition most conducive to this sea breeze is afternoon in summer, when the pressure gradient is light. In mid-latitudes wind speeds may be of the order of 15–25 km/h; in low latitudes the speeds may be 30–40 km/h. The winds may extend vertically upward for about 300 m, and their influence may extend as far as 25 to 30 kilometres inland. (See Fig. 30.)

Land breezes blow towards the sea when the sea, being relatively warmer than the land, creates a condition of rising air and draws cooler air from the land surface. This is prevalent at night or early morning in autumn (and in winter, when the pressure gradient is again light). (See Fig. 31.) The sea-breeze effect may be strong enough to mask the wind created by the atmospheric pressure gradient. In this case the undisturbed wind will be found above the sea breeze.

The cause of the sea breeze is the reduced pressure over the land resulting from the presence of the warmer and lighter air above it. At night the conditions are reversed. The idea of warm, rising air over the land does not appear entirely to be the answer. Motion in the sea breeze is mainly horizontal and is due to horizontal differences in pressure. The simple suggestion that hot air rises over the land and cool air flows in to take its place cannot be wholly accepted, and a more elaborate explanation is necessary. Provided one remembers that wind is due to horizontal

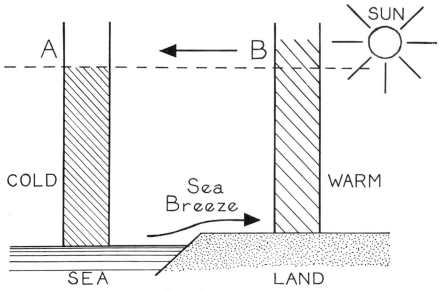

FIG. 30. SEA BREEZES

Air over land becomes warmer than that over the sea. Air in column B will expand, and the pressure at B will be greater than that at A. Air will commence to flow from B to A, as shown by the top arrow. The surface pressure over the land will fall, while that over the sea will rise. Air will now begin to flow towards the land, as shown by the lower arrow. A sea breeze has set in.

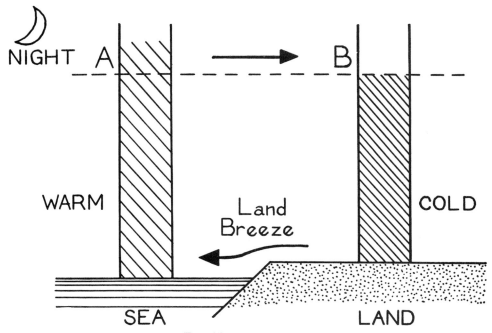

FIG. 31. LAND BREEZES

Air over the land is cooler than that over the sea, and the surface pressure in column B tends to become greater than that at the base of column A. An air flow now develops from land to sea.

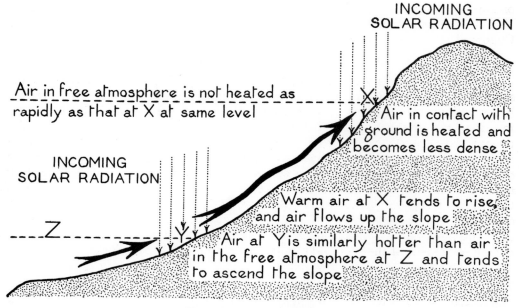

FIG. 32. ANABATIC WINDS

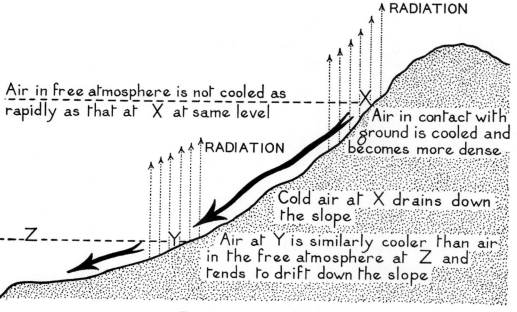

FIG. 33. KATABATIC WINDS

differences in pressure, and that air moves from regions of high to regions of low pressure, then one can readily appreciate the phenomena of sea and land breezes. The Asiatic monsoons are but an enlarged system of sea and land breezes (see Chapter 15).

ANABATIC AND KATABATIC WINDS

These surface winds are associated with hill slopes. If the slope is heated by the sun the air in contact with it becomes warmer than the air at the same level over the lower land surface; it is less dense and tends to rise. There is a tendency, therefore, for air to rise up the slope: such winds are called 'anabatic winds' (Fig. 32). The reverse effect (producing downward movements of air) occurs when the hill slope is cooling and it cools the air in contact with it to a lower temperature than the air at the same level over the lower land surfaces. The cold air along the hill slope tends to flow down the incline, so producing the 'katabatic wind' (Fig. 33). The speed of the wind is not great, being of the order of a few metres per second. There are, of course, exceptions, such as the bora of the Adriatic coast, which is an off-shore wind from the mountains of the Balkan peninsula. This is not a purely katabatic wind, but funnel effects of the mountain valleys do emphasize the air flow.

THE FÖHN WIND

The föhn wind (Fig. 34) is a mountain wind experienced in Switzerland. It is caused by surface air which is forced to move up and over mountain barriers. In so

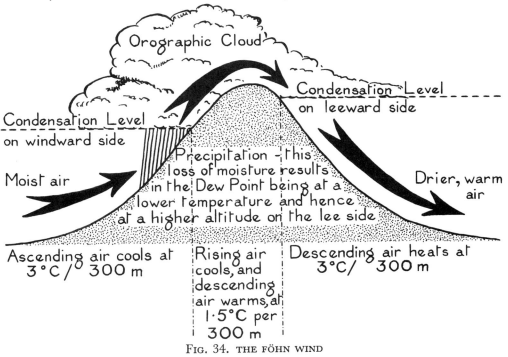

FIG. 34. THE FÖHN WIND

The graphical interpretation of the föhn effect is illustrated in Fig. 48. For a definition of dew point see p. 170.

doing the air cools adiabatically, and, if the vertical movement is large enough, condensation occurs and precipitation may result. The latent heat released is transferred to the air, which descends again to the other side of the mountain as a relatively dry and warm wind.

Winds of the Upper Atmosphere

The wind at any level is related to the pressure distribution at that level, in the same way as the wind at six hundred metres is related to the pressure distribution at the surface. It is therefore necessary to consider the factors that influence the pressure distribution at an upper level.

Atmospheric pressure always decreases with height, the difference of pressure between any two points on the same vertical line being equal to the weight of a column of air of unit cross-section whose ends contain those points. But warm air

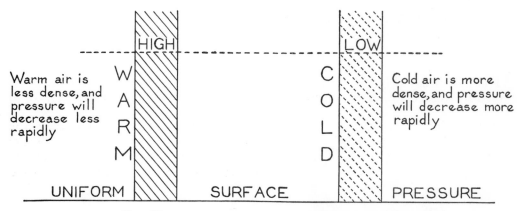

FIG. 35. PRESSURE DIFFERENCES IN THE UPPER ATMOSPHERE

is lighter than cold, volume for volume. Hence the decrease in pressure with altitude takes place more slowly in warm air than in cold.

It follows that if the surface pressure over a portion of the earth were uniform, but the temperature of the atmosphere above were not, then, at any upper level, relatively high pressure would exist in places where the air below this level was comparatively warm, and relatively low pressure would exist where the air below was comparatively cold. (See Fig. 35.) Isobars, and therefore winds, would exist at the upper level even in the absence of winds at the surface (Fig. 36). The upper wind in such circumstances, being closely associated with temperature differences, is called a 'thermal wind.'

Usually, of course, pressure differences do exist at the surface; then there will be a system of isobars there, with an associated system of winds. But if the overlying atmosphere were not of the same vertical temperature structure everywhere the horizontal pressure distribution would gradually change from one level to another during change of altitude—that is, the isobaric pattern at any level would be slightly different from that at any neighbouring level. It follows that the winds would also change with altitude.

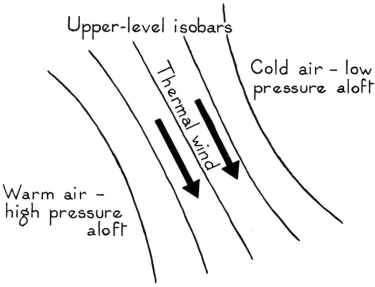

FIG. 36. UPPER-LEVEL ISOBARS, RESULTING FROM PRESSURE DIFFERENCES

Nevertheless, in order to determine the wind at any particular point above the earth's surface it is not necessary first to construct an isobaric chart for the level of the point. Instead, the hypothetical wind that would exist at the point in the absence of any pressure differences at the earth's surface—that is, the appropriate thermal

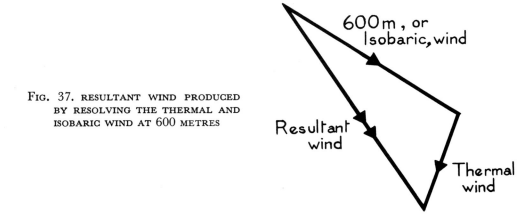

FIG. 37. RESULTANT WIND PRODUCED BY RESOLVING THE THERMAL AND ISOBARIC WIND AT 600 METRES

wind—could be calculated and then compounded with the actual wind below the point at six hundred metres above sea-level (see Fig. 37). The 'thermal wind' is now simply one component of the resultant wind, but a component which becomes more and more important with increasing altitude. At great heights, in fact, it may by itself be an adequate approximation to the true wind. Near the tropopause winds as strong as 300 km/h, owing largely to the thermal effect, are not unknown.

It follows from the above that, with increase in altitude above six hundred metres, the wind can veer or back, increase or decrease, according to the position of warm or cold air relative to the run of the surface isobars. Generally speaking, however, warm air lies to the south in the Northern Hemisphere, so that the thermal component of the wind at any height will, as a rule, be westerly. Hence upper winds tend to become increasingly westerly with increase in height.

Upper winds may be determined by observing the path followed in space by a free balloon, either by using one or two theodolites or by means of radio and radar apparatus. The latter methods permit of wind determination to great heights, and even in cloudy conditions. Pressures in the upper air may be calculated from measured surface pressures and upper-air temperatures.

By plotting upper winds and pressures it is possible to draw upper-level isobars, which then enable upper winds to be forecast over areas for which specific measurements are not available. In addition, future upper-level isobars—and, therefore, future upper winds—can then be forecast. In practice, however, instead of drawing lines of equal pressure on a surface of constant altitude it is found more useful to draw lines of equal altitude on a surface of constant pressure—that is, instead of isobars for a specific altitude contour lines for a surface of constant pressure are used. These contours are plotted on a working chart and, for purposes of wind determination, can be used in much the same way as are isobars.

Today, the forecasting of upper-level winds has become of the utmost importance. Modern high-flying jet aircraft, which daily cross the Atlantic at 12 000 to 15 000 metres, are flying within the tropopause and consequently experience these high-level winds. Indeed, the supersonic Concorde is now flying regularly in the lower stratosphere where conditions are somewhat different again.

The general tendency for the westerlies continues throughout the tropopause, but in the stratosphere the temperature distribution changes, and hence the thermal-wind component changes also. In the stratosphere the coldest air is situated at low latitudes; the horizontal temperature gradient is reversed, and the thermal winds are similarly reversed. It follows, then, that, while the westerlies may increase with height into the tropopause, the increase does not continue into the stratosphere. Little information is as yet available about air movements in the stratosphere, but what evidence there is suggests that winds at these levels are no more constant in speed or direction than those winds nearer the earth's surface. Turbulence effects and buffeting of aircraft suggest that strange, unaccountable movements of air are taking place. 'Jet streams,' or narrow belts of extremely rapid air movement, occur at the level of the tropopause, where differing air-mass types lie adjacent to one another. Navigation in these regions, however, is becoming more commonplace in aviation, and in recent years attempts have been made to glean more and more information about the behaviour of the atmosphere on the edge of the stratosphere.

The satellite projects of the United States and Russia have thrown light upon this problem. The large amount of statistical data relating to stratospheric conditions which satellites now provide is being analysed by computer as a matter of routine. Activities on the edge of space directly affect the troposphere, and atmospheric circulation at lower levels is now being predicted with greater accuracy as a result of the successful interpretation of meteorological situations in the stratosphere and mesosphere.

Chapter 5

WATER VAPOUR IN THE ATMOSPHERE

ALTHOUGH water vapour represents only a very small proportion of the earth's atmosphere, being approximately 2 per cent. of the total mass, it is the most important constituent of the air in deciding weather and climate. Water may be present in the atmosphere as an invisible gas, as water droplets, or as ice, but it is the invisible vapour form which concerns the meteorologist. The term 'humidity' refers only to this invisible gas, or vapour, and humidity is highly inconstant throughout the atmosphere. This variability in the water-vapour content of the atmosphere, in both place and time, is of great significance for several reasons:

1. The amount of water vapour present in a given volume of air is an indication of the atmosphere's potential capacity for precipitation.

2. Water vapour, in its power to absorb radiation, is a regulator of heat loss from the earth.

3. The amount of water vapour present decides the quantity of latent energy stored up in the atmosphere for the growth of storms.

4. The amount of water vapour present is an important factor affecting the human body's rate of cooling.

The source of the water vapour in the atmosphere is the great oceans which cover almost three-quarters of the earth's surface. By wind and other atmospheric movements the vapour evaporated from these masses of water is carried in over the continents, where it may become condensed again and may ultimately fall as rain or snow and hail.

There is a definite maximum amount of water vapour that a given quantity of air can hold at a certain temperature. When the air contains this maximum amount it is said to be saturated, and the amount of vapour present is called the 'saturation water-vapour content.' This saturation content increases with temperature—that is, warm air can hold more water vapour than cold air. Thus, if warm air which contains moisture, but is not yet saturated, is cooled it will ultimately reach a temperature at which it will become saturated. Any further cooling will produce condensation, and some moisture will be deposited in liquid or solid form. The temperature at which the air becomes saturated is termed the 'dew point.'

Table 9 shows how the amount of water which can be held in a given volume of air is controlled by the temperature. The moisture content is expressed in grams per cubic metre and represents the amount of water necessary to saturate the air at the appropriate temperature.

The total amount of water vapour that a given volume of air contains, usually expressed in grams per cubic metre, is called the 'absolute humidity.' Since it gives the actual content of water vapour in the air, it is of some significance in assessing the atmosphere's possibilities for precipitation. Absolute humidity is usually highest in low latitudes and decreases towards the Poles. It does, of course, vary with distance from oceans. Absolute humidity is higher in summer than in winter and is usually greater during the day than at night.

It is often more convenient to know to what degree the air is partially saturated instead of stating how much vapour is present in the air in grammes. The actual

TABLE 9.—VALUES OF MOISTURE CONTENT AT SATURATION POINT FOR GIVEN TEMPERATURES

TEMPERATURE	MOISTURE CONTENT
° C	g/m³
—15	1·6
—10	2·3
— 5	3·4
0	4·8
5	6·8
10	9·4
15	12·8
20	17·3
25	22·9
30	30·3
35	39·6
40	50·6

weight of water vapour in a given volume of air at a given temperature is expressed as a ratio of the maximum possible amount of water vapour that could be held in the same volume of air at the same temperature. This ratio, expressed as a percentage, is defined as the fraction of saturation and is known as the 'relative humidity.' This can be expressed more concisely:

$$\frac{\text{relative humidity}}{100} = \frac{\text{absolute humidity}}{\text{saturation content at the same temperature}}$$

Relative humidity depends both upon the absolute humidity and the temperature; if the moisture content remains the same, then the relative humidity will decrease as the temperature rises and will increase as the temperature falls. Table 10 shows how air, which is saturated at 5° C, acquires successively lower relative humidities merely by increasing its temperature.

If unsaturated air is cooled sufficiently its capacity for holding moisture is thus reduced, and a temperature will be reached at which the relative humidity of that air will be 100 per cent., even though the amount of water vapour has not itself altered. This critical temperature, we have already seen, is called the 'dew point.' If air is cooled below this dew point the excess of water vapour, over and above that which the air could contain at that temperature, will become visible as minute particles of water or ice (depending on the temperature being above or below 0° C), and condensation will have taken place.

TABLE 10.—TEMPERATURE AS A CONTROLLING FACTOR
IN RELATIVE HUMIDITIES

TEMPERATURE	ABSOLUTE HUMIDITY	RELATIVE HUMIDITY
° C	g/m³	per cent.
5	6·8	100
10	6·8	72
15	6·8	53
20	6·8	39
25	6·8	30
30	6·8	22

CONDENSATION

The process by which invisible water vapour, evaporated from the water surfaces of the earth, is condensed and ultimately returned to the surface as precipitation is of the utmost importance to the study of meteorology, and it is necessary to examine the effects of condensation closely and try to relate these to precipitation.

Significant amounts of water vapour in the atmosphere can only be changed into either the liquid or solid state if the temperature of the air is reduced to the dew point. The dew point of any mass of air is closely related to its relative humidity. When the relative humidity is high and the air is nearly saturated, then only a small amount of cooling will be necessary before the dew point is reached and condensation commences. Conversely, when the relative humidity is low a large amount of cooling is necessary before the dew point is reached. Condensation therefore depends upon

1. The amount of cooling.
2. The relative humidity of the air.

Fig. 38 shows a graph which plots the absolute humidity when the air is saturated against temperature. It will be seen that the curve steepens sharply as the temperature increases and changes of temperature produce great variations in the amount of water vapour released. For example, less water vapour will condense out of air cooling from 10° C to 5° C than will be condensed from air which is cooled from 35° C to 30° C. The application of this fact can be made in the assessment of precipitation amounts in the various climates of the world, and in the types and heights of clouds in various localities of the world. These facts will be discussed more fully in the following chapters.

Moisture is often precipitated directly from the atmosphere without passing through the stage of visible cloud. Condensation is frequently noticed when warm, moist air comes into contact with a cold surface. The misting of car windows in winter is one example. A similar effect may be noticed on house windows: warm, humid air indoors comes into contact with the cold pane of glass, and moisture condenses directly. When the temperature of the surface of the earth is below the dew point of the air above, condensation takes place directly, and dew is formed. If the condensation temperature is below freezing-point, then ice or frost is deposited

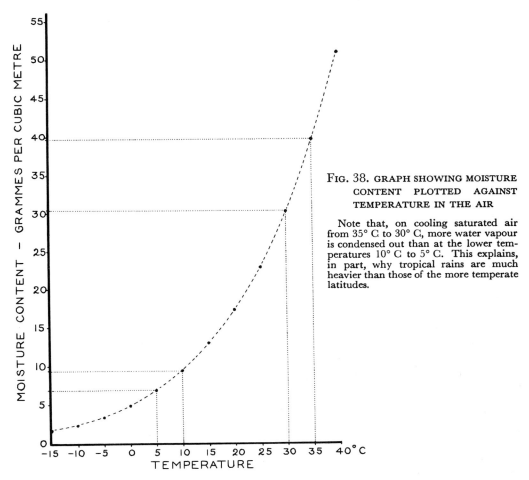

FIG. 38. GRAPH SHOWING MOISTURE CONTENT PLOTTED AGAINST TEMPERATURE IN THE AIR

Note that, on cooling saturated air from 35° C to 30° C, more water vapour is condensed out than at the lower temperatures 10° C to 5° C. This explains, in part, why tropical rains are much heavier than those of the more temperate latitudes.

directly. Hoar-frost is the ordinary white coating of ice which is often seen on ground and exposed surfaces on any winter's morning after a clear, cold night.

Cooling of the atmosphere so as to cause condensation of the water vapour present may be brought about by several methods. By direct radiation and conduction relatively shallow layers of air may have their temperatures reduced to below the dew point. The condensation products (dew, frost, fog) resulting from this cooling are usually confined to air in close proximity to the earth's surface, and they are located in relatively small areas. Precipitation on any large scale never results from this type of cooling. Cooling sufficient to reduce the temperature of large masses of air (so that abundant precipitation results from the condensation) is associated with rising air currents. The expansion of air gives rise to cooling of an adiabatic nature, and condensation may occur in large air masses and up to great vertical extent.

Summarizing the main points mentioned above, it may be stated that the essential cause of all condensation is the reduction of the air temperature below its dew point. This may be brought about in any one of the following ways:

1. Loss of heat by direct radiation from the air.
2. Loss of heat by conduction to a cold surface.
3. The mixing of two masses of air at different temperatures.
4. Adiabatic cooling due to ascent.

According to theory, it is considered that water vapour in the atmosphere is entirely vapour until 100 per cent. relative humidity is reached: further cooling results in a portion of the vapour being condensed into liquid or solid form. In addition, it is assumed that liquid droplets do not exist freely in the atmosphere at temperatures below freezing-point, and any such droplets are immediately frozen into ice particles as soon as freezing-point is reached. Furthermore, theory suggests that at temperatures below freezing-point all condensation is directly from the gas to the solid state—that is, that a process of sublimation occurs. In actual fact, the three theoretical assumptions are only partially correct.

Fog, and even some cloud formation, are likely to commence before 100 per cent. relative humidity is reached. Naturally the process increases in speed as complete saturation is approached. In some industrial smoke fogs, colloquially referred to as 'smog,' the humidities may be below 90 per cent. It is now known that condensation occurs only when microscopic nuclei, around which the droplets could form, are present. These particles, in order to cause condensation, must have a high affinity with water—that is, they must be hygroscopic nuclei. The most common hygroscopic nuclei are salt, which is derived from the oceans and seas, and smoke, especially that associated with the combustion of coal and oil. The particles are extremely small, being of the order of one-millionth of a metre in diameter (10^{-6} m). This is less than the wave-length of ordinary light, and therefore the nuclei are quite invisible. They themselves do not affect the clarity of the atmosphere.

Liquid condensation droplets do exist in large numbers in the atmosphere at temperatures below freezing-point, and fogs composed of water droplets have been observed at temperatures ten degrees below freezing-point. It is now generally accepted that the majority of clouds down to a temperature of $-20°$ C (except those in which there are rapidly ascending currents) are composed predominantly of water particles. The agitation of the air which is associated with this condition rapidly produces a solidification of the water droplets. (For a closer examination of this effect see Chapter 9.)

Condensation appears to be a continuous process, and hygroscopic nuclei begin to attract water to them at relatively low humidities. A slight haze is the first sign of such condensation, and as the relative humidity approaches 100 per cent. the growth of these particles becomes rapid, and fog conditions develop.

WATER DROPLETS

Gravity acts upon water droplets in the same way that it acts upon any other body having mass and weight. Thus, whatever the size of a water particle, it must tend to fall through the air under the force of gravity. A droplet, allowed to fall through still air, will rapidly reach a maximum downward velocity until the resistance of the air just balances its weight. This terminal velocity is shown for droplets of various diameters in Table 11.

TABLE 11.—THE SIZE OF WATER DROPLETS AND THEIR TERMINAL VELOCITIES

Diameter of Droplet, in mm	0·01	0·1	1·0	2·0	3·0	4·0	5·0	5·5
Terminal velocity of droplet, in m/s	0·003	0·32	4·4	5·9	6·9	7·7	8·0	8·0

In the average cloud water droplets have a diameter of about 0·01 mm. Needing no vertical motion of the air to support them, they are carried in all directions along with the air. As these smaller droplets collide with each other, they coalesce until larger droplets are formed. It has been found that the largest size to which water droplets can grow is approximately 5·5 mm in diameter. Any larger droplets cannot attain their terminal velocity without being disintegrated by the effects of air resistance. Any droplets which do in fact grow larger than 5·5 mm are speedily broken up into smaller droplets.

The point at which the water droplets overcome the effects of vertical currents and do commence to fall under the force of gravity may take place at any time. Droplets having the maximum diameter of 5·5 mm can be kept aloft by upward currents of eight metres per second. This speed of vertical air movement is quite common, and therefore droplets of any size up to the maximum may be found in the mass of a cloud. Only when the up-currents are insufficient to support the droplets will these fall as precipitation.

Chapter 6

CLOUDS AND CLOUD FORMATION

CLOUD study is one of the most fascinating aspects of meteorology, and even the person who has no knowledge of the physics behind cloud formation can derive immense pleasure from an examination of the infinite forms which clouds take. Cloud forms clearly reflect the physical processes which are taking place in the atmosphere, and they are therefore obvious indicators of weather conditions. But before an attempt is made to give a classification of cloud types, the outlines of the physics of cloud formation will be considered.

Clouds are caused mainly by the adiabatic cooling of air below its dew point; this cooling process is most effectively created by upward movements of air, which in

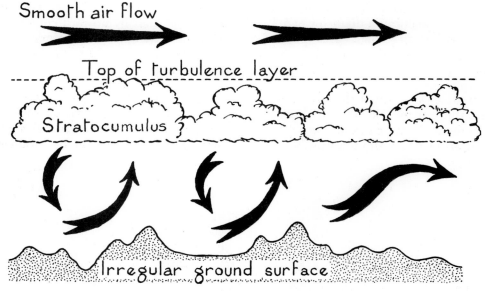

FIG. 39. TURBULENCE CLOUD

The turbulence may be sufficient in unstable air to produce larger cumulus cloud which becomes embedded within the stratocumulus layer.

turn produce reductions in pressure. The various types of cloud and their associated precipitation can then be accounted for entirely by the various forms of upward motion:

1. Turbulence effects (Fig. 39).
2. Uplift due to relief effects: orographic uplift (Fig. 40).
3. Convectional effects (Fig. 41).
4. General uplift over wide areas (Fig. 42).

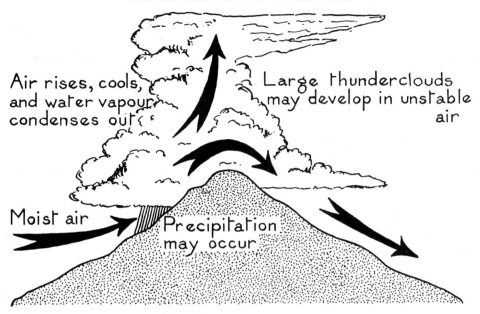

FIG. 40. OROGRAPHIC CLOUD

In some cases two or three of these types of vertical motion may operate together, but each process will be considered in turn, and the simple cloud types associated with them illustrated in outline. Where two or more of the types of vertical movement of air occur simultaneously a wide variety of cloud forms may be produced

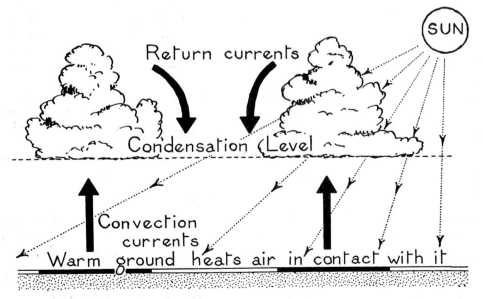

FIG. 41. CONVECTION CLOUD

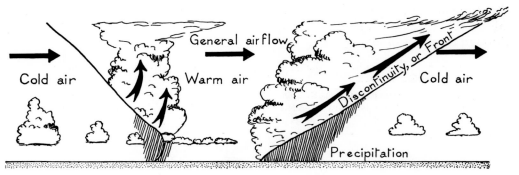

FIG. 42. FRONTAL CLOUD

which do not fit into any simple class. At this point it is necessary to enlarge upon the meaning of the term 'adiabatic' and give further attention to lapse rates and the stability of the atmosphere.

ADIABATIC COOLING

In Chapter 3 it was explained that it is a property of all gases that when they are compressed the temperature rises, and when they are allowed to expand the temperature decreases; also, changes of temperature due to expansion and compression within the gas system were explained as being adiabatic changes. It is now necessary to elaborate upon the remarks made in that chapter.

'Adiabatic' is a term used in thermodynamics which applies to changes in the pressure and density of a gas when heat can neither enter nor leave the system. In other words, the system is 'thermally insulated,' and when the gas expands or contracts no heat can be given out or taken in. In the atmosphere such a system is obtained in the interior of an air mass which is rising to a position of lower pressure or descending to one of higher pressure. As a consequence of this, there is a mechanical change of temperature. This change of temperature is of vital importance in the study of clouds, because it accounts largely for their formation and disappearance—and probably for the entire precipitation received by the earth.

A thermally insulated system is difficult to envisage in practice, and we have to suppose the gas to be contained in a case which is impermeable to heat. Changes of temperature produced in such a system are quite considerable, and Table 12 illustrates these changes most effectively.

We saw in Chapter 3 that there was a distinct relationship between temperature and pressure changes, and that this could be expressed by the formula:

$$\log T - \log T_0 = 0 \cdot 288(\log p - \log p_0)$$

where T_0 and p_0 are the initial absolute temperature and pressure and T is the new temperature when the pressure has changed to p. We saw further that unsaturated air—i.e., dry air in meteorological terminology—cooled at a rate of 3° C per three hundred metres rise. It was clear that this rate of cooling of ascending air was considerably more rapid than the normal environmental rate of cooling. Here it is important to differentiate between the two. The dry adiabatic lapse rate represents the rising and cooling of a moving mass of air. The environmental lapse rate is the falling off in temperature as recorded by a thermometer which is carried aloft through the layer of air.

TABLE 12.—FALLS IN TEMPERATURE FOR ADIABATIC PRESSURE CHANGES

ADIABATIC CHANGE OF PRESSURE DECREASING FROM 1000 MB BY	FALL IN TEMPERATURE FROM 17° C., IN ° C.
10	0·89
100	8·7
200	18·2
300	28·4
400	39·9
Mb ⎨ 500	52·8
600	67·8
700	85·5
800	108·2
900	141·4

The rate of cooling for unsaturated air which is forced upward is a fixed value and may be calculated from the expression:

$$\frac{v-1}{v} \cdot \frac{g}{R}$$

where R = the gas constant = $2\cdot8703 \times 10^6$.
    g = acceleration of gravity = $9\cdot8062$ m/s² at 45° latitude at mean sea-level.
    v = the ratio of the specific heats of dry air at constant pressure and constant volume respectively = $1\cdot402$.

The value calculated from this expression gives a dry adiabatic lapse rate of 0·98° C per hundred metres, which approximates to 3° C per three hundred metres.

Once rising air reaches the level at which condensation occurs—that is, the level of the dew point and the level where clouds begin to form—the rising saturated air cools at a somewhat lower rate: the saturated adiabatic lapse rate. Heated air will continue to rise until it reaches those layers in which the air has similar characteristics of temperature and density. This process of cooling by the expansion of rising air currents is the only one capable of reducing the temperature of large masses of air to the dew point and below. The direct and obvious result of cooling due to the upward movement of air is clouds. One can therefore define clouds as being a form of condensation in air at altitude. Fog and cloud are identical in their characteristics; the only difference is the height at which these condensation products are situated.

STABILITY AND INSTABILITY OF THE ATMOSPHERE

It has already been indicated that almost all precipitation is due to vertical movements within the atmosphere. Consequently all conditions which encourage or hinder such movements are of great importance. Mention was made of stability and instability within the atmosphere in those sections of the book dealing with the temperature of the atmosphere, but it is essential to explore the subject further, because these characteristics of the atmosphere are directly related to condensation and precipitation.

Air is said to be stable if it resists vertical uplift and if, when forced to rise, it tends to return to its former position. Vertical currents of air are virtually absent in stable air. If, however, displacement upward results in a tendency for the air to continue

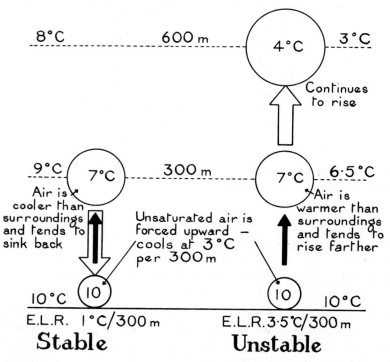

FIG. 43. A COMPARISON BETWEEN STABLE AND UNSTABLE AIR CONDITIONS

to rise, then a condition of instability exists. Vertical movement of air is most prevalent in these conditions. (See Fig. 43.)

An air mass is stable or unstable according to the relationship between its environmental lapse rate and its adiabatic lapse rates (see Chapter 3, pp. 41, 42). If the environmental lapse rate is greater than 3° C per three hundred metres, then the air will be unstable whether the air is saturated or not. If the environmental lapse rate is less than 1·5° C per three hundred metres the air will be stable, whether it is unsaturated or saturated. If, however, the environmental lapse rate is between 1·5° C and 3·0° C per three hundred metres the air will be stable if it is unsaturated and unstable if it is saturated.

The environmental lapse rate may exceed the dry adiabatic lapse rate on such occasions as a bright, hot afternoon. The surface air will be unstable and will be inclined to rise. Conversely, on cold, clear winter nights the environmental lapse rate may be less than the adiabatic rate; the air will be stable, and there will be no tendency to rise.

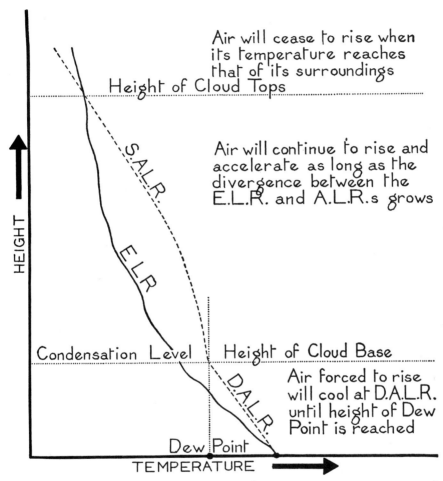

FIG. 44. PRINCIPLE OF CLOUD FORMATION (A.L.R. = ADIABATIC LAPSE RATE)

The theory of cloud formation (see Fig. 44) is therefore based upon the relationships between the environmental lapse rate and the dry and wet adiabatic lapse rates. The general thermodynamics of rising air can be understood in the light of what has just been considered. A mass of warm, unsaturated air can be forced aloft, and its conditions with regard to temperature and condensation of the water vapour present can be examined through the various stages of ascent. The first stage can be called the 'dry stage.' Here the ascending air cools at the normal dry adiabatic lapse rate of 3° C per three hundred metres rise, but, since dew point has not been reached, there is no moisture in either solid or liquid form present in the atmosphere.

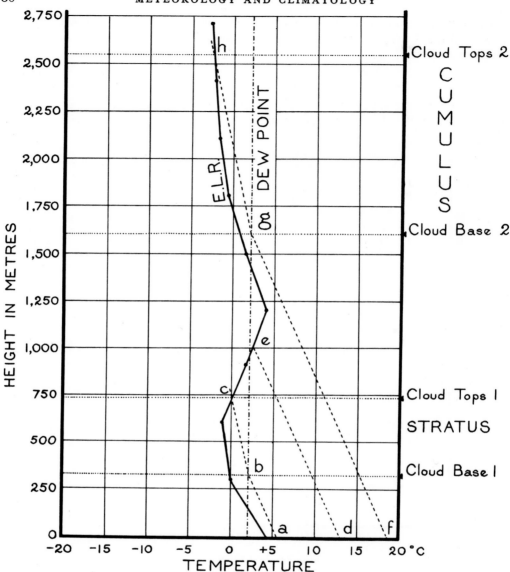

FIG. 45. GRAPH SHOWING HOW CLOUD HEIGHTS, TYPES, AND THICKNESS MAY BE CALCULATED

If the air near the surface reaches a temperature of 5·5° C, and if that air is given an upward stimulus, then it will rise and cool at the D.A.L.R. along line a–b. At b the air has reached the dew point, and condensation will occur. The air will continue to rise, cooling at the S.A.L.R. along line b–c. At c the air is now at the same temperature as its surroundings (E.L.R.) and thus the air ceases to rise farther. The cloud so formed is likely to be of the layer type.

If the ground temperature rises still higher to 13° C the rising air would cool along line d–e. This rising air never reaches its dew point before it reaches the temperature of its surroundings. Any cloud previously formed will now disperse.

A further temperature increase to 18·5° C will cause any rising air to cool along line f–g. At g the air has reached the dew point, and condensation will commence again. The air continues to rise to h, where once more the air reaches the temperature of its environment, and the upward movement is curtailed. This corresponds with the cloud tops. The condition is likely to lead to the formation of fair-weather cumulus.

Eventually the ascending and cooling air will reach the height of the dew point. (This altitude varies with the time of the year.) Condensation commences, and the ascending air enters the 'cloud-and-rain stage.' At this level the clouds are composed of minute water droplets. For this condensation to occur latent heat has been released, and consequently the air, in rising farther, will cool at the saturated adiabatic lapse rate. Continued condensation will take place until the rising air eventually reaches the temperature of the surrounding air—that is, until the rising

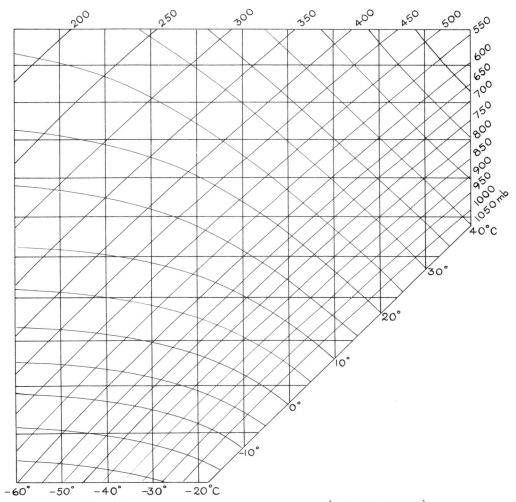

FIG. 46. A REPRODUCTION OF A TEPHIGRAM (REDUCED IN SIZE)

The tephigram differs from conventional graphs in that the axes are not at right angles. The vertical lines represent temperature in degrees Celsius. The other axis is that of pressure, which is plotted on the diagonal lines running upward from left to right. The environmental lapse rate (E.L.R.) is plotted on these axes. Superimposed on the basic axes are two other sets of lines: the horizontal lines represent the gradient of the dry adiabatic lapse rate, that is, a fall in temperature of 3° C per three hundred-metre rise in height; the curved lines sloping upward from right to left represent the gradient of the saturated adiabatic lapse rate. It is possible to compare the plotted E.L.R. directly with the S.A.L.R. or D.A.L.R., and thus assess the stability of the atmosphere.

air, cooling at the saturated adiabatic lapse rate, reaches the same temperature as the environmental lapse rate. This level will indicate the cloud tops. It is conceivable that the air will not reach the temperature of its surroundings before the temperature reaches 0° C. When the ascending and cooling air reaches the freezing-point the condensed particles become ice crystals. Beyond this level continued adiabatic cooling may result in additional condensation, and, since the temperatures are below freezing-point, the remaining water vapour theoretically passes directly into the solid state.

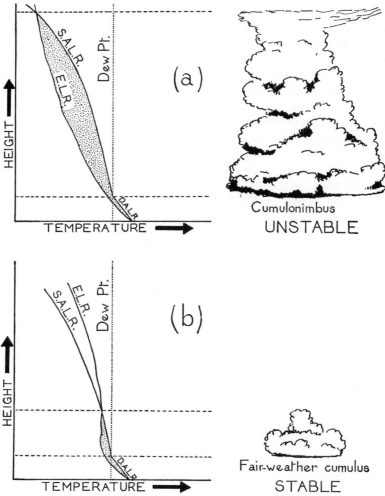

FIG. 47. A COMPARISON BETWEEN GRAPHS. ONE SHOWS UNSTABLE CONDITIONS, THE OTHER ILLUSTRATES STABLE CONDITIONS

The area enclosed by the graph lines of the environmental lapse rate and the adiabatic lapse rate is a measure of the stability of the atmosphere. The larger the area, then the more unstable is the air.

The above theory of cloud formation is only applicable in part. Condensation may in fact commence before the complete saturation occurs, and the water droplets may exist at temperatures much below 0° C. From the evidence available it would appear that supercooled droplets are the rule rather than the exception at temperatures below freezing-point. But the theory does indicate the general principles of cloud formation, and it can be seen from Fig. 45 that cloud types and thicknesses can be calculated by comparison of the environmental lapse rate with the dry adiabatic and saturated adiabatic lapse rate. In the meteorological service the fullest possible use is made of upper-air temperatures and humidities. More elaborate graphical methods than those shown in Fig. 45 have been evolved to assess cloud amounts and heights. The most common type of graph employed by the Meteorological Office is the 'tephigram.' This is merely a convenient method of plotting air temperature against pressure, as observed in upper-air recordings. A specimen chart is shown in Fig. 46. The horizontal lines represent the dry adiabatic lapse rate, while the curved lines indicate the saturated adiabatic lapse rate. If the environmental lapse rate is then plotted one can see readily how it compares with the dry adiabatic or saturated adiabatic lapse rates. From this one can obtain an idea of the degree of stability or instability of the atmosphere.

Fig. 47 shows the comparisons between the environmental lapse rate and the dry adiabatic and saturated adiabatic lapse rates. In Fig. 47 (a) the environmental lapse rate is considerably steeper than the adiabatic lapse rates, and consequently the cloud depth and instability layer are of some magnitude. In Fig. 47 (b) the environmental lapse rate is not so steep, and the saturated adiabatic lapse rate crosses it at a low altitude; the cloud is of small vertical extent.

TURBULENCE CLOUD

Turbulence is a feature of the surface winds, and extends upwards of five hundred to six hundred metres. Physical obstructions and friction effects are responsible for the creation of eddies and irregular movements within the general air flow. The ultimate result of turbulence is the mixing of layers of air so that the water vapour is fairly evenly distributed throughout the air mass. Adiabatic changes in the rising and falling air produce conditions where cloud may form. The irregular turbulence tends to produce a layer of cloud which is continually being formed in the up-currents and dispersed in the down-currents. There are two conditions which enable turbulence cloud to form:

1. The humidity must be high enough for the dew point to be reached near to the surface.
2. Turbulence must be sufficient for the air to be carried up to the dew-point level.

If the layer immediately above the turbulence level is unstable, then large up-currents would commence, and the turbulence cloud would rapidly change from a layer type, so producing large, towering, heap-type clouds (see Fig. 39).

Turbulence cloud, by the very character of its formation, is low cloud, and it is usually of the layer type. The base may be between the surface and six hundred metres; the vertical thickness may vary from a few metres up to 1000 or 1500 metres, depending upon the degree of stability of the lower layers. Since the clouds are continually undergoing formation in the ascending currents and dispersal in the down-currents, there is rarely sufficient activity within them to produce precipitation.

Turbulence cloud is quite common in Britain when moist air from the Atlantic arrives in our temperate latitudes; it produces those characteristically dull, overcast days with little rain.

OROGRAPHIC CLOUD

Air which is compelled to rise over a barrier of hills or mountains may be forced aloft until the dew-point level is reached. Condensation will occur, and cloud will form on the hills. The amount of ascent necessary to produce condensation will depend upon the degree of humidity of the air. In Britain, where moist south-

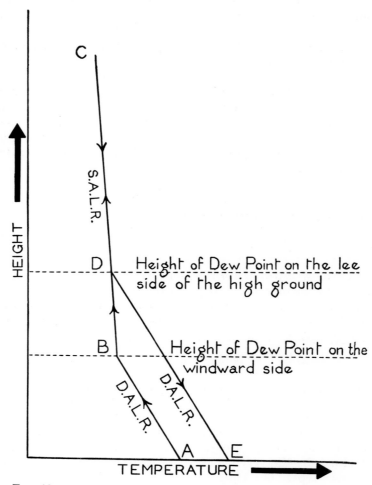

FIG. 48. GRAPH TO ILLUSTRATE THE EFFECT OF THE FÖHN WIND

Moist air, on rising, will cool as indicated by the graph A–B–C, but, on returning downward on the leeward side of the high ground, will heat up along the graph line C–D–E. Thus the temperature to the leeward side of the hill will rise from A to E.

westerly air moves up and over the coastal cliffs, cloud may be formed where the ascent is as small as a hundred metres.

The degree of stability controls the cloud types. If the air is comparatively stable, then layer cloud with a flat base is formed (see Fig. 40). Where there is marked instability within the air mass the air may go on ascending, and cloud of great vertical thickness may result.

The Föhn Effect. Air which is forced to rise over a range of hills will cool at the dry adiabatic lapse rate until the level of the dew point is reached. At this level condensation occurs, and cooling now takes place at the saturated adiabatic lapse rate. If the ascent is sufficient some moisture may fall out as rain. Consequently, on descent over the leeward side of the hills, there will be less moisture in the air mass than there was on the windward side. The air will warm up at the saturated adiabatic lapse rate until the level of the dew point is reached again. Because there is less moisture now present the temperature of the dew point on the windward side will be less than it was; this means that the level of the dew point on the leeward side will be higher, and therefore moisture will be reabsorbed at a greater altitude than that at which it was condensed on the windward side. The descending air will now heat up at the dry adiabatic lapse rate, and, if the downward flow brings the air to the same level as it was originally before orographic uplift, the temperature will be correspondingly higher. (See Fig. 48.) High ranges of mountains may produce warming of some 8°–10° C on the leeward side. In the Alps the local name for these warm, dry winds is the föhn, and this name has been applied to all winds created in this way. The Chinook of the Rockies is a good example.

CONVECTION CLOUD

Convection currents are formed in two ways:

1. Air may be heated and forced to rise by direct heating from ground surfaces.
2. Air may become vertically unstable.

If the air is forced to ascend to the level of its dew point, then cloud will form. The thickness of the cloud layer will again depend upon the stability of the air mass. In unstable conditions the cloud may be of great vertical extent; in stable conditions the clouds may be small and quite innocuous (see Fig. 41). Fair-weather cumulus is a good example of convection cloud which is formed under stable conditions; violent summer thunderstorms are the result of convection cloud which has formed under unstable conditions. Wherever air is heated from below some convection will occur. Fig. 49 (a) shows the effect of air being heated by direct contact with the ground; Fig. 49 (b) shows how air, in moving from higher latitudes to lower latitudes, may be heated from below, so bringing about conditions under which convection currents may develop. Shower conditions associated with the frequent cold north-westerly air streams over Britain are a good example of this latter type of convection cloud.

CLOUD FORMED BY GENERAL UPLIFT OF AIR OVER WIDE AREAS

Air which originated in warm, moist regions may be forced to move up towards colder air which originated in other regions. By the common laws of physics, the warmer, moist air will be compelled to ride up and over the colder air mass. This

(a) CONVECTION OVER LAND

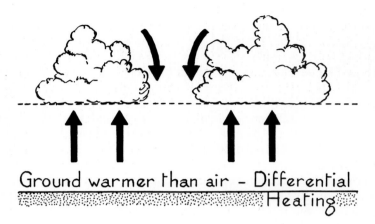

Ground warmer than air - Differential
Heating

(b) AIR IS HEATED FROM BELOW ON ITS WAY FROM NORTH TO SOUTH

Moist air from polar regions

Broken cumulus

FIG. 49. CONVECTION CLOUD

(*a*) Forming as a direct result of heating from the surface. (*b*) Forming where air moves from high to low latitudes.

gradual ascent of the moist air can produce conditions under which condensation and cloud formation develops over wide areas. Conversely, cold air may force its way under a warmer and moist air mass. In being forced aloft, the moist air is cooled; ultimately the level of the dew point may be reached, when cloud will form. Details of this type of cloud will be discussed fully in Chapter 10, since an examination of air masses and their characteristics must be fully appreciated before cloud formations can be understood. Fig. 42 (p. 76), which indicates the mode of formation of this 'frontal' cloud, suffices at this stage.

THE CLASSIFICATION OF CLOUDS

It will have been seen from the preceding sections that cloud depends upon the environmental and adiabatic lapse rates. The cloud base is governed by the height

A LAYER OF STRATOCUMULUS, WITH CUMULUS BUILDING UP WITHIN IT

Crown copyright reserved

Pl. I

Pl. II

AN ALTOCUMULUS LAYER
SEEN FROM 7500 METRES

Note the cirrostratus layer above.

Pl. III

A LAYER OF STRATO-
CUMULUS AT 450 METRES

of the dew point, and the degree of stability and consequent cloud thickness is controlled by the steepness of the environmental lapse rate by comparison with the adiabatic rates. Cloud base and thickness therefore form convenient criteria by which to classify cloud types and their characteristics.

The Three Main Groups. The classification commences with three main groups (Table 13), arranged according to the average heights of their bases. Each group is further divided according to the form of the cloud and its vertical extent. In all, there are ten fundamental types of cloud.

TABLE 13.—THE CLASSIFICATION OF CLOUDS

Group	Mean Upper and Lower Levels	Types of Cloud
High clouds	6000–12 000 m	Cirrus Cirrocumulus Cirrostratus
Medium clouds	2000–6000 m	Altocumulus Altostratus
Low clouds	Ground level– 2000 m	Stratocumulus Stratus Nimbostratus Cumulus Cumulonimbus

Both cumulus and cumulonimbus may be cloud of considerable vertical thickness, and, though they can be included in the low-cloud group, their tops often far exceed the two-thousand-metre level. *N.B.* the term 'cirrus' and the prefix 'cirro' indicate high cloud; 'alto' indicates medium cloud; 'cumulus' and 'cumulo' indicate a heap cloud; 'stratus' and 'strato' indicate a layer cloud.

The Ten Major Types of Cloud. The descriptions which follow have been adapted from the *International Atlas of Clouds*.

Cirrus are detached, featherlike clouds with a delicate and fibrous structure. An irregular arrangement of these shadowless, white wisps of cloud often indicates fair weather. When they are formed into bands or lines they usually indicate approaching frontal clouds and bad weather. They are invariably composed of ice crystals.

Cirrocumulus clouds are composed of small white flakes or globular masses, without shadows, and are arranged in groups or lines or, more often, in ripples resembling those of the sand on the sea-shore. Such a sky is called a 'mackerel sky.'

Cirrostratus forms a thin white sheet which covers the whole sky and gives it a milky appearance. This veil of cloud does not blur the outline of the sun or moon and gives rise to haloes. These clouds often herald the approach of a warm-frontal condition (see Chapter 10).

Altocumulus are layers, or patches, of cloud, composed of thin flakes or flattened globular masses which are arranged in lines or waves. Shadows may or may not be noticeable.

Altostratus is usually in a uniform sheet, more or less grey in colour. It resembles thick cirrostratus and often merges with it. The sun is barely visible through altostratus cloud.

Stratocumulus consists of large, globular masses, soft and grey in appearance. The masses are often arranged in a regular pattern.

Stratus is a uniform layer of cloud which resembles fog, but which is above ground-level.

Nimbostratus is a dense, shapeless, and rainy layer of cloud. It is dark grey in colour and appears uniform in texture.

Cumulus are thick clouds, with some vertical development; the upper surface is dome-shaped, with 'cauliflower' tops, and the base is almost horizontal.

Cumulonimbus are heavy masses of cloud, having great vertical development, whose summits rise like mountains and towers. The upper parts have a fibrous nature and often spread out in the form of an anvil. They are accompanied by heavy showers and sometimes thunder and hail.

Subdivisions of the Ten Major Types of Cloud. The ten major types of cloud are often subdivided into other varieties. The more common of these subdivisions are as follows:

Castellatus. Altocumulus clouds may often assume a turreted structure similar to that of the larger 'cumulo' forms. It is not common, but it is a good indication of upper atmospheric instability. These conditions are usually associated with thunderstorms.

Fracto Clouds. The prefix 'fracto,' added to cloud forms, suggests that the cloud is composed of broken fragments. It is usually employed to describe the small, low, and ragged cumulus associated with the approach of bad weather.

Lenticular Clouds. Often one may see cloud whose shape resembles that of a lens—that is, the section has clear-cut edges. Certain clouds of orographic origin have these characteristics.

Estimating the Amount of Cloud. The amount of cloud is given by the number of eighths of the sky which is covered by cloud. It is only with experience that this figure can be estimated with any degree of accuracy.

Estimating the Height of Cloud. It is, of course, of great interest to know the height of cloud, especially that of its base. In practice it is only the low clouds whose heights can be estimated with some accuracy by ground observers. There are, however, a number of methods by which cloud heights may be determined:

1. Comparisons with hills and mountains of known height.
2. Altimeter observations from aircraft.
3. Simultaneous sighting of clouds by two observers at the ends of a measured base line.
4. Observation of pilot balloons.
5. Cloud-searchlight observations at night. This method is practicable only for estimating the height of the cloud base of low cloud. A beam of light is projected vertically, and the base of any low cloud becomes illuminated. The angle of elevation of the spot of light from a position at a known distance from the light is recorded. The height of the cloud base can be determined by simple trigonometry.

Chapter 7

THE PRINCIPLE OF FOG FORMATION

ONE of the important elements of weather recorded by the meteorologist is that of atmospheric transparency. The layman often talks of fog when he is referring to the lack of visibility, but to the meteorologist fog is a specific condition of the atmosphere. The expert distinguishes between the various causes of atmospheric obscurity, and to him fog is usually a condition which arises when liquid water is present in the air at ground-level. (It is true that other solid particles do often induce condensation to take place.) Here only the principle of formation of water droplets at ground-level will be considered in detail; reference to the other causes of atmospheric obscurity will be brief.

Unlike clouds, fogs are formed by cooling processes which do not involve ascent and consequent adiabatic cooling of the rising air. A fog composed of water droplets may be considered as being a cloud at the surface, and it is perhaps necessary to point out that, over hills, fog may be merely orographic cloud which is moving over the summits. But condensation of water vapour which gives rise to fog is produced almost entirely by the direct effect of cooling from a cold surface. Three types of cooling processes can be distinguished:

1. Radiation, due to cooling of the ground by radiation. This effect is confined almost entirely to the night.
2. Movement, when moist air moves over a colder surface on land or sea.
3. Advection, when air moves gradually from a region of higher temperatures to regions of lower temperatures.

RADIATION FOG

The development of radiation fog (Fig. 50) depends on the cooling of the ground surfaces at night. It is confined to ground areas, since the daily variation in sea-surface temperatures does not ordinarily become sufficient to cool the lower layer of the air to its dew point. By direct conduction and radiation, the cold land surface cools the lower layers of the air. Provided that the temperature of the air is reduced to below its dew point, condensation will occur at ground-level.

Three conditions are necessary for the production of radiation fog:

1. There must be a clear sky with little or no cloud to permit free radiation. A layer of cloud reflects some of the earth's outgoing radiation and sends some of it back to the ground again. This reduces the net loss of heat and hence reduces the rate of cooling of the air. Continued cooling from below produces temperature inversions which effectively prevent upward dispersion of the cooling air at ground-level.

2. There must be sufficient moisture in the air. The air temperature must not be too far above that of the dew point; then only a little cooling will be required to produce condensation.

3. The winds must be light (of less than 5 m/s). With a light wind, the cooling will be spread upward by slight turbulence. Strong winds will create deep turbulence, and a greater depth of air will be cooled less, so producing less suitable conditions for radiation fog.

Radiation fog is worst in autumn and winter, when there are long nights, with more cooling and higher relative humidities in consequence. The fog is a condition associated with winter anticyclonic or col pressure types, and is worst at night and in the early morning. It is most likely to occur in valleys and low-lying marsh

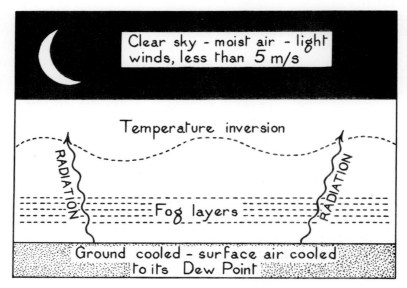

FIG. 50. RADIATION FOG

ground—also in industrial areas, where there are abundant hygroscopic nuclei associated with the smoke. In these latter areas these minute condensation particles result in tinier fog droplets, which produce fog of a greater density. The London fogs are especially noted for this condition. The darkness and persistence of the fog are dependent on the pall of smoke which collects beneath the inversion layer.

The fog can be dispersed either by the warming from the sun or by an increase in wind strength, which accentuates the turbulence effects. The mixing will thus bring down warmer air from above and so bring about a reabsorption of the water droplets.

MOVEMENT AND ADVECTION FOG

There is very little essential difference between movement and advection fog. ('Movement fog' is a term often used for that fog localized over small areas.) In both cases the mode of cooling is the transfer of air across a surface which is cold enough to reduce the air to its dew point.

Fog in warm air moving over a colder surface may occur over either land or sea. Its most frequent occurrence is over land in winter after a cold spell, when milder air arrives from the sea. The moist, south-westerly air stream moves over the colder land surface, and the cooling of the lower layers of air eventually produces saturation. Over the sea, this type of fog develops when warm air moves from land over a colder sea. This occurs around the coasts of Britain in spring or early summer. Further, air may move from a warmer part of the oceans over a cold water current. One of the outstanding examples of this condition is along the Grand Banks of Newfoundland. Here warm air from the south-westerly air stream blows over the cold Labrador current.

(a) SEA FOG

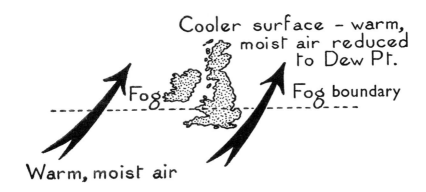

(b) THAW FOG

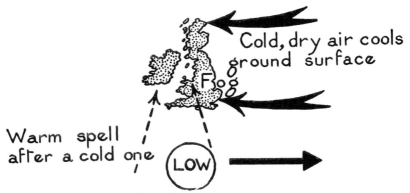

FIG. 51. ADVECTION FOG

N.B. A depression conveys mild, moist air. If this air passes over the British Isles which have previously been subjected to cold, dry air from the Continent it is cooled from below, and fog often develops.

Advection fog which occurs in air moving from warmer to colder regions tends to be much more widespread than other types. Basically, the mode of formation is similar to that of movement fog, which has just been considered. The best example of this type of fog is to be found where air of tropical and sub-tropical origin is carried high into temperate latitudes. Over the sea this fog may occur at any season, but over land it is confined to autumn and winter.

It is clear that wind speed does not matter so much in the formation of advection or movement fog, although a moderate wind will usually lift the fog off the surface and create low cloud. Nor is it essential to have clear skies. The fog may develop at any time of the day, and it is not a feature of any particular pressure type.

Two other types of fog—'steaming fog' and 'mixing fog'—should now be mentioned.

STEAMING FOG

This type of fog forms when water vapour from relatively warm water mixes with colder air which is passing over the water surface. The essential feature is that the air is cooler than the water. This is a rare phenomenon in nature, but suitable conditions of temperature and humidity appear frequently in polar and sub-polar regions, and the fog so produced, which rapidly disappears in the rising air currents, is known to sailors as 'sea smoke.' The common, yet small, example of this fog type is the steaming of roads in the sunshine after rain.

MIXING FOG

It is a physical fact that if warm and nearly saturated air is mixed with colder air the resultant mixture can become over-saturated. Consequently it is possible for condensation at ground-level to occur when two air masses, one warm and moist and the other cold and relatively dry, meet along a boundary. Mixing fog, therefore, often accompanies a warm front, which is a boundary between warm, moist air and cooler air.

OTHER CAUSES OF ATMOSPHERIC OBSCURITY

Apart from the visible forms of water which are present in the atmosphere and which cause atmospheric obscurity, two other causes may be classified:

1. Smoke particles.
2. Dust.

Industrial regions and large urban areas are responsible for the addition of phenomenal amounts of carbon and smoke particles to the atmosphere. In recent years legislation has done something to reduce this unnecessary pollution of the air (the Clean Air Acts, 1956 and 1968), since it has been proved smoke adversely affects the health of the inhabitants, the injurious ingredients producing lung and other respiratory ailments. But as long as open fires and smoky fuels are burnt, the atmosphere over large built-up areas will continue to suffer pollution by carbon particles. The larger particles readily drop out from the atmosphere, as anyone who lives in an industrial area will have noticed only too well. The finer particles will remain in suspension; they will reach the ground only when they are washed out by rain.

The degree of obscurity due to smoke haze depends on the rate at which it is dispersed through the air. The dispersion may occur through

1. Vertical movements of air by convection.
2. Horizontal movements of air.

But it is not so much the obscurity due to solid particles that is important; it is the effect which smoke particles have in increasing the likelihood of fog formation. Mention has already been made of the effect which hygroscopic nuclei have upon the condensation of water vapour from the atmosphere, and the air does not have to reach saturation before some condensation takes place.

Ideal conditions for smoke fogs ('smog') are associated with anti-cyclonic pressure systems, where the winds are light and the air is tending to sink. In winter cold conditions may also occur, and persistent fogs develop in the industrial zones of Britain.

Dust particles get into the atmosphere in two forms: solid matter thrown out from volcanoes, and wind-blown material from arid surfaces. Volcanic dust may be carried for great distances, and, though it is of little significance as an element in fog formation, it is an important factor in the control of climates, owing to its effects on the intensity of solar radiation. Dust from arid areas is of some importance in the matter of atmospheric visibility. When the wind raises sufficient dust from the ground to cause considerable deterioration in visibility, then a 'dust-storm' is evident. The degree to which the visibility is reduced depends upon a number of factors which are outside the scope of this book, but, according to meteorological definitions, fog conditions may exist in some circumstances. (*N.B.* 'Fog' is said to exist when the horizontal visibility is less than one thousand metres.)

Chapter 8

THUNDERSTORMS AND OPTICAL EFFECTS

THUNDERSTORMS

THUNDERSTORMS are caused by intensely powerful up-currents of air occurring within dense, moist cumulonimbus clouds, which themselves result from great atmospheric instability. A thunderstorm is a local storm characterized by lightning and thunder, these two latter elements being the result, rather than the cause, of the storm. The rapid vertical up-currents of air are usually associated with high surface temperatures and intense convection air flow, but wherever extreme instability occurs, such as along frontal zones within cyclonic pressure areas, conditions suitable for the development of thunderstorms are often found.

The conditions which most favour the occurrence of thunderstorms are as follows:

1. Warm, moist, unstable air. The degree of instability controls the intensity of the storm.
2. An extensive vertical depth of cloud. Usually the thickness of the cloud exceeds three thousand metres. The greater the distance between the cloud base and the freezing level, the more powerful will be the energy released on condensation.
3. Some agency by which the unstable air is made to rise. The lapse rate must be in excess of the saturated adiabatic lapse rate through a range of height of at least three thousand metres.

The rainfall in thunderstorms is of the heavy, shower type. The downpour is related to the more rapid vertical up-currents, which are capable of maintaining quite large water droplets in suspension within the cloud. Occasionally, in the very intense storms, hail is developed. When convection is violent, and the air is moving vertically upward at rates above 45 km/h (12·5 m/s), the raindrops are carried into temperatures below freezing-point. As the strength of the up-currents diminishes the droplets, or globules, of ice fall towards the earth again. They may descend below the freezing level and become coated with clear ice from the water droplets with which they come in contact. The convective currents may take these masses of ice and water upward and downward several times within the main cloud. The size of the ice particles will depend upon the strength of the up-currents; occasionally hail-stones as large as golf balls are experienced in tropical and sub-tropical storms. It has been estimated that up-currents of 95 km/h will keep aloft hail-stones of 2·5 cm diameter.

Since the Second World War great advances have been made in the understanding of conditions within thunderclouds. The main exploratory investigation has been carried out over a number of years by the United States Weather Bureau with the co-operation of Air Force and Navy aircraft. Ground and airborne radar equipment has enabled examination of convection clouds to be made, and it has been possible to observe the development of thunderstorms.

The essential result of the work has been to prove that the unit of thunder activity is not the cumulonimbus cloud as a whole but a vertical 'cell' which, when fully grown, extends through the full height of the cloud. A thundercloud can be composed of several cells each of which develops along a given pattern: the life cycle of each cell, independent of adjoining cells, may vary from one to two hours, but the period of greatest activity can be as little as twenty minutes. A number of stages can be recognized in the life cycle of each thunder cell:

1. *The Growth Stage.* In a developing cell a small cumulus may begin to grow into a large cumulus whose base may be over six kilometres in diameter. There is a main up-draught throughout the cell, the vigorous currents being of the order of 110–120 km/h. To feed the up-currents air flows into the cell through the sides as well as at the base of the cloud.

2. *The Mature Stage.* The cloud now assumes a vertical thickness in excess of 6000 metres, the last few hundred metres being below freezing-point. The character of the cell development is such that there is a fall of precipitation. The precipitation now produces a down draught where previously there had been an up-current. Descending currents may be as much as 50 km/h. Therefore at this stage up and down movements proceed side by side within the cloud. Water droplets, hail, and snow may be moving up and down, and it is in these complex and changing conditions that the process of electricity generation operates.

Several theories have been put forward to account for the build-up of electricity within the cloud. The view generally held at present is that strong positive and negative charges of static electricity build up as a result of the vigorous ascending currents and the consequent break-up or collision of the precipitation particles within the cloud. Raindrops continue to grow in the up-currents until they reach such a size that the limit of their cohesion is reached; at this stage, which is usually above the freezing level, they begin to disintegrate as supercooled water and collide with ice crystals and hail-stones. The tiny droplet of water is almost instantaneously converted into ice, but there is a fraction of an instant when the outer shell is ice whilst the interior remains liquid. Owing to the latent heat of fusion of ice, the ice shell is fractionally warmer than the liquid centre, and there is a rapid movement of positive charges to the outer surface of the freezing droplet. The up-currents carry these small ice crystals aloft, and the top of the cloud becomes positively charged. The lower section is negatively charged, the whole cloud now having a positive polarity.

The continuous disruption of countless raindrops builds up enormous electrical charges within the cumulonimbus cloud. The charges grow in size until the difference in electrical potential reaches a critical value depending on the conductivity of the air and the distance between the charges. Once the field strength within the cloud approaches a million volts per metre an electrical discharge occurs. The flash produced by this discharge is the lightning associated with thunderstorms. Usually the discharge takes place from one part of the cloud to another, but sometimes the discharge is made direct to the earth.

3. *The Declining Stage.* The life cycle of the thunderstorm cell ends when the down draughts have spread across the lower sections of the cloud and the up-currents are of secondary importance. The mechanism by which the generation of electricity operates has been removed, the lower portion of the cloud dissipates, and all that remains

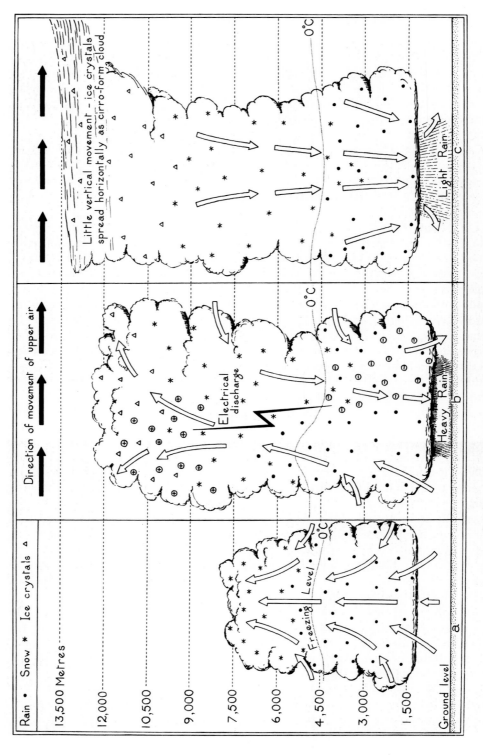

Fig. 52. STAGES IN THE DEVELOPMENT OF THE THUNDER CELL

(a) Growth; (b) maturity; (c) declining of cell.

FAIR-WEATHER CUMULUS

Pl. IV

A LARGE CUMULONIMBUS CLOUD SHOWING THE ANVIL CIRRUS

Pl. V

ALTOCUMULUS CASTELLATUS FROM ABOVE

In the far distance there is a layer of cirrus and some lenticular altostratus.

Crown copyright reserved

Pl. VI

is a wide cover of cirro-form cloud of ice crystals formerly associated with the cumulonimbus cirrus anvil.

Fig. 52 illustrates the stages in the life cycle of a thunderstorm cell.

Thunder is merely the noise created by the violent expansion of the air caused by the intense heat of the lightning, followed almost immediately by rapid cooling and consequent contraction. The long, continuous rumbling of thunder is explained by the fact that the sound from one flash of lightning, which extends over considerable lengths, has different distances to travel to the listener. The maximum distance at which thunder can usually be heard—15 kilometres—is surprisingly small. But the distance depends upon a number of factors, and thunder has been heard at distances of over 50 kilometres.

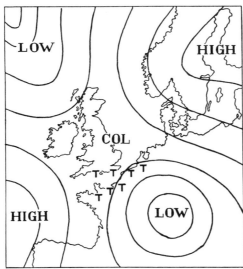

FIG. 53. SUMMER-HEAT THUNDERSTORMS OVER N.W. EUROPE

Perhaps the most significant feature of thunder cloud is the extreme turbulence which is produced within the main mass. The squall is associated with the dark-grey body of the cloud, and the wind is a strong onrush of cold air which precedes the main cloud mass. The velocity of the wind is sometimes of hurricane force, and is produced by the spreading out of cold air which has been brought down from aloft and which undermines the warmer air at ground-levels. Assisting this velocity is the forward movement of the storm cloud itself. It can be realized, therefore, that flying conditions within these clouds are very unpleasant; the fluctuations in the velocity and direction of the air currents are hazards to aircraft, and structural damage may result from flying through such conditions.

The Classification of Thunderstorms

Thunderstorms may be classified according to the conditions which produce them:

1. Frontal thunderstorms.
2. Air-mass thunderstorms.

Frontal Thunderstorms. Frontal thunderstorms are associated with boundary surfaces between two air masses having different characteristics, also with unstable belts along both cold and warm fronts. (Fronts will be considered in detail in Chapter 10.)

Air-mass Thunderstorms. Air-mass thunderstorms are those which develop within relatively homogeneous air masses; the commonest storm of this type is the summer-heat storm, where heating from below increases the instability of the air.

The Summer-heat Thunderstorm crops up over land and is associated with cols and shallow lows which develop over the northern regions of the Continent (Fig. 53). They are usually medium-level storms and wander irregularly across the country. Quite often they follow the line of contours. Several may indeed join up to form one large storm. They are most frequent in afternoon and evening and often continue into the night. Altocumulus castellatus is a forewarning of thunder conditions of this type.

Orographic Thunderstorms develop where air is made to rise over a mountain mass, and where the air is sufficiently unstable for cumulonimbus cloud to grow. Such storms remain almost stationary over the hill regions, because the up-currents are localized in those areas.

OPTICAL EFFECTS

Rainbows

The common rainbow consists of a circle, or part of a circle, of coloured light, formed by the splitting up of the sun's light by the prismatic action of individual rain-drops, and the accompanied reflection from these raindrops. (See Fig. 54a.) The colours of the spectrum always follow the same order: red is on the outside of the bow and blue and violet on the inner portion. The intermediate reds and yellows are ranged between. Sometimes the light is reflected twice within the raindrops before it emerges again, and so a second bow can be seen. The order of colours of this subsidiary rainbow is reversed, and the intermediate spacing between the two bows appears much darker than that beyond the outer bow.

The raindrops may be at any distance from the observer, varying from a few metres to several kilometres. As the sunlight falls on the raindrops some light enters each one, is reflected from the rear side by internal reflection, and so re-emerges from the near side. In doing this the rays of light are refracted and split up into the colours of the spectrum. The brighter, inner, primary bow and the outer, secondary bow are both circles, or parts of circles whose centres are at an 'anti-solar point'— that is, a point down sun along a straight line from the sun through the observer. (See Fig. 54b.) The primary and secondary bows have angular distances from this point of 42° and 51° respectively, these angles representing the rays of minimum deviation within the raindrops for each bow. Light rays reflected along directions other than those of minimum deviation travel either inside the primary bow or outside the secondary bow, and thus the region in between is relatively dark.

Mirages

Rays of light, in passing through the atmosphere, are subject to refraction. This is the result of differences in the density of the atmospheric layers, and rays of light,

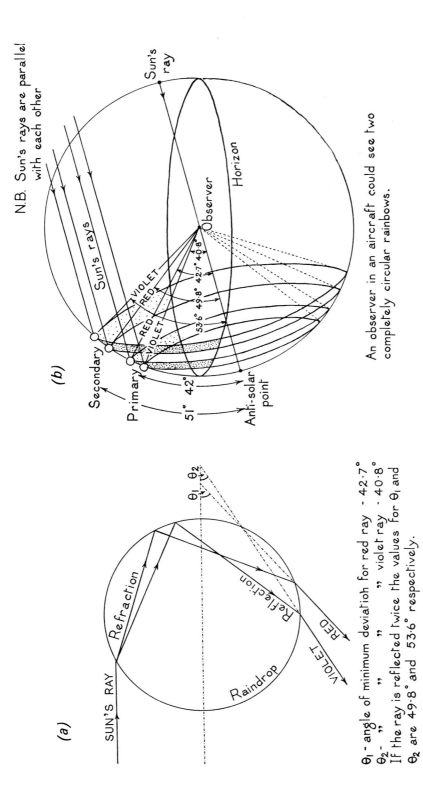

N.B. Sun's rays are parallel with each other

(b)

Sun's ray

Horizon

Observer

VIOLET
RED
RED
VIOLET

53·6° 49·8° 42·7° 40·8°

Sun's rays

Secondary

Primary

51° 42°

Anti-solar point

An observer in an aircraft could see two completely circular rainbows.

(a)

SUN'S RAY

Refraction

Reflection

Raindrop

RED

VIOLET

θ₁ θ₂

θ_1 - angle of minimum deviation for red ray - 42·7°
θ_2 - ,, ,, ,, ,, violet ray - 40·8°
If the ray is reflected twice the values for θ_1 and θ_2 are 49·8° and 53·6° respectively.

FIG. 54. THE PHYSICS OF RAINBOWS

in passing from one layer which is less dense to another which is of greater density, are bent (Fig. 55). For this reason objects which are below the observer's horizon may become visible, and other curious phenomena are produced. These phenomena include the illusion of sheets of water on desert surfaces, distortions of the sun's shape near the horizon, and the images of ships at sea seen in duplicate and even in triplicate. Simple mirage effects are noticeable in Britain. Over heated ground in summer the air very close to the ground is less dense than that above it, so that the

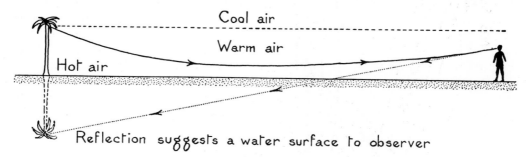

FIG. 55. THE MIRAGE

speed of light is greatest close to the ground. Rays coming down from the sky at a slight inclination may be bent up again towards the observer. This gives the appearance of a bright water surface and is often visible along smooth Tarmac roads on hot days. Sometimes hills may appear as detached masses which are floating on a lake-like surface.

Haloes

To the meteorologist, a halo is a circle of light (produced by refraction through ice crystals) around a luminous body. The most frequent example of a halo is the luminous ring which surrounds the sun or moon as they shine through a layer of cirrostratus cloud. The ring is white and subtends an arc of 22°, this being the critical angle for light which passes through a prism of ice. If the halo is very pronounced the inner edge is coloured red.

There are several similar phenomena, and haloes of 46°, mock suns, and curved arcs of various radii have been recorded.

Since the halo is most common in Britain when a cover of cirrostratus cloud is present, it has been suggested that the halo is a forewarning of bad weather associated with warm-frontal conditions. But the occurrence of halo phenomena is too frequent to suggest that they may be good indicators of weather developments.

Chapter 9

ICE IN THE ATMOSPHERE

WATER vapour in the atmosphere was discussed in some detail in Chapter 5, where it was indicated that the invisible vapour is present in some small measure in the troposphere over much of the earth's surface. It was also stated that this water vapour could remain in that state even if the temperature became reduced to freezing-point and below, but would under certain conditions be precipitated out directly as solid ice. Such ice, forming on ground surfaces, gives the typical frost conditions of winter mornings. Other forms of ice in the atmosphere which have already been mentioned include hail and the ice clouds of cirrus types. In this chapter a closer examination of ice formation in the atmosphere will be made, and more precise definitions of the ice types will be given.

HOAR FROST

Hoar frost is merely a covering of thin ice crystals (in the form of needles) which is deposited on surfaces cooled by radiation. Provided that the condensation temperature of the air—*i.e.*, the dew point—is below freezing-point, any air cooled below the dew point will deposit its condensed water vapour directly, in the form of ice. The conditions required for this ice to form are

1. Clear sky, to allow radiation from the ground surfaces to take place.
2. No wind to disturb the cold air forming at ground-level.
3. Sufficient moisture in the air to condense at temperatures below freezing-point.

Initially, if there is sufficient moisture present in the air, dew may form, but as the temperature is reduced below freezing-point the dew will freeze, and any further condensation will occur directly as hoar frost.

GLAZED FROST

Glazed frost occurs when rain falls from a warm upper layer of air on to surfaces which are at temperatures below freezing-point. The thickness of this type of ice may be considerable, and it is often sufficient to break telephone-wires. The conditions suitable for the formation of this frost are infrequent, but they do occur here when a warm front approaches Britain after a long spell of cold. The ground surfaces are below freezing-point while the upper air mass is at temperatures above freezing-point. Any precipitation falls as rain, but, on contact with the cold ground, immediately turns to ice. The running of transport is very difficult under such conditions. Aircraft, flying in air below freezing-point, may find themselves approaching air masses from which rain is falling. If this rain is converted to ice on the surfaces of the aircraft serious icing problems may be experienced.

Snow

Snow is precipitation in the solid state which forms at temperatures less than 0° C. In the snow-forming process the water vapour passes directly from the gas to the solid state. A snowflake is simply a mass of ice particles matted together in a flat triangular or hexagonal plate. These aggregates of crystals are presumably built up by the joining together of ice particles with water droplets on the way to earth. Heavy snowfalls are usually associated with temperatures not much below freezing-point, since very cold air contains very small amounts of moisture. Thirty cm of freshly fallen snow is equivalent to thirty mm of rain—although this is but an approximation, since the figure depends upon the type of snow which has fallen. The ratio may vary from five to one to fifty to one, depending upon the density of the snow.

Sleet

Sleet is merely the transition stage between rain and snow. It may be a mixture of snow and rain or merely partially melted snow. This type of precipitation occurs only when the surface temperatures are at or just above freezing-point.

Hail

Mention has already been made of hail conditions. These occur in unstable cloud, where the vertical air currents are strong enough to carry condensed water droplets above the height of the freezing-level. Hail-stones are composed of concentric layers of clear and opaque ice. These layers indicate the successive vertical movements of the droplet in the intense vertical currents within heavy, thunder-type clouds.

The theory of hail formation suggests a number of points concerning the processes of condensation at temperatures below freezing-point. In order that a hail-stone may grow it must be kept aloft by strong vertical currents, and these are associated with instability systems. Once the initial water droplet has been frozen (this will take place when the particle has been carried well above the freezing-level) the ice particle may grow by three processes:

1. Further condensation may take place on the particle from saturated air around it.

2. Minute droplets of water of a supercooled nature may coalesce with the particle. They will freeze and with a white soft hail, build up the particle.

3. Droplets may be picked up at temperatures near freezing-point and, when frozen, cover the particle with clear ice.

The character of the hail-stone suggests that a number of processes are involved. The conditions favourable for the growth of soft ice are found high in the cloud, while those suitable for the formation of clear ice occur at lower levels. The concentric layers of clear and opaque ice indicate that the ice particles must have been formed at both high and low levels, and the number of the trips up and down within the cloud can be fairly accurately estimated by counting the number of these layers.

RIME

Ice crystals are often formed on exposed surfaces when frost and wet fog occur together. Supercooled drops of water in the fog immediately freeze on coming into contact with the solid surface.

ICE ACCRETION ON AIRCRAFT

Ice formation on aircraft is in no way different from that on ground surfaces, and an aircraft may come into contact with snow, sleet, hail, frost, rime, or glazed frost. Dry snow and hail do not affect an aircraft's performance, because they do not adhere to the flying surfaces. Sleet sometimes sticks to an aircraft, but, being wet, is usually harmless. Hoar frost and rime are of little significance, but glazed frost is extremely dangerous. As was stated earlier, this type of ice forms when surfaces which are at temperatures below freezing-point come into contact with rain falling from a warm upper layer of air. Often aircraft surfaces are at temperatures below freezing-point, and they may enter cloud in which water droplets are held freely in suspension. On striking the aircraft, these water particles freeze, and, if there are enough of them, they may render the controlling surfaces of the aircraft inoperative. Dangerous ice accretion occurs only when the aircraft is flying through rain or cloud composed of water droplets at temperatures below 0° C. These conditions are typical of large cumulus and cumulonimbus clouds.

Chapter 10

AIR MASSES AND THEIR CHARACTERISTICS

AIR masses are related to the general circulation of the atmosphere, and consequently they play a large part in deciding weather and climate over great areas of the earth's surface. An air mass may be defined as being a widespread expanse of homogeneous air in a horizontal direction. That is, the temperature and humidity of the air mass are similar throughout the surface layers. Normally the horizontal

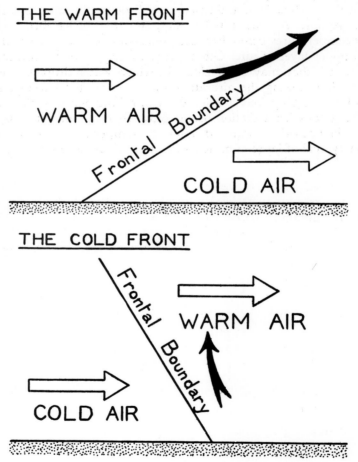

FIG. 56. A DIAGRAM TO SHOW THE DIFFERENCE BETWEEN A WARM AND COLD FRONT

dimensions are quite large, being of the order of hundreds of kilometres. Surface air masses may be caused by the stagnation of air or by the long continued motion of the same air, stagnant areas of high and low pressures being examples of the former, and trade-wind zones of the latter. Regions where homogeneous air masses tend to be created are called 'source regions.' Those surface areas of the earth where uniform conditions are to be found provide the most suitable localities for the development of air masses.

In the areas of sub-tropical high pressures both requirements are fulfilled: there is an area of uniformity of condition and there is also quiescence within the atmosphere. These regions are the source areas of tropical air. Similarly, homogeneous conditions develop over polar and large continental regions. Sometimes the air masses become very thick and extend upward to the stratosphere, depending upon the period during which the air remains within the source region. But these masses of homogeneous air often migrate from their source region and profoundly affect the climate of the areas over which they pass. Such a body of air is able to travel for great distances over the earth's surface from its region of origin and still retain many of the physical properties which it obtained at its source. Consequently, although an air mass, in moving away from its source region, is somewhat modified by its new environment, it does in turn modify the weather of the region into which it is moving.

When air masses which have different characteristics are brought together they do not mix freely with each other; they tend to remain separate, with sloping boundary surfaces between them. These boundary surfaces are called 'fronts,' and they usually separate masses of air having very different temperature and humidity features. The location of the surfaces of discontinuity within the atmosphere is of great significance in meteorology, because it is along such fronts that changes in weather occur. Fronts may be distinguished by the movements of the two air masses which are in juxtaposition. Usually one air mass begins to advance into the region occupied by the other. Where the lighter, warmer air moves against the colder and more dense air there is a tendency for the air at the higher temperature to ride up over the colder mass. Such a front is called a 'warm front.' Conversely, where cold air forces its way under a mass of warmer air, and pushes the latter upward, there is said to be a 'cold front.' (See Fig. 56.)

The Classification of Air Masses

Air masses are classified according to their source origins and the paths over which they have moved after leaving them. Three main types of air mass, each divided into two subsidiary types, can be distinguished:

1. Arctic. Air which has originated in extremely high latitudes and which proceeds equatorward over

    (a) Maritime regions (A_m).
    (b) Continental areas (A_c).

2. Polar. Air which has originated over unfrozen land or water in high latitudes and which proceeds equatorward over

    (a) Maritime regions (P_m).
    (b) Continental areas (P_c).

3. Tropical. Air which has originated over low latitudes and which moves poleward over

(*a*) Maritime regions (T$_m$).
(*b*) Continental areas (T$_c$).

N.B. Sometimes 'equatorial air masses' are differentiated, but for the sake of simplicity it will be assumed in this book that 'tropical air masses' include any air which has its source in equatorial regions.

The 'arctic air masses' are typical of the high-pressure belts which are situated over the snow and ice fields of the polar regions. The so-called 'polar air masses' originate over land or water surfaces in the high latitudes. 'Tropical air masses' develop in the regions of the sub-tropical high-pressure belts, while the 'equatorial air masses' originate in the doldrums. Further modifications can be noted according to the route over which the air mass travels, and subsequent changes in temperature and humidity. If the route has crossed ocean surfaces there will be a marked change of humidity, while air which has travelled across continental areas will probably show greater changes in temperature.

Four main types of air mass affect the British Isles:

Polar maritime (P$_m$) (Fig. 57).
Polar continental (P$_c$) (Fig. 58).
Tropical maritime (T$_m$) (Fig. 59).
Tropical continental (T$_c$) (Fig. 60).

Polar Maritime. Originally this air is cold and relatively dry. As it moves southward it picks up moisture and becomes heated from below. Ultimately the air becomes unstable. The weather associated with this air mass gives broken

FIG. 57. POLAR MARITIME AIR
OVER BRITAIN

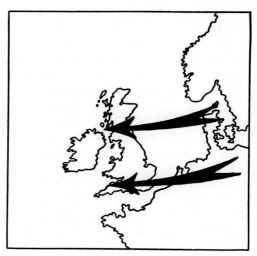

FIG. 58. POLAR CONTINENTAL AIR
OVER BRITAIN

cumulus and cumulonimbus; local showers, heavy at times, with bright periods and good visibility are typical.

Polar Continental. This air too is cold and dry, and, as its passage towards Britain carries it over land, it remains dry. In summer the weather is warm, and

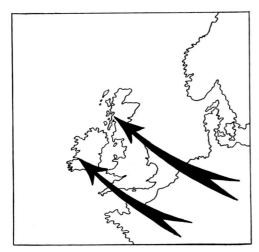

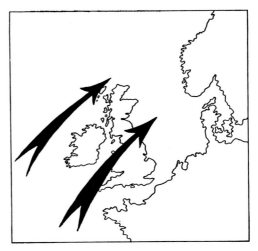

FIG. 59. TROPICAL CONTINENTAL AIR
OVER BRITAIN

FIG. 60. TROPICAL MARITIME AIR
OVER BRITAIN

fair-weather cumulus is the typical cloud type; in winter the air is very cold and stable. Stratus cloud develops (especially in the eastern parts of the country) as a result of moisture which is picked up over the North Sea. *N.B.* If the Arctic variant reaches the British Isles, then the air is much more unstable and usually gives snow showers in winter.

Tropical Maritime. This air usually originates in the Atlantic Ocean at 35° to 40° N. It is warm, moist air, which cools as it moves north over the sea. There is a high relative humidity, but, with the consequent surface cooling of the lower layers, the air becomes stable. One associates muggy, humid conditions with this type of air mass. Low layer cloud develops, and drizzle or sea fog often occur over coastal districts. In winter mist and low cloud are common.

Tropical Continental. This is air which has originated in latitudes 35° to 40° N., but which has travelled northward over North Africa and the Mediterranean. It commences as warm, dry air; it cools over the Mediterranean and picks up some moisture, which it drops as rain over the Continent. It finally reaches the British Isles as warm, dry air. This type of air produces cloudless days, with poor visibility. Fog often develops over the North Sea.

The above details are merely simplified classifications. Some air masses which arrive over Britain do not fit into any of these descriptions; a common, and therefore important, example is that of returning polar maritime air. This type of air reaches Britain when there is a slow-moving depression situated to the south of Iceland. The polar air flows all the way round the west and south sides of the depression before it finally arrives over the British Isles. It arrives as a south-west wind, bringing mild conditions in winter and cool ones in summer. This type of air mass is largely responsible for the extreme variability of weather conditions which one associates with south-west winds.

FRONTS

It has already been stated that well-defined boundaries may exist where air masses possessing different characteristics lie in juxtaposition. Therefore wherever air masses which have different features of temperature and humidity lie adjacent to one another, there will be the slow ascent of warmer air over colder air or the more rapid forcing of warm air upward by cold air pushing in. It follows that adiabatic cooling of the warm air will occur, and ultimately condensation will take place. Thus, fronts are among the most important features of weather in both temperate and equatorial zones. In the temperate latitudes fronts are responsible for most of the precipitation and low cloud, while in the equatorial areas fronts may produce the violent tropical storms.

Two obvious frontal zones can be distinguished on the earth's surface:

1. The polar front.
2. The intertropical front.

The 'polar front' is the boundary area which separates the polar air masses from the tropical air masses. The position of this front varies from season to season (Fig. 61). In winter the front is situated well to the south and extends approximately

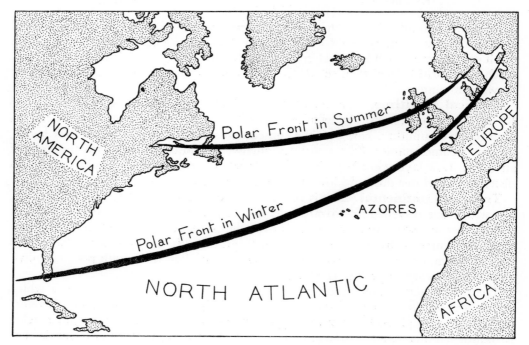

FIG. 61. THE POSITION OF THE POLAR FRONT IN THE NORTH ATLANTIC—WINTER AND SUMMER

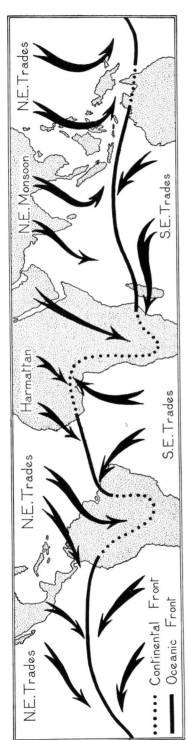

FIG. 62. THE POSITION OF THE INTERTROPICAL FRONT—JANUARY

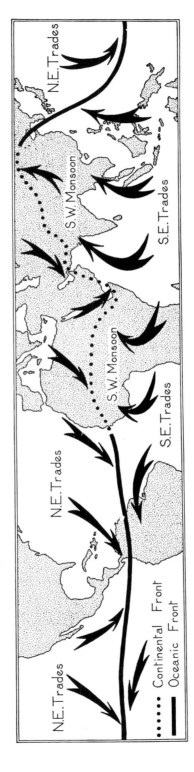

FIG. 63. THE POSITION OF THE INTERTROPICAL FRONT—JULY

Adapted from diagrams by J. S. Sawyer in 'Memorandum on Intertropical Front'.

from the central-eastern seaboard of North America to Spain; in summer the front moves northward and stretches from Newfoundland across to Norway. Of course, the positions of these lines are variable, and no clear-cut location for each season of the year can be predicted with certainty. Over the large continental regions in the Northern Hemisphere the polar front is considerably displaced by the radiation effects of the land masses. A polar front can also be distinguished in the Southern Hemisphere. But its normal position lies over the great oceans of the south, and it is much less in evidence than the northern polar front.

The 'intertropical front' is situated within the equatorial belt, and is the region where the trade-wind belt of the northern latitudes meets the trade-wind belt of the southern latitudes. Figs. 62 and 63 show the mean position of the intertropical front in January and July. The essential characteristics of this front vary with the locality; over the oceans there will be a different weather situation from that associated with the frontal system as it exists over the continents. A more detailed description of the weather associated with this front will be given later.

The Development of Cyclonic Conditions along the Polar Front. Frontology, or the study of fronts by Norwegian meteorologists, led to the theory of frontal depressions, or cyclones. The observed facts clearly substantiate the theory, although the reasons for certain events which take place cannot satisfactorily be explained at present. According to the theory, mid-latitude depressions originate as a direct result of the interaction between two contrasting air masses, one of tropical and the other of polar origin. Fig. 64, Stage 1, indicates such a condition.

A state of equilibrium exists between the cold polar air, which is flowing in a general westerly direction, and the tropical air, which is moving towards the east. The front is stationary, because the air currents are parallel to it. The polar air, which is colder than that of tropical origin, underlies the warm air in the form of a wedge, at an inclination of approximately 1:100. There is no vertical movement of the warm air, and consequently there is no condensation or precipitation. Possibly friction effects of the wind flows which are in opposition to each other create strong wind shears. The result of this is to create a wave along the frontal surface. (See Fig. 64, Stage 2.)

The wave form, which always bulges towards the colder air, rapidly becomes larger. Simultaneously pressure in the area begins to fall, the largest fall occurring at the crest, or tip, of the wave. A closed system of isobars develops, so that an anticlockwise circulation of winds blows around the centre of low pressure. The whole system now moves eastward along the front, and, as it proceeds, the wave grows, and the pressure at the centre continues to fall. In Fig. 64, Stage 3, the wave is shown, and two sections of the front can now be distinguished.

The boundary, shown along the line AC, is that section where warm air of tropical origin is slowly moving upward over the colder air of polar origin. This is a warm front. The line BC is the section where colder air is undercutting warmer air; this line demarcates the cold front. The region of warm air lying in between the warm and cold fronts is known as the 'warm sector.' Fig. 65 shows a typical depression associated with the North Atlantic polar front and the distribution of cloud and rain around it. Fig. 66 shows a cross-section through the depression and indicates the type of cloud associated with each front. Any station which is situated along the

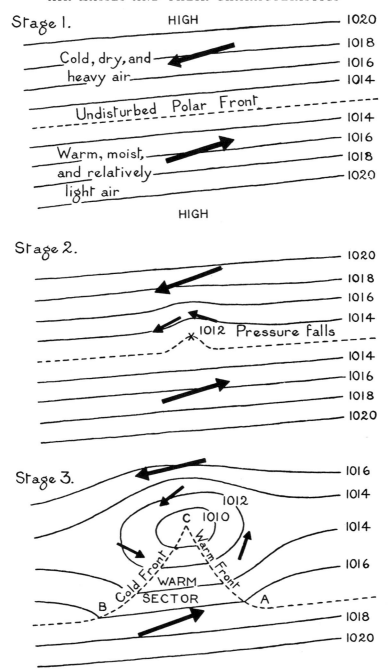

Stage 1.   HIGH —— 1020
—— 1018
Cold, dry, and —— 1016
heavy air —— 1014

Undisturbed Polar Front ------ 1014

Warm, moist, —— 1016
and relatively —— 1018
light air —— 1020

HIGH

Stage 2. —— 1020
—— 1018
—— 1016
—— 1014
1012 Pressure falls
—— 1014
—— 1016
—— 1018
—— 1020

Stage 3. —— 1016
—— 1014
1012
C 1010
—— 1014
Cold Front   Warm Front
WARM
B   SECTOR   A
—— 1018
—— 1020

FIG. 64. THE GROWTH OF A POLAR FRONTAL DEPRESSION

Stage 1. Two air masses in equilibrium.
Stage 2. The growth of the wave form along the polar front.
Stage 3. The development of the warm and cold fronts and the warm sector

line of movement of the whole depressional system will experience a succession of weather conditions. If the station is at point A in Fig. 65, ahead of the warm front, and the depression moves in the direction of the isobars in the warm sector, then all

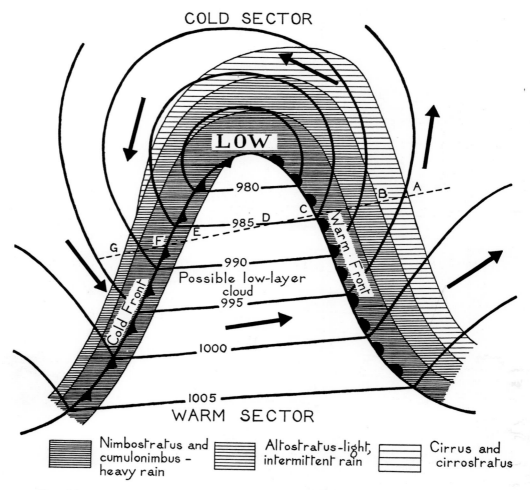

FIG. 65. A TYPICAL POLAR FRONTAL DEPRESSION AND THE RAIN BELTS ASSOCIATED WITH IT

A: High cirrus clouds slowly thickening into cirrostratus.
B: Cloud base lowers, and cloud is of the altostratus type. Slight, intermittent rain may occur.
C: Warm front at the ground level. Nimbostratus cloud gives continuous, moderate-to-heavy rain.
D: Stratus cloud is often found within the moist warm sector area.
E: Cold front at ground level. Cumulonimbus cloud gives heavy thunder showers.
F: Cumulonimbus belt thins out and the cloud becomes more broken. Showers are less frequent.
G: Patches of altostratus and scattered cumulus.

the points on the line AG will pass in succession over the station. At A the weather is fine, and the winds are light westerlies. The first sign of the approaching warm front will be a slight backing of the wind—that is, the wind will become more south-

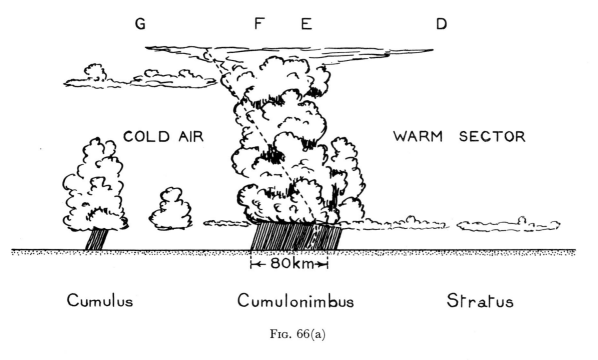

G   F   E   D

COLD AIR   WARM SECTOR

|← 80km →|

Cumulus   Cumulonimbus   Stratus

Fig. 66(a)

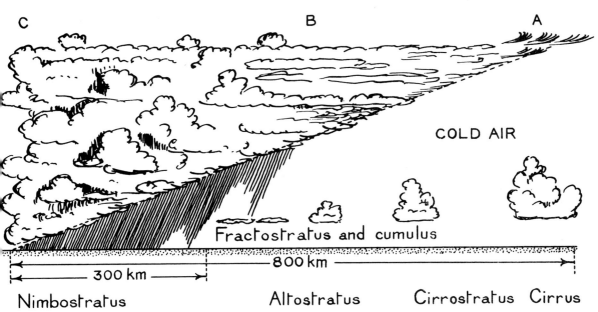

C   B   A

COLD AIR

Fractostratus and cumulus

←————— 800 km —————→

←— 300 km —→

Nimbostratus   Altostratus   Cirrostratus Cirrus

Fig. 66(b). A CROSS-SECTION THROUGH A DEPRESSION. (LINE AG FIG. 65.)

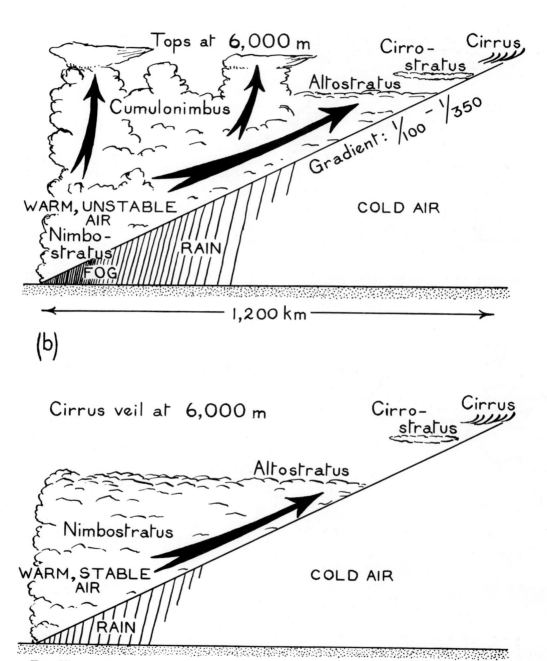

FIG. 67. SECTIONS THROUGH WARM FRONTS UNDER (a) UNSTABLE CONDITIONS OF WARM AIR; (b) STABLE CONDITIONS OF WARM AIR

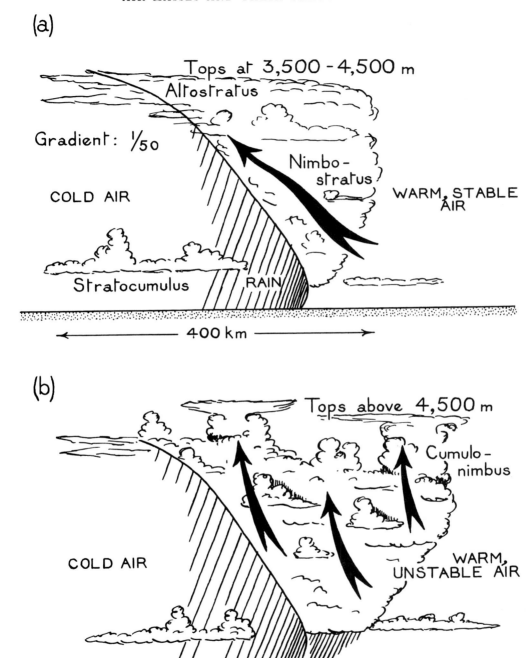

FIG. 68. SECTIONS THROUGH COLD FRONTS UNDER (a) STABLE CONDITIONS OF WARM AIR;
(b) UNSTABLE CONDITIONS OF WARM AIR

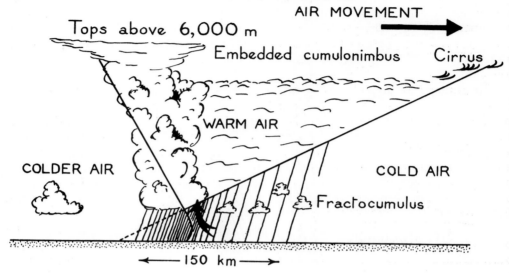

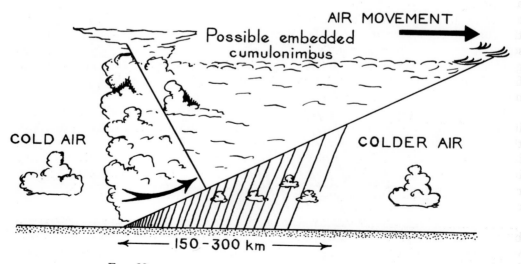

FIG. 69. THE TWO FORMS WHICH OCCLUSIONS MAY TAKE

westerly. It will also increase slightly in strength. High cirrus cloud will form in the west. The cloud will gradually thicken and lower, and eventually rain will fall. The barometer will fall steadily, and the wind continue to back and increase in speed. At the warm front the wind will veer to south-west, the pressure will steady, and there will be a perceptible rise in temperature and humidity. In the warm sector the warm, moist air of tropical origin gives generally dull conditions, with low stratus cloud and some drizzle. Inland, heating from the ground may disperse the low cloud.

The changes at the cold front are much more rapid, because the boundary is inclined at a much steeper angle. The belt of cloud and rain is quite narrow. The precipitation is usually heavy, and is often accompanied by hail and thunder. The actual cold front is marked by a sharp wind veer, and quite often there is a line of squall conditions. As the front moves through there is a sudden drop in temperature, and the pressure rises. The wind generally moderates, the rain ceases, and there is a period of fair weather, with good visibility. As the air becomes progressively more unstable in its movement southward, cumulus clouds begin to build up, the wind freshens from the north-west, and showers occur.

The inclination of the surface of the warm front is relatively gentle, usually of the order of 1 : 100 to 1 : 350. Consequently the width of the front may be of the order of eight hundred kilometres. The characteristics of warm-front cloud depend upon the degree of stability of the warm air. Fig. 67 shows the activity of unstable and stable warm air along a warm front.

In the cold front the warm air is forced to rise by the action of the cold air—that is, cold air is replacing the original warm air. The slope of the discontinuity layer is about 1:50 or less. Once again the characteristics of the cold-frontal cloud depend upon the stability of the warm air. Fig. 68 shows a vertical section through two cold fronts: in one the air is stable; in the other, unstable.

Both the warm and cold fronts within the depressional system move anticlockwise around the centre. The speed of a front is normally measured along a line at right angles to the front, and it approximates to the geostrophic wind speed. Generally the cold front moves more rapidly than the warm front, and therefore the warm sector becomes smaller as the cold catches up the warm front. The two fronts gradually close in and squeeze out the warm air. The line where the cold and warm fronts have met is called an 'occlusion.' The two possible forms which an occlusion may take are shown in Fig. 69.

This is a normal development in the life-history of the mid-latitude cyclones, and it marks the filling-up of the depression. As the occlusion continues the depth of the cold air along the occluded front increases, and the warm air is forced higher into the atmosphere until it spreads out laterally over the cold air masses enclosing it. When this occurs the uplift of the warm air ceases, and the air mass is no longer responsible for further cloud and rain. From now on the weather conditions are controlled by the characteristics of the two cold air masses.

The centre of the depression slows down soon after the occlusion develops and soon becomes stationary. The whole cycle of events from the formation of the initial wave along the polar front until the occlusion usually takes about three or four days. With the occlusion comes the slow filling-up of the depression. This dying-away may take ten days or so, but more usually the remains of the system are absorbed into some neighbouring pressure pattern.

The waves which give rise to the depressions along the polar front may occur in families, and a whole series of depressions may move across from west to east. Secondary depressions (see Fig. 14, p. 35) are usually second waves along a polar-frontal bulge associated with a primary cyclonic disturbance.

Similar depressions are created along the polar front in the Southern Hemisphere, the bulge, or wave, again extending towards the cold air mass. The general circulation is reversed, and the air moves clockwise around the cyclone. The whole system moves from west to east.

The Characteristics and Structure of the Intertropical Front. An examination of the world pressure distribution will show that two of the main features are the belts of high pressure which encircle the earth at about 30° N. and 30° S. Separating these two belts of high pressure is the equatorial low-pressure belt. It is likely that, were the earth's surface uniform, these pressure belts would be continuous around the globe. But there are marked breaks in the belts along the land regions. Over the oceans the high-pressure belts are clearly defined, and the equatorial trough is most obvious. Here the north-east trade winds of the Northern Hemisphere and the south-east trade winds of the Southern Hemisphere blow with great regularity towards the equatorial low-pressure zone. Over the land masses, on the other hand, these systems are not clearly defined, and in summer they may break down entirely over Asia, North Africa, and Australia.

Thus, in the general circulation of the atmosphere a belt encircles the earth into

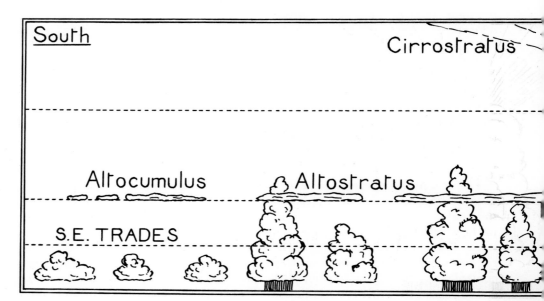

FIG. 70. A CROSS-SE
Adapted fr

This is a typical cross-section through the intertropical
The rain belt varies in width

which air streams of the lower atmosphere converge. In the oceanic areas the air streams are the trade winds. Over the continents one air stream is a slow-moving mass of continental air, and the other is a monsoon wind. Wherever air streams converge conditions are favourable for the formation of fronts, especially if the air masses possess different properties. Over the land masses the discontinuity surfaces may be evident on account of distinct temperature differences, but over the oceans temperature and humidity differences between the two trade winds are small. Nevertheless, a belt of convergence does exist, and a major air-mass boundary may be distinguished. This boundary is the 'intertropical front.' (See Figs. 62 and 63.)

The air masses which converge towards the intertropical front over the oceans are moist in the lower layers and relatively dry at higher levels. Usually the lapse rate slightly exceeds the saturated adiabatic lapse rate. If such air masses are slowly lifted by the general low-level convergence, instability results and large cumulus clouds form. These clouds will continue to develop into cumulonimbus and will give rise to intense shower and thunder conditions. A typical cross-section through the inter-tropical front over the ocean is shown in Fig. 70.

TROPICAL CYCLONES

It is along the convergence of the intertropical front that tropical cyclones form, but, because there are seldom great temperature contrasts in the air masses along the zone of confluence of the trade winds, they do not show sharply defined warm and cold fronts as in the extra-tropical depressions of middle latitudes. The intensity of tropical cyclones varies considerably, and the majority have weak pressure gradients.

ERTROPICAL FRONT

awyer

s. The diagram extends about five hundred kilometres north–south.
erity of the frontal conditions.

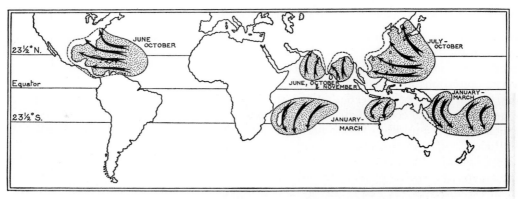

FIG. 71. THE REGIONS AND TRACKS OF TROPICAL STORMS

However, it is the vigorous and destructive form which is much better known, although, fortunately, it is much less common.

Tropical revolving storms, originating in the vicinity of the intertropical front, probably result from the marked instability which is a common feature of the atmosphere in this equatorial region. They form over all the tropical oceans except the South Atlantic, where the equatorial belt of convergence seldom moves far enough south of the equator. They never originate over land surfaces. In the Caribbean and off the Pacific coast of Mexico they are known as *hurricanes*; in the seas off China, the Philippines, and Japan they are called *typhoons*; in the Indian Ocean they are *cyclones*, and off Northern Australia they are known locally as *willy-willies*. The regions affected are shown in Fig. 71.

The energy of a hurricane depends upon an abundant supply of moisture in the warm tropical air and the consequent latent heat set free by the condensation of the water vapour. As is evident from Fig. 71, the tropical cyclone occurs mainly over the western regions of the oceans where the trade winds have journeyed for a long passage over waters having the highest sea-surface temperatures. Lapse rates are frequently steep in equatorial air masses, and consequently there is great instability in comparatively deep layers of the atmosphere. Therefore there are all the conditions for highly convective development.

Waves develop along the intertropical convergence in much the same way as waves are created on the polar front, and there is a resulting drop in barometric pressure. The vertical movement associated with the surface of separation of the two air masses is accelerated as intense condensation from the saturated warm air takes place. Air must necessarily flow in at the base of the depression so formed, and, as this air is very warm and moist, more and more water vapour is brought into the centre. Consequently as long as there is an unlimited supply of moisture at the base of the developing cyclone the energy of latent heat released by condensation is maintained, and this is converted into an intense circulatory air motion. Since the whirling motion is the result of geostrophic forces, which are least at the equator, the cyclone is most likely to form in the late summer when the intertropical front is situated at some distance from the equator. Tropical storms are a phenomenon from July to October in the Northern Hemisphere and from January to April in the Southern.

The pressure at the centre of a tropical cyclone may be as low as 900 millibars, but

AN EXTENSIVE LAYER OF ALTOCUMULUS

Crown copyright reserved

Pl. VII

CIRROCUMULUS AND HIGH ALTOCUMULUS
The sun is shining through a veil of cirrus.

Crown copyright reserved

Pl. VIII

generally it is of the same order as that of the polar frontal depression. However, whereas the latter may measure over 2000 kilometres in diameter, the isobars of the tropical cyclone are crowded into a diameter varying from 150 to 750 kilometres. Some hurricanes may, in fact, have diameters as small as 40 to 50 kilometres.

The associated winds at low levels may be of devastating force, and velocities of 200 km/h are by no means uncommon. In nearly all tropical cyclones the highest winds are those which immediately surround the calm centre, or 'eye of the storm.' In the calm centre the conditions are comparatively clear and warm with light, variable winds. During the passage of the calm centre, which is about 15 to 25 kilometres across, the roar of the hurricane winds on all sides may sometimes be heard. When the centre moves away the winds begin again, blowing with great violence once more from the opposite direction. See Fig. 73 for the structure of a hurricane.

The high degree of instability within the system produces vigorous vertical up-currents to 15 kilometres in height, and these too may be of the order of 200 km/h. Resulting heavy condensation from cumulonimbus-type clouds produces torrential rain which is often accompanied by thunder and lightning.

Despite the strong winds, the movement of the system is only 15 to 25 km/h in the early stages of the cyclone's development. However, as the system moves poleward the speed of travel increases. Initially the cyclones tend to move from east to west, but the direction becomes gradually northerly (in the Northern Hemisphere) and then more north-easterly. See Fig. 72 for paths of hurricanes in the Caribbean and South China Seas. The point at which the direction of motion changes from being westerly to easterly is known as 'the point of recurvature.' This position usually marks the stage at which the system begins to fill—that is, the pressure at the centre begins to rise. The recurvature of typhoon tracks in the Southern Hemisphere is in the opposite direction, centres moving south-west and then later to the south-east.

Tropical hurricanes may pass well into temperate latitudes, when their speed of movement may be 45 to 50 km/h. However, their isobars are becoming more widely spaced and their winds are slackening. Decayed Caribbean hurricanes frequently reach the coasts of West Europe and are recorded merely as deep depressions. Fortunately for the British Isles, the wind force rarely exceeds 100 km/h.

A cyclone fills rapidly once it passes over land. As the inflow of air to the storm takes place at the base and the continuation of the system depends on an adequate supply of moisture, the source of energy is removed over the land, where the humidity is much less. A second factor is undoubtedly the increased surface friction which unbalances the forces acting on the system.

There is sufficient evidence to say that the frequency of tropical cyclones has not changed much since Columbus sailed in the Caribbean or Magellan reached the Philippines. Frequency tables of the occurrences of storms in different parts are available. In the China Seas about 20 typhoons are recorded annually; in the West Indies and North Indian Ocean 10 per year, but only 2 or 3 in Northern Australia.

There appear to be fluctuations in the annual numbers, however; in some years there are many and in others few storms. The apparent increasing frequency of tropical storms is perhaps more a reflection of the growth of facilities for reporting them. During the hurricane season meteorologists at key stations in the Caribbean, Indian, and Pacific Oceans keep a close watch on upper-air temperatures and

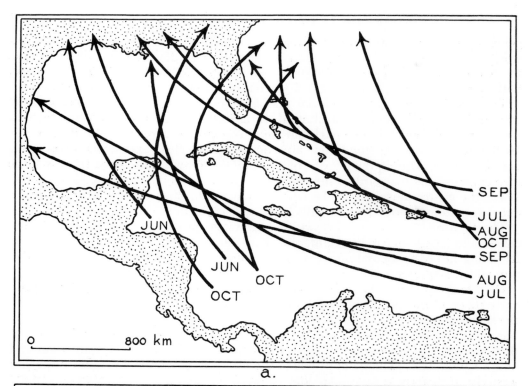

SEP
JUL
AUG
OCT
SEP
AUG
JUL

JUN
JUN
OCT
OCT

0   800 km

a.

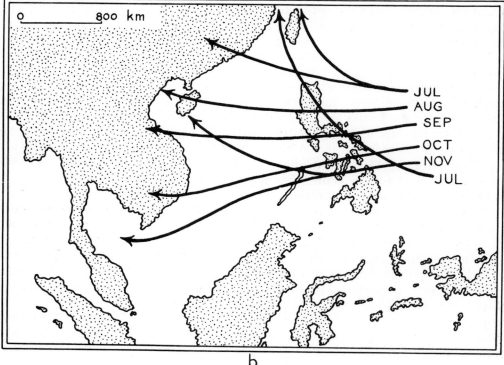

0   800 km

JUL
AUG
SEP
OCT
NOV
JUL

b.

FIG. 72. THE PATHS OF TROPICAL STORMS
(a) The West Indies; (b) South China Seas.

pressures. Any slight deviation from the normal at heights of 18 to 20 km is sufficient to start a complex of warning and spotting systems throughout the affected region.

Spotting aircraft report on cloud forms, pressure patterns, and wind strengths. Indeed, the United States regularly send aircraft, equipped with recording apparatus, directly into tropical storms in efforts to find out more about the processes at work within the system. Modern radar equipment, established on ships, aircraft, or on shore, allows observers to plot cloud patterns over wide areas. Circular patterns would indicate the presence of developing hurricanes. Even more recent refinements include, first, weather satellites whose equipment allows cloud photographs to be

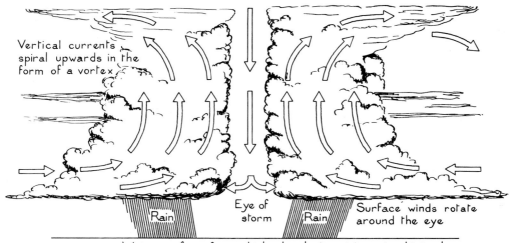

Vertical currents spiral upwards in the form of a vortex

Eye of storm

Rain   Rain

Surface winds rotate around the eye

Water surface from which abundant moisture is obtained

N.B. The rainfall often exceeds 500 mm in twenty-four hours.

FIG. 73. THE STRUCTURE OF A HURRICANE

taken over wide sea areas in which tropical storms may develop, and, second, the recording of microseismic waves imparted to the ocean by hurricane-force winds. At sea the long, distinctive heavy swell in advance of an approaching hurricane is one of the most valuable warning signs to mariners. As a matter of convenience in tracking the paths of hurricanes in the Atlantic and typhoons in the Pacific, the meteorological services use girls' names to designate the storms alphabetically.

Owing to the tremendous destructive power of the tropical storm, which often leaves island settlements and coastal communities in its path completely devastated, man, in addition to taking well-organized preparatory action, is now looking for ways of controlling the hurricane. One promising method is to convert super-saturated moisture to ice by dropping canisters of silver iodide or dry ice (solid carbon dioxide) from aircraft into the 'heat chimney' of the storm. The excessive latent heat of fusion of ice released by this process produces some dissipation of cloud at critical points in the storm, and there is an upsetting of the energy balance within the system. This method has been only partially and momentarily successful. Another suggestion is to drop a nuclear bomb into the 'eye' of the storm. This is unlikely to have the desired effect, because the energy produced from one bomb is comparatively slight.

Chapter 11

THE METEOROLOGY OF THE UPPER ATMOSPHERE

No textbook on meteorology would be complete without some reference to high-altitude meteorology. The rapid development of flying since the Second World War has been responsible for the creation of aircraft which now operate outside the troposphere and well within the tropopause. A great deal of military-aircraft flying now takes place at heights above twelve kilometres. Even civilian airliners are crossing the Atlantic at similar heights, where the ordinary phenomena of the weather are rarely encountered. Even at these levels, however, there are still meteorological factors which must be considered by aircrews who operate on the edge of the stratosphere. Aircraft performances, navigational problems, and other operational factors must be considered, and an understanding of the meteorological phenomena associated with high-altitude flying is essential to the safe and efficient use of modern jet aircraft.

In Chapter 2 brief reference was made to the tropopause. It was defined simply as "the upper limit of the atmosphere, where the troposphere borders the stratosphere." Few real meteorological data are as yet available about the tropopause, but it is apparent that there are two distinct lapse rates in this transition zone between the lower atmosphere and the stratosphere. The first tropopause layer exists at about nine kilometres—a level at which the lapse rate is very small, being of the order of 1·8° C per kilometre-rise in altitude. A second tropopause layer appears to exist at just under fourteen kilometres—a level at which the lapse rate is steeper, being of the order of 3° C per kilometre-rise in altitude. No complete explanation of this temperature distribution within the tropopause has been offered, but it is generally accepted that convection is responsible, whereas in the stratosphere heat is transferred merely by radiation.

The height of the tropopause varies with the latitude, the season, and the weather situation within the troposphere. Table 14 shows the average heights of the tropopause for the various latitudes.

Weather situations within the troposphere do considerably affect the height of the tropopause. A moving air mass has a tropopause which is apparently carried along with the system, and there is little change in the altitude of the boundary. Thus polar air masses which move equatorward bring a lower tropopause, characteristic of polar latitudes. Similarly, warm air of tropical origin brings a high tropopause. It becomes obvious, therefore, that, with the passage of a frontal system associated with mid-latitude depressions, there may be a change in the height of the tropopause amounting to several hundreds of metres.

Differences of temperature which exist at the surface between two air masses are almost always reversed at the tropopause. The air mass which is the warmer of the two when near the ground becomes the colder of the two at high altitudes. The reason for this is obvious. A high ground temperature, such as is typical of tropical regions, is usually associated with a high tropopause. The temperature continues to fall with increasing altitude up to the tropopause. Consequently, the higher the tropopause the greater the fall in temperature. The total effect generally is more important than any differences in surface temperatures. It is a fact that the air

TABLE 14.—HEIGHT OF THE TROPOPAUSE IN VARIOUS LATITUDES

LATITUDE	HEIGHT OF THE TROPOPAUSE, IN KM	
	WINTER	SUMMER
0°	17·1	16·8
10°	16·8	15·8
20°	15·8	15·5
30°	13·7	14·3
40°	11·6	13·1
50°	10·7	11·6
60°	10·0	10·7
70°	8·9	9·4
80°	7·6	8·9

N.B. In Great Britain the average height of the tropopause is about 10·5 km, but there are individual values which range from 4·5 km to 15 km.

above the equator at 15 kilometres is much colder than air at a similar height above the Poles. (This is shown effectively in Fig. 20.) Another remarkable feature is that, at 20 to 25 kilometres above the earth's surface, temperature increases with increasing altitude. This is due to the absorption of ultra-violet light from the sun.

In Chapter 4 it was indicated how winds in the upper atmosphere were calculated; they may be determined from the path followed in space by a free balloon. This path is usually tracked by radar and radio observations, but it is clear that the winds so found apply only to a line defined by the movement of the balloon. For the accurate estimation of winds over a wide area of the tropopause it is necessary to construct isobaric charts similar to those used for calculating surface wind speeds and wind directions. In actual practice the meteorologist does not construct charts showing the pressure distribution at varying heights above the earth's surface. He uses 'contour charts,' which serve the same purpose and which are much easier to construct.

In a vertical ascent from any place on the earth's surface a height will eventually be reached where the pressure is, for example, three hundred millibars. The height at which this pressure occurs will vary from place to place, and the shape of a layer having the pressure can be represented by a system of contour lines, like those used on ordinary topographical maps. A series of contour lines is shown in Fig. 74. In this diagram the contour chart is drawn for the three-hundred-millibar pressure layer at approximately the nine-thousand-metre level. Contours may be interpreted in the same way as isobars: wind flows along them, and the spacing of the lines may be related to wind strengths. In the diagram there is a pronounced westerly wind which covers the British Isles at about nine thousand metres. This is an example of the fast-flowing 'jet stream' which was referred to in Chapter 4. The axis of the jet

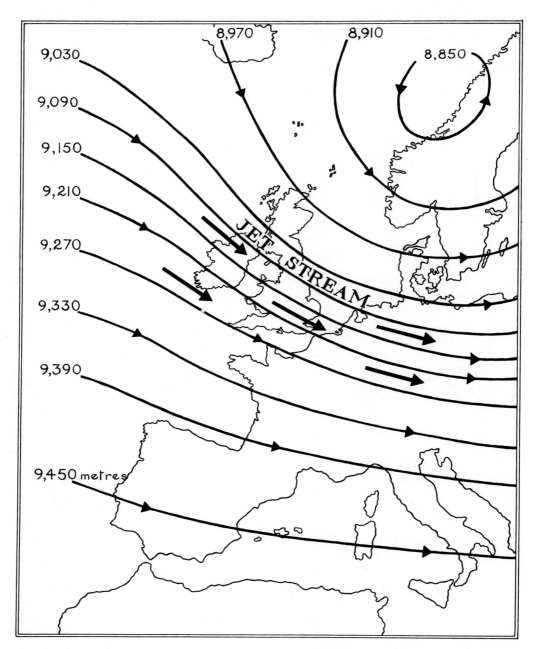

FIG. 74. A CONTOUR CHART FOR 300 MILLIBARS, SHOWING A JET STREAM

stream is located where the contour lines are packed together most closely, and is situated just below the tropopause. Hence the maximum winds are to be found at about 10 kilometres in the temperate latitudes.

Jet streams are frequently associated with the cyclonic disturbances along the polar front. The jet axis usually stretches parallel with the front (see Fig. 75) and

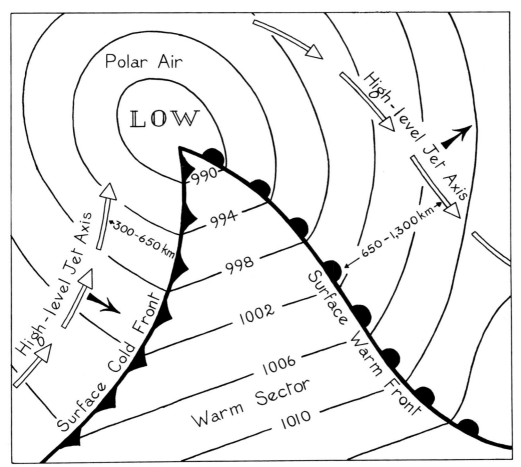

FIG. 75. JET STREAMS NEAR FRONTS
Based on diagrams in 'Elementary Meteorology for Aircrew' (H.M.S.O.)

occurs where there is a marked discontinuity within the troposphere. In Fig. 76 a cross-section of a jet stream is shown. The lines indicate the wind speeds at the various heights, and the wind is blowing at right angles to the plane of the paper. The cross-section shows clearly the change in height of the tropopause at either side of the front. Over Britain wind speeds in a jet stream are greater during the winter season and may be of the order of 240 km/h. (The greatest speed so far recorded is 370 km/h.) The streams occur at any season, but are much more frequent in winter than in summer. The strongest jet streams appear to be situated over the

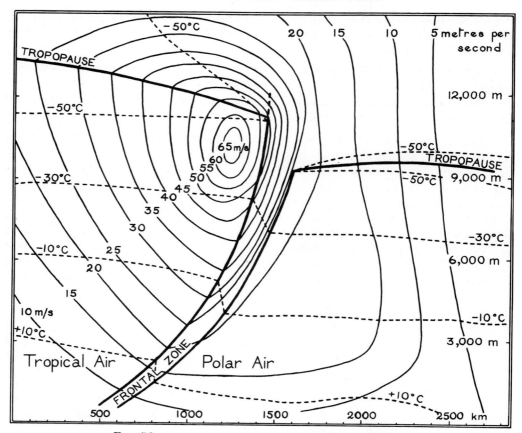

FIG. 76. A VERTICAL CROSS-SECTION OF A JET STREAM

Based on diagrams in 'Elementary Meteorology for Aircrew' (H.M.S.O).

This figure shows the cross-section of a typical jet stream. The speed with which the wind is blowing is shown by a series of lines. The wind is blowing at right-angles to the plane of the paper—*i.e.*, towards the reader.

Note the change in the height of the tropopause—this is higher over the warm-air side of the front than over the polar-air side.

The wind speeds are shown in knots because the nautical mile per hour continues to be the meteorological unit of wind speed. For conversion to S.I. units

$$1 \text{ knot} = 0.514 \text{ metres per second}$$

eastern seaboards of Asia and North America, where wind velocities approaching 650 km/h are not uncommon.

CONDENSATION TRAILS

Britain's first real introduction to condensation trails was effected in 1940, when high-flying German bombers were intercepted over the south-eastern counties. Visible trails were produced which contrasted sharply with the deep-blue skies of the English summer. This trail, often known as a 'contrail,' results from the condensation of water vapour produced by the combustion of fuel.

Condensation trails are thus the result of a change in the relative humidity of the air immediately behind the engines of a high-flying aircraft. The humidity is changed in two ways:

1. The exhaust gases contain a large amount of water, and this tends to raise the relative humidity.

2. The exhaust gases are also hot and raise the temperature of the air. This inevitably results in a lowering of the humidity.

Which of these two effects is of greater importance depends entirely upon the temperature of the air through which the aircraft is flying. But it is reasonable to say that only a very small amount of water requires to be ejected by the aircraft engine to saturate the very cold air at high altitudes. Any additional moisture will condense and appear as a trail behind the aircraft.

Over Britain condensation trails rarely form below 7500 metres in summer or 5500 metres in winter. In tropical zones, however, trails are unlikely to develop below 10 000 metres. Under certain atmospheric conditions trails persist; they may spread out across the sky, so producing a cirro-type cloud formation. On other occasions the trails are merely transitory and soon disperse behind the aircraft.

Chapter 12

WEATHER FORECASTING AND WEATHER MAPS

In the preceding chapters an attempt has been made to analyse weather. The under-lying principles of physics have been used to explain the elements of weather, and the foundations have been laid upon which to build our knowledge of the atmo-sphere. At this stage it should perhaps be possible for us to appreciate more fully something of the vagaries of weather, and we may be more sympathetic towards the meteorologist when he attempts to forecast future weather developments. In this chapter an attempt will be made to show how the meteorologist collects information about the weather and how (using the physical principles which have been outlined in the earlier chapters of this book) he endeavours to predict future conditions of the atmosphere.

We are often critical of the meteorologist's forecast and say that he is never right. What we fail to appreciate is that he is trying to predict future weather from informa-tion he has which concerns only the present weather situation. If his knowledge of the present conditions is comprehensive and concerns a wide area he may be able to offer a fairly accurate forecast for the next twenty-four or forty-eight hours. Thus it appears essential that the meteorologist should have an accurate picture of the present weather over a wide area in order that he may produce his forecast of the future conditions.

Weather reports form the basis upon which all meteorological services are built. The collection and interpretation of meteorological information is complex and depends largely upon the availability of weather observations and records. Inter-national collaboration is most necessary, and national frontiers must not interfere with the issue of meteorological data. It can in truth be said that the World Meteoro-logical Organization is one of the finest existing examples of international co-operation, free from political and economic stress. The main purpose of the Organization is to provide a universal recording system, the information being available to all member countries. The British Isles is a typical member country, and it serves the Organization by its provision of the following services:

1. The maintenance of a network of observing stations.
2. The use of unified methods of observation and adherence to fixed times at which observations are to be made.
3. The compilation of the observations in accordance with a code which is used for the sake of brevity and the need to overcome language difficulties.
4. A system of communication which allows the reports from all observing stations to be available to the forecasting services as soon as possible.
5. A uniform method of indicating weather elements on a map or chart, so that the information can be understood by all, irrespective of nationality.

OBSERVING STATIONS IN BRITAIN

In Britain the observing stations alluded to above fall into several classes:

Principal, or Full-reporting, Stations. These are sited uniformly over the country and are usually Royal Air Force airfields or Naval stations (see Fig. 77). A full-time reporting service is maintained, and hourly observations of the weather elements are recorded, coded, and dispatched by telephone or teleprinter to the main Meteorological Office at Bracknell, Berkshire. Each station has an international number by which it is identified when the coded information is broadcast back from Bracknell to the forecasting services.

Auxiliary Stations. These supplement the information of the principal stations and are also Royal Air Force airfields or Naval stations which operate on a part-time basis. Normally they supply hourly observations only for the daylight hours.

Ship Stations. In addition to fixed weather-reporting ships sited at strategic positions in the North Atlantic, there are many ocean-going liners which make weather reports and broadcast their information by means of the international code. Gaps in the information are, of course, unavoidable, but even one report may have some value to the forecaster.

Aircraft. Long-distance aircraft also send abbreviated reports of the weather conditions experienced along their route. Brief though these reports may be, they are of immense value to the forecaster, since the aircraft routes often traverse those areas which are not covered by surface observations.

After they are received at a forecasting office the observations are decoded and plotted on a chart (see Fig. 77). This chart provides a synopsis of the weather observations made at the same time over a wide area, and is therefore referred to as a 'synoptic chart.'

Satellites. Today direct photographic observations from satellites are becoming increasingly available. See Chapter 13.

THE CODING OF THE METEOROLOGICAL INFORMATION

By international agreement, a unified system of weather recording has been adopted. Once he understands the code, an observer of any nationality may interpret correctly the information conveyed by the system. The message outlining the facts concerning the weather elements takes the form of a series of five-figure groups; these groups are arranged in a definite order, so that each figure refers to a specific element. The following series of five-figure groups is that used by the principal reporting stations:

$$iiIII \quad Nddff \quad VVwwW \quad PPPTT \quad N_hC_LhC_MC_H \quad T_dT_dapp \quad 7RRjj \quad 8N_sC_hh_s$$

ii	Block No.—for example, British Isles.
III	Station No.
N	Fraction of sky covered by cloud (in eighths, or oktas).
dd	Surface wind direction, in tens of degrees.

Note. The World Meteorological Organization, whilst using knots at present for wind speed, will change to metres per second as soon as international civil aeronautics organizations will agree. At present (1978) there is no intention on the part of the I.C.A.O., the R.A.F., or marine services to change from knots.

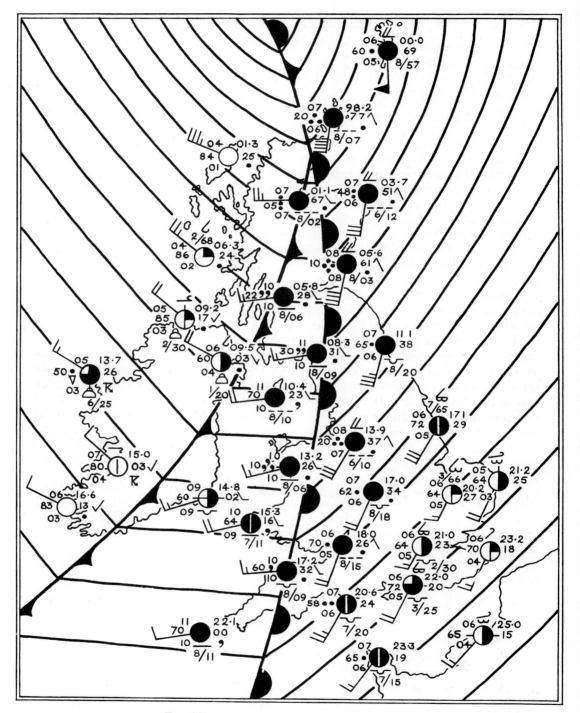

FIG. 77. AN EXAMPLE OF A SYNOPTIC CHART

N.B. By convention, certain symbols and figures are plotted in red. However, in view of the growing use of printed facsimile charts in the meteorological service, the plotting is often executed in black only.

ff   Surface wind speed, in knots.

VV   Visibility, in metres.

ww   Present weather.

W   Past weather.

PPP   Mean sea-level pressure, in millibars.

TT   Dry-bulb temperature, in ° C.

N_h Amount of cloud, with base given by h—*i.e.*, amount of low cloud.

C_L Type of low cloud.

h   Height of base of low cloud.

C_M Type of medium cloud.

C_H Type of high cloud.

T_dT_d Dew-point temperature.

a   Characteristic of barometric tendency (increasing or decreasing).

pp   Amount of pressure tendency.

7   Indicator figure of seventh group.

RR	Rainfall, in millimetres.	N_s	Amount of lowest cloud.
jj	Maximum temperature.	Ch_s	Type of lowest cloud.
8	Indicator figure of eighth group.	h_s	Height of lowest cloud.

A number of other five-figure groups may be employed, but these are applicable at special stations only. The ninth group, for example, refers to special phenomena experienced which require a report.

The above Synoptic Code consists of some weather elements which can be reported directly—for example, temperature, wind speed, and wind direction can be denoted by the figures observed. Certain elements, however, can be reported only in code form. Visibility and present weather, for example, must be coded in such a way that a number can be interpreted correctly by all who read the code. Fig. 78 indicates the code figures from 0 to 9 for certain weather elements reported in the Synoptic Code. The symbols indicate cloud amounts, past weather, cloud types, the state of the ground, and the barometric tendency. Code figure 6 for N (cloud amount) indicates that three-quarters of the sky is covered. The same number (6) for W (past weather) tells the observer that rain has been falling during the past hour. The following tables explain the symbols shown in Fig. 78.

N (CLOUD AMOUNT)

0	Clear sky.	5	Five-eighths cover.
1	One-eighth cover.	6	Three-quarters cover.
2	Two-eighths cover.	7	Seven-eighths cover.
3	Three-eighths cover.	8	Complete cloud cover.
4	Half of sky covered.	9	Sky obscured (fog condition).

W (PAST WEATHER)

0	Clear conditions.	5	Drizzle.
1	Cloud covering half of sky.	6	Rain.
2	Cloud covering whole sky.	7	Snow.
3	Sand- or dust storm.	8	Showers.
4	Fog.	9	Thunderstorm.

C_L (Types of Low Cloud)

0 No low-cloud type.
1 Small cumulus.
2 Large cumulus.
3 Cumulonimbus.
4 Stratocumulus.

5 Stratus, with some cumuloform.
6 Stratus.
7 Broken stratus.
8 Cumulus and stratocumulus.
9 Cumulonimbus, with anvil top.

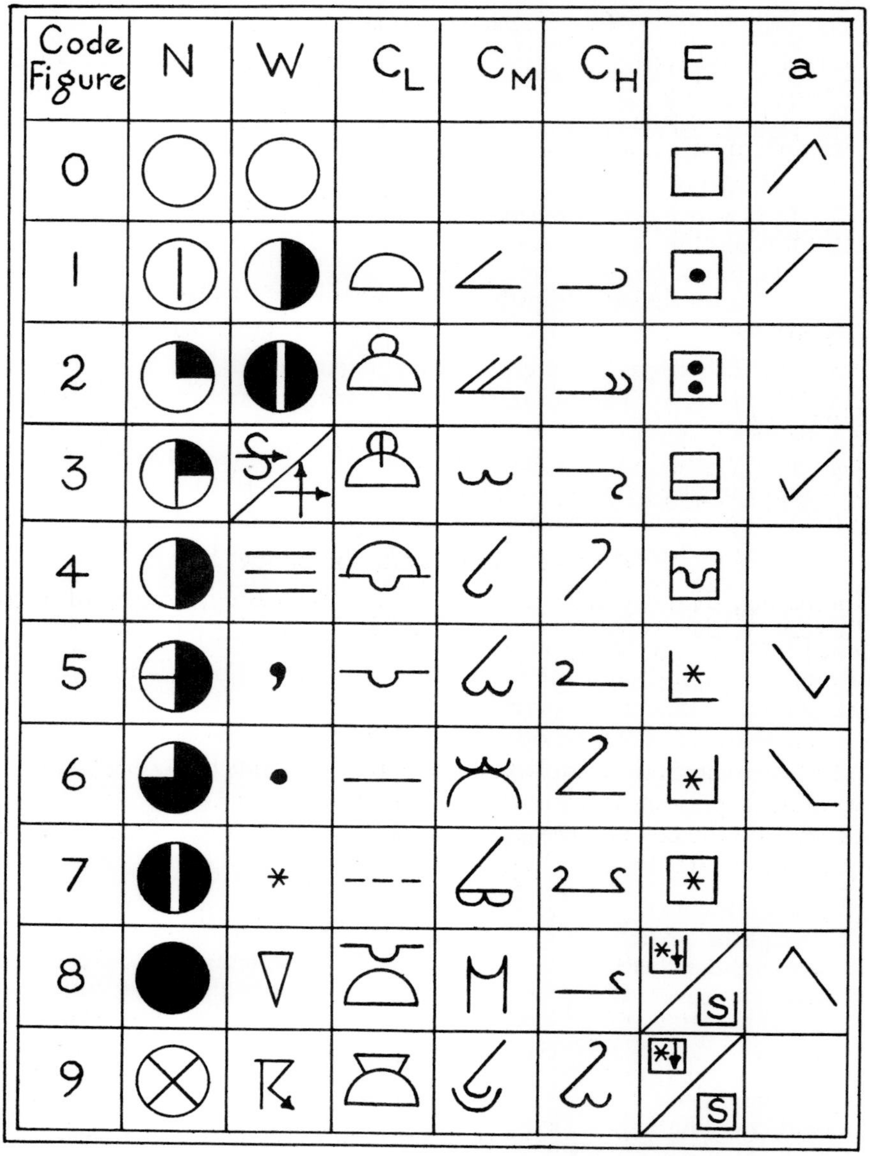

FIG. 78. CODE FIGURES AND SYMBOLS FOR VARIOUS WEATHER ELEMENTS

All symbols for past weather—W—and for high cloud—C_H—are plotted on the chart in red. In addition, the figures 5, 6, and 8 for the barometric tendency—a—are coloured red.

C_M (TYPES OF MEDIUM CLOUD)

0 No medium-cloud type.	5 Bands of altocumulus.
1 Altostratus—transparent.	6 Altocumulus developing from cumulus.
2 Dense altostratus.	7 Altocumulus in two layers.
3 Altocumulus—transparent.	8 Turreted altocumulus.
4 Patches of altocumulus.	9 Many layers of altocumulus.

C_H (TYPES OF HIGH CLOUD)

0 No high-cloud type.	6 Dense cirrus, covering all the sky.
1 Cirrus in patches.	7 Veil of cirrostratus, covering all the sky.
2 Dense cirrus in patches.	8 Cirrostratus, not covering all the sky.
3 Cirrus from cumulonimbus tops.	9 Cirrocumulus.
4 Dense cirrus, covering much of the sky.	
5 Continuous cirrus cover.	

E (STATE OF THE GROUND—not often used)

0 Dry surface.	7 Ice or snow—covering all the ground.
1 Moist surface.	8 Loose dry snow, dust, or sand—half-cover.
2 Wet surface.	9 Loose dry snow, dust, or sand—covered.
3 Frozen surface.	
4 Glaze on the ground.	
5 Ice or snow—less than half-cover.	
6 Ice or snow—more than half-cover.	

a (THE BAROMETRIC TENDENCY)

0 Increasing, then decreasing.	5 Decreasing, then slightly increasing.
1 Increasing, then steady.	6 Decreasing, then steady.
2 Increasing steadily or unsteadily.	7 Decreasing steadily or unsteadily.
3 Decreasing, then increasing steadily.	8 Increasing, then decreasing rapidly.
4 Steady.	

In 1–3 the atmospheric pressure is higher than it was three hours before. In 6–8 the atmospheric pressure is lower than it was three hours before.

In addition to the code figures and symbols indicated in Fig. 78, a further code is employed to indicate the height of the low-cloud base:

h (HEIGHT OF BASE OF LOW CLOUD, OF TYPE C_L, Figures in Metres)

0	0–50	5	600–1000
1	50–100	6	1000–1500
2	100–200	7	1500–2000
3	200–300	8	2000–2500
4	300–600	9	Above 2500

In Fig. 79 the code table for the symbols indicating the present weather (ww) is shown. It is not practicable to list here all the descriptions for the values of ww from 00 to 99, and it is sufficient to mention that each row describes one aspect of the

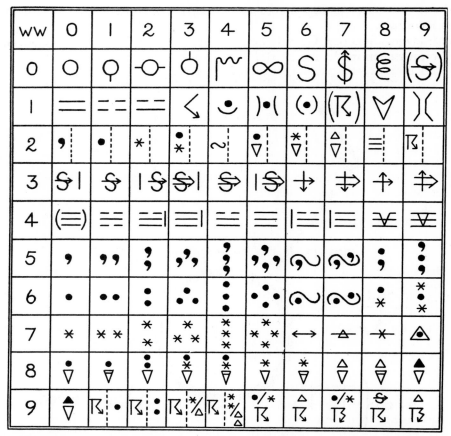

FIG. 79. LIST OF PRESENT WEATHER SYMBOLS (SEE APPENDIX VI FOR DESCRIPTIONS OF SYMBOLS)

present weather. Figures 61–70, for example, describe the details of rainfall. (See Appendix VI for details of the present weather symbols.)

The complete code is explained in a pamphlet issued by the Meteorological Office (M.O. 515), and anyone requiring to know the finer details should consult this publication. Enough material has been listed to show the methods by which certain weather elements are coded, and it is now possible to explain how the coded information is plotted on the weather map.

THE PLOTTING OF WEATHER INFORMATION

The technique of plotting the information recorded in the Synoptic Code is based upon an international station model (see Fig. 80), on which the positions of the figures and symbols to be plotted are shown in either black or red ink. Fig. 80 shows the location around the station circle of all the more important weather elements. For each station report given in the Synoptic Code a plot of the figures and symbols is made, so that an observer may see at a glance the weather at that station for the time of recording.

The following Synoptic Code figures, shown in their five-figure groupings, are plotted on a station model in Fig. 81:

03772   61815   40188   10211   52460   09020   70655

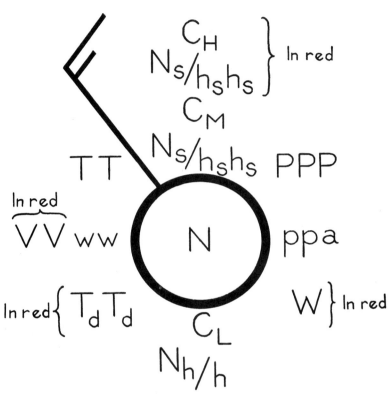

FIG. 80. THE STATION MODEL

N	Cloud amount.	a	Characteristic of tendency.
W	Past weather.	PPP	Barometric pressure.
C_L	Type of low cloud.	N_s	Used when there are two layers of cloud. One
C_M	Type of medium cloud.		layer is plotted as N_h, and the other layer
C_H	Type of high cloud.		is shown as N_s. The position of the
TT	Air temperature.		plotting of N_s depends upon the classifica-
$T_d T_d$	Dew point.		tion of cloud in this layer.
VV	Visibility.	h_s	Height of cloud amount N_s.
ww	Present weather.	N_h	Amount of low cloud.
pp	Barometric tendency.	h	Height of low cloud.

The wind speed and wind direction are shown by an arrow attached to the station circle. The direction is indicated by the position of the line in relation to the north, and the speed is shown by feathers on the shaft of the arrow. The full feathers represent 10 knots, the half-feathers represent 5 knots, and the solid pennants represent 50 knots. (See Fig. 82.)

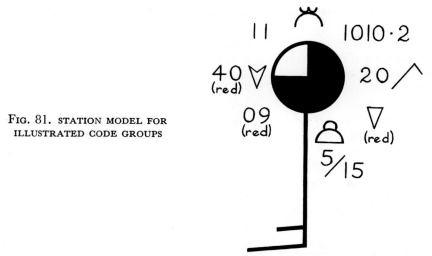

FIG. 81. STATION MODEL FOR
ILLUSTRATED CODE GROUPS

KNOTS	AS PLOTTED	KNOTS	AS PLOTTED
Calm	◎		
1-2	——	33-37	
3-7		38-42	
8-12		43-47	
13-17		48-52	
18-22		53-57	
23-27		58-62	
28-32		63-67	

FIG. 82. WIND-SPEED SYMBOLS ON WIND ARROW
(See note on p. 137 regarding the use of knots)

Each station receives the complete observations of all stations in the British Isles for every hour. This information is obtained from a teleprinter machine which types the stations' weather elements in the Synoptic Code, as they were received by the Meteorological Office a few minutes earlier. Speed is the essential feature of the system, and the observations, taken every hour, coded, and dispatched to Bracknell, are collected, co-ordinated, and rebroadcast from Bracknell within twenty minutes. The information can then be plotted on charts, and a complete picture of the weather of an hour earlier can be placed before a meteorologist. The hourly receipt of this information enables the forecaster to appreciate how the weather is moving, what developments are likely to take place, and what the prospects will be during the next few hours. It is from the charts that the prediction of future weather is therefore made, and, although many pieces of other information are available to the meteorologist in assisting him in his forecast, he is often compelled to make intelligent guesses about future developments from his synoptic charts alone.

Meteorology is still a most uncertain science, and since it depends upon the interpretation of the weather elements on a global scale, even further international co-operation is needed in order to produce fuller records. A great deal has been accomplished since the formation of the World Meteorological Organization in 1951, and the weather satellites launched by the United States and the Soviet Union have added a new dimension to tropospheric analysis. Details of upper atmospheric conditions are still very meagre; the answers to the problems of weather-forecasting may well be found in the analysis of the upper atmosphere. Studies of the sun will enable us to understand many weather phenomena on the earth. It has been definitely established that the charged particles emitted by the sun are responsible for considerable changes in the composition of the troposphere. A new science, called aeronomics, today investigates the upper atmosphere as a whole, and various methods have now been developed to determine the physical characteristics of the atmosphere, both in its horizontal and its vertical dimensions.

Only satellites could give meteorologists a coherent and comprehensive image of the circulation of the atmosphere and of the earth's cloud cover. The world's lower layers of the atmosphere have been laid out like a map. Cloud over vast areas of the earth's surface has become visible, and the tracking of bad-weather situations has become commonplace. Results of investigations at great altitudes are now enabling meteorologists to revise their theories. We are beginning to understand more about the reasons for weather change, and to predict future situations with growing confidence. In making future predictions meteorology is becoming increasingly computer-based. Nevertheless, many years will elapse before computers will be programmed to forecast actual weather situations. Even in weather forecasting much remains to be done manually, and trained meteorologists will continue to be required to forecast weather, to make allowances for local topographical weather controls, and to apply logic in the evaluation of the mass of new data being provided. For many years in the future we shall remain dependent upon the meteorologist to record the weather elements and to make a forecast in the light of past experience and the elementary principles of physics. Physics, which forms the basis of meteorology, remains the same, and the content of the preceding chapters will not be materially invalidated by any new discoveries about the conditions of the atmosphere.

Chapter 13

WEATHER WATCHERS IN SPACE

THE world entered the space age on 4 October 1957, when the Soviet Union launched Sputnik 1, the earth's first artificial satellite. An aluminium sphere, some 58 centimetres in diameter and weighing about 83½ kilogrammes, was projected into an elliptical orbit with an apogee of about 900 kilometres. The satellite represented the successful conclusion to a long technical programme in rocket research, initiated by scientists of several nations during the International Geophysical Year July 1957 to December 1958. After some initial disappointments in their own rocket programme, the United States hurled their Explorer 1, weighing 13·6 kg with its instrument load, into orbit on 31 January 1958. Ordinary folk listened to their radios with astonishment and admiration as the strange, high-pitched 'bleeps' were transmitted from outer space, while scientists proceeded to make numerous observations.

Explorer 1 was a major scientific success, since this first American satellite made one of the greatest discoveries of our time. Two hitherto unknown radiation belts surrounding the earth were located: the Van Allen belts, named after the scientist who investigated them. Other Explorer satellites, specifically designed to investigate further these radiation belts, were launched. Explorer 4 had a very elongated orbit which enabled the satellite to venture over 40 000 kilometres into space. In addition to the Geiger counters capable of measuring the Van Allen radiation, the satellite also carried a rudimentary television system which, for the first time in meteorological history, allowed a crude picture to be obtained of the earth's cloud cover as viewed from space.

Not long after the launching of the first satellites the United States, and doubtless Russia also, began to study the practical uses of artificial satellites. While more than 50 per cent of the American satellites launched are secret, and have military implications, the remainder have been designed essentially for technical and scientific purposes. After the squandering of effort between the armed services, the United States Government decided, in summer 1958, to set up a single official authority, the National Aeronautics and Space Administration (NASA), whose task it became to co-ordinate all programmes relating to space rocketry and satellite launchings. Thus, in addition to satisfying the need for applying results of space investigation to national defence, NASA spends much money and effort in advancing the knowledge of the earth, solar system, and man himself.

The number of satellites that have been successfully placed in orbit now runs into several hundreds, and many 'applications satellites' have been sent on missions of direct value in connection with man's daily life on earth. Among these meteorological satellites figure largely. President Johnson once quoted the annual savings which meteorological satellites would bring to the American economy if weather could be forecast accurately five days in advance. In terms of money saved for agriculture, transport, and water-supply, the total was estimated to be over

5000 million dollars per year. NASA's budget in 1977 was 4500 million dollars, so it is evident that the special meteorological satellite programme may alone repay the greater part of the cost of the American civil space administration.

The close relationship existing between weather forecasting and weather observation was stressed in the preceding chapter. Predictions of future weather are based on interpretations of past and present atmospheric conditions. Forecasting depends on what is known of the interaction of the various forms of energy which determine atmospheric movement. To obtain this knowledge, measurements must be taken of the condition of the atmosphere at any given time. These measurements must then be collated and analysed. It was underlined in Chapter 12 that day-to-day weather forecasting depends on:

1. The observation and collection of weather data.
2. The rapid transmission of that data to a collecting and analysing centre.

The first meteorological observations were made by skilled personnel on the ground. Then balloons and aeroplanes extended the observations by enabling measurements to be made at increasingly high altitudes in the atmosphere. Later, radio-sonde balloons and rockets made it possible to carry out observations at even greater altitudes bordering on the stratosphere. The stage has now been reached at which meteorological information is gathered by satellites and transmitted to collecting and processing centres.

Satellites differ significantly from the more conventional means of gathering weather information. A single satellite can provide global coverage, whereas the normal earth-bound weather reporting network covers only a small portion of the world's surface area. There are large regions of deserts, oceans, and the polar latitudes for which no man-made observations are possible. These, comprising almost three-quarters of the earth's surface, are the very areas from which much of the world's bad weather originates. Covering these remote and difficult regions with manned meteorological observation stations would be economically prohibitive. A better method, clearly, is by satellite, which can locate tropical storms, frontal systems, and weather of continental and oceanic dimensions. Forecasts have been materially improved by the use of photographs taken by satellite. Utilizing this information from space, forecasts made for public service twenty-four to forty-eight hours in advance are now 85–90 per cent accurate.

The TIROS Meteorological Satellites

On 1 April 1960 the first American satellite specially designed to record weather, TIROS 1, was put in orbit. This launching represented the culmination of a decade of theory and planning. The name TIROS is an acronym for 'Television and Infra-Red Observation Satellite'. Two hours after launching into an almost circular orbit nearly 700 kilometres above the earth, TIROS 1 sent back its first television pictures of the earth's surface. This satellite gave meteorologists their first overall view of the 'weather', and, until 12 July 1960, transmitted 22 952 pictures.

The TIROS family consisted of ten satellites. They were cylindrical in shape, about one metre in diameter and 0·5 metre deep. They weighed almost 135 kg, and were powered by nickel-cadmium batteries charged by over 9000 solar cells mounted on the top and sides. Two television cameras were carried. The first eight TIROS were stabilized in space by rotation about their vertical axis. Each satellite thus in effect formed a gyroscope with its axis fixed with respect to a point in space.

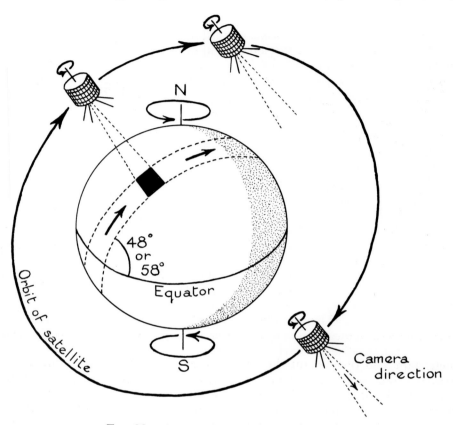

FIG. 83. SPACE-ORIENTED TIROS SATELLITE

N.B. By being launched in the same direction as the rotation of the earth—viz., eastward—the satellites start with the benefit of the earth's rotational velocity.

As they moved round in orbit the satellites presented a different face to the earth on each half-revolution. Consequently, cloud photographs could be taken only during that part of each orbit when the base of the satellite containing the camera lenses was pointing to the earth. TIROS 9 and 10 were spin-stabilized (see Fig. 84), such that they rolled along their orbits like wheels. In these two satellites the cameras were positioned on the rim, and thus each of them pointed towards the earth once during each revolution of the satellite about its central axis.

Each satellite camera consists of two parts, a Vidicon television tube and a focal plane shutter which allows pictures to be stored temporarily on the tube screen. An electron beam converts each stored picture into an electronic signal, which is then either transmitted to the ground station or stored on a magnetic tape recorder for later relay. On the ground, the television pictures are simultaneously recorded on

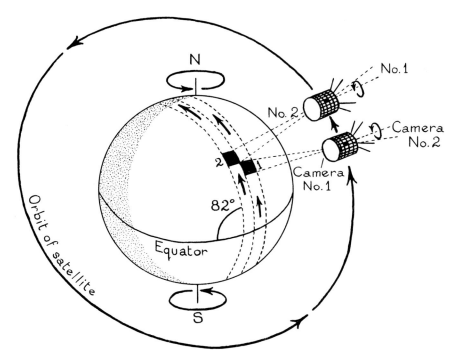

FIG. 84. "CARTWHEEL" TIROS SATELLITE

N.B. This is a retrograde orbit, i.e. the satellite is launched in the opposite direction to the rotation of the earth.

magnetic tape and re-constituted on a television tube, known as a kinescope. The kinescope is photographed, and within a quarter of an hour of reception the film has been developed and printed. Overprinted with the latitude and longitude grid which has been determined from computer calculations of the earth's graticule at the time of the satellite observation, the photographs can easily be assembled in the form of a mosaic giving an analysis of the earth's cloud cover—the 'nephelosphere'.

The disadvantage of the first eight TIROS satellites was that the photographs were confined to relatively low latitudes. The orbits' inclination to the equator varied between 48° and 58°, and thus high latitudes and polar regions were unobserved. TIROS 9 and 10, besides being of 'cartwheel' motion, were placed in quasi-polar orbits of 96·4° and 98·7° respectively, and retrograde to the earth's spin in order to improve the extent of the daily photographic coverage. The table in Appendix VII provides the statistical information of the TIROS satellites.

THE NIMBUS METEOROLOGICAL SATELLITES

The NIMBUS family of American satellites represents further development in the techniques for improving constant surveillance of the earth's surface. Four satellites have so far been launched, and each was put into a polar orbit, retrograde to the earth's axial rotation. Moreover, they were permanently stabilized, so that they

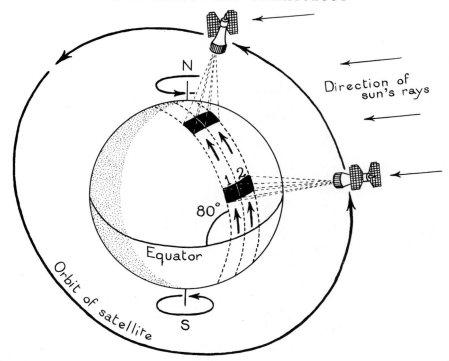

FIG. 85. NIMBUS SATELLITE WITH SUN-ORIENTED PADDLES CARRYING SOLAR CELLS

maintained a fixed camera angle with the earth's surface. The solar cells were deployed as two large paddles which were oriented constantly towards the sun. Thus, although the orientation system was complicated, it was accurate in performance. Infra-red equipment, greatly superior to that of the TIROS satellites, gave photographic data a third dimension by reporting temperature in the atmosphere with respect to altitude.

Launched on 28 August 1964, NIMBUS 1 made 380 orbits. It exceeded all expectations as a research vehicle and weather tracker. In its first day of orbit it had photographed several Caribbean and Pacific hurricanes. By means of its high-resolution infra-red spectrometer it became the first satellite to provide night-time pictures of the earth's cloud cover. Using both the Advanced Vidicon Camera System (AVCS) and Automatic Picture Transmission equipment (APT), NIMBUS 1 took well over a thousand pictures daily. Before becoming unusable on 23 September 1964, the satellite had sent back more than 27 000 day and night-time photographs.

NIMBUS 2, launched on 15 May 1966, provided a continuous stream of weather information for almost three years, amounting to over 112 000 pictures. This second satellite in the family differed little from its predecessor. NIMBUS 3, launched in April 1969, incorporated new systems for obtaining quantitative weather measurements. In all, nine experiments were carried, which proved extremely successful:

1. A Satellite Infra-Red Spectrometer (SIRS), designed to measure the atmosphere's vertical temperature from the earth's surface up to 24 kilometres.

Pl. IX

ESSA 7 SATELLITE

ESSA photo

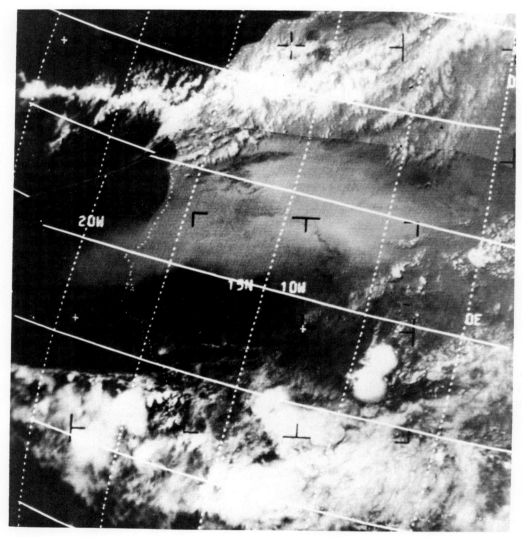

Pl. X   SANDSTORM ACROSS THE SAHARA
ESSA photo

2. An Infra-Red Interferometer Spectrometer (IRIS), for measuring the
atmosphere's vertical temperature, water-vapour content, and ozone
distribution.

3. A Monitor of Ultra-Violet Solar Energy (MUSE), for measuring the ultra-violet radiation flux from the sun.
4. An Interrogation, Recording, and Location System (IRLS), for collecting global data from remote weather stations such as balloons, buoys, and automatic weather instruments.
5. An Image Dissector Camera System (IDCS), for providing regional daylight cloud cover and earth-surface pictures.
6. A High Resolution Infra-Red Radiometer (HRIR), for producing night-time photographs of the earth's cloud cover.
7. A Medium Resolution Infra-Red Radiometer (MRIR), for measuring the entire earth's heat balance daily.
8. A Rate Measuring Package (RMP), for evaluating the performance of special gyroscopes in space.
9. A Radio-Isotope Thermonuclear Generator (RTG), for evaluating a nuclear-power system for weather satellites.

The use of SIRS was of tremendous importance to meteorologists in that the system, incorporated in a single satellite, gave full global coverage of atmospheric temperatures at all levels within the troposphere.

NIMBUS 4, sent into a 1100-kilometre orbit on 8 April 1970, observes the entire planet twice daily. It further develops the experiments to monitor the distribution of ozone, water vapour, and radiation from the earth. Continuous mapping of the earth's surface, including its cloud cover, is provided by the IDCS.

NIMBUS 5 and 6 complete the family of satellites. Weighing 700 kg and 1600 kg respectively, compared with the 270 kg of NIMBUS 1 and 2, both have had their electrical power increased from 200 to 400 watts. NIMBUS 5 was launched on 11 December, 1972 and is the first satellite capable of making vertical temperature measurements of the atmosphere. NIMBUS 6, which has over twenty experiments on board, was launched on 12th June, 1975.

THE ESSA AND ATS SATELLITES

It should be remembered that both the TIROS and NIMBUS satellites were essentially experimental platforms for scientific equipment. The apparatus carried into orbit set out to satisfy five major requirements for the substantial improvement of weather satellites:

1. To provide meteorological information concerning the regions of sparse data such as the oceans, deserts, and polar regions.
2. To scan large-scale weather patterns and their movement.
3. To obtain more data about the upper levels of the troposphere.
4. To observe night-time weather in detail.
5. To improve the statistical models that are being increasingly used in weather forecasting by computer.

As the NIMBUS satellites continue to test new scientific equipment and recording systems, operational satellites have been put into orbit whose essential task is to observe the earth environment using apparatus which has already proved to be successful. Within the United States Department of Commerce there is the Environmental Science Services Administration (ESSA). One of ESSA'S responsibilities is to describe, understand, and predict the state of the atmosphere. Consequently the Administration has two major sub-units, the National Environmental Satellite Centre and the American Weather Bureau, whose combined task it is to investigate the atmosphere.

On 3 February 1966 the successful experiments associated with the first six years of satellite meteorology finally were incorporated in the satellite ESSA 1. Each satellite, in the series of nine launched by ESSA, carried either an Advanced Vidicon Camera System or an Automatic Picture Transmission System. They therefore fulfilled one of the main objectives of the United States National Meteorological Satellite System—namely, the daily observation of global weather conditions. Unfortunately, the series does not permit night-time observations of cloud patterns or temperature distribution.

The AVCS cameras of the ESSA satellites send cloud pictures directly to two Command and Data Acquisition Stations (CDA) at Wallops Island, Virginia, and Gilmore Creek near Fairbanks, in Alaska, or they can store the photographs on a tape recorder for read-out when the satellites pass within line-of-sight range of one of the stations. After receipt the signals are processed. Cloud-cover maps, or 'nephanalyses', are then prepared and, combined with weather information obtained by conventional means, form the basis of weather forecasts. Fig. 88 and the accompanying photograph illustrate this combination of a cloud map and a conventional synoptic chart. The nephanalyses are drawn symbolically in much the same way as the ordinary synoptic chart, and this information is then available to all members within the World Meteorological Organization who have facsimile reproduction facilities.

The Automatic Picture Transmission cameras (APT) can take and immediately transmit pictures of an area of $10\frac{1}{4}$ million square kilometres ($10\cdot25 \times 10^6$ km²) beneath the satellite to simply equipped ground stations within 2400 kilometres of the spacecraft. The APT pictures employ radio facsimile methods of reproduction instead of the costly television processes. Images are built up in dots, rather than in line, using the ordinary equipment similar to that used by the national newspapers for the receipt of photographs by radio from all parts of the world. The APT pictures therefore furnish local meteorological forecasters with a fresh (within 200 seconds) view of the cloud patterns over or adjacent to the local area.

The last ESSA satellite—ESSA 9—was launched on 26 February 1969. Along with ESSA 2, ESSA 3, ESSA 6, and ESSA 8, it has continued to work efficiently, giving world-wide weather information.

As meteorological research and supply of weather information continued in the TIROS, NIMBUS, and ESSA satellites, a further series, not exclusively confined to meteorology, also began to contribute information. These were the ATS satellites—Applications Technology Satellites—launched as a NASA project in conjunction with a civil firm, Hughes Aircraft Company, Space Systems Division. Five satellites were planned, to be launched over a period of two and a half years from December 1966, each carrying a large number of scientific instruments, including some which were meteorological.

ATS 1 was launched on 7 December 1966, and contained two pieces of meteorological apparatus for scientific evaluation:

    a. A Spin Scan Cloud Camera (SSCC), designed to monitor weather phenomena over a large area of the earth's surface during selected intervals of time, to illustrate the feasibility of continuous coverage.

    b. A Weather Dissemination Project (WEFAX), designed to test satellite transmission of facsimile cloud pictures, so increasing the amount of data available to over 500 ground stations in some fifty different countries which possess the recording equipment. This includes the British Central Meteorological Office at Bracknell.

The satellite was placed in a geo-synchronous orbit over Christmas Island in the Pacific (0° Latitude, 151° W.) at an altitude varying between 35 782 and 35 766 kilometres. A geo-synchronous orbit is one in which the speed of the satellite in its revolution coincides exactly with the rotational speed of the earth about its axis. In this way a satellite in synchronous orbit appears stationary relative to the earth, and permits continuous observation of short-duration weather changes over a large area of the globe.

Not all the satellites in the ATS series were successfully launched, and ATS 2, ATS 4, and ATS 5 were eventually discarded. However, ATS 3, launched successfully on 5 November 1967, was placed in a geo-stationary orbit over the mouth of the Amazon. This satellite carried both a black-and-white and colour spin scan camera system. Cloud pictures, covering the entire disc of the earth and supplied every twenty minutes by the SSCC system, have provided meteorologists with a true 'moving picture' of the evolution of weather systems.

THE ITOS SATELLITES

With the launch of ITOS 1—Improved TIROS Operational Satellite—on 23 January 1970, operational weather satellites entered a second generation. The ITOS system is jointly planned by NASA and ESSA, and six satellites are envisaged.

Weighing 305 kg, ITOS 1 compresses the AVC and APT systems into a single satellite, instead of in two separate spacecraft as in the ESSA series. There are two advanced AVCS and two APT systems for day-time cloud observation, as well as two scanning infra-red radiometers to provide global day and night pictures. In addition, there are other radiometers which provide cloud-top and surface temperatures, and a Solar Proton Monitor (SPM) to measure solar flares.

The orbit of ITOS 1 is near-circular at 1450 kilometres altitude, and is inclined at 102° to the equator—*i.e.*, it is retrograde to the earth's spin. It takes about 115 minutes to complete each orbit, and is sun-synchronous. The sun is thus always at the same angle relative to the craft, giving the best condition for photography and solar-cell exposure. The satellite is finally stabilized in all three axes, so that it constantly faces towards the earth.

ITOS 2 was launched on 11 December 1970, to become operational under the recently formed National Oceanic and Atmospheric Administration in the U.S.A. The equipment is identical with that on board ITOS 1.

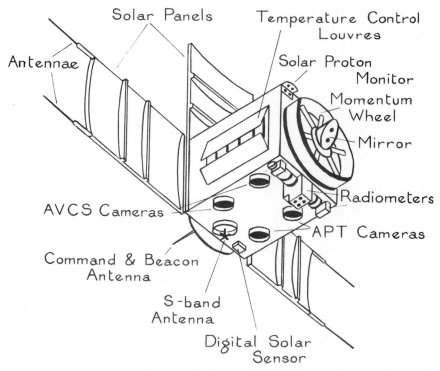

FIG. 86. ITOS I—SCHEMATIC DIAGRAM

SOVIET METEOROLOGICAL SATELLITES

Despite the fact that Soviet Russia was the first nation to place an artificial satellite in orbit around the earth, in 1957, it was not until 25 June 1966 that COSMOS 122, a satellite officially designated meteorological, was launched. The Russians indicated that the satellite provided data on global cloud cover, surface temperature distributions on the earth, and information about the polar ice-caps.

The satellites in the COSMOS series are very versatile and all-embracing, being engaged in every kind of scientific investigation. Since the first was launched in March 1962, over 400 COSMOS craft have been placed in orbit, many of which contain space research equipment which has some meteorological significance. Experiments have included research into the radiation belts of the earth, the intensity of the geo-magnetic fields, and infra-red and ultra-violet radiation reflected from the earth. However, between February 1967 and June 1968 five more COSMOS satellites specially designed for meteorological investigation were launched, and these became the forerunners of the Soviet Union's current METEOR satellite programme.

The METEOR satellites, in many ways similar to the American NIMBUS series, collect meteorological information by means of three systems: television, infra-red

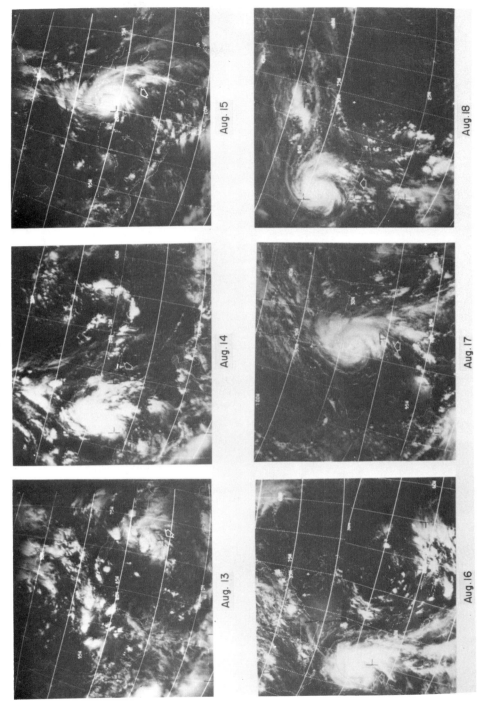

Pl. XI   TRACK OF HURRICANE CAMILLE, AUGUST 1969
ESSA photo

Pl. XII   A CYCLONIC STORM NEAR HAWAII FROM APOLLO 9
NASA photo

equipment, and actinometric equipment. The object of the actinometric apparatus is to measure the intensity of the radiant heat reflected and emitted from the earth's atmosphere. In addition it also measures the radiation temperatures of the earth's surface and the cloud tops. Six operational METEOR satellites are now in orbit, each carrying identical equipment. Each craft also carries a radio and telemetry system for the exact measurement of the orbital parameters and the transmission of the data to ground control stations.

The Soviet Union, during the past few years, has also launched scientific satellites in two other series, the ELEKTRON and PROTON programmes. These craft together have investigated low- and high-energy particles making up the radiation belts surrounding the earth, cosmic rays, and the short-wave solar emissions. There is no doubt that these Soviet satellites have contributed much valuable and accurate information on the content and character of cosmic rays, and have presented meteorologists with data on the ionosphere and cosmos leading to a deeper understanding of the factors conditioning the atmosphere and global weather.

THE WORLD WEATHER WATCH

International co-operation in meteorology began as early as 1853, when a meeting of maritime nations took place to consider collaboration in this field. In 1878 the International Meteorological Organization was formed, and it continued to encourage the growth of international co-operation in weather study until the end of the Second World War. The creation of the United Nations presented new opportunities for joint meteorological investigation, and in 1947 the World Meteorological Convention was adopted in Washington. As a result a new organization, the World Meteorological Organization (WMO), was set up in March 1950 as a specialized agency within the United Nations Organization.

The World Meteorological Organization, based in Geneva, has as its function to 'co-ordinate, standardize and improve the services rendered by meteorology throughout the world to various human activities'. At present 139 nations are members, as well as certain colonial territories such as Hong Kong. The main exceptions are the People's Republic of China and East Germany. Every four years the supreme organ of the WMO meets to fix the policy and draw up a programme.

The first two nations to have a successful satellite programme were the United States and the Union of Soviet Socialist Republics. Bilateral co-operation between these two major contributors to space technology was initiated as early as 1962 in an exchange of letters between President Kennedy and Nikita Krushchev. This resulted in a memorandum of understanding between NASA and the Soviet Academy of Sciences, and a positive decision was made to exchange meteorological satellite information. The initial exchange of photographs took place on 11 September 1966, the Soviet pictures coming from their first weather satellite, COSMOS 122, which was launched on 25 June 1966.

In 1968 the WMO launched its World Weather Watch programme (WWW), the aim of which was to bring about improved meteorological services in all countries by the application of all the modern scientific and technical devices, including satellites.

Three basic requirements are necessary to provide an efficient global weather service:

1. Sufficient data on a world-wide scale. (The WMO considers that the network of observing over three-quarters of the earth's surface is inadequate.)
2. Facilities for processing the data.
3. Efficient and adequate communication for the rapid dissemination of the processed data.

The World Weather Watch is attempting to fulfil the three main requirements. It is developing a Global Observing System (GOS), a Global Data Processing System

(GDPS), and a Global Telecommunication System (GTS). Satellites, although obviously suited to the GOS programme, can assist materially in satisfying the other two conditions. We have already seen how NIMBUS 3 carried equipment (IRLS) which successfully demonstrated that satellites could collect data from remote weather locations. Having proved that satellites can contribute significantly to the satisfying of the three basic requirements for a comprehensive and efficient global weather service, the United States has proceeded to initiate a satellite programme which will provide 'the cornerstone of a sophisticated data gathering and distribution system'.

The first in a series of Geo-Stationary Operational Environmental Satellites (GOES) was launched on the 16th October 1975. Cylindrical in shape, one and a half metres in diameter, and about the same in depth, these satellites will be placed in a geo-stationary orbit at altitudes of about 37 000 kilometres. To remain in orbit in the same position relative to a point on earth, the satellites must be over

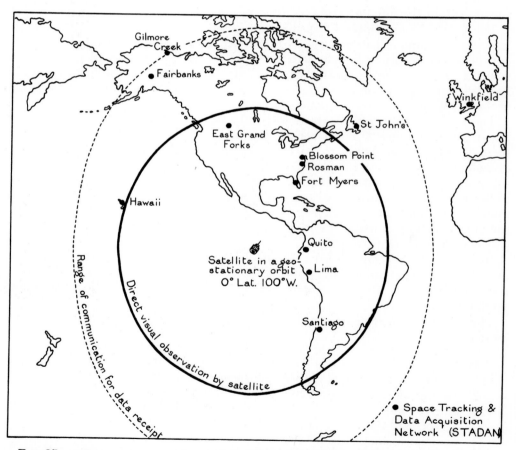

FIG. 87. GEO-STATIONARY OPERATIONAL ENVIRONMENTAL SATELLITE—GOES I—TO BE PLACED NEAR THE EQUATOR AT 100° W

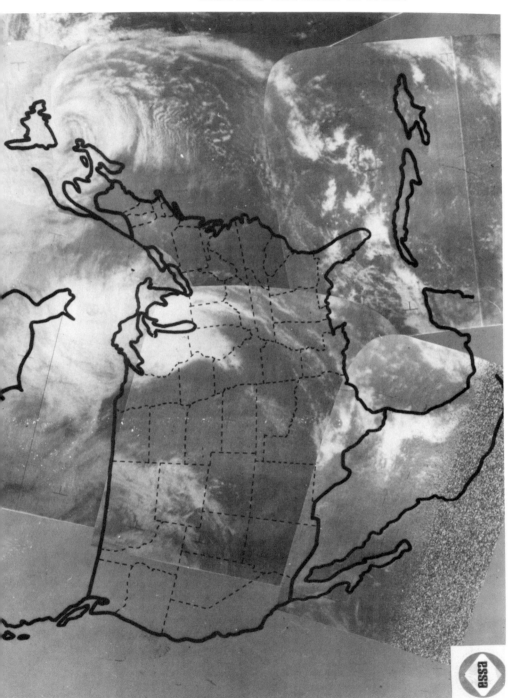

AMERICAN WEATHER FROM ESSA SATELLITE, 22 OCTOBER 1968
ESSA photo

Pl. XIII

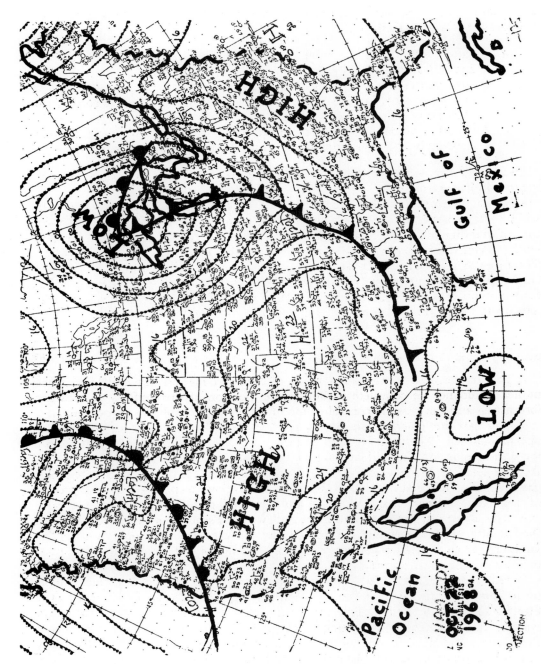

Fig. 88. SYNOPTIC CHART OF AMERICAN WEATHER FOR 22 OCTOBER 1968

American Weather Bureau

the equator. The first has been placed near the 100° W. line of longitude, and provides the following facilities:

a. It contains a visual observing system covering an area between 50° N. and 50° S. (See Fig. 87.)
b. It also carries some form of IRLS equipment for receiving and retransmitting observational data from a very large number of meteorological platforms.
c. There is a third capability of broadcasting certain meteorological data to suitably equipped ground recording stations within line of sight.

Other member countries in the WWW, including Britain and France, aim to launch similar satellites.

The final dissemination of this comprehensive accumulation of global weather data will be carried out by an efficient telecommunication link. The WWW plan to make the information available to all member countries in the WMO via a system of world, regional, and national meteorological centres (WMCs, RMCs, and NMCs). The three WMCs are located at Washington, Moscow, and Melbourne, and they act as the service centres for the analyses of large-scale atmospheric processes. Main circuits connect the WMCs with the RMCs, and subsidiary communications links oin up the individual national networks.

SATELLITES, WEATHER FORECASTING, AND WEATHER MODIFICATION

A chapter devoted to an examination of the most modern meterological techniques would not be complete without some mention of their effects on weather forecasting and the possible control or modification of atmospheric phenomena.

Today satellite cloud photographs are processed as a matter of routine for operational use. The pictures are digitized, rectified, and fit into a global mosaic for transmission via facsimile to national weather centres throughout the world. Routine and reliable receipt of meteorological data has resulted in the widespread use of satellite information in daily weather observation. Nephanalyses have proved of great value in short-term forecasting, and now APT pictures, received regularly by over fifty countries, provide almost 'instant' weather situations over large areas in the vicinity of the receiving stations. These pictures are used operationally for analyses, for local and area forecasts, and for briefing pilots on weather conditions over long trans-ocean routes.

Weather forecasting is fast becoming computer-based, and the modern, high-speed computer may well be the key to accurate global weather forecasting in the future. The WWW, besides developing the global observing and data distribution systems, also promotes a research programme, the Global Atmospheric Research Programme (GARP). The aims of the programme are directed towards the study of physical processes in the troposphere, and atmosphere as a whole, essential for understanding large-scale fluctuations in atmospheric behaviour and those factors that determine statistical properties of atmospheric circulation.

Weather satellites provide such vast amounts of data concerning the above factors that only modern computers can solve speedily the complex mathematical equations which describe the atmosphere's behaviour. Already the Meteorological Office at Bracknell use their IBM computer for running routine numerical forecast programmes. Two series of forecast programmes, utilizing meteorological information from the northern hemisphere, are daily run through the computer. The machine calculates the future values of pressure and wind for some ten levels in the atmosphere. Temperatures, humidities and certain other parameters may also be calculated. Perhaps by the early 1980s we may know with some degree of certainty how predictable the atmosphere is, and then how to predict it.

The feasibility of large-scale weather modification is still very much in its infancy. Up until recently the main hindrance to weather modification has been the immensity of the phenomena involved, and the great dearth of information over extensive areas of the globe. The meteorological satellites are now filling these gaps, and it is hoped that extreme weather conditions can be located before they reach unmanageable proportions. Satellites have become essential tools in the study of weather. From the information they present we are now comprehending more and more about atmospheric conditions. Comprehension will doubtless lead eventually to control. However, control is as yet scarcely in sight, but this still remains the ultimate goal of meteorologists.

APPENDICES TO PART ONE

Appendix I

SUMMARY OF CLOUD CHARACTERISTICS

Name of Cloud	Usual Abbreviation	Range of Height of Cloud Base in Great Britain, in Metres	Vertical Thickness of Cloud	Significant Features
Cirrus	Ci	6000–12 000	Often a few hundred metres.	Usually indicates an approaching frontal system.
Cirrostratus	Cs	6000–12 000	Often a few hundred metres.	Usually indicates an approaching frontal system. Is accompanied by haloes around the sun.
Cirrocumulus	Cc	6000–12 000	Fairly thin.	—
Altocumulus	Ac	2000–6000	A few hundred metres.	Bands are often seen ahead of fronts. The castellated types are associated with thunder.
Altostratus	As	2000–6000. Base often merges into nimbostratus	Thick — may be up to 3500 metres.	Indicates closeness to precipitation area of frontal system.
Nimbostratus	Ns	100–600	Thick — may be up to 4500 metres.	Associated with precipitation. Tops merge with altostratus.
Stratus	St	150–600	Thin — from 30 to 300 metres.	May cover high ground.
Stratocumulus	Sc	300–1350	Thin — from 150 to 900 metres.	—
Cumulus	Cu	300–1400	May be thick —1400 to 4500 metres.	Is some indication of atmospheric stability. Strong vertical currents in large types.
Cumulonimbus	Cb	600–1400	Very thick— may be 3000 to 9000 metres.	Very turbulent cloud, accompanied by heavy showers, perhaps of hail, lightning, and thunder.

PROPERTIES OF MAIN AIR MASSES AROUND GREAT BRITAIN

TYPE OF AIR MASS	TYPICAL CHARACTERISTICS IN WINTER	TYPICAL CHARACTERISTICS IN SUMMER
Polar maritime	Cumulus or cumulonimbus clouds. Showers, often of sleet or snow. Good visibility, except in the showers. Clouds may clear inland.	Cool conditions. Showers are prevalent, often with hail and thunder.
Polar continental	Very cold conditions. Dry air. Seldom produces showers—except along the east coast, where air comes in from the North Sea.	Warm and dry. Little cloud develops. Dust haze from the Continent reaches south-eastern counties.
Tropical maritime	Warm and moist air. Low stratus cloud, often bringing drizzle and fog.	Warm, moist, and low cloud develops over coastal areas. Fog is often a feature over the sea and coastal districts. Layer cloud usually disperses over the land during the day.
Tropical continental	Warm and fairly dry.	Very warm and dry. Clear skies are usual, but haze is most apparent.

SUMMARY OF FRONTAL CHARACTERISTICS

ELEMENT	IN ADVANCE	AT THE FRONT	IN THE REAR
WARM FRONT			
Pressure	Steady fall.	Fall ceases.	Little change.
Wind	Backs and increases.	Veers and decreases.	Steady.
Temperature	Steady or slow rise.	Rises slowly.	Little change.
Humidity	Gradual increase.	Rapid rise.	Little change.
Cloud	Ci, Cs, As, Ns in succession.	Low nimbostratus and fractostratus.	Stratus and strato-cumulus.
Weather	Continuous rain (or snow in winter).	Precipitation almost stops.	Fair conditions, or intermittent slight rain or drizzle.
Visibility	Good, except in rain.	Poor—mist and low cloud produce poor visibility.	Often poor, with low cloud and mist or fog.
COLD FRONT			
Pressure	Falls.	Sudden rise.	Slow, continuous rise.
Wind	Backs and increases.	Veers suddenly—often accompanied by line squalls—*i.e.*, severe winds along frontal boundary.	Slow backing after squall, then steady.
Temperature	Steady—sometimes a slight fall in rain.	Sudden fall.	Little change.
Humidity	No great change.	Sudden fall.	Generally low.
Cloud	Altocumulus and altostratus, followed by cumulonimbus.	Cumulonimbus, with fractocumulus or low nimbostratus.	Lifts rapidly, but cumulus or cumulonimbus may develop.
Weather	Some rain, with possible thunder.	Heavy rain, often accompanied by hail and thunder.	Heavy rain for a short period; fine spell, followed by further showers.
Visibility	Poor—some fog.	Temporary deterioration—rapid improvement.	Very good.

SUMMARY OF FOG CHARACTERISTICS

Type of Fog	Season	Areas affected	Mode of Formation	Mode of Dispersal
Radiation fog	October to March	Inland areas, especially low-lying, moist ground.	Cooling due to radiation from the ground on clear nights when the wind is light. Is a feature of anti-cyclonic weather.	Dispersed by the sun's radiation or by increased wind.
Advection fog 1. Over land	Winter or spring	Often widespread in inland regions.	Cooling of warm air by passage over cold ground—typical when warm air arrives after a cold spell.	Increased wind produces a lift in the cloud base. The fog is dispersed by a change in air mass or by the gradual warming of the ground.
2. Over sea and coastline	Spring and early summer	Sea and coasts adjacent. May penetrate for a few kilometres inland.	Cooling of warmer air by passage over colder sea.	Dispersed by a change in air mass. May be cleared over coast by the sun's heating.
Frontal fog	At all seasons	High ground.	Lowering of the cloud base along the line of the front.	Dispersed as the front moves and brings a change of air mass.
Smoke fog ('Smog')	Winter	Near industrial areas and large conurbations.	Conditions for formation are similar to those for radiation fog.	Dispersed by wind increase or by convection. Is often slow to clear in stable anticyclonic air.

Appendix V

SHORT GLOSSARY OF METEOROLOGICAL TERMS

Absolute Humidity. The mass of water vapour present in a unit-volume of air. It is usually expressed in grammes per cubic metre of air.

Adiabatic Change. A term employed in thermodynamics for changes which take place in the pressure and temperature of a gas when no heat is added or extracted from the system.

Advection. The transfer of heat by the horizontal movement of air.

Air Mass. A mass of almost homogeneous air, in which the horizontal changes of temperature and humidity are small over wide areas.

Albedo. The proportion of radiation falling upon a non-luminous body which is reflected from that body. The earth's albedo is approximately 0·4. This means that four-tenths of the sun's radiation is reflected back to space.

Anabatic. The term used to describe air which flows upward as a result of convection.

Anemometer. An instrument for measuring the speed of the wind.

Anomaly. The difference between the value of a meteorological element and its normal value. It is used chiefly in connexion with temperature, to indicate the departure from the mean temperature for a given latitude.

Anticyclone. A region in which the atmospheric pressure is high relative to its surroundings.

Backing. A wind is said to back when its direction changes in an anticlockwise manner. For example, a wind blowing originally from the south will back towards the south-east.

Bar. The unit of atmospheric pressure, equal to the pressure of 1 000 000 dynes per square centimetre. (A dyne is a C.G.S. (Centimetre-Gram System) unit of force; it represents the force which, when applied to a mass of one gramme during one second, will produce a velocity of one centimetre per second.) A bar is equal to a pressure of 76 cm of mercury at 0° C at latitude 45°. 1 bar = 10^5 newtons per square metre.

Barometer. An instrument for measuring atmospheric pressure.

Beaufort Scale. A code of letters and numbers, indicating the state of the weather and the speed of the wind respectively. It was originally introduced by one Admiral Beaufort for use at sea.

Buys–Ballot's Law. If, in the Northern Hemisphere, an observer stands with his back to the wind, the region of low atmospheric pressure will be situated to his left. In the Southern Hemisphere low pressure will be on his right.

Clouds. Merely condensed water vapour in the atmosphere. They may be composed of liquid or ice particles, depending upon the height of the condensation level and the time of the year.

Col. A region of almost uniform atmospheric pressure, situated between two high- and two low-pressure zones.

Cold Front. A boundary line between an advancing cold air mass and a warm air mass. The pushing effect of the cold air forces the warm air aloft, so producing a belt of rising moist air which gives heavy cloud.

Conduction. The process by which heat is transferred through matter from places of high to places of low temperature, without movement of the matter itself. Heat is merely conveyed from molecule to molecule within the substance.

Convection. The process by which heat is conveyed from one place to another by the bodily transfer of the material containing that heat.

Cyclone. A region where the atmospheric pressure is lower than that of adjoining areas. More usually the term 'depression' is used to denote an area of low pressure, the term 'cyclone' being used to refer to tropical revolving storms of the Arabian Sea and the Bay of Bengal.

Dew Point. The temperature to which air must be cooled in order to reach saturation level.

Diurnal. This term, which simply means 'daily,' is usually employed when the meteorologist wishes to refer to daily changes in temperature; then he speaks of "diurnal variations in temperature."

Föhn. A warm, dry wind which descends on the leeward side of mountains. Air which is forced to rise over a ridge of mountains cools, and associated condensation and precipitation occur. When the air descends on the other side of the range, having lost its moisture, it is warmed at a greater rate than it was originally cooled. So it reaches the lower slopes as a warm, dry wind. (The air cools at the saturated adiabatic lapse rate on the windward side, but heats up at the dry adiabatic lapse rate on the leeward side.)

Gradient. The change in meteorological elements per unit-horizontal-distance. It is usually applied to pressure and temperature changes along the earth's surface.

Hygrometer. An instrument for measuring the humidity of the air.

Insolation. The solar radiation received by the earth.

Instability. Air which, when given an initial impetus upward, continues to move upward with increasing vigour, is said to be unstable.

Intertropical Front. The boundary between two air masses produced within the trade-wind systems.

Inversion. That condition of the atmosphere when temperature increases, rather than decreases, with height.

Isobar. A line on a chart which joins all places having the same barometric pressure (usually pressure at mean sea-level).

Isohyet. A line on a chart which joins all places having the same amount of rainfall.

Isotherm. A line on a chart which joins all places having the same temperature (usually temperature at mean sea-level).

Katabatic. The term applied to winds which flow down a slope that is cooled by radiation.

Lapse Rate. The rate at which temperature decreases with height.

Millibar. A thousandth part of a bar; or 10^2 newtons per square metre.

Occlusion. The line of weather associated with a depression where the cold-front conditions have coalesced with the warm-front conditions.

Orographic Rain. The rainfall associated with cloud formed by uplift of moist air over a high-relief feature.

Polar Front. The boundary between air masses originating in high latitudes and those originating in low latitudes. It is along this boundary that depressions develop.

Radiation. The movement of heat from one region to another by means of electro-magnetic waves. For example, heat from the sun is transmitted to the earth's surface by means of short-wave transmission. Heat is re-radiated back from the earth by means of long-wave radiation.

Radio-sonde. A free balloon which carries aloft special meteorological instruments which transmit messages by radio-telegraphy direct to the observer. Upper-air pressures and temperatures are transmitted at regular intervals.

Relative Humidity. The actual weight of the water vapour present in a given volume of air at a given temperature, expressed as a percentage of the maximum possible amount of water vapour which could be held in the same volume of air at the same temperature.

Ridge. An extension of a high-pressure region.

Secondary Depression. A small area of low pressure, accompanying a larger primary low-pressure area.

Stability. The term applied to the condition of the atmosphere when air which is given an initial impetus upward tends to remain in its original position—in other words, the conditions when convection currents do not readily form within the air mass.

Stratosphere. The region of the atmosphere where the temperature does not decrease appreciably with increase in height. It is also that zone in which no convection occurs. The average height at which the stratosphere commences is ten kilometres.

Synoptic. A term derived from the noun 'synopsis,' which is a brief statement presenting a general view of something. It is applied in meteorology in the statement of probable weather conditions. A 'synoptic chart' shows the weather conditions over a wide area for a given time.

Tephigram. A graphical means of assessing the stability of the atmosphere at different heights.

Tropopause. The boundary layer between the zone of the atmosphere in which weather occurs (the troposphere) and the stratosphere.

Troposphere. The lower layer of the atmosphere, where temperature generally decreases with increasing height. In the temperate latitudes it is about 11 km thick.

Trough. An extension of a low-pressure region. It is the opposite of a ridge of high pressure.

Turbulence. The irregular flow of air which results from the movement of the air over obstacles at low levels. It is also the term used to describe the bumpiness associated with severe vertical currents of air within convective-type cloud.

Veering. A wind is said to veer when its direction changes in a clockwise manner. For example, a wind blowing originally from the south will veer towards the south-west.

Warm Front. A boundary line between an advancing warm air mass and a cold air mass. The warm air rides up over the colder air; any moisture present is condensed to form warm frontal cloud.

DESCRIPTION OF CODE FIGURES FOR PRESENT WEATHER (ww)

(See Fig. 79 for the symbols)

00 Cloud development not observed during the past hour.
01 Cloud becoming less developed during the past hour.
02 State of the sky has been unchanged during the past hour.
03 Clouds generally developing during the past hour.
04 Visibility reduced by smoke (for example, forest fire, industrial smoke).
05 Haze.
06 Widespread dust in the air.
07 Dust or sand raised by the wind.
08 Well-developed dust-devils during the past hour.
09 Dust or sand-storm during the past hour.
10 Mist.
11 Shallow fog in patches.
12 Shallow continuous fog.
13 Lightning.
14 Precipitation in sight, but not reaching the ground.
15 Distant precipitation reaching the ground.
16 Precipitation reaching ground near to station.
17 Thunder heard, but no precipitation at the station.
18 Squalls during the past hour.
19 Funnel clouds seen during the past hour.
20 Drizzle during the past hour.
21 Rain during the past hour.
22 Snow during the past hour.
23 Rain and snow during the past hour.
24 Freezing drizzle or rain during the past hour.
25 Showers of rain during the past hour.
26 Showers of snow, or rain and snow, during the past hour.
27 Showers of hail, or hail and rain, during the past hour.
28 Fog during the past hour.
29 Thunderstorm during the past hour.
30 Slight or moderate dust or sand-storm has decreased during the past hour.
31 Slight or moderate dust or sand-storm, no change during the past hour.
32 Slight or moderate dust or sand-storm has increased during the past hour.
33 Severe dust or sand-storm has decreased during the past hour.
34 Severe dust or sand-storm, no change during the past hour.
35 Severe dust or sand-storm has increased during the past hour.
36 Slight or moderate drifting snow below eye-level.
37 Heavy drifting snow below eye-level.
38 Slight or moderate drifting snow above eye-level.
39 Heavy drifting snow above eye-level.
40 Distant fog during the past hour.
41 Fog in patches.
42 Fog, sky discernible, has become thinner during the past hour.
43 Fog, sky obscured, has become thinner during the past hour.
44 Fog, sky discernible, no change during the past hour.
45 Fog, sky obscured, no change during the past hour.

46 Fog, sky discernible, has become thicker during the past hour.
47 Fog, sky obscured, has become thicker during the past hour.
48 Fog, depositing rime. Sky discernible.
49 Fog, depositing rime. Sky obscured.
50 Intermittent slight drizzle.
51 Continuous slight drizzle.
52 Intermittent moderate drizzle.
53 Continuous moderate drizzle.
54 Intermittent thick drizzle.
55 Continuous thick drizzle.
56 Slight freezing drizzle.
57 Moderate or thick freezing drizzle.
58 Slight drizzle and rain.
59 Moderate or heavy drizzle and rain.
60 Intermittent slight rain.
61 Continuous slight rain.
62 Intermittent moderate rain.
63 Continuous moderate rain.
64 Intermittent heavy rain.
65 Continuous heavy rain.
66 Slight freezing rain.
67 Moderate or heavy freezing rain.
68 Slight rain or drizzle and snow.
69 Moderate or heavy rain or drizzle and snow.
70 Intermittent slight snow.
71 Continuous slight snow.
72 Intermittent moderate snow.
73 Continuous moderate snow.
74 Intermittent heavy snow.
75 Continuous heavy snow.
76 Ice needles.
77 Granular snow.
78 Isolated snow crystals.
79 Ice pellets.
80 Slight showers of rain.
81 Moderate or heavy showers of rain.
82 Violent showers of rain.
83 Slight showers of rain and snow.
84 Moderate or heavy showers of rain and snow.
85 Slight showers of snow.
86 Moderate or heavy showers of snow.
87 Slight showers of soft or small hail.
88 Moderate or heavy showers of soft or small hail.
89 Slight showers of hail.
90 Moderate or heavy showers of hail.
91 Slight rain. Thunderstorm during the past hour.
92 Moderate or heavy rain. Thunderstorm during the past hour.
93 Slight snow, or rain and snow, or hail. Thunderstorm during the past hour.
94 Moderate or heavy snow, or rain and snow, or hail. Thunderstorm during the past hour.
95 Slight or moderate thunderstorm with rain and/or snow.
96 Slight or moderate thunderstorm with hail.
97 Heavy thunderstorm with rain and/or snow.
98 Thunderstorm with dust or sand-storm.
99 Heavy thunderstorm with hail.

WEATHER SATELLITES LAUNCHED UP TO JULY 1975

1. AMERICAN SATELLITES

SATELLITE	LAUNCH DATE	ORBITAL PERIOD (minutes)	INCLINATION TO EQUATOR (°)	PERIGEE (kilometres)
TIROS 1	1 April 1960	98·3	48·4	690
TIROS 2	23 November 1960	99·2	48·5	625
TIROS 3	12 July 1961	100·4	47·8	740
TIROS 4	8 February 1962	100·4	48·3	710
TIROS 5	19 June 1962	100·5	58·1	590
TIROS 6	18 September 1962	98·7	58·3	683
TIROS 7	19 June 1963	97·4	58·2	621
TIROS 8	21 December 1963	99·4	58·5	700
TIROS 9	22 January 1965	119·2	96·4	705
TIROS 10	2 July 1965	100·7	98·7	710
ESSA 1	3 February 1966	100·2	81·1	683
ESSA 2	28 February 1966	113·6	101·0	1430
ESSA 3	2 October 1966	114·6	101·1	1385
ESSA 4	26 January 1967	113·5	102·0	1330
ESSA 5	20 April 1967	113·6	102·0	1360
ESSA 6	10 November 1967	114·8	102·1	1507
ESSA 7	16 August 1968	115·3	101·7	1469
ESSA 8	15 December 1968	114·7	101·9	1410
ESSA 9	26 February 1969	115·3	101·8	1427
NIMBUS 1	28 August 1964	98·4	98·7	430
NIMBUS 2	15 May 1966	108·1	100·3	1142
NIMBUS 3	14 April 1969	107·4	99·9	1075
NIMBUS 4	8 April 1970	107·3	99·9	1095
NIMBUS 5	11 December 1972	107·2	99·9	1089
NIMBUS 6	12 June 1975	107·3	99·9	1092
ATS 1	6 December 1966	1465·9	0·2	36 000
ATS 2	6 April 1967	218·9	28·4	178
ATS 3	5 November 1967	1436·4	0·4	38 400
ATS 4	10 August 1968	93·9	29·0	219
ATS 5	12 August 1969	1463·8	2·6	35 760
ITOS 1	23 January 1970	115·1	102·0	1436
ITOS 2	11 December 1970	115·0	102·0	1440
ITOS D (NOAA 2)	15 October 1972	114·9	101·7	1451
ITOS F (NOAA 3)	6 November 1973	116·1	102·1	1500
SMS–A*	17 May 1974	576·4	24·47	182
ATS 6	30 May 1974	1436·1	1·6	163
NOAA 4 (ITOS)	15 November 1974	115·0	101·75	1447
SMS–B	6 February 1975	1456·4	1·1	35 680

Satellite	Launch Date	Orbital Period (minutes)	Inclination to equator (°)	Perigee (kilometres)
GOES–A	16 October 1975	1435·9	1·00	35 196
NOAA 5 (ITOS)	29 July 1976	116·34	102·1	1509
AMS+	11 September 1976	101·6	98·7	818

* SMS – Synchronous Meteorological Satellite
+ AMS – Advanced Meteorological Satellite (launched for USAF)

2. Russian Satellites

Satellite	Launch Date	Orbital Period (minutes)	Inclination to equator (°)	Perigee (kilometres)
COSMOS 122	25 June 1966	97·1	65·0	625
COSMOS 144	28 February 1967	96·9	81·2	625
COSMOS 156	27 April 1967	97·0	81·2	630
COSMOS 184	25 October 1967	97·1	81·2	635
COSMOS 206	14 March 1968	97·0	81·0	630
COSMOS 226	12 June 1968	96·9	81·2	600
METEOR 1	26 March 1969	97·9	81·2	645
METEOR 2	7 October 1969	97·7	81·2	630
METEOR 3	17 March 1970	96·4	81·2	555
METEOR 4	28 April 1970	98·1	81·2	640
METEOR 5	23 June 1970	102·0	81·2	860
METEOR 6	15 October 1970	97·5	81·2	635
COSMOS 389	18 December 1970	98·1	81·2	642
METEOR 7	20 January 1971	97·6	81·2	629
COSMOS 405	7 April 1971	98·3	81·2	673
METEOR 8	17 April 1971	97·2	81·2	610
METEOR 9	16 July 1971	97·3	81·2	614
METEOR 10	29 December 1971	102·7	81·3	845
METEOR 11	30 March 1972	102·6	81·2	868
METEOR 12	30 June 1972	102·9	81·2	889
METEOR 13	26 October 1972	102·6	81·3	867
METEOR 14	20 March 1973	102·6	81·3	873
METEOR 15	29 May 1973	102·5	81·2	853
METEOR 16	5 March 1974	102·23	81·23	832
METEOR 17	24 April 1974	102·58	81·23	865
METEOR 18	9 July 1974	102·57	81·23	865
METEOR 19	28 October 1974	102·48	81·18	843
METEOR 20	17 December 1974	102·38	81·24	842
METEOR 21	1 April 1975	102·6	81·2	867
METEOR 2–01	11 July 1975	102·4	81·3	855
METEOR 22	18 September 1975	102·4	81·3	838
METEOR 23	25 December 1975	102·4	81·3	842
METEOR 24	7 April 1976	102·3	81·3	827
METEOR 25	15 May 1976	102·4	81·2	846
METEOR 26	15 October 1976	102·5	81·3	836

PART TWO

Climatology

Chapter 14

GENERAL ATMOSPHERIC CIRCULATION AND ITS RELATION TO WORLD CLIMATES

In Part One the individual elements out of which climates are composed have been examined. The climate of any region is a survey of the average weather of that area, and, therefore, the changing combinations of these elements will produce a wide variety of climatic types. The simplest classification of climates is that produced by the Greeks, who divided the earth into three zones: the summerless zone in high latitudes, the winterless zone in low latitudes, and an intermediate, or temperate, zone in mid-latitudes. This broad classification takes into account the general distribution of world temperatures, but does not consider world rainfall distribution. The geographer and climatologist must take into consideration all the elements of weather, and a more detailed and refined classification of climates, based upon precipitation as well as upon temperature characteristics, must be developed.

Were the surface of the earth composed of a uniform material, and were it of the same altitude and not affected by the variable heating of the sun, it is clear that the atmosphere would remain stagnant and of uniform depth. The evidence shows, however, that, under the influence of differential heating from the sun, and as a result of the different materials which comprise the earth's surface, the atmosphere moves constantly in a complicated way. Nevertheless, these atmospheric movements do show some rhythmic cycles, and they may be related directly to the seasonal changes of the sun over the earth's surface. Therefore, in discussing the actual distribution of world climates, it is perhaps convenient to assume initially that the earth's surface is composed of a uniform material, and to endeavour to assess what circulatory movements of the atmosphere would occur in such a hypothetical circumstance. This idealized circulation does form a useful background against which the observed facts may be considered, and it simplifies the discussion of the part played by the contrasting land and sea surfaces in deciding the character of climates.

If the earth were composed entirely of a homogeneous surface material the average temperature would vary only with latitude. The lowest temperatures would be found at the Poles, and there would be a gradual increase in temperature with approach towards the equator. The warm air would rise over the equatorial regions, and the colder polar air would sink. The general atmospheric circulation would be as shown in Fig. 89. At the surface there would be a gradual drift of air from high latitudes to the lower latitudes. At higher altitudes there would be a compensating air flow from low towards high latitudes. This idealized flow of air would only

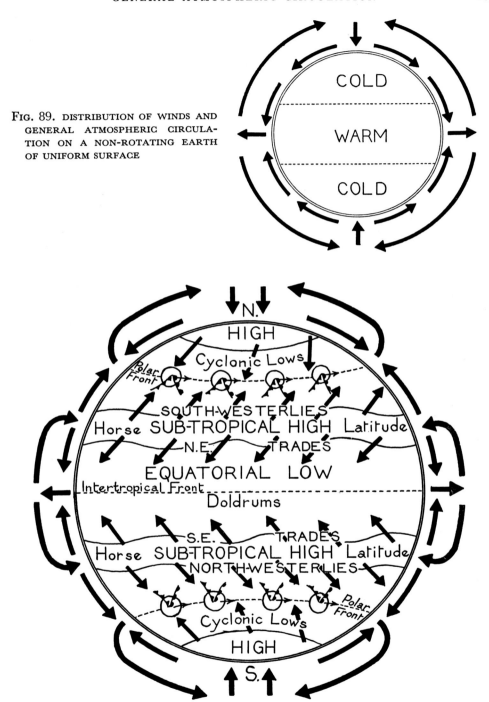

FIG. 89. DISTRIBUTION OF WINDS AND GENERAL ATMOSPHERIC CIRCULATION ON A NON-ROTATING EARTH OF UNIFORM SURFACE

FIG. 90. DISTRIBUTION OF PRESSURES AND WINDS ON A ROTATING EARTH OF UNIFORM SURFACE

occur if the earth did not rotate upon its axis. The effect of the earth's rotation would be to complicate this general air movement, and the circulation would probably present the complex arrangement shown in Fig. 90. It is clear that there is an interaction between air flow and pressure. Fig. 90 is a very diagrammatic representation of the zonal sea-level pressures which might exist on a homogeneous earth composed of either all land or all sea.

The equatorial region would be one of low pressure and ascending air. The general surface air flow at low latitudes would therefore be towards the equator from both hemispheres. The cold polar areas would be regions of high pressure, where the air would be descending and flowing out towards the lower latitudes. At sub-tropical latitudes there would be another high-pressure belt. This subsiding air would flow outward to both the north and south. On one side the air flow would add to the air flow towards the equator; on the other side air would move poleward. These latter air flows, coming from tropical regions, would move up against the cold polar air coming from the higher latitudes. The boundary between these two air masses has already been described as the 'polar front,' and is that zone along which the frontal depressions develop.

This general circulation is confined to the troposphere, and the location of these pressure belts does vary somewhat from season to season as the sun's apparent position changes with regard to the equator. In the northern summer the 'thermal equator'—that is, the belt of highest temperature—would be located north of the geographical equator, and the pressure belts also would correspondingly shift northward. In the southern summer the reverse movements of the pressure belts would occur.

The climatic belts in this idealized system of pressure and wind distribution would be simple. In the areas of ascending air there would be precipitation—that is, along the equator and at the temperate frontal belt. Over the Poles and the sub-tropical high-pressure belts there would be dry, arid conditions. The descriptions of these main climatic belts can be listed as follows:

1. Polar climate (subsiding air; mainly fair weather).
2. Temperate climate (disturbed conditions; frontal weather and variable conditions).
3. Sub-tropical climate (subsiding air; clear skies and arid conditions).
4. Equatorial climate (two main rain seasons as sun crosses the equator; no real dry season).

There would also, of course, be transition climates as one belt gradually merged into the next.

The above idealized layout of climatic zones will serve as a background against which the actual conditions can be assessed. There are marked divergences from this theoretical pattern, the predominating factor governing these differences being the dissimilar thermal properties of land and sea. The hypothetical layout of pressures and winds can be recognized to some degree in Figs. 28 and 29—especially in the Southern Hemisphere, where there is an almost homogeneous water surface. To understand the main differences we must next turn to the consideration of a hypothetical triangular land mass, situated in the sea and symmetrically placed about the equator. Owing to the unequal rates of heating and cooling of the two surface materials, disturbances will be produced in the pressure patterns. Fig. 91 indicates the distribution of pressures and winds in January and July over a non-homogeneous earth's surface.

In January the sun is overhead somewhere south of the equator, and consequently the thermal equator will rest in southern latitudes. In the Northern Hemisphere the land mass will cool more rapidly than the sea around it, and the central area will receive little moderating influence from the oceans. The temperature of this northern continental mass will become low. The result will be the formation of a high-pressure region. This anticyclonic pressure region will amalgamate with the sub-tropical high- and the polar high-pressure zones (see Fig. 91 (a)). The cyclonic low-pressure belt of the northern mid-latitudes will be broken by the high pressure over the continent.

In the Southern Hemisphere the land mass will tend to heat up more quickly than the sea, and a thermal low-pressure area will tend to form over the land surface. The effect will be to break the continuity of the sub-tropical high-pressure belt of the Southern Hemisphere. The distribution of wind belts is not widely different from that of the theoretical situation, in which there are three distinct wind belts— namely, the south-east trades, the north-westerlies, and the polar south-easterlies (see Fig. 90).

In July the reverse effects take shape. The sun is now overhead somewhere north of the equator, and the interior of the northern continental land mass becomes very hot. The thermal low produced is very intense, and there are no moderating effects from the oceans, which are remote from the centre of the land surface. The cyclonic low-pressure belt associated with the polar front joins up with the thermal low-pressure zone of the continent; further, the equatorial low-pressure region is absorbed into the continental low. (See Fig. 91 (b).) The sub-tropical high-pressure belt of the Northern Hemisphere is broken; it can be distinguished over the oceans, but its place is taken by the continental low-pressure belt over the northern land mass. In the Southern Hemisphere the pressure and wind belts do not differ substantially from those associated with a homogeneous surface.

A study of Figs. 28 and 29 (pp. 56–59) will show that the pressure and wind belts which cover the earth's surface do reflect the conditions outlined in the previous paragraphs. The large land masses of Asia and North America can be regarded as equivalent to the base of the triangular mass in the hypothetical case, and South America and South Africa as equivalent to the apex.

It is clear, then, that the world pressure and wind distributions are related closely to the temperature distributions, and in order to understand the layout of the former some examination must be made of the latter. The broad features of surface air-temperature distribution may be considered in relation to latitude: the temperatures decrease gradually from equatorial to polar regions, but they are greatly modified by the distribution of land and sea. At the same time the whole is controlled by the apparent movements of the sun over the earth's surface; there are complicated variations, according to the season of the year.

Figs. 23 and 24 show the general surface temperature distribution for January and July. In both diagrams all temperatures have been reduced to sea-level, so that the effects of altitude are eliminated. Complications created by variations in relief

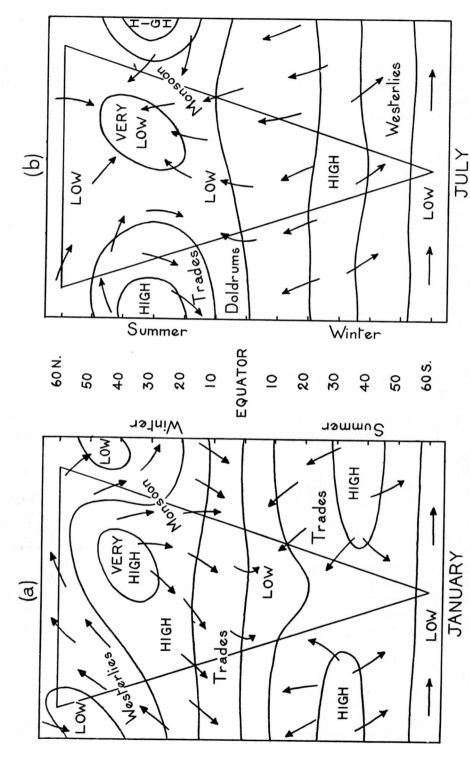

Fig. 91. LAYOUT OF PRESSURES AND WINDS ON A NON-HOMOGENEOUS EARTH'S SURFACE: (a) JANUARY; (b) JULY

would render maps so confusing that effects of latitude and land–sea relationships would be difficult to appreciate. In general the isotherms run from east to west. Since all places along the same latitude receive identical amounts of solar energy, this is easily understood. Consequently it is true to assume that *latitude is the greatest single factor governing world temperature distribution.*

The main features of world temperature distribution can be summarized as follows:

1. Highest average annual temperatures are in low latitudes.
2. Lowest average annual temperatures are in high latitudes.
3. Isotherms are straighter and more widely spaced in the Southern Hemisphere, where there is a more nearly homogeneous surface.
4. Greatest deviations from the east/west trend occur in the Northern Hemisphere, where isotherms pass from ocean to land surfaces.
5. Comparison of January and July isotherms shows the marked latitudinal shift of temperatures. (This is due to the latitudinal migration of the sun's rays, and hence to the variation in insolation received.)
6. Migrations of isotherms are greater over the continents than over the oceans.
7. Highest temperatures are over land areas.
8. Lowest temperatures in January are in the central regions of North America and Asia.
9. In the Northern Hemisphere the January isotherms bend equatorward over the colder continents and poleward over the warmer oceans. (In July the opposite situation prevails.)
10. The largest annual temperature ranges occur over the northern continents.
11. Temperature ranges are small near the equator and over large water masses.
12. In January positive temperature anomalies exist over the northern oceans, and negative temperature anomalies are found over the land masses of the Northern Hemisphere.
13. In July the oceans of the Northern Hemisphere have negative temperature anomalies, and the land masses have positive temperature anomalies.

For climatic studies it is often necessary to examine the temperature means for each month of the year. These figures indicate certain characteristics:

1. The difference between the temperature of the hottest month and that of the coldest month.
2. The phase—that is, the time—of the year with the highest temperature and that with the lowest.
3. The degree of symmetry of the annual temperature curve.

There are certain recognized temperatures which control the various aspects of plant and human geography:

1. 0° C is the freezing-point of water.
2. 4·4° C is the temperature at which plants commence to germinate.
3. 10° C is the lower limit of the comfort zone for human beings.

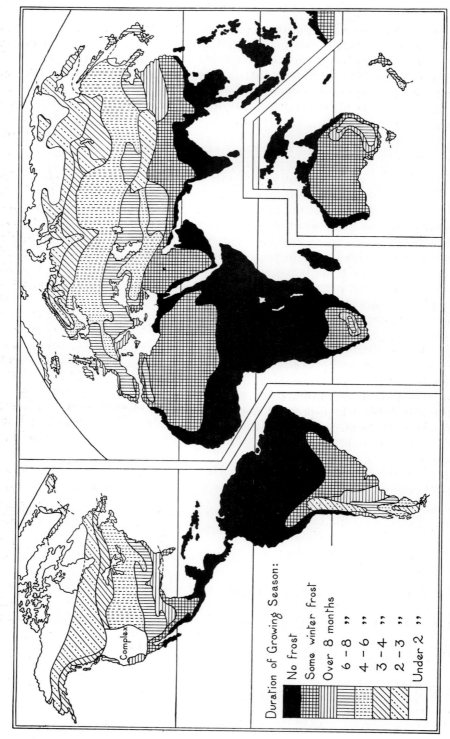

Duration of Growing Season:

No frost
Some winter frost
Over 8 months
6 – 8 ,, ,,
4 – 6 ,, ,,
3 – 4 ,, ,,
2 – 3 ,, ,,
Under 2 ,, ,,

Complex

FIG. 92. DURATION OF FROST-FREE PERIODS (EFFECT OF HIGHLANDS IS NOT CONSIDERED IN TROPICAL AREAS)

The period during which the temperature remains above 0° C is known as the 'frost-free period,' or the 'growing season.' Fig. 92 shows the duration of frost-free periods for the land surfaces of the earth.

Figs. 28 and 29 show the general pressure distribution for January and July. The isobars have been reduced to sea-level, and thus the effects of altitude are eliminated. The essential characteristics of pressure distribution over the earth's surface are as follows:

1. Pressure belts migrate north or south as the position of the sun moves during the year. (The latitudinal pressure movements are greater over the land masses than over the oceans.)

2. The sub-tropical high-pressure belts are divided into sections by the warm continents during the summer.

3. The sub-tropical high-pressure belts in winter join up over the northern land mass with the polar high-pressure zone, so dividing the cyclonic low-pressure belt.

4. The sub-tropical high-pressure zones remain over the oceans.

5. The relationship of high temperatures to low pressures and low temperatures to high pressures is to be seen over the continental masses during summer and winter respectively.

6. The zonal distribution of pressures (as illustrated in the hypothetical case) is more or less maintained in the Southern Hemisphere.

The atmospheric horizontal circulation is indicated in Figs. 28 and 29. The basic fact of air moving from high- to low-pressure regions is still apparent, and the following wind systems can be recognized:

1. The north-east and south-east trade winds blow into the equatorial low-pressure area. (The north-east trades are reversed over southern Asia during the northern

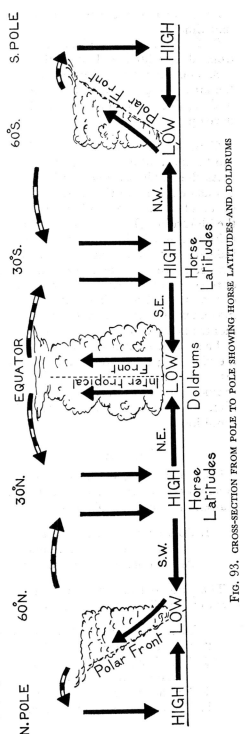

FIG. 93. CROSS-SECTION FROM POLE TO POLE SHOWING HORSE LATITUDES AND DOLDRUMS

summer, owing to the seasonal low pressure which is established in central Asia at that time.)

2. The south-west and north-west winds blow on the poleward side of the sub-tropical high-pressure belts in the Northern and Southern Hemispheres respectively.

3. There is a flow of air equatorward from the polar regions. These winds meet the air flowing poleward from the sub-tropical high belts along the polar front. It is along this polar front (45° to 60° N. or S.) that the cyclonic low-pressure systems develop.

Certain areas of the earth's surface are associated with vertical air movement; the most important are the 'doldrums' and the 'horse latitudes.'

As the north-east and south-east trades converge towards the equator there is a tendency for air to rise along the intertropical front. The trades leave a condition of calm between them at low altitudes. This region of low pressure gradient is called the 'doldrums' (Fig. 93). It is not clearly marked all round the equator, nor does it exist all through the year, and the general convectional, showery weather conditions indicate that the upward movement of air may be intermittent rather than steady. The belts are variable in position and move north or south with the annual changes of the sun's declination. The movement is not so extensive as that of the sun, being of the order of 5° either side of the equator. There is also a delay in the time of movement of the doldrum belt with that of the sun, the belt lagging about two months behind the passage of the sun.

There is also a zone of light, variable winds and calms, occupying a position between the diverging trade winds and stormy westerlies, along the crest of the sub-tropical high-pressure belts. In this zone the air is subsiding and, on account of the compression due to its subsiding, relatively dry. This region, called the 'horse latitudes' (Fig. 93), is characterized by clear skies, abundant sunshine, low rainfall, and calm conditions.

The World Distribution of Precipitation

Fig. 94 shows the mean annual amount of precipitation. Practically all the precipitation of the earth is the result of the adiabatic cooling of ascending air masses. The major regions of ascent are:

1. Zones of converging horizontal air flow (equatorial and cyclonic low-pressure areas giving convectional and frontal rains).
2. Areas along the windward sides of mountain ranges (orographic rainfall).

The principal factors which influence the distribution of precipitation over the earth can be listed as follows:

1. The location of the belts of ascending air.
2. The character of the moisture-bearing winds.
3. The distance from the ocean—that is, the distance from the main source of water in the atmosphere.
4. The height of the land over which the moisture-laden winds blow.
5. The temperature of the air; this governs the moisture content.

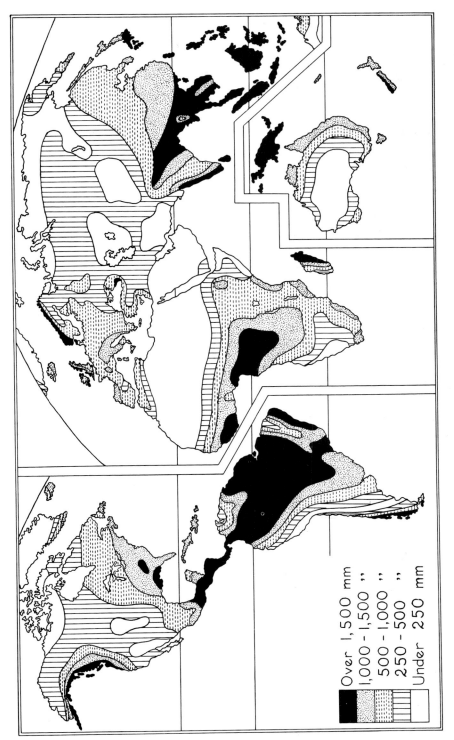

Over 1,500 mm
1,000 - 1,500 ,,
500 - 1,000 ,,
250 - 500 ,,
Under 250 mm

FIG. 94. THE DISTRIBUTION OF ANNUAL WORLD RAINFALL

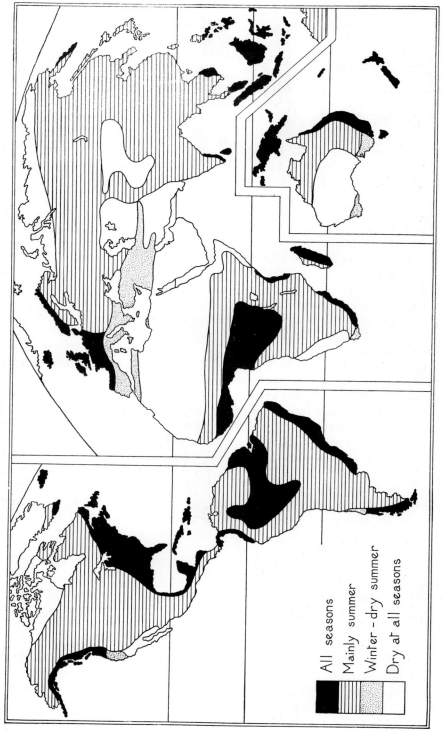

All seasons

Mainly summer

Winter - dry summer

Dry at all seasons

FIG. 95. SEASONAL DISTRIBUTION OF RAINFALL

The Principal Rainfall Regimes. The principal rainfall regimes are outlined below, but their main characteristics will be considered more fully under the respective climates. Fig. 95 shows the seasonal distribution of rainfall-types.

Equatorial Rainfall. This is characterized by abundant precipitation and the absence of a dry season. The rainfall is chiefly convectional, but may be frontal where the convergence of the air masses along the intertropical front occurs.

Savanna Rainfall. This is located in latitudes 5° to 20° north or south of the equator. The rainfall 'follows the sun,' hence the convectional rain is concentrated into those months during the high-sun season. Drought occurs during the low-sun period.

Tropical-desert Rainfall. This is characterized by low rainfall at all seasons. The drought is associated with the subsiding air masses of the sub-tropical high-pressure belts.

Mediterranean Rainfall. The precipitation is confined mainly to the winter season, when the areas (western sides of land masses 30° to 40° of latitude) come under the influence of the cyclonic low-pressure belts. The dry summers are associated with the subsiding air of the sub-tropical high-pressure belts.

West European Rainfall. The western sides of the land masses (poleward from about 40° of latitude to 60°) are influenced by the stormy westerlies and the cyclonic low-pressure areas. The precipitation is abundant, the amount depending largely upon the height of the coast. There is no dry season, although there tends to be more rain in winter than in summer.

Continental Rainfall. The distance from the oceans is the chief factor governing precipitation. Normally the main rainfall is in summer, when the high seasonal temperature results in a maximum absolute humidity, and when there is a flow of air into the continental low-pressure area.

East-coast Rainfall. In low latitudes the east-coast belts tend to have a high rainfall. This precipitation results from the on-shore trade winds. In mid-latitudes the precipitation is the result of monsoon wind systems, with the inflowing mass of warm, moist air in summer, and cyclonic low-pressure conditions in winter.

Polar Rainfall. Low temperatures and the consequent low absolute humidities give rise to small precipitation amounts. Anticyclonic pressure controls and also militates against the conditions favouring precipitation. The maximum precipitation probably occurs during the season of higher temperatures, when there is more moisture in the air, and when the cyclonic influence can reach farther poleward.

OCEAN CURRENTS AND THEIR EFFECTS UPON WORLD CLIMATES

In the climatological section of this book consideration must be given to the movement of the waters of the oceans, because ocean currents are among the controllers of climate. A knowledge of their movements is important in understanding some world climates. It is important to add that the surface drift of ocean waters is climatically induced; so, while to a great extent the atmosphere controls the oceanic circulation, the latter in turn exerts some considerable influence upon world climates. It is sufficient here to consider the water movements as they exist, and to assess their total effects upon the world climates. The origin of water movements being somewhat outside the scope of this book, it is necessary merely to state that the primary causes of ocean circulation are as follows:

1. Owing to the frictional effects of the winds upon the ocean surface, the thin layer of top water is driven slowly in the general direction of the air movement.

2. Contrasting densities of sea-water, due to different temperatures and salinities, are responsible for slow movements or currents within a large water mass.

Fig. 96 illustrates the main ocean currents of the world. Poleward-flowing waters are inclined to be warm relative to the waters on either side, and equatorward-flowing waters are usually cooler than the sea on either side. Thus, ocean currents may be broadly classified into

1. Warm-water currents (poleward-flowing water).
2. Cold-water currents (equatorward-flowing water).
3. Return, or compensating, currents.

In Fig. 96 the warm and cold currents are indicated. It will be seen that, in the lower latitudes, warm ocean currents tend to flow parallel with the eastern sides of the land masses, and cool ocean currents flow along the western sides. At 4° S., for example, the water temperature along the S. American west coast may be only 15·0° C, but at the same latitude along the New Guinea coast the surface temperature may be over 27·0° C. Similarly, at about 40° N. the surface water may be about 10° C along the west coast of North America, yet, at the same latitude on the east coast of Japan, the sea temperature may be 11·0° C higher. In the mid- and high latitudes the warm ocean currents tend to flow towards the western sides of the land-masses, and the cool ones appear to affect the eastern sides.

A current of water either warms or cools the prevailing winds that pass over it and, if these winds blow on shore, indirectly affects the climate of the lands which are washed by it. A good example of this is to be found in North-west Europe, where westerly winds throughout the year carry the warmth from the North Atlantic Drift far into the Continent. Similarly, along the coast of Peru a cooling effect is produced by the cold Peru current. Table 15 illustrates some temperature contrasts for stations on the east and west coasts in similar tropical and sub-tropical latitudes.

TABLE 15.—TEMPERATURE CONTRASTS FOR STATIONS ON EAST AND WEST COASTS IN SIMILAR TROPICAL AND SUB-TROPICAL LATITUDES

EAST COAST		DIFFERENCE E.–W.	WEST COAST	
STATION	WARM MONTH		STATION	WARM MONTH
	° C			° C
Jacksonville	27·8	7·8° C	Mogador	20
South Brazil	24·4	8·9° C	Port Nolloth	15·6
Shanghai	27·2	6·7° C	San Diego	20·6
Port Darwin	28·9	5·6° C	Lima	23·3

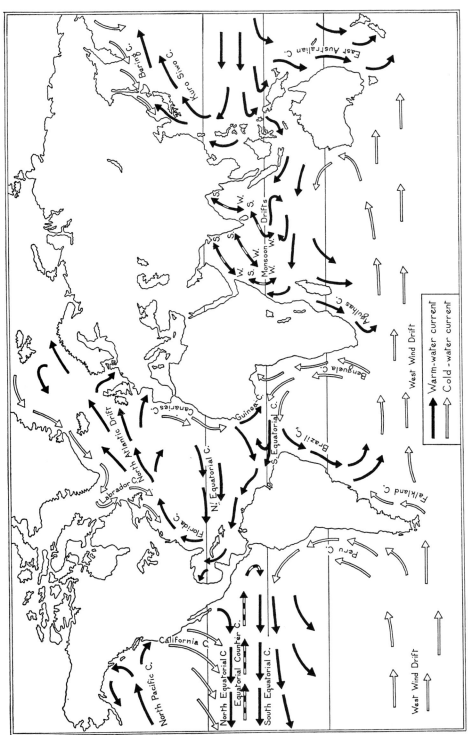

FIG. 96. THE OCEAN CURRENTS OF THE WORLD

In the North Indian Ocean the water currents vary with the seasons.
In the northern winter the winds generally blow from the north-east; the ocean currents thus flow approximately towards the south-west. (The arrows marked with W.)
In the northern summer the south-west monsoon winds blow on to the sub-continent of India; the ocean currents now flow in a north-easterly direction. (The arrows marked with S.)

The following summary indicates the main climatic influences of the ocean waters:

1. West coasts in tropical latitudes are bordered by cool waters; thus they have low average temperatures, with small annual and diurnal ranges. The general conditions are arid and foggy.

2. West coasts in mid- and high latitudes are affected by warm waters and have oceanic climates. The moderate rainfall is associated with the westerly winds. The winters are mild, and the summers are cool.

3. East coasts in low latitudes are bordered by warm currents, which give warm, rainy climates as a result of the moist, on-shore trade winds.

4. East coasts in mid-latitudes are bordered by warm waters, but have modified continental climates, with relatively cold winters and hot summers.

5. East coasts in high latitudes are bordered by cold-water currents. The shores are characterized by long, cold winters and cool summers.

Chapter 15

THE CLASSIFICATION OF WORLD CLIMATES

ANY portion of the earth's surface over which the climatic elements (and hence the climatic characteristics) are similar is described as a 'climatic region.' There is frequently a duplication of climates in corresponding locations on the continents which shows that there is order in the layout of climatic characteristics. In view of this the classification of climatic types may be confined to a relatively few categories.

A considerable number of classifications of world climates have been made, but the system devised by W. Köppen is the one which will be used and discussed here. This scheme of climatic classification is quantitative, and the divisions between groups and types are made on an analysis of temperature and rainfall statistics.

Köppen's classification is based primarily upon annual and monthly means of temperature and precipitation. The distinctive feature of the system is the use of symbols to designate the climatic types, so making unnecessary the employment of descriptive terms. Although the system has its shortcomings (areas for which few records are available are classified, and there are certain discrepancies in the categorization of climatic zones) its merits outweigh its deficiencies. It is a simple classification, and it has been widely accepted by climatologists. Fig. 97 shows a simplified distribution of the world's climates, based upon the Köppen classification.

Köppen recognizes five principal climatic groups and endeavours to correlate them with the five major vegetation types. The five climatic groups are given below, each prefaced by its symbol.

A Tropical rainy climates, with no cool season.
B Dry climates.
C Mid-latitude rainy climates, with mild winters.
D Mid-latitude rainy climates, with cold winters.
E Polar climates, having no warm season.

Each of these major groups is further subdivided, the subdivisions being based upon temperature and precipitation differences.

The following tables illustrate the symbols which differentiate the climatic elements within the major groups:

'A' CLIMATES (TROPICAL RAINY CLIMATES)

The coolest month is above 18° C.

Af Tropical rain-forest climate. The minimum monthly rainfall is at least 60 mm.
Aw Tropical savanna climate. There is a distinct dry season in the low-sun period.
 m Monsoon. There is a short dry season, but there is sufficient rainfall to support rain forest.
 w′ The rainfall is in the autumn.
 w″ Two rainfall maxima separated by two dry seasons can be distinguished.

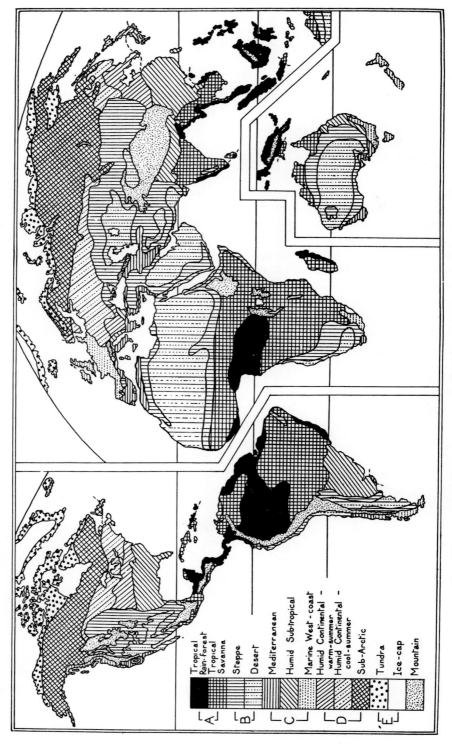

FIG. 97. A SIMPLIFIED VERSION OF KÖPPEN'S CLASSIFICATION OF WORLD CLIMATES

Legend:

A {
Tropical Rain-forest
Tropical Savanna
}

B {
Steppe
Desert
}

C {
Mediterranean
Humid Subtropical
Marine West-coast
}

D {
Humid Continental – warm-summer
Humid Continental – cool-summer
Sub-Arctic
}

E {
Tundra
Ice-cap
}

Mountain

s   There is a dry season during the high-sun period.
i   The temperature range is less than 5° C.
g   The hottest month comes before the solstice and the summer wet season.

'B' CLIMATES (DRY CLIMATES)

The evaporation exceeds the rainfall.

BW   Arid, or desert, climate.
BS   Semi-arid, or steppe, climate.
 h   The average annual temperature is above 18° C.
 k   The average annual temperature is below 18° C. (*N.B.* Subdivisions 'h' and
     'k,' thus differentiated, represent the distinction between hot and cold deserts.)
 s   There is a summer drought.
 w   There is a winter drought.
 n   There is frequent fog. (This is usually associated with cool-water currents flow-
     ing along desert coasts.)

'C' CLIMATES (WARM-TEMPERATURE RAINY CLIMATES)

The coldest month is below 18° C but above −3° C. The warmest month is
over 10° C.

Cf   No dry season is apparent.
Cw   There is a winter dry season.
Cs   There is a summer dry season.
 a   There is a hot summer; the warmest month is over 22° C.
 b   There is a cool summer; the warmest month is under 22° C.
 c   There is a short, cool summer.
 i   The range is less than 5° C.
 g   The hottest month comes before the solstice.
 x   The rainfall is greatest in late spring or early summer.
 n   There is frequent fog.

'D' CLIMATES (COLD FOREST CLIMATES)

The coldest month is below −3° C. The warmest month is above 10° C.

Df   A cold climate, humid winters.
Dw   A cold climate, with dry winters.
 d   The coldest month is below −38° C.
 s   There is a summer drought.
 a   There is a hot summer; the warmest month is over 22° C.
 b   There is a cool summer; the warmest month is below 22° C.
 c   There is a short, cool summer.

'E' CLIMATES (POLAR CLIMATES)

The warmest month is below 10° C.

ET   A tundra climate; the warmest month is below 10° C but above 0° C.
EF   There is perpetual frost.

The chapters which follow are devoted to a consideration of the world's major
climatic types. But in order to simplify the classification, it has been decided to
consider the climates under the following headings:

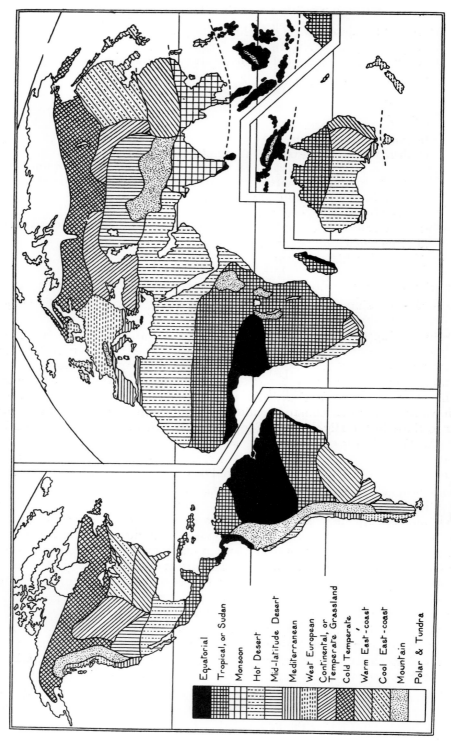

Fig. 98. A SIMPLIFIED DISTRIBUTION OF WORLD CLIMATES

Equatorial
Tropical, or Sudan
Monsoon
Hot Desert
Mid-latitude Desert
Mediterranean
West European
Continental, or Temperate Grassland
Cold Temperate
Warm East-coast
Cool East-coast
Mountain
Polar & Tundra

1. Tropical rain climates:

    (*a*) The equatorial climate.
    (*b*) The tropical, savanna, or Sudan climate.
    (*c*) The monsoon climate.
    (*d*) The warm east-coast climate.

2. Desert climates:

    (*a*) Low-latitude deserts.
    (*b*) Mid-latitude deserts.

3. Temperate climates:

    (*a*) The Mediterranean climate.
    (*b*) The West European climate.
    (*c*) The cold-temperate, or taïga, climate.
    (*d*) The cool east-coast, or Laurentian, climate.
    (*e*) The continental climate.

4. Polar and Mountain.

Fig. 98 shows a simplified layout of world climates, on the lines of the list given above.

Microclimatology. The fundamental problem in classifying climates is the search for factors which constitute distinctive climatic types. There are no fixed boundaries in the atmosphere, and the lines drawn on maps represent only transition zones. More important is the fact that climatic classification merely attempts to distinguish areas in which the prevailing conditions have some similarity. However, even in Britain we are aware that climatic conditions in Southern England are by no means similar to those in the Highlands of Scotland, although both regions are said to be within the West European climatic zone. Indeed, the conditions which exist in Central London are very different from those at Kew Gardens in the suburbs.

Slight contrasts of climate result from small differences of aspect, slope and form of the ground, colour of the soil and its texture, and the vegetation and plant cover. Every difference in degree of slope with respect to the sun's rays produces a different set of climatic conditions. Variable conditions are commonly effected by local topography and the relation of the regions to exposure and altitude. Human landscapes, adjacent buildings, local water surfaces, and industrial wastes all produce deviations in climatic conditions for small areas. Microclimatology, the study of these local contrasts from the prevailing conditions, is becoming more significant as man makes major changes in his environment. Occasional extremes, overstepping critical values, may substantially affect plant, animal, and even human life.

In conclusion, therefore, it is important to remember that, however efficient is a world climatic classification, it can never wholly explain local variations and extremes from prevailing conditions. Principles of microclimatology must in the end be used if a detailed assessment of any region's climate is to be of real significance.

Chapter 16

THE TROPICAL RAIN CLIMATES

THE tropics may be said to occupy half of the earth's surface, and over 20 per cent. of the land and 40 per cent. of the ocean surface have tropical rainy climates. They are considered as lying between the mean annual isotherm of 20° C, both north and south of the equator. Certain areas coming within these temperature bounds—*e.g.*, the hot deserts of North Africa and Arabia—must be excluded from this climatic group on account of their extreme aridity. This isotherm corresponds with the mean polar limit of the growth of palms; it is also the polar limit of the trade winds, averaging from 30° N. to 26° S.

In the tropical belts the temperatures are very uniform; consequently these climates must often be studied from rainfall figures. Insolation is relatively even throughout the year, and weather sequences are very regular. There are few unexpected weather changes in the tropics. Temperature ranges are usually very small, and the diurnal range always exceeds the annual range. Barometric pressures vary little; storms are rare, but those that do occur are violent and are confined to the end of the hot season. Winds are simple; they are, in fact, the trades, with a belt of equatorial calms situated in between. The only exception to these trade-wind belts is the summer monsoon wind in the Indian Ocean.

Rain is the most important single element in the climate of the tropics. It is relatively abundant, being well over 750 mm annually. Most of the precipitation is convectional in origin and is often accompanied by thunderstorms. Some cyclonic rain also results from frontal cloud which develops along the intertropical front— that is, along the boundary of convergence between the south-east and north-east trade winds. Unlike the temperature conditions, rainfall is much more variable in amount and seasonal distribution. Where the land is low-lying the trade winds tend to be dry, but where there is the slightest tendency for the ground to rise they cause remarkable rainfalls. In Dominica, for example, the windward side of the island has a fall of 2500 mm, whereas some small Pacific islands are almost arid.

Fig. 99 illustrates graphically the annual distribution of rainfall throughout the tropical latitudes. The graph shows the effect of the two passages of the sun across the tropical latitudes. Two principal climatic types within the humid tropics can be distinguished from each other on the basis of their seasonal distribution of rainfall:

1. The tropical rain-forest climate. Here there is abundant rainfall all the year.
2. The tropical savanna climate. Here there are distinct wet and dry seasons.

There is also the 'tropical monsoon climate.' This may be classified with the tropical savanna climate, although its dry season is somewhat shorter and less severe.

In this chapter the three main tropical climates will be considered in detail. The 'warm, east-coast, sub-tropical climate' will also be dealt with here; although its climatic conditions are somewhat different from those elaborated earlier in this chapter, it is appropriate to consider this climate in the tropical rain group. According to Köppen's classification, the warm east-coast climate rightfully belongs to the 'C' groups, and not to the 'A' groups, of climates. But in the description of the

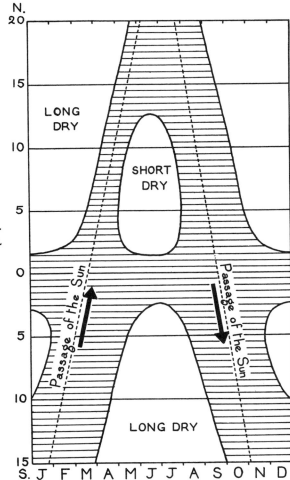

FIG. 99. THE ANNUAL DISTRIBUTION OF RAINFALL IN TROPICAL LATITUDES

climates illustrated in Fig. 98 for the simplicity of young students the warm east-coast climate is considered as a sub-tropical rather than a temperate climate.

THE EQUATORIAL, OR TROPICAL RAIN-FOREST, CLIMATE

This climate has the following characteristics:

1. Temperatures are uniformly high throughout the year. (The yearly average lies between 24° C and 27° C.)

2. Rainfall is heavy, and is distributed throughout the year. (The yearly average is of the order of 2000 to 2500 mm.)

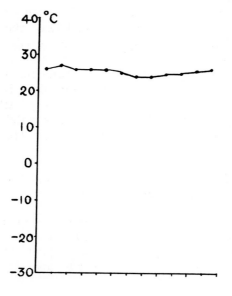

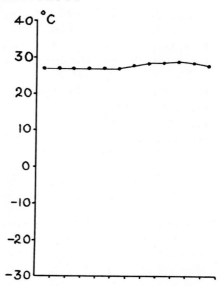

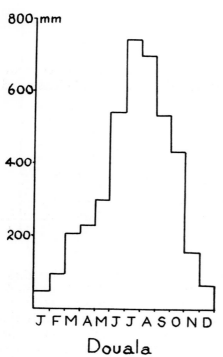

Douala

FIG. 100. AN EQUATORIAL
STATION

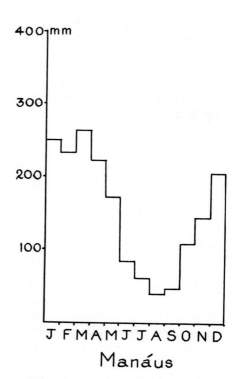

Manáus

FIG. 101. AN EQUATORIAL
STATION

The climate is located astride the equator, extending about 5° to 10° north or south. The region coincides with the equatorial low-pressure belt and follows the area of calms between the trade winds. Along the windward margins of the continents this climate may extend up to 20° from the equator.

The area is located in the belt of greatest insolation, and, since the sun's noon altitude is never far from vertical and the variation in length of day and night is small, the annual temperatures are always high. The annual range is usually less than 5°, although the diurnal range may be 10° to 25°. There is no distinct dry season, and the rainfall is both heavy and distributed throughout the year. The causes of the heavy precipitation are:

1. Convergence of tropical air masses at the doldrums, along the intertropical front.
2. Abundant local convection in the humid, unstable equatorial air.

The maximum rainfall occurs during the afternoon—hottest part of the day—when convectional effects are greatest. The seasonal distribution is not even throughout the year. There are usually two periods of maximum and two corresponding periods of minimum rainfall. This rainfall curve may follow the insolation curve closely.

Areas having an equatorial climate are shown in Fig. 98:

1. The *Selvas* of the Amazon basin in South America.
2. The Congo basin in Africa.
3. The East Indian islands.

The graphs shown in Figs. 100, 101, and 102 are representative of the three areas. The seasonal distribution of rainfall, as described in the text, is not fully illustrated by these graphs.

The Tropical, or Savanna, Climate

The major characteristics of this climate can be summarized as follows:

1. Rainfall is less than in the equatorial climate, being 1000 to 1500 mm.
2. There are distinct wet and dry seasons. The rainfall distribution coincides with the period of greatest insolation.
3. There are high temperatures throughout the year.

The tropical climate is located poleward of the equatorial climate and lies approximately 5° to 15° north or south of it. The exception to this is the east plateau of Africa, where the tropical climate is located on the equator. Altitude is the main reason for this distribution. It therefore lies between the humid, unstable equatorial air and the drier, stable air masses associated with the sub-tropical high-pressure belts.

The noon sun is never far from the vertical position, and the variation between day and night is small from one part of the year to another. Consequently the annual temperatures are fairly high, although the range is somewhat greater than that of the equatorial climate: the annual range is 3° C to 8° C. These larger ranges are the result of the high-sun months being hotter, and the low-sun months being cooler,

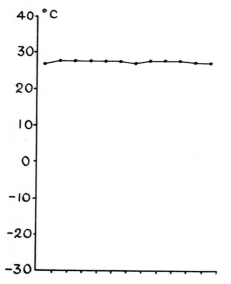

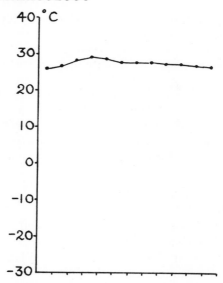

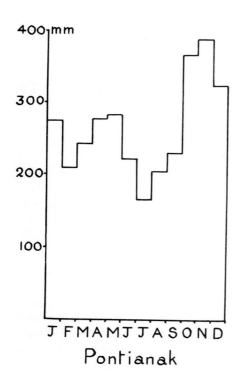

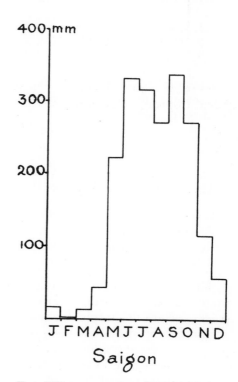

Pontianak

Saigon

FIG. 102. AN EQUATORIAL
STATION

FIG. 103. A TROPICAL (SAVANNA)
STATION

than similar seasons nearer the equator. Three distinct temperature seasons can be distinguished:

1. A cool, dry season which coincides with the low-sun period (27° to 32° C in the afternoon).
2. A hot, dry season immediately preceding the rains (38° C during the hottest part of the day).
3. A hot, wet season which coincides with the high-sun period.

Since the tropical climate is on the margin of the doldrums and the drier, subsiding tropical air masses, it follows that the rainfall distribution will be controlled by the location of these types of air mass. As the sun's vertical rays move north or south, according to the time of the year, so the doldrums and high-pressure belts influence the latitudes of the tropical, or savanna, regions at the different seasons. The doldrums and convectional effects will predominate during the high-sun period; consequently this will be the season of heavy rainfall. During the low-sun period the drier, subsiding air of the sub-tropical high-pressure belt will give a dry season. It should be emphasized, therefore, that *the rainfall follows the sun.*

Areas having a tropical, or savanna, climate are:

1. The Sudan and veld plateau of Africa.
2. The tropical grasslands of northern Australia.
3. The *llanos* of the Guiana highlands of South America.
4. The *campos* of Brazil.

Fig. 98 shows these locations; Figs. 103, 104, and 105 show climatic statistics for typical tropical, or savanna, areas.

THE MONSOON CLIMATE

The monsoon climate is characterized by

1. A wet season, with on-shore winds which coincide with the period of high sun.
2. A dry season, with off-shore winds which occur during the period of low sun. (The rainfall of this climate therefore resembles that of the tropical savanna.)
3. A hot season.
4. A cool season.

Temperatures are high during the wet season, but the winter temperatures vary considerably, from cold in the monsoon regions of China to hot in peninsular India. Thus, the monsoon climate can in reality be divided into two types: the 'tropical monsoon climate' and the 'temperate monsoon climate.'

The rainfall distribution is governed by on-shore or off-shore winds, which themselves are controlled by low- or high-pressure systems. Figs. 106 and 107 show in a simple form the pressure conditions which give rise to the monsoon winds of South-east Asia.

It is during the period of low sun over India and South-east Asia that the sub-tropical high-pressure belt has its greatest influence. The excessive cooling in Central Asia intensifies the high-pressure belt, and the off-shore north-east trades

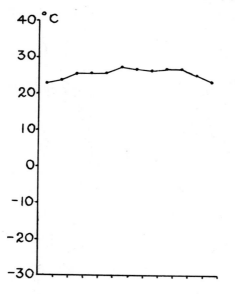

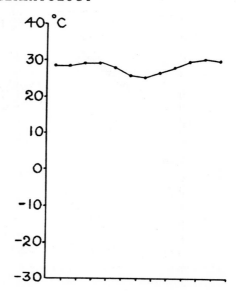

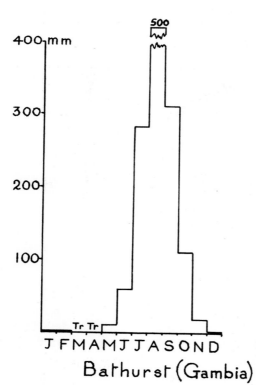

Bathurst (Gambia)

FIG. 104. A TROPICAL (SAVANNA)
STATION

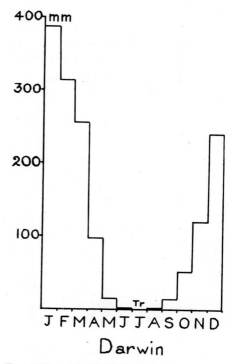

Darwin

FIG. 105. A TROPICAL (SAVANNA)
STATION

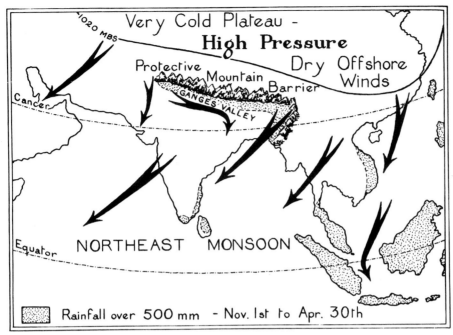

FIG. 106. THE NORTH-EAST MONSOON

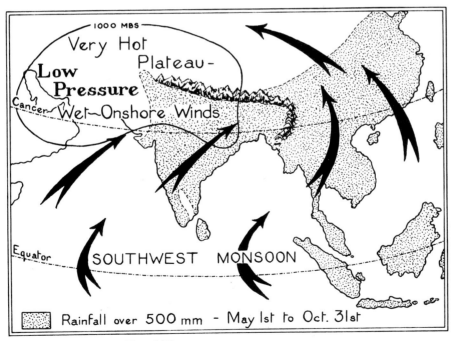

FIG. 107. THE SOUTH-WEST MONSOON

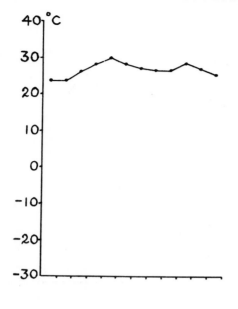

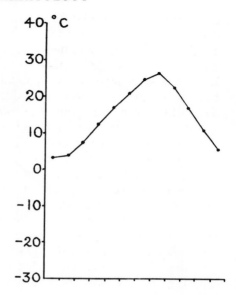

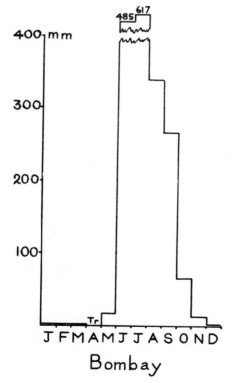

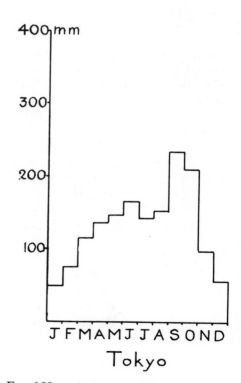

Bombay

Tokyo

FIG. 108. A TROPICAL MONSOON
CLIMATE

FIG. 109. A TEMPERATE MONSOON
CLIMATE

The more uniform distribution of rainfall in Tokyo is due to small depressional disturbances
and to marine influences, which occur throughout the year.

cover most of South-east Asia. In China the cold air comes directly from the centre of the continent; hence temperatures are low during this season. In India the Himalayas act as a mountain barrier and prevent the cold air from descending into the peninsula; consequently the temperatures are higher.

During the high-sun period the sub-tropical high pressure belt is replaced by a region of low pressure. The intense heating of Central Asia produces an area of very low pressure, which combines with the low pressure associated with the doldrums. A steep pressure gradient now exists between the sub-tropical high pressure of the Southern Hemisphere and the low pressure of Central Asia. The south-east trades pass over the Indian Ocean, cross the equator, are deflected to the right, and reach India and South-east Asia as on-shore south and south-westerly winds. The long ocean passage allows the winds to pick up a good deal of moisture, which they deposit over India and South-east Asia.

The areas having a 'tropical monsoon climate' are:

1. South-east Asia (excluding central and northern China).
2. Northern Australia.
3. The Guinea coast of West Africa.
4. The Pacific coast of Colombia.

The 'temperate monsoon climate' is associated with C. and N. China and, in a modified form the Japanese islands.

Figs. 108 and 109 show the temperature and rainfall for typical tropical and temperate monsoon areas.

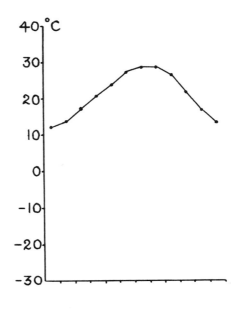

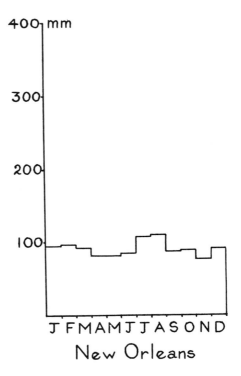

New Orleans

FIG. 110. A WARM EAST-COAST STATION

THE WARM EAST-COAST CLIMATE

This climate is distinguished from the tropical savanna climate which has a dry season by two facts:

1. There is a greater amount of rainfall.
2. The precipitation is well distributed throughout the year.

The main cause of this greater and more evenly distributed rainfall is the location of the areas within the south-east trade-wind belt. On-shore winds blow for much of the year, and consequently there is rain at all seasons.

Temperatures are affected by the warm-water currents which wash the littoral. The summer temperatures may be between 27° C and 31° C. Not only is the temperature high in summer, but the humidity is also well up, and the resulting condition is one of sultry oppressiveness. Winters are, of course, mild, being of the order of 10° C. Annual ranges are therefore usually small along the coasts, although there is some variation, depending upon latitude and size of continent. At Buenos Aires, for example, the range is 14° C, at Shanghai it is 24° C, and at Sydney it is 10° C. The effect of the large Asiatic continent is clearly seen in the case of Shanghai, and it is more usual, therefore, to consider this location as having a 'temperate monsoon climate': the temperatures differ from those of the average station on warm east coasts, and the rainfall is distinctly seasonal, coming primarily during the summer.

Fig. 110 shows the main features of the warm east-coast climate.

Chapter 17

THE DESERT CLIMATES

THE chief feature of any desert climate is the scarcity of water, and the fact that evaporation exceeds precipitation. Less than 125 mm of annual rainfall gives a true desert. As a result of the prevailing rainfall deficiency, there is no water supply with which to maintain regular plant and animal life. Deserts are regions where agriculture is impossible, unless man-made adaptations to the local conditions have been produced.

Since the lack of rain depends upon evaporation as well as upon the actual precipitation, it is clear that no specific amount of rain can be accepted as a limit covering all desert conditions. The rate of evaporation depends upon temperature, less water evaporating at low than at high temperatures. Consequently rainfall amounts which give humid conditions in temperate climates may produce semi-arid conditions in tropical regions. The boundary separating dry from moist climates is determined by the combined effects of rainfall and temperature, and not by precipitation alone. In fact, some climatologists suggest that it is impossible to define a desert in terms of climatic statistics and that it is more appropriate to indicate these dry areas in terms of plants and animals and their adaptations.

The dry climates can be subdivided into:

1. The arid, or desert, type.
2. The semi-arid, or steppe, type.

The steppe is merely a transition belt separating the true desert from the humid climates. It is difficult to suggest any obvious line of demarcation between steppe and true desert conditions. Köppen defined the boundary as being that line at which the rainfall was 50 per cent. of that separating steppe from humid climates— that is, if a rainfall of 500 mm separated the outer boundary of the dry climate from its adjoining humid one, then 250 mm could be taken as the boundary separating the steppe from true desert.

Dry climates cover at least 25 per cent. of the continental areas of the earth. They are widely located over the surface of the earth and can be broadly distinguished as

1. The cold-water deserts of the west coasts of the Southern Hemisphere continents.
2. The interior deserts.

Another form of subdivision can be more conveniently considered here:

1. Hot, or low-latitude, deserts.
2. Mid-latitude deserts.

These two types of climate are illustrated in Fig. 98.

LOW-LATITUDE DESERTS

The low-latitude deserts are the most arid regions on earth. Their location coincides with the warm, dry, stable air masses associated with the sub-tropical high pressures, where the conditions are not favourable for the development of convectional rain. In addition, the low-latitude deserts are outside the areas of rain-bringing conditions of either the doldrums or the mid-latitude cyclones. Some of the extensive low-latitude deserts, particularly the Sahara and the western desert of Australia, are important source areas for tropical continental air masses.

No clear-cut figure for precipitation can be given, but the rainfall amount probably lies somewhere between 250 mm and 400 mm, while over much of the Sahara, Kalahari, Atacama, Western Australian, and Thar deserts the precipitation is under 125 mm. The rainfall is also very erratic; over most low-latitude deserts the rainfall variability shows 40–50 per cent. departures from the normal. Average or typical rainfall figures are therefore very difficult to assess. Widespread rain is unknown; most precipitation comes in heavy convectional showers. The figures in Table 16 show the great variations in rainfall amounts for selected desert stations.

TABLE 16.—VARIATIONS IN RAINFALL AMOUNTS AT DESERT STATIONS

PLACE	ANNUAL RAINFALL, IN 10^{-3} METRES		
	MINIMUM	AVERAGE	MAXIMUM
Salton Sea (California)	Trace	68·6	180·0
El Paso (Texas)	56·0	234·0	465·0
Ouargla (Sahara)	0	89·0	210·3
Basra (Iraq)	53·0	167·5	272·0
Roebourne (Australia)	0·3	?	106·7

Skies are usually clear, and sunshine is abundant. Strong surface heating will occur during the day, owing to the intense insolation which is received. At night excessive radiation will take place, and low temperatures will result. Daily temperature ranges may be very great; the largest diurnal range recorded was at Bir Milrha in Tripoli, where a change of 40° C once occurred within twelve hours. In spite of the very low relative humidity, the intense cooling at night may produce surface dew. Dew probably plays a large part in the life of desert vegetation. The annual range of temperature varies from 10° C to 18° C. This range is greater than that of some mid-latitude climates and results from

1. The clear skies.
2. The bare earth (the lack of vegetation cover).
3. The low humidity and lack of cloud.
4. The greater variations in insolation received during the seasons.

At Wadi Halfa the following temperature figures have been recorded:

Lowest mean reading 7·8° C; Highest mean temperature 41·1° C; Lowest absolute reading −2·2° C; Highest absolute reading 54·4° C.

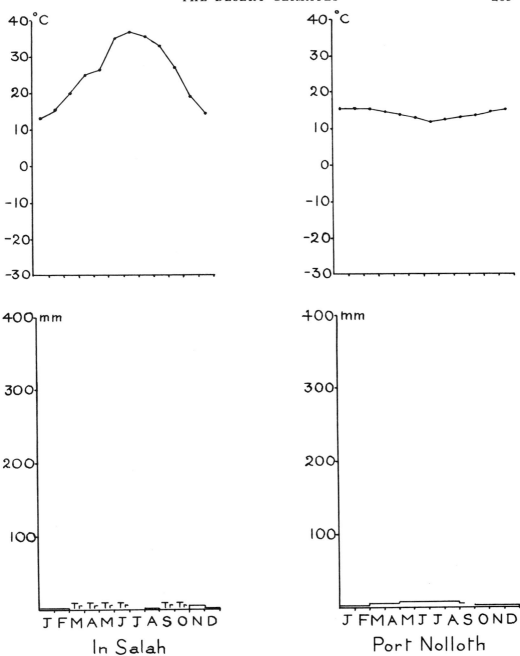

Fig. 111. LOW-LATITUDE DESERT—
SAHARA

Fig. 112. LOW-LATITUDE DESERT—
A WESTERN LITTORAL

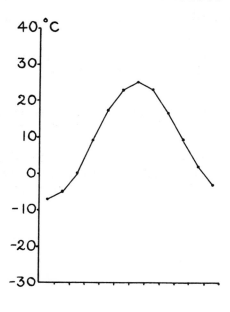

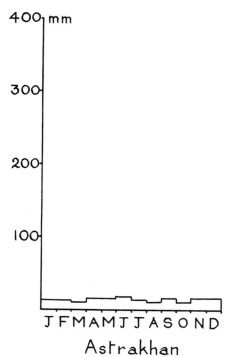

FIG. 113. A MID-LATITUDE DESERT
STATION

The characteristics of tropical deserts are modified along the coasts of several of the low-latitude deserts, where cool ocean currents wash the shores. These modifications are to be seen along the Peruvian and Kalahari deserts, where temperatures may be 10° or more lower than the normal for the latitude. The annual ranges are usually smaller, due mainly to lower summer temperatures rather than to higher winter temperatures. Rainfall is extremely low along these coasts, but the humidity is high, and the cooling effect of the ocean surface produces abundant fog. The *garua* of Peru is a typical example of such fog conditions.

Figs. 111 and 112 give climatic details for two low-latitude deserts, one centred in the Sahara and the other situated along a cool western coast respectively.

MID-LATITUDE DESERTS

The lower temperatures (and consequent reduced evaporation rates) produce lower rainfalls along the boundaries of the mid-latitude deserts. There is no indication, however, that these deserts themselves are more arid. In fact, some precipitation falls in mid-latitude deserts every year; in this, these deserts are quite unlike their low-latitude counterparts, where some regions are almost rainless. The mid-latitude deserts are located:

1. In the low-altitude continental basins of Central Asia and in the Great Basin of the United States.
2. In the rain-shadow regions in temperate latitudes of South America (Patagonia).

The essential characteristics of the climates of the mid-latitude deserts

situated in the continental interiors are indicated in Fig. 113. They can be summarized as follows:

1. There are excessively high summer temperatures (32·2° C has been recorded).
2. The winter temperatures are very low (−12·2 C has been measured).
3. The annual range is large (over 28° C).

In Patagonia the temperature range is much smaller, since maritime influences
play a greater part. Summer temperatures are thus fairly low, while the winters are
unusually mild for the latitude.

It is evident that the mid-latitude deserts are to be found either in the deep
interiors of continents—far from the oceans, which are the main source of water
vapour—or in the rain-shadow areas of extremely high mountain barriers which are
influenced by westerly winds. (See Fig. 98.)

Chapter 18

THE TEMPERATE CLIMATES

MID-LATITUDE climates are characterized by their definite seasonal rhythm in the general weather conditions. There is, for example, an obvious seasonal cycle of change in temperature; whereas, in the tropics, seasons are distinguished by their differences in rainfall, in the temperate climates the chief features differentiating one season from another are to be found in temperature changes. In the tropics seasons are designated wet or dry; in the mid-latitudes they are called winter or summer. In the intermediate zone within the temperate belt the weather is noted for its variability. This is the direct result of the location with respect to the contrasting air masses of tropical or polar origin.

Temperate climates fall into two distinct classes:

1. Humid climates having moderate temperatures.
2. Humid climates having low temperatures.

In this chapter the following climates will be discussed, and they will be grouped according to 1 or 2 above:

1. Humid climates having moderate temperatures.

    (*a*) The Mediterranean climate.
    (*b*) The West European climate.

2. Humid climates having low temperatures.

    (*a*) The cold-temperate, or taïga, climate.
    (*b*) The cool east-coast, or Laurentian, climate.
    (*c*) The continental climate.

THE MEDITERRANEAN CLIMATE

As its name suggests, this climate is typical of the areas bordering the Mediterranean Sea. But it is also located on the tropical margins of the mid-latitudes (30° to 40°), along the western sides of the continents. It is thus intermediate in position between the dry, subsiding air of the sub-tropical high-pressure belt and the rain-bringing fronts of the cyclonic low-pressure zone. As there is a seasonal shift of these pressure belts with the annual movements of the sun, the Mediterranean latitudes are influenced by the sub-tropical high-weather conditions in summer and by the cyclonic frontal weather in the winter. This climate is therefore a transition type between the arid low-latitude desert type and the changeable marine West-European climate, situated poleward.

The general features of the climate are as follows:

1. There is a moderate rainfall, concentrated in the winter season.
2. There are warm to hot summers which are almost dry.

3. The winters are mild.
4. There is a high percentage of sunshine, especially in summer.

This climate is characteristic of only 1·7 per cent. of the earth's land surface, yet it is the best known of the climatic types. The following five regions are among those where this climate exists:

1. The borderlands of the Mediterranean Sea.
2. Central and coastal southern California.
3. Central coastal Chile.
4. The Cape area of South Africa.
5. The extreme south-west and portions of southern Australia.

The climate is sub-tropical in character. Frost is rare, and winter temperatures lie between 4° C and 10° C. In summer the temperatures may be between 20° C and 27° C. The annual range is thus about 10° C to 17° C. High diurnal variations are noticeable in interior locations. Rain is low, on the whole, varying from 400 to 600 mm; 80 per cent. of the precipitation is received between December and March, and originates from the travelling lows associated with the polar front. Fig. 114 illustrates the main characteristics of the Mediterranean climate.

THE MARINE WEST EUROPEAN CLIMATE (TEMPERATE OCEANIC)

This climate characteristically occupies positions on the west, or windward, side of the mid-latitude continents, poleward from about 40°, where on-shore westerly winds bring oceanic conditions. Equatorward, the climate is adjacent to the Mediterranean type, but, unlike the latter, is rarely affected by the sub-tropical high pressure. Hence there is no pronounced dry season, and the cyclonic low-pressure systems bring variable conditions throughout the year. The coasts are paralleled by warm-water currents. Poleward, consequently, the climate may terminate directly in sub-Arctic, or tundra, type. The depth to which the climate may be felt inland depends entirely upon local relief. In Europe (excluding Scandinavia) the climate extends well into the continent, but in North America and Scandinavia there is only a narrow belt of land which experiences a temperate oceanic effect. On the landward side this climate is bordered by the more extreme continental-type conditions. Fig. 98 shows the chief areas of the world in which the climate predominates.

The summer temperatures are moderately cool and are often too low for the growth of many cereal types. In winter the conditions are abnormally mild for the latitude: this is due entirely to the effects of the south-west winds as they traverse the warm-water currents. In Western Europe the temperatures are 10° C to 17° C too warm for the latitude in January. In other words, there is a positive temperature anomaly. The isotherms around the coast of Europe run parallel with the coast rather than from east to west. The cooling is, therefore, from west to east rather than from south to north. Temperatures for Paris and Brest show that, in January, the former is 4° C cooler than the latter. Similarly, the heads of the fjords in Norway may be 5·5° C cooler than the open coastal regions. Frosts can be severe and frequent; the frost-free season is much shorter than that of the Mediterranean climate. Nevertheless, the growing season is unusually long for the latitude, 180 to 200 days

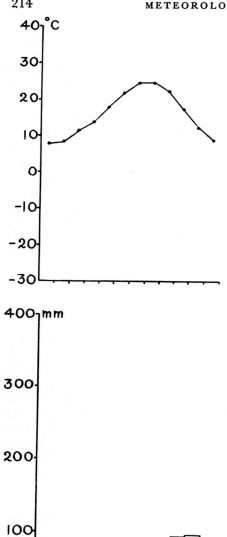

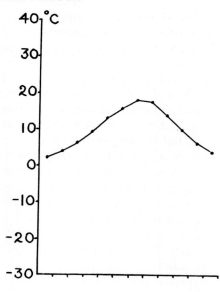

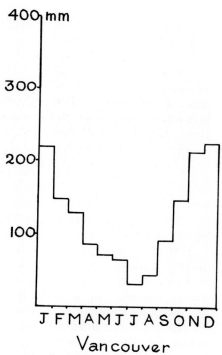

Rome

FIG. 114. A MEDITERRANEAN
CLIMATE

Vancouver

FIG. 115. A WEST EUROPEAN
CLIMATE

being characteristic—that is, the average temperature remains above 4·4° C for that period of time. Periodic cold spells cover the regions. These are due to invasions of cold air from the continental interior.

There is adequate rainfall at all seasons, the total depending upon the relief of the locality. In lowland areas the figures may vary from 500 mm to 1000 mm, but in regions of high relief near the coasts the precipitation may be in excess of 2500 mm. The rainfall is greatest in the winter months, when the cyclonic low-pressure systems are most frequent. About 59 per cent. occurs between October and April. Snow does fall, but it rarely settles for long periods. In Paris there are, on the average, fourteen snowy days per year; in north-east Britain, twenty-five days; in south-west Britain, less than four. The rainfall tends to be cyclonic in origin, although considerable orographic rain occurs on the seaward side. Even convectional rainfall does occur in eastern Britain, away from the sea influences. Relative humidities are always high, especially in winter; much cloud is typical—in fact, it is the cloudiest climate on earth (60 to 70 per cent. of the year). Sunshine is greater in summer than in winter; Britain receives 40 per cent. of the possible in summer as against 15 per cent. in winter.

Fig. 115 illustrates some of the main characteristics of the West European climate.

THE COLD-TEMPERATE, OR TAÏGA, CLIMATE

This type of climate is found only in the higher middle latitudes of the large continents situated in the Northern Hemisphere. On the poleward side it is adjacent to the sub-Arctic, or tundra, climate; the boundary is approximately that of the isotherm of 10° C for the warmest month. This line closely follows the poleward limit of tree growth. The vegetation associated with this climatic type is coniferous soft-wood forest, to which the name 'taïga' has been applied, and this climate is sometimes, therefore, called the 'taïga.' Its locations are shown on Fig. 98. In North America the belt stretches from Labrador and Newfoundland to Alaska. In Europe and Asia the climate extends from Sweden and Finland across the whole of the continent to Siberia and the Pacific coast.

The general features of the climate can be summarized as follows:

1. The summers are short; July is usually the warmest month, and is between 10° C and 15° C.

2. The winters are long and very cold; frosts arrive in late August, and the minimum temperatures in mid-winter may be as much as −50° C.

3. The precipitation is small, but varies from 400 mm over much of the taïga to 500 mm to 600 mm over the western margins of this climatic belt.

The short summers are compensated by the long days in the higher latitudes. Thus, the large number of hours during which the sun shines is a counterbalancing feature. Similarly, the short nights do not allow long periods of cooling. In June the days average seventeen hours of possible sunshine at 55° N., and at 65° N. the figure increases to twenty-two.

The autumn also is short, and winter quickly follows upon the summer. The excessively low winter temperatures (−50° C at Verkhoyansk in January) are responsible for the large annual temperature ranges. The excessive and long-continued cold of these winters causes large areas of the taïga to be frozen permanently, down to great depths. Long nights are characteristic of the winters, and at 65° N. the maximum possible amount of sunshine is only three hours. These periods of darkness are to a large degree responsible for the low winter temperatures. In North America the winters are not quite so cold as those of Asia; the largeness of the Asian land mass results in the formation of a region of intensively high pressure, and this, together with the remoteness from oceanic influences, produces an accumulation of stagnant, but very cold, air.

The precipitation is low and is usually concentrated into the warmer months. But, though the amounts are low, they are sufficient for tree growth. In many mid-latitude climates the precipitation amounts (such as those associated with the taïga) would give rise to semi-arid conditions; where the temperatures are so low, however, and the evaporation rates are also very small, there is sufficient precipitation for tree growth. The low precipitation is associated with:

1. The low temperatures.
2. The intense winter anticyclone.
3. The largeness of the land masses.

Fig. 116 illustrates some of the main characteristics of the cold-temperate, or taïga, climate.

The Cool East-coast, or Laurentian, Climate

This climate is sometimes called the humid continental warm-summer type. It is located along the north-eastern seaboard of the United States, and across into the 'corn-belt' states. It may also be identified in northern China, Japan, Korea, and within the plains of the lower Danube.

The characteristics of the Laurentian climate can be summarized as follows:

1. The summers are long, hot, and humid; tropical maritime air masses are responsible for these features. July temperatures may average 24° C to 27° C.

2. The winters are cold; but there are great variations in temperature, due to the influence of travelling masses of tropical air. Temperatures between —4° C and 0° C are the usual averages in January.

3. The precipitation varies with the localities: in New York over 1000 mm is usually recorded; in Bucharest only 580 mm is received. Most of the precipitation comes in summer, although a fair proportion of the winter precipitation comes as snow. Twenty-five to 100 cm of snow are recorded in the American states.

The summer temperatures are sub-tropical in character. In St Louis (Missouri) the average July temperature is 26° C; in New York, on the eastern seaboard, it is 24° C. The high humidity in summer is responsible for a large number of hot, sultry, and very oppressive days. The high absolute humidity does not allow rapid cooling during the night, and temperatures at this time are also fairly high. The summers are long, and the frost-free period can exceed two hundred days.

The winters are relatively cold; New York's January average is —0·5° C,

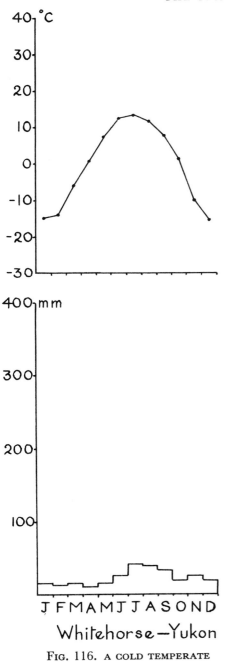

FIG. 116. A COLD TEMPERATE
CLIMATE

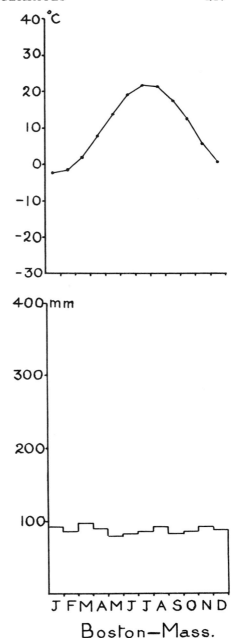

FIG. 117. A COOL EAST-COAST
STATION

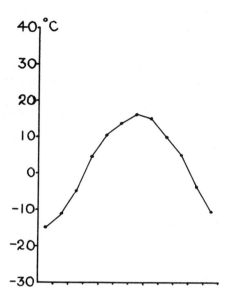

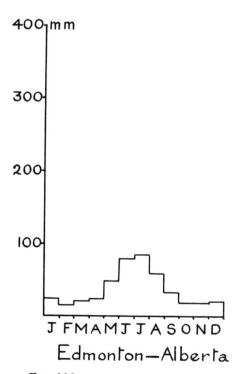

Edmonton—Alberta

FIG. 118. A CONTINENTAL CLIMATE

while that of Bucharest is 3·3° C. But influxes of warmer air of tropical origin do result in greater temperature variations during the winter months.

The precipitation is variable, and most of the areas experiencing this type of climate suffer from too little, rather than too much, rainfall. Summer rainfall is characteristic and is convectional in type. High sunshine amounts are recorded, and conditions throughout the summer are conducive to good agricultural growth. Thunderstorms are numerous, and the 'corn-belt' states of the United States experience as many as fifty a year. In winter the precipitation is usually less than in summer, and what comes usually falls as snow. The number of days in the year on which snow falls varies from fifteen to thirty, and the number of days with snow cover on the ground varies from ten on the southern margins to sixty on the poleward margins of the climatic zones. Cyclonic disturbances are responsible for much of this winter precipitation, although in the northern Chinese areas the intense winter anticyclones preclude rainfall and snow conditions, and precipitation is therefore meagre.

Fig. 117 indicates the chief characteristics of this climate.

THE CONTINENTAL CLIMATE

This climate could be described as the humid continental cool-summer type; in North America and central Russia it coincides with the 'spring-wheat belts.' Its main locations are shown in Fig. 98. In Eurasia the climate extends from Poland and the Baltic states to the central Russian plain; beyond the Ural mountains the belt is narrow, being situated along the 55° parallel and separating the cold-temperate climate from the mid-latitude deserts of Turkestan.

In North America the climate is situated in the northern states of the United States and within the southern zones of the central states of Canada.

The essential characteristics of the continental climate are as follows:

1. The higher latitudes are responsible for temperatures which are lower than those of the cool east-coast climate, but higher than those of the cold-temperate climate.

2. Summers are warm, being of the order of 18° C to 21° C. The duration of the summer is short.

3. Winter is the dominant season. In January the highest temperatures are often well below freezing-point. The average January temperature for Montreal is −10° C; for Winnipeg, −20° C.

4. Precipitation varies considerably with the localities, and it is difficult to generalize about amounts. Usually most rainfall comes in the summer, caused by the surface heating of conditionally unstable air and by frontal conditions. Being nearer to the polar front, these climatic regions receive more frontal precipitation. Amounts vary from 1000 mm at Quebec to 500 mm at Winnipeg.

Fig. 118 shows the main features of this climate.

Chapter 19

POLAR AND MOUNTAIN CLIMATES

POLAR CLIMATES

POLAR climates are characterized by the absence of a warm period, and by monotonous and long-continued cold conditions. These climates are, as their name suggests, confined to the high latitudes, but there are great differences between the Arctic climates and those associated with the Antarctic. Since the Arctic is almost a land-locked sea, while the Antarctic is a seagirt land, certain important differences of climate are to be expected between these two regions. The Antarctic shows much greater uniformity in its climate: wind and pressure systems are symmetrically developed about the South Pole, and there appears to be little change in the climatic elements throughout the year. In the Arctic, on the other hand, the atmospheric conditions are less symmetrical, and seasonal variations of climatic controls are characteristic of the North Pole.

A distinctive feature of the polar climates is their peculiarity with respect to hours of day and night. The sun is below the horizon for approximately six months of the year, and is constantly above the horizon for a similar period. Along the Arctic and Antarctic Circles the daily period of sunlight varies from twenty-four hours at the summer solstice to zero at the winter solstice. Between these latitudes (*i.e.*, $66\frac{1}{2}°$ N. and $66\frac{1}{2}°$ S.) and the Poles the durations of day and night vary between the two extremes. These peculiarities in solar radiation receipts are inevitably reflected in the temperatures of the regions. The effects of solar radiation depend upon its duration—that is, upon the length of day—and also upon the angle at which the sun's rays reach the earth. Fig. 18 shows how the sun's radiation is received and reflected by the earth's atmosphere. (This reflection is known as the earth's 'albedo'—see p. 36.) It is calculated that 42 per cent. of the total insolation is scattered at the outer limits of the atmosphere: 9 per cent. is reflected direct from the atmosphere, 25 per cent. is reflected from the clouds, and the remaining 8 per cent. is reflected from the earth's surface. The atmosphere absorbs a further 15 per cent. Thus the rest (43 per cent.) reaches the earth and is absorbed by it.

The amount of solar radiation which reaches any particular part of the earth's surface in any one day depends upon a number of factors:

1. The solar constant—that is, the intensity of the sun's radiation in space at the earth's average distance from the sun. (The value of the constant can be taken as 1354 J/m²/s or 1354 W/m².)
2. The area of the surface upon which the radiation falls.
3. The inclination of that surface to the sun's rays.
4. The transparency of the atmosphere.
5. The position of the earth in its orbit—that is, the season.

It will be seen from Table 17 that the sun's radiation depends upon the obliqueness of the ray of sunlight. When the sun is only 5° above the horizon its rays have to penetrate an atmosphere almost eleven times thicker than that which exists when its altitude is 90°. It is clear, therefore, that in higher latitudes this becomes of some significance; in spite of the sun being above the horizon for almost six months of the year, the amount of solar radiation reaching the Poles is less than that reaching the equator. Additionally, the angle at which the sun's rays strike the surface affects the amount of insolation received per unit area. Oblique rays of a low-angle sun are

TABLE 17.—THE INTENSITY OF INSOLATION AT DIFFERENT ELEVATIONS OF THE SUN

ALTITUDE OF THE SUN	RELATIVE LENGTHS OF THE PATHS OF RAYS THROUGH THE ATMOSPHERE, GIVEN IN ATMOSPHERES	INTENSITY OF INSOLATION ON A SURFACE PERPENDICULAR TO THE RAYS, GIVEN IN PERCENTAGE—COEFFICIENT OF TRANSMISSION	INTENSITY OF INSOLATION ON A HORIZONTAL SURFACE
90°	1·00	78	78
80°	1·02	77	76
70°	1·06	76	72
60°	1·15	75	65
50°	1·31	72	55
40°	1·56	68	44
30°	2·00	62	31
20°	2·92	51	17
10°	5·70	31	5
5°	10·80	15	1
0°	45·00	0	0

(*N.B.* The coefficient of transmission is 78 per cent.)

spread over a larger surface area than are vertical rays, and consequently they produce less heating per unit area. Insolation varies with the latitude, and, though the North Pole receives more insolation than the equator during June, there are five months of the year when it receives no insolation. Table 18 shows the calculated insolation which reaches the Poles and the equator for each month of the year.

TABLE 18.—CALCULATED INSOLATION REACHING THE EARTH, IN kW/M²

LATITUDE	J.	F.	M.	A.	M.	J.	J.	A.	S.	O.	N.	D.	YEARLY TOTAL
90° N.	0·0	0·0	1·3	12·2	22·0	25·4	22·9	14·7	3·2	0·0	0·0	0·0	101·7
Equator	20·5	21·2	21·4	20·7	24·6	18·9	19·3	20·0	21·0	21·1	20·6	20·2	249·5
90° S.	24·2	14·4	2·2	0·0	0·0	0·0	0·0	0·0	0·3	10·9	22·0	27·0	101·0

N.B. The earth is at its nearest to the sun at the end of December and during early January; hence the amount of insolation received at the South Pole will be greater in this month than it will be at the North Pole in June, when the earth is farthest away from the sun. The movement of the sun north and south of the equator is also reflected in these figures.

It is evident from the above details that the insolation reaching the surface of the earth at the Poles is small and unevenly distributed throughout the year. Loss of heat by terrestrial radiation goes on continuously, and, during the period of total darkness, the temperature will continue to fall. The minimum temperature should therefore be reached some time before the spring equinox. Once the temperature is below

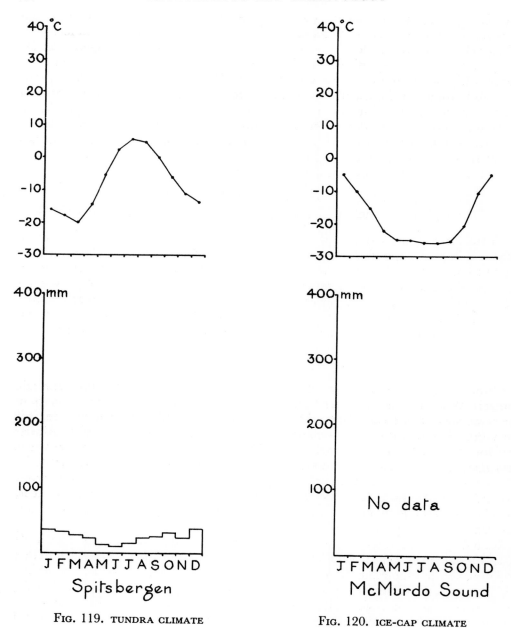

FIG. 119. TUNDRA CLIMATE   FIG. 120. ICE-CAP CLIMATE

freezing-point the seas and oceans will freeze, and all precipitation will be in the form of snow. If we assume that the total insolation reaches the surface in summer, then all the energy will be used in melting the snow and ice which have accumulated during the past six months. Snow and ice are good reflecting surfaces, and 80 per cent. of the insolation is reflected back from the surface. Consequently there is insufficient energy to melt all the snow and ice, and an accumulation of snow and ice takes place each year. The formation of the ice caps is thus accounted for.

Polar climates have the lowest mean annual and lowest summer temperatures for any part of the earth's surface. Winters are bitterly cold, and summers are cool. Hence fairly large annual ranges are recorded. Precipitation is small throughout the high latitudes, being usually less than 250 mm. Because of the low evaporation and the small amount of melting permanent snow and ice fields have accumulated. In some cases these ice fields may be several hundred metres thick: in Greenland the ice is over two thousand metres thick, and recent evidence suggests that in Antarctica the ice is as much as three thousand metres thick.

Polar climates are usually divided into two classes:

1. The regions in which the warmest month is below 0° C.
2. The regions in which the warmest month is above 0° C but below 10° C.

Where the average monthly temperature is below freezing-point all vegetation growth is impossible, and there is a permanent snow and ice cover. Such an area is said to have an 'ice-cap climate.' Where the temperature of the warmest month does rise above 0° C but never above 10° C the ground may be free of snow for a short period, and a sparse sort of vegetation is possible. In this latter case the area is said to have a 'tundra climate.' Figs. 119 and 120 show the temperature and precipitation figures for selected stations in ice-cap and tundra climatic zones.

MOUNTAIN CLIMATES

Altitude, next to distribution of land and sea, is the most important climatic control. While it is not possible to distinguish one particular mountain climate in the same way as one can distinguish a continental or Mediterranean climate, it is clear that elevation does play a most important part as a climatic control. Almost endless varieties of local climates exist within a mountain mass, the atmospheric conditions varying with the altitude and the exposure as well as with the latitude. The climate of an enclosed valley is very different from that of an exposed peak. Conditions on leeward slopes differ greatly from those on windward slopes. It is, therefore, impossible to produce representative figures for highland climates, and one can make very few generalizations.

Sunlight becomes more intense as height increases in the thinner and cleaner air of the mountains. On a cloudless day about 75 per cent. of the solar radiation penetrates to two thousand metres, but this figure falls to less than 50 per cent. at sea-level. Also, the receipt of ultra-violet rays is greater at higher altitudes. But the most fundamental change resulting from an increase in altitude is the decrease in air temperature (approximately 0·6° C per hundred metres), in spite of the increased intensity of insolation. It is obvious that the temperature gradient is steep as one rises vertically, and this is responsible for the existence of the several zones of climate which one encounters as one ascends the mountain. In tropical regions there will be a change from tropical climates at ground-level to temperate and sub-arctic climatic types at high altitude. (Fig. 121 illustrates this change on a tropical mountain; Fig. 122 shows similar changes in climate for a mountain in temperate

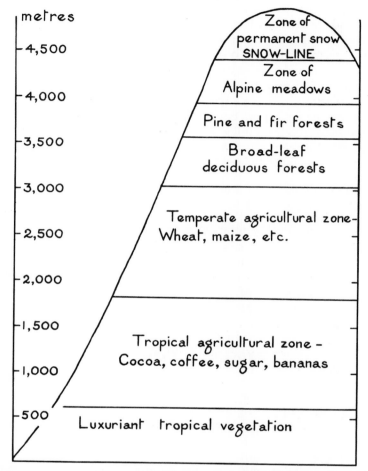

FIG. 121. ILLUSTRATION TO SHOW HOW VEGETATION, AND HENCE CLIMATE, CHANGES AS
ELEVATION INCREASES ON A TROPICAL MOUNTAIN

zones.) As one would expect, the snow line is considerably lower in the temperate
areas, and the climates are solely of the temperate and alpine type.

Precipitation is usually much heavier in the mountainous areas; this is explained by:

1. Orographic uplift of moist air over the mountain ranges.
2. Convectional uplift along the sunny slopes of mountains.

Above two thousand metres the absolute humidity is fairly small, and consequently
the specific, or relative humidity is also always small. This means that at heights
greater than two thousand metres there is a distinct falling-off in precipitation
amounts.

Winds are usually strong along mountain ridges and peaks, but the valleys are
sheltered and well protected against violent winds. The great variety of relief and
mountain contour patterns result in a number of local wind characteristics. Anabatic

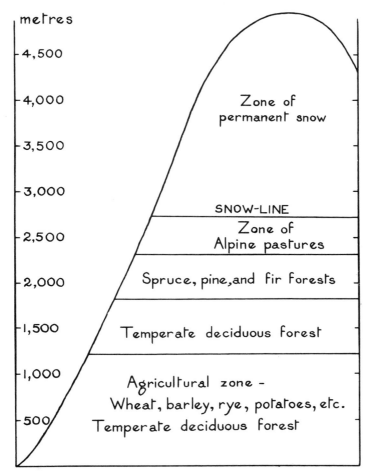

metres

4,500

4,000 — Zone of permanent snow

3,500

3,000

SNOW-LINE

2,500 — Zone of Alpine pastures

2,000 — Spruce, pine, and fir forests

1,500 — Temperate deciduous forest

1,000 — Agricultural zone –
Wheat, barley, rye, potatoes, etc.

500 — Temperate deciduous forest

FIG. 122. ILLUSTRATION TO SHOW HOW VEGETATION, AND HENCE CLIMATE, CHANGES AS ELEVATION INCREASES ON A TEMPERATE MOUNTAIN

and katabatic winds have already been considered in Chapter 4. The föhn effect has also been dealt with at some length, both in Chapter 4 and in Chapter 6.

Weather changes are much more rapid in mountain areas than at lower altitudes. Violent changes in temperature in the sun and in the shade have their effects upon air movements and upon cloud formations. Diurnal changes are quite erratic, but a general pattern can be discerned. Mornings on the mountain slopes are cold and raw, but then, as the sun rises, the temperature of the air soon goes up. At midday it will be hot in the sun, but relatively cold in the shade. Clouds commence to build up in the early afternoon, and rain, hail, or even snow may be precipitated. Thunder is quite common. As the sun sets the convectional heating ceases, the clouds tend to die away, and the mountain peaks once again become visible.

The major areas of the world which have mountain climates are shown in Fig. 98.

Chapter 20

WEATHER, CLIMATE, AND LIFE

IT is an accepted fact that climate, and particularly weather, are subjects of universal conversation, and even our daily salutations frequently express the wish that the day will be good. But, as is often the case with the common experiences of human beings, this natural element of our environment is usually taken for granted. Insufficient attention is paid to-day to the systematic relationship existing between weather, climate, and the other environmental elements of the earth and living organisms, particularly man.

Of all the geographical influences to which living organisms are subjected climate is probably the most powerful. There is a most decisive relationship between climate and plant life. Soils result from the interplay of a number of environmental factors, but climate is probably the most significant of these because it generally affects all the other factors. Climate influences animals, who, owing to their mobility, change their habitat as fluctuations in climatic conditions affect their mode of life. Above all, man is subjected to climatic influence. In large measure climate affects man's choice of location, his food crops, the type of house in which he lives, the kind of clothing he needs, and what diseases he has to combat. Climate therefore influences all aspects of social, political, and cultural life of man, and it is the dominant factor affecting all other life forms.

THE INFLUENCE OF CLIMATE UPON VEGETATION

Any excursion into the countryside will show how plant distribution is controlled by physical surroundings. The influence of water is readily noticeable; one can differentiate between plants which flourish in abundant moisture and those which are able to grow in drought conditions. Again, one can see those plants which grow only in light and those which like shady, dark places. Temperature also is a major control; one can see the effects of this when ascending a mountain. In fact, it becomes clear after frequent excursions into different areas having a wide variety of physical conditions that certain plants, quite unrelated to each other, will be found growing side by side. These associations must be based upon common needs: some plants have adapted themselves to abundant moisture, others to more than average light or cold, and others to special types of soil. Before examining the influence of climate upon vegetation it is important to consider the mechanism of the physical influences whose action upon plant life is noticeable.

The conditions of plant life are rigidly determined by temperature. For every species of plant there is a minimum and a maximum temperature: if the temperature remains for any length of time either below the minimum or above the maximum, then the plant will surely die. There is also an optimum temperature, at which the plant will grow the most vigorously. Plants have in many cases adapted themselves to periods of cold or heat: at such times certain plants may relapse into a period of retarded growth, others may lose their leaves, and others may even arrest certain functions associated with their growth.

No plants can live without some water, but many species have adapted themselves to a scarcity of it, while others can survive in an excess. Plants which live in water are called 'hygrophytes.' Their leaves are long, thin strips attached to long stalks, which allow them to reach the surface. The stomata are small or absent altogether, and the tissue itself is full of holes, which allow the air to circulate directly within the plant.

In contrast to the hygrophytes are the 'xerophytes' (plants which have adapted themselves to drought conditions). Their roots are very long, and they reach down well towards the subsoil in their search for water. The stems are woody and usually short; the leaves are thick, with a small surface area; stomata are few, and sometimes even absent altogether. All these features are designed to reduce transpiration and to increase the water supply. Some plants adapt themselves to drought by storing water in modified tissue; often, in these cases, the distinction between leaf and stem disappears, and the whole plant becomes very thick. (Cactus plants are a good example of this type of water-storing feature.)

Certain climates have distinct dry and wet seasons—the monsoon climate, for example—and consequently the plants must adapt themselves to two different conditions. Most trees drop their leaves in the dry season and conserve water in their woody tissue. In the wet season the leaves develop. Such plants are called 'tropophilous.'

The type of soil is another very important factor governing the distribution of plant species, because the moisture content and temperature of the soil are controlled by the soil's texture and composition. All soils contain two important ingredients: humus, or decayed organic material, and inorganic minerals. The essential characteristic of soil is that it is influenced by vegetation which, after being fed at its expense, necessarily modifies the composition of the soil. The influence of climate determines the humus content: some soils may be leached by excess moisture, others may be saline due to lack of water, and others may contain excesses of minerals. One of the best soils is the 'chernozem,' found in the grassland belts of N. America, Asia and in parts of S.E. Europe—e.g., the Ukraine. It consists of a balanced composition of mineral and humus and provides a good 'black earth,' which forms the granaries of the world.

Having briefly outlined the main characteristics of and conditions for plant growth, it is now necessary to examine the conditions under which each type of vegetation will grow. It is possible to define the main features of the earth's mantle of vegetation and to sum them up in classes, according to the physical conditions to which they are adapted. For the sake of simplicity the types of vegetation will be considered under the following headings:

1. Forest vegetation.
2. Grassland vegetation.
3. Mediterranean vegetation.
4. Desert vegetation.
5. Tundra vegetation.
6. Alpine vegetation.

FOREST VEGETATION

The tree is the most powerful, yet the most exacting, type of plant within the vegetable kingdom. Its great stature demands a support of considerable strength, and woody tissue is very necessary. A tree should be hygrophilous, because transpiration amounts may be high. Full-grown beeches may well transpire amounts of water equivalent to 250 mm of rain per year. Because of its long and deep roots, which reach down well into the subsoil, a tree is not as sensitive as smaller plants to an absence of surface water. A tree can endure a dry period after a wet season if some check is made upon transpiration during the drought.

True hygrophilous types exist only in the tropical forests, where there is an abundance of moisture. These trees are characterized by rapid, continuous growth; the leaves tend to be large, and there is less woody tissue than the average. Lianas, or rope-like plants, entwine themselves around the taller trees. These grow rapidly and demand high temperatures and heavy rainfall. Vegetation of this type is therefore absent from temperate forests.

In equatorial, humid conditions forests contain much decaying material, and 'saprophytes' are to be found existing on (and sustained by) this dying vegetation. An example of such a plant is the mushroom. Other types include 'parasites' (which feed upon the sap of other plants) and 'epiphytes.' These latter grow attached to the leaf stem of other plants (from which, however, unlike parasites, they draw no sustenance). They possess hanging roots and absorb moisture directly from the air.

In the tropical savanna climate some tree growth is noticeable, but, since there is a distinct dry season, the trees must adapt themselves to drought. This they do either by storing water—e.g., the baobab—or by having waxy, polished leaf surfaces and an umbrella-shaped foliage to shade their roots from the drying effects of the sun—e.g., the acacia.

In the temperate belt most of the land was formerly covered by forest. Unfortunately, much of this virgin growth has disappeared as man has progressively cleared a way for agriculture, and little now remains in its natural state. What does remain is to be found in the taïga of Russia, Canada and the N.W. United States. Two main types of forest can be recognized. There is 'deciduous' forest, consisting of trees which lose their leaves in winter, and 'coniferous' forest, which consists of evergreen trees. In each case there is a period when growth is arrested.

In the southern regions of the temperate climates the summers are hot enough for transpiration to occur rapidly, and the leaves must therefore be of the broad type. In winter, however, there are cold spells, and frosts are not uncommon. Hence some protection must be afforded the tree to prevent the sap freezing in the leaves. The winter may be looked upon as a period of drought, in that the tree becomes dormant, and it loses its leaves in the autumn in preparation for the cold season.

Farther north, in the cold-temperate climates, the tree protects itself by having tiny, needle-like leaves which resist transpiration. They are also thick enough to prevent the sap freezing in the capillaries. Evaporation rates are never very high, and broad leaves are unnecessary. The conical shape of the conifer assists by compelling the snow to fall off the foliage. During the winter season this tree too is dormant.

Grassland Vegetation

Most herbaceous plants are either xerophilous or tropophilous. They are low in stature and, having short roots, very sensitive to changes in humidity and rainfall. They cannot, therefore, endure drought during their growing period.

Adaptation to drought conditions can be achieved by:

1. Reducing the size of the leaves.
2. Changing the leaf-form (long and narrow).
3. Sometimes developing a hair covering on the leaf.
4. Developing the woody tissue, or producing prickles (as in thistles).

Tropophilous plants are quite widespread: they may be perennial types, having hibernating shoots or bulbous growths.

Herbaceous plants tend to die down during the winter season, or during the dry spell, and to complete their main growth in a single season. Such annual plants are very common in the temperate belt. Generally, herbaceous vegetation adapts itself to moderate temperatures and requires a soil which is damp at the surface, but it can endure a considerable dryness of the atmosphere.

Grasslands can be found in both tropical and temperate regions of the world. Savanna grass is found in the tropical savanna climatic areas and illustrates the effect of high evaporation rates, high temperatures, and dry seasonal conditions upon vegetation types. Tropical savanna is a discontinuous carpet of grasses which grow in tufts. The grasses spring up quickly during the wet season, often reaching heights of two to three metres, but in the dry season they soon wither away. In the continental climatic zones grassland vegetation types are again characteristic. Here there is a lack of the moisture which is important for tree growth; snow cover is another handicap for trees, although it protects grass from the extreme cold, and the desiccating winds do not affect herbaceous plants so readily. The steppes of Russia and the prairies of Canada are excellent examples of temperate grasslands.

Mediterranean Vegetation

Mediterranean climatic conditions have been summarized as mild, damp winters and hot, dry summers. Consequently vegetation types must be xerophilous in character. Forests are composed of conifers and trees with thick bark (such as cork oak) and gnarled trunks. Their leaves are small and often wax-covered, and the general growth tends to be limited. The stunted evergreen oak and sparse, tufted herbaceous plants form the typical *maquis* country of the southern regions of Mediterranean Europe. Grass in Mediterranean regions is anything but lush, and the hot, dry summer causes any growth to be very limited. The *mallee* of southern Australia is the local name for the Mediterranean vegetation of similar climatic areas in that continent.

Desert Vegetation

Desert vegetation occurs only in small patches and is very much controlled by the appearance of water. Consequently it is liable to disappear for several seasons during those years in which no rainfall is received, but will spring forth rapidly as some moisture is derived from the occasional convectional showers. Plants with a very short period of growth exist in deserts; grasses and other herbaceous types of a xerophilous character can grow, but they nearly all tend to develop underground. The roots are enormous, the stem is undersized, and there are hardly any leaves. Fleshy plants are numerous in the tropical deserts, but in the mid-latitude deserts thorny shrubs are more characteristic.

TUNDRA VEGETATION

Excessive cold has much the same effect upon plant growth as excessive drought. Thus, tundra vegetation is similar to that found in the deserts. Snow cover for long periods of the year, frozen soils and subsoils, and dry air all prevent the growth of plants. Some stunted trees exist on the southern boundary of the tundra region, but the characteristic vegetation type is the scrubland and peatland called 'tundra,' from which the region receives its name. Plants with small roots may thrive in the short summer, during which the top few centimetres of soil may be warmed above freezing-point and yield some water. Mosses, lichens, and alpine plants of diminutive size are typical of tundra conditions.

ALPINE VEGETATION

It has already been noted (p. 223) that there is no one characteristic type of mountain climate. Conditions depend entirely upon height, latitude, and the relationship of the relief to the prevailing winds. In many ways Alpine vegetation is related to the arctic and tundra types, and those plants found near the snow-line are tundra in character. But mountain climates do have a real summer, when insolation is high and the period of time during which temperatures are above freezing-point is long. There are usually no trees, because of the likely damage by frost and exposure, but xerophilous bushes and grasses do survive.

The lower limit of the Alpine zone coincides with the upper limit of the temperate forest zone. This tree line depends upon latitude and the climatic zone in which the mountains are situated. In the true European Alps the tree line is at about 2000 metres, but this rises from 4500 to 5000 metres in the Himalayas and the tropical Andes. The location of the mountain slope in relation to the sun also influences tree lines. Trees may be anything up to 150 metres higher up the slopes on the southward-facing side than on the shaded north slopes.

SUMMARY

Forest, grassland, and desert differ greatly in their climatic requirements, and a clue to the type of climate which prevails in a particular area can often be obtained by an examination of the vegetation.

Trees demand more water than other plants. In hot regions trees need a heavy rainfall to make up for the great loss by evaporation, but in temperate regions a moderate precipitation is sufficient for tree growth. For a region to be thickly covered by forest the rainfall must be well distributed throughout the year. Thus it is possible to assume that wherever forest vegetation occurs the following climatic features are to be found:

1. Rain falls at all seasons.
2. Under temperate conditions the annual rainfall is 500 mm to 1000 mm.
3. In tropical regions the rainfall is heavy (1000 to 1500 mm). Often the figure is above 1500 mm.

There are, of course, exceptions; trees do grow in monsoon lands and other areas where water is available in one season and can be stored up for the drought period, and where the plants can also adapt themselves to the dry spell.

Two mean monthly temperatures assist in controlling the growth of trees: 5·5° C in winter and 10° C in summer. Trees cannot grow unless the temperature for the warmest months reaches at least 10° C, and the mean monthly temperature of 5·5° C stops the growth of all plants. The type of forest which covers an area is decided by the number of months where the mean is below 5·5° C.

1. If there are no months when the temperature falls below 5·5° C, then the forest consists of broad-leaved evergreens. Leaf-shedding is not necessary to check transpiration in any season.
2. When the average monthly mean is below 5·5° C for anything up to six months of the year the forest is of the deciduous type. Cold-weather drought occurs, and leaf-shedding must take place to protect the tree from frost. In summer there is sufficient time for new foliage to grow.
3. Where there are over six months of the year in which the mean is below 5·5° C the forest is of the evergreen, coniferous type.

Wherever grassland is the natural vegetation there are generally two main climatic features:

1. The majority of rain falls in the summer season.
2. The annual rainfall is less than that required for forest growth. In temperate areas the amounts vary between 250 mm to 500 mm. In tropical climates, where the evaporation is rapid, grass will require 500 mm to 1000 mm.

Fig. 123 shows the distribution of natural vegetation throughout the world.

CLIMATE AS A FACTOR IN SOIL FORMATION

Soil is a mixture of inorganic and organic material at the surface of land areas of the earth that is capable of sustaining plant life. It is a layer of material that undergoes constant change and development, these dynamic processes which form soils being physical, chemical, and biological in character. Five natural factors influence soil formation—climate, relief, parent rock material, plant and animal life, and time. Of these factors climate is the most important. The physical and chemical processes are directly the result of climatic conditions, and the biological actions are indirectly caused by climate influencing both vegetation and animal life.

The various soil-forming processes combine to produce layers or horizons, and the mature soil is then said to have a distinctive profile. These profiles provide the means

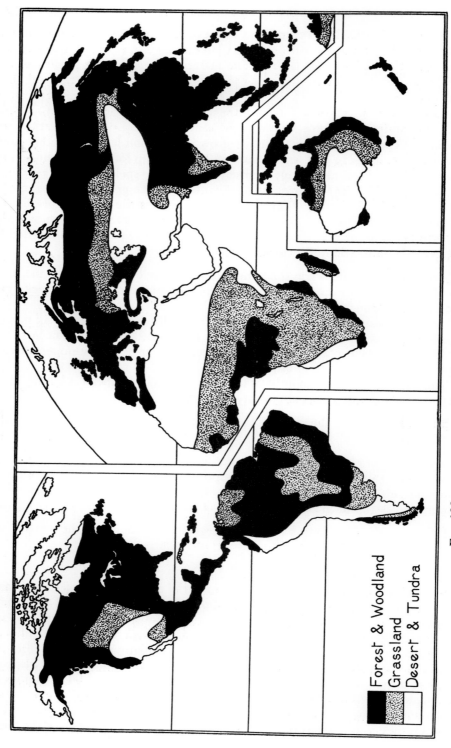

FIG. 123. MAP TO SHOW DISTRIBUTION OF NATURAL VEGETATION

Forest & Woodland
Grassland
Desert & Tundra

by which soils are identified and classified. Some soils, which develop under humid conditions where the prevailing natural vegetation usually is forest, tend to have thick B and relatively thin A horizons. The soluble materials on which the fertility of the soil depends are removed by leaching. Such soils are called 'pedalfers,' and they tend to be impoverished soils containing an overabundance of insoluble sesquioxides of aluminium and iron. Podsols and laterites are examples of leached soils. Soils which develop under conditions where there is a deficiency of precipitation are

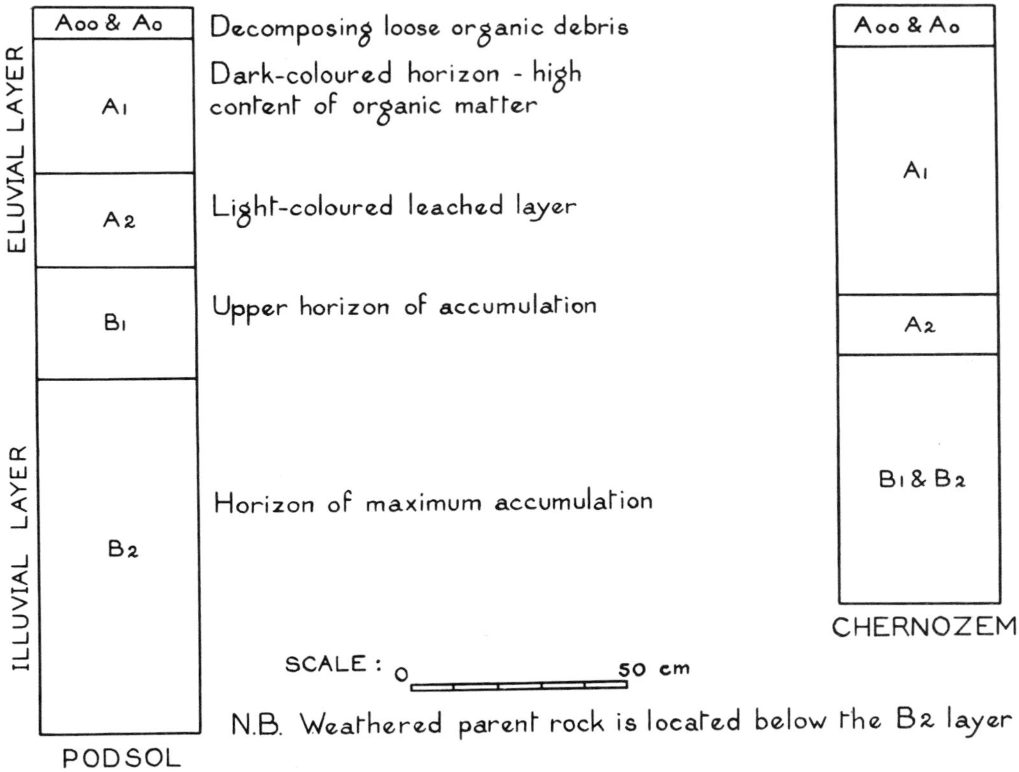

SCALE : 0 _____ 50 cm

N.B. Weathered parent rock is located below the B2 layer

FIG. 124. SOIL PROFILES OF A PODSOL AND A CHERNOZEM

called 'pedocals.' The climatic conditions are such that the soil water tends to seep upward by capillary action. The natural vegetation is non-forest in character, being grasses, bushes, and scrub. Chemically, these soils have retained all the soluble substances on which their fertility depends. Hence they are usually good soils. Chernozems, or black earths, are examples of pedocals, and in these soils the A horizons are much thicker than the B sections of the profile.

The importance of climate as a soil-forming factor is appreciated when one compares maps showing world climates, vegetation, and soils. It will be seen from the map showing the world distribution of soils that a very large portion of the earth's surface contains what may be described as naturally unusable soils for present-known techniques of cultivation. Mountain and desert soils cover a significant area of the

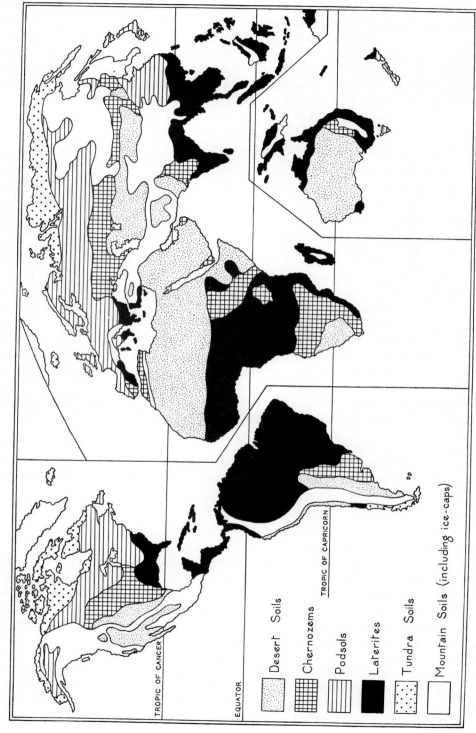

TROPIC OF CANCER

EQUATOR

TROPIC OF CAPRICORN

Desert Soils

Chernozems

Podsols

Laterites

Tundra Soils

Mountain Soils (including ice-caps)

FIG. 125. THE WORLD DISTRIBUTION OF SOILS

land surfaces. Even podsolic and chernozem-type soils are not always of great agricultural value: the former may be found in regions having an excess of rainfall and the latter in those areas having a deficiency of rainfall, so rendering them unsuitable for cultivation. Consequently soils must be wisely used by man. If he acts foolishly and accelerates the natural processes he becomes responsible for the rapid removal of these few centimetres of lifegiving materials.

CLIMATE AND AGRICULTURE

As climate largely controls the vegetation cover on the land surfaces of the earth, so it sets limits for crop production and pastoral activities. The main climatic factors affecting cultivation are exactly the same as those influencing all vegetation, but they must be considered in relation to the behaviour of man as an agriculturist. Man has cultivated crops in environments which are not exactly those for which the plant is naturally adapted. In many cases the plants could not survive without direct assistance from man. Agriculture is therefore a combination of processes designed by man to create favourable environments for growth. Perhaps it is true to say that economics is the only factor limiting these processes. We accept that if man is prepared to pay the price he can grow his bananas in the polar regions. But if we are to remain in the realms of practicability, then all crops have their climatic limits for economic production.

Similarly, the stock-raising of domestic animals is greatly influenced by climatic factors. Animals are completely dependent upon the availability of feedstuffs, and these latter are directly controlled by the climatic conditions prevailing. Additionally, all animal stock breeds have optimum climatic requirements. Climate directly affects the normal bodily functions of animals; for example, cows produce much less milk under high temperatures, and generally they suffer discomfort in heat just as man does.

Many of the restrictions on cultivation and stock-raising can be pathological— that is, they result from bacterial diseases and insect pests. Here again climate exerts an indirect influence because insects and disease-producing organisms have very narrow climatic limits for full development.

CLIMATE AND MAN

Climate probably affects man as an individual more than any other element of his physical environment. His health, energy, comfort, and perhaps his mental vigour and emotional outlook are all conditioned by the state of the weather and climate. Nevertheless, by virtue of his cultural advancement, man shows considerable adaptability to climatic conditions. Climate may be a limiting factor in his actions, and it is unquestionably a factor in his efficiency, but care must be taken not to overstress the influence of climate on man's activities, particularly those which indicate his failures.

Of the climatic elements which affect the human body, the most important ones are temperature, sunshine, and humidity. If man were cold-blooded his responses to changes in temperature would be very different. However, man is warm-blooded, and he must always keep his body temperature at a reasonably constant figure

(36·9° C). The main source of heat to maintain this temperature is food. Over 80 per cent. of energy produced from food intake is used for this purpose, the remaining 20 per cent. being utilized in muscular activity. Foods vary in their heating capacity, fats providing over twice as much heat value per unit quantity as carbohydrates. For example, 1 oz (28·4 g) of fat will provide 1150 joules, whereas the same quantity of carbohydrates will give 500 joules. It becomes evident, therefore, that man will find it necessary to adjust his intake of food and diet to the temperature conditions in which he finds himself. The Eskimo's diet consists of a much greater proportion of fatty foods, whereas the inhabitants of the tropical climates have a diet almost exclusively of starchy carbohydrate foods, such as rice, yams, and manioc. The starch provides the body with the energy for muscular action without that for body heat.

However, man does possess certain body mechanisms which allow him to regulate his temperature in climatic conditions which tend to upset his heat balance. The human body can lose heat in a variety of ways:

1. His body loses heat by radiation all the time.
2. He may lose heat by convection of the air in contact with the skin.
3. He loses heat by evaporation of perspiration from the skin. The body is always losing heat in this manner, but it is not until the temperature of the skin reaches 26·5° C that perspiration becomes visible as beads of liquid.

When the air temperature is in excess of 33·5° C the air is then a warming agent, and evaporation is the only way of getting rid of body heat. During the Second World War the Americans conducted research into man's water requirements under high-temperature conditions and found that a soldier carrying out normal military duties in a temperature of 38° C required a minimum of three-quarters of a pint of water every hour. It is easy to appreciate the logistics involved in supplying a military force with adequate water whilst it is fighting in hot desert conditions.

In cold weather loss of heat takes place by radiation and convection. Wind will naturally increase the effect of cold. The body's involuntary reaction to serious loss of heat is a muscular spasm which is termed 'shivering.'

Air temperature is not in itself a completely reliable guide to the reactions felt by a human being, and one must try to assess the sensible temperature, which is governed by other factors, such as humidity. The degree of humidity directly affects the cooling processes of the body: if the temperature and humidity are high the evaporation of perspiration will be seriously impeded and the body will experience discomfort; if the relative humidity is low and the temperature remains high the sensible temperature will be reduced because the rate of evaporation is increased, and body cooling can take place.

It is obvious that a definition of the comfort zone in relation to temperature and humidity is difficult because it must vary with individuals and their living and social habits. However, it is apparent that everyone experiences discomfort when wet-bulb temperatures are in excess of 29·5° C, and most human beings would consider 15·5° C to be cool whatever the relative humidity. Man, by virtue of his capacity to reason, makes some limited adaptations to his climatic environment. He adapts his clothing to temperature changes, excessive sunshine, and precipitation. Indeed, as man enters more and more extreme environments—polar regions, high altitudes, and even space around the earth—he takes greater precautions to ensure that his clothing prevents his body from losing or gaining excessive amounts of heat. Aviators to-day use electrically heated garments for use in extremely low temperatures at 15 000 metres, and in regions of high temperature aircrew are provided with special suits fitted with air-ducts which allow a passage of air over the skin to assist evaporation of perspiration. Astronauts in outer space must be equipped with either a space capsule or space suit which provide a built-in earth-type atmosphere. In addition they must be protected from the effects of cosmic radiation.

The extent to which climate influences the physical energy and mental vigour of man is difficult to assess. It is a problem which has been considered by geographers since classical times, and in the nineteenth century the 'environmentalist' school of geographers were prepared to state categorically that man was a product of the geographical conditions in which he found himself. Doubtless it is true to say that the ideal air temperature for a clothed person to carry out muscular work is that which is conducive to the easy maintenance of the body's heat balance. 18·0° C has been suggested as the best air temperature, with a daytime humidity of 80 per cent. But this suggestion neglects to consider the age, state of health, and psychological differences of human beings.

Emotional behaviour is undoubtedly affected by changes in the weather. Variability of conditions is considered to stimulate physical and mental energy, but there are extremes of conditions which seriously impair man's mental efficiency. Thunder, dullness, and dreary grey cloud cover all affect man's emotions, and everyone knows how a pleasantly warm, sunny day gives us a complete sense of wellbeing and contentment. Seasonal changes of climate are also important; in Northern Europe man begins to feel some elation as the winter nights commence to draw out and the sun climbs higher in the sky with the approach of spring.

Climate and Disease

Amongst social and nutritional factors, climate also must be considered in the complex relationship between environment and disease. There are two basic aspects of climatic influence on disease: first, there is the relation of climate to disease-carrying organisms, and, second, there are the effects of climate and weather on man's resistance to disease.

Diseases fall into categories according to mode of development and propagation:

1. Those diseases associated with particular climates where the conditions favour the growth of bacteria and of other causative organisms. Bronchitis and rheumatic fever are almost exclusively diseases of cool temperate climates, whilst yaws and leprosy flourish in the tropics. Rheumatic fever, a complaint that is common in children, is a bacterial infection. Leprosy is caused by a bacillus which is transmitted from one human being to another in hot humid lands. Yaws is caused by a spirochaetic germ which enters the body through cuts and open wounds, producing open sores and ulcers.

2. The diseases associated with parasites which live in certain climatic zones.

Hookworm is a tropical parasite worm which lives in the human intestine. The eggs of the worms leave the body as excreta, and the larvae develop in the ground. They enter into man's lymphatic system through the skin of his feet and find their way into his bowels. The larvae require a temperature of more than 21° C and high moisture. Hence the disease is limited to those tropical climates between 36° N. and 30° S. where there is sufficient moisture in the ground.

3. Diseases spread by carriers which themselves live in specific climatic regions. The best-known example of a carrier disease is malaria, it being notorious because of its capacity as a great killer of man. In India there are over 3 000 000 deaths per year from malaria. The disease is due to a parasite, a unicellular organism which lives part of its life in the 'Anopheles' mosquito and part in man. At regular intervals the parasite 'Plasmodium' liberates toxins which have the effect of raising the body temperature. The life cycle of the parasite is complicated, and there are distinct geographical controls on the life of the organism as well as that of the mosquito. The climate that would be suitable for both parasite and mosquito is decided by temperature. At 14° C no development of the organism can take place, but at 14·5° C there is some commencement. The higher the temperature the speedier becomes the development. At 30° C the organism develops in seven days. If the development time of the Plasmodium is greater than the life cycle of the mosquito the malaria will die out. Thus it is clear that certain climatic conditions only provide the suitable environment for the development and propagation of malaria by the mosquito.

It is correct to say that no diseases are caused directly by climate. As has been shown, climatic conditions may allow certain disease-producing organisms to grow and flourish. But, in addition, climatic elements may significantly affect man's ability to resist disease. Climatic conditions may affect his body functions and his mental outlook so that his resistance to disease is altered. Man's resistance may be weakened by chilling, low humidity and dust conditions, smog and high-altitude low pressures. Conversely, his resistance can be greatly strengthened by fresh air, sunshine, and moderate humidities. Psychological ailments, which often lead to physical disorders, also result from certain climatic conditions.

The Relationship between Climate and Aspects of Man's Social and Economic Activities

Climate and Commerce. Research into the effects of climate on man's economic and commercial life is only now beginning to advance beyond mere descriptive lines of thought. Climate and weather undoubtedly determine fluctuations in sales of particular goods. Endless lists of examples can be given: the period of extreme cold in the winter of 1962–63 gave an immense boost to the supply of electrical and oil heating apparatus, and coal merchants' bunkers were quickly exhausted of supplies; the fine summer spell in 1964 encouraged greater sales of light warm-weather clothes, soft drinks, and ice-cream; the first cold spells of autumn make householders decide to order fuel supplies and to have heating appliances installed. In the motor-car age the first air frosts compel anxious motorists to fill their car radiators with anti-freeze solutions. Sudden storms bring trade to the suppliers of umbrellas, raincoats, boots, and the like. So one can go on, quoting examples which suggest a direct link between climatic and weather conditions and economic activities.

Climate and Communications. More than anything climatic conditions affect communications, and in Britain one is frequently made painfully aware of interruptions to road, rail, sea, and air services because of adverse weather. Icy roads, snow, fog, gales, and heavy rainfall all play havoc with the day-to-day activities in the country. They interfere with rail services and interrupt city life; even the farmers' daily cycle of activities can be seriously upset by snow and gales. Air communications are particularly vulnerable to the adverse conditions which weather and climate can produce. The very process of air navigation must take into account both meteorological and climatological phenomena that are experienced on the routes flown by the trans-world airlines. For example, the seasonal movement of the polar and intertropical fronts is of vital importance to the aviator. Not only does he become aware of the location of weather belts, but also he may take advantage of following winds in his flight-planning.

Climate and Housing. It is axiomatic that man builds a house to protect and shelter himself and his family from the climatic elements. He must concern himself with sunshine, rain, wind, humidity, and their seasonal variations. He considers the local micro-climatic conditions when choosing his site, and the materials he selects for his house are chosen specifically in an attempt to overcome many of the climatic disadvantages. Wherever possible, man favourably orientates his building with respect to prevailing winds, exposure, and sunlight.

The design of his house is conditioned by climatic elements. This climatic conditioning is evident in design features such as shape, layout of rooms, roof slopes, and overhang of eaves. The character of the precipitation and its seasonal distribution influences window design, roof overhangs, and the material used. For example, hail damage to roofs is often very great, hence, in climates where heavy hail is common, roofing materials must be resistant to the battering of the ice. Similarly, in regions of heavy snowfall roofs must be strong enough to support considerable weights of snow.

In recent years much more attention has been paid to house design, especially in Britain, which experiences such variable climatic conditions. Only when the country finds itself suffering extremes of temperature does its population realize the inadequacy of most British homes. Badly designed, ill-fitting windows allow cold winter draughts to enter the building; external drainage and water-supply pipes fracture in the freezing temperatures, and usually most of the heat supplied by the traditional open coal fire disappears up the chimney. In summer the same houses often become unbearably hot in the occasional heat wave.

Rarely, therefore, can site selection, orientation, materials, and design provide the perfect house having the desired indoor climate all the year. Thus some form of internal conditioning has become a feature of many modern homes. Central heating, double glazing of windows, insulation of roofs, and internal waste and water pipes are being fitted more extensively into British houses. In America houses are being artificially cooled in those areas where uncomfortably high summer temperatures are experienced, and in the overseas tropical humid zones Service personnel now live and work in air-conditioned and de-humidified buildings.

CONCLUSION

Man is already something of a planetary engineer, and everywhere one looks there is evidence of his own influences on the landscape. His scientific advances make it possible for him to effect a large measure of control over his surroundings, and, provided he is prepared to pay the price, his influences are almost unlimited. So far, however, his control over weather and climate is small. Experimental meteorology is a new science, but already, through his intelligence and inventiveness, man overcomes many of the handicaps of an unfavourable climate. Man's very development of civilization is due in very large measure to his success in overcoming the difficulties imposed by climate. All science is based on the belief that there is order in natural phenomena, and that, by research into the foundations, a finite set of laws will emerge. Perhaps man in his quest for the fundamentals of meteorological science will one day reach this finite. Then the control of weather and climate will become a reality.

Chapter 21

CLIMATIC CHANGES

No ONE who lives in Britain can deny the existence of diurnal and seasonal weather changes, and it is all too certain that the only constant thing about weather is the extreme variability. These weather changes which collectively make up climate are taken for granted, but what is frequently overlooked is the evidence which points to fluctuations in climate as well. Whilst climatic change during the life-span of one man is unlikely to be identifiable, fluctuations over generations and longer periods of earth history can be recorded.

The periods of time and the associated evidence of climatic change can be classified into three categories:

1. Periods of geological time in the order of millions of years. The study of climate over such periods is known as 'palaeoclimatology.'
2. Periods during the last few thousand years where climatic changes may be interpreted in terms of organic life of recent geological time. For this study the term 'geochronology' is used.
3. The historic period which may include documentary evidence of climatic conditions.

PALAEOCLIMATOLOGY

Developments in geological and stratigraphical techniques have provided considerable evidence of conditions in the past. In the Pre-Cambrian era, which lasted for at least three thousand million years from the birth of the earth until the first signs of organic life presented themselves, we are unable as yet to effect any palaeo-climatological calendar. However, it is possible to examine rock strata and fossil evidence much more closely at the beginning of Palaeozoic times, and as we approach recent geological time the available information becomes more abundant.

In the remote Palaeozoic times, some 500 million years ago, the aquatic form of most fossils is not very useful in identifying climatic types, but at the beginning of the Mesozoic era the greater development of organic life allows the palaeoclimatologist to distinguish both temperate and tropical types. However, palaeoclimatology is primarily based on the nature of rock strata. Coal measures indicate tropical forest vegetation, coral limestones were laid down in tropical warm waters, and boulder clay represents the evidence of glacial climates.

To explain climatic changes since Cambrian times several theories have been developed. They may be classified as either geographical or astronomical.

Geographical Theories. The simplest theory attempts to explain climatic changes in geological time in terms of conspicuous variations in the amount of solar energy received by the earth. The change in receipt of insolation may have been due to a change in the amount of energy released by the sun itself. In other words, the solar constant changed. Alternatively, activities on the earth may have significantly

TABLE 19.—THE GEOLOGICAL TIME SCALE

Eras	Geological Periods or Systems	Derivation of the Name	Approximate Duration (in years)	Thickness of Strata (in metres)	Orogenic or Mountain-building Movements	Conditions and Distinctive Life in the British Isles	Approximate Date (in years)
QUATERNARY	Recent or Holocene Pleistocene	Holos—whole Pleistos—most ('cene' from Kainos—new; refers to the abundance of modern fossil shell types)	10 000 1 000 000	900		Post-glacial; milder climate; *Homo sapiens*; Glaciation of N. Europe and N. America; arctic fauna and flora; mammoth, woolly rhinoceros; early man. Interglacial periods: cool temperate fauna and flora in N. Europe	1 000 000
TERTIARY or CAINOZOIC (Kainos—new; Zoé—life)	Pliocene	Pleion—more	15 000 000	3600		Some mountain-building; climate cooling with approach of Pleistocene Ice Age; apes and hominid creatures; elephants and hoofed animals are numerous	16 000 000
	Miocene	Meion—less	20 000 000	6000	ALPINE	Modern world mountain chains created affecting south-east England; some volcanic activity off north-west Britain; warm climate, forests give way to grassland; modern mammals flourish	36 000 000
	Oligocene	Oligos—few	10 000 000	4500		Commencement of mountain-building; warm temperate climate; beginning of modern mammals and flowering plants; modern insects	46 000 000
	Eocene	Eos—dawn	20 000 000	4500		Basaltic lava flows over chalk in Antrim; very warm climate; primitive forms of mammalian life. Tranquil marine conditions over much of south-east England	65 000 000
SECONDARY or MESOZOIC The Age of Reptiles (Mesos—middle)	Cretaceous	Creta—chalk	55 000 000	21 000		Dry, mild climate; dinosaurs dominant at the beginning of period, but die out towards end; ammonites die out during this period. Primitive forms of flowering plants and insects; mammals developing	120 000 000
	Jurassic	Jura mountains in Europe	30 000 000	6000		Very warm climate; many reptiles developing; crabs and ammonites abundant; first birds and mammals appear	150 000 000
	Triassic (including Rhaetic)	Based on the threefold division of Central Europe	40 000 000	7500		Dry desert climate; ferns and cycads develop as scale trees die out. First air and sea reptiles develop	190 000 000

Era	Period	Derivation of name	Duration (years)	Thickness	Mountain building	Climate and Life	Years ago
PRIMARY or PALAEOZOIC — The Age of Invertebrates (Palaios—ancient)	Permian	The ancient kingdom of Permia near the Volga river	30 000 000	3600	ARMORICAN or HERGYNIAN	Dry-warm climate; reptiles and fishes appear; primitive coniferous trees. Mountain-building at beginning of period	220 000 000
	Carboniferous	Coal-bearing	60 000 000	12 000		Warm tropical climate, becoming damper towards end of the period. Shallow seas at first with coral reefs; small amphibians on the land; upper strata indicate vast forests of ferns, scale trees, and large amphibians	280 000 000
	Devonian or Old Red Sandstone	Devon where marine sediments are located	40 000 000	12 000		Warm sub-tropical climate; earth movements and volcanic activity; spread of primitive plants; fishes and cephalopods in the seas	320 000 000
	Silurian	Ancient Welsh tribe called the Silures	30 000 000	4500	CALEDONIAN	Tropical conditions; shallow seas in which corals, crinoids, and molluscs abound; primitive fishes; first primitive plants. Orogenic uplift begins at end of period and spreads into next system	350 000 000
	Ordovician	Ancient tribe of North Wales—the Ordovices	50 000 000	12 000		Warm climate; a period of marine transgression; first fishes and corals; invertebrates become more varied; plant life consisted mainly of sea-weeds	400 000 000
	Cambrian	Cambria was the Roman name for Wales	100 000 000	12 000		Tropical and sub-tropical climate; large number of invertebrates came into existence; plant life only of calcareous algae types. Is that period first providing abundant fossils	500 000 000
PRE-CAMBRIAN	Pre-Cambrian: 1. Proterozoic 2. Archaeozoic 3. Azoic	Proteros—earlier Archaeos—primaeval Azoos—lifeless	These periods cover the time interval between the formation of the first rocks and the Cambrian system, estimated to be more than 2 000 000 000 years		CHARNIAN 600 000 000 years KARELIAN 800 000 000 years MAREALBIAN 1 600 000 000 years	Life must have originated in the warm seas of late Pre-Cambrian times. Scanty evidence is in the form of fossil sponges and sea-weeds. The land crust formed early in this era and the water vapour condensed as rain	2 500 000 000
	Origin of the Earth—estimated to be at least 4 500 000 000 years ago						3 500 000 000 +

changed the amount of solar radiation which reached the surface of the globe. Variations in the amount of dust, volcanic ash, or atmospheric gases such as carbon dioxide and ozone would result in corresponding variations of the amount of insolation reaching the earth's surface.

The assumption that the radiation output from the sun has changed periodically so as to produce climatic fluctuations throughout geological history cannot be proved, and therefore cannot be regarded as satisfactory. However, if other known observable factors can be found which explain simply the fluctuation of climate they are to be preferred. Certain geological evidence does provide more positive lines of thought.

One of the more controversial geographical theories to explain palaeoclimatological change is that of continental drift. Changes in the world distribution of land and ocean areas on the surface of the earth have occurred throughout geological time. Whilst most geographers and geologists will accept the general principle of continental drift, based on direct geological evidence, they are by no means in agreement on the earth mechanisms which have brought about these movements. If continental surfaces are recognized as always having been such and as having, throughout geological history, migrated over the surface of the earth, then the theory appears to supply the key to most palaeoclimates.

Changes in the elevation of the land in the geological past may also have been responsible for climatological changes. It has been described how temperature decreases with altitude. If similar lapse rates prevailed in past geological eras, then changes in the elevation of land, associated with either orogenic movements or erosional processes, might be directly responsible for alterations in both climate and vegetation cover.

Astronomical Theories. Four principal known astronomical factors exist which can be described as possible explanations of palaeoclimatological change:

(*a*) *Changes in the Obliquity of the Ecliptic.* At present the earth's axis is vertically displaced by $23\frac{1}{2}°$ from the plane of the ecliptic. This means that the earth, revolving along its path round the sun throughout the year, is inclined at this angle to the orbit. The seasons are the direct result of this fact. Therefore if there had been astronomical changes in the angle which the earth's axis makes with the plane of the ecliptic there would also have been changes in the seasons. A decrease in the obliquity of the ecliptic (compared with the present $23\frac{1}{2}°$) would diminish the seasonal differences, but would certainly increase the distinction of climatic zones. On the other hand, an increase in the angle would result in marked seasonal differences, but geographical zones would disappear.

(*b*) *Changes in the Eccentricity of the Earth's Orbit.* A second element which, by its fluctuations, influences the receipt of solar radiation by the earth is the eccentricity of the orbit. The earth moves round the sun in an elliptical orbit, the sun occupying one focus of that ellipse. It is easy to understand that it is the sun's distance from the centre of the ellipse that controls the distance of the earth from the sun at different times of the year and the length of the four seasons.

Because the sun is not located in the centre of the orbit, there is a time of the year when the earth is nearer to the sun than during the remainder of the year. Perihelion, the point of the orbit when the earth is nearest to the sun, occurs on January 4th, and aphelion, when the earth is farthest from the sun, is July 4th. In the Northern Hemisphere the summer portion of the orbit is thus longer than the winter portion: the summer half of the year in the Northern Hemisphere is at present $7\frac{1}{2}$ days longer than the winter half.

Clearly, the smaller the eccentricity of the elliptical orbit the smaller will be the differences in the length of the seasons, and the greater the eccentricity the greater will be the variation between the seasons. Astronomers have calculated that the eccentricity fluctuates, having a period of 92 000 years. Therefore in about 50 000 years the earth, in its orbit, will be nearest to the sun in July and not January as at present. There is a good astronomical reason, consequently, why the summers in the Northern Hemisphere may become warmer and the winters colder during the next 50 000 years.

(c) *The Precession of the Equinoxes.* Evidence shows that there is a gradual migration of the four cardinal seasonal points (spring and autumn equinoxes and the winter and summer solstices) along the orbit. At present these seasonal points occur as follows: spring equinox—21st March; summer solstice—21st June; autumn equinox—23rd September; winter solstice—21st December. The angle which the earth's axis makes with the plane of the orbit is responsible for the change of noon-day altitude of the sun throughout the year. On the 21st of June the sun is overhead somewhere along the Tropic of Cancer, this date defining midsummer in the Northern Hemisphere. On the 21st of December the sun is overhead on the Tropic of Capricorn, this date defining midwinter in the Northern Hemisphere. The displacement of the four seasonal points will result in the migration of the seasons along the orbit.

The cause of the displacement is to be found in gravitational attraction between the sun, moon, and earth. The attractions of the sun and moon on the earth are unbalanced about the centre of the earth, owing to its oblate spheroidal shape. One part of the equatorial bulge, being nearer the sun or moon, experiences a greater gravitational force than other parts. This force can be represented as a primary force applied to the earth's axis, which, by reason of the gyroscopic effect of the earth's rotation, moves in a direction at right angles to the direction of the primary force. The effects of these forces are to produce a rotation of the earth's axis in a conical form, in much the same way as a spinning top wobbles with an uneven load. The complete cycle takes 25 800 years. It is thus within this period that the precession of the equinoxes influences the amount of solar radiation received by the earth.

(d) *The Movement of the Earth's Axis.* Theories have been put forward suggesting that the geographical poles have migrated to their present locations from what are now lower latitudes. The resultant effects would be a shift of climatic zones. However, all propounders of this theory neglected to consider the dynamical forces required to change the direction of spin of the earth. It is generally agreed, therefore, that movement of the poles on a scale sufficient to bring about important climatic changes is not very probable.

So far the explanation of climatic changes in the geological past has not advanced beyond the stage of theory. Suffice it to say that both the geographical and astronomical factors may well have worked together to produce the palaeoclimatical changes, the evidence of which is present in the sequences of rock strata and their incorporated fossil organisms.

THE PLEISTOCENE ICE AGE

Superficial geological materials, fauna and flora remains, all provide environmental evidence indicating that during the last million years or so of earth history large areas of the Northern Hemisphere have been subjected to periodic ice ages. The main divisions of the Pleistocene period in to-day's temperate Northern Europe are based on moraines and fluvioglacial deposits. The evidence derived from careful examination of these superficial layers and their associated organic debris shows that the ice advanced more than once and that in the intervals the climate was temperate and even sub-tropical.

Four major glacial periods can be distinguished—the Günz, Mindel, Riss, and Würm—the names being those of places where the glacial debris was examined in the Alps. The last glacial period ended about twenty thousand years ago, so we may be within one more interglacial phase. Whilst it is comparatively easy to assess geologically the duration of the interglacial periods, there is no means of estimating the duration of the glacial phases, since their intensity does not necessarily determine their length.

Very recently American scientists have been examining silt cores lying on the ocean beds. Like land deposits, the silt records the fossil accumulations of time, and it has been easy to recognize the deposits of the last glaciation. The American results indicate the four cold spells, but their dating, based on accumulations of silt at the rate of 2·5 cm per 1000 years, places the beginning of the Pleistocene Ice Age as early as 1 500 000 years ago. This suggests that the Ice Age may have in fact commenced before the end of Pliocene times.

GEOCHRONOLOGY

Before the more recent submarine geological surveys mentioned above, the longest and most authentic climatic record for the last few thousand years was found in cores extracted from silt and clay floors of lakes and ponds that annually freeze in winter and thaw in summer. *Varves*, as these accumulations are called, consist of sand, silt, and clay in a definite order. Each varve, averaging from 3 to 12 mm in thickness, has the coarser material at the base and represents that which settled during the maximum summer drainage. The fine clay at the top is that which settled out slowly during the winter.

Because of climatic fluctuations, no two successive years have the same thickness of deposits. Therefore dating of lake beds in the same region is possible by correlating the relative thickness of the varves. Furthermore, if all the varves could be counted from the time the ice of the Pleistocene period held its most advanced position, some light could be thrown on the number of years since the retreat of the ice. The technique of correlating varves was developed by de Geer in Scandinavia, and some 14 000 years are represented in varve records. In the United States varve analysis shows that some 5000 years elapsed during the retreat of the Würm ice-sheet a distance of four hundred kilometres in New England.

Another technique of geochronology is based on the annual growth of tree-trunks. Records of living and fossil trees allow for the construction of a chronology dating back nearly 5000 years. A close relationship between growth rings of tree-trunks and rainfall has been established. Analysis of ring growth therefore can give some clear indications of climatic conditions in the recent geological past.

Analysis of old soils which have been buried by more recent deposits also provides evidence of the nature of past climates, because climate is the chief factor in the formation of soils. Identification of pollen grains indicates the type of plants associated with a particular soil. The succession of plant types in peat deposits shows the climatic fluctuations that have occurred since the last glacial period. More recently, the radio-isotope methods for climatic study have been developed. The most important of these methods is the Carbon-14 process of analysis which is applicable to both animal and plant remains.

The table on pp. 248–249 shows how all these studies may be correlated with the cultural development of man.

CLIMATE DURING RECORDED HISTORY

During the period of written and recorded history evidence has accumulated which allows some analysis to be made of past climates. However, it is important to remember that many historical documents and manuscripts were written for purposes other than climatic description, and it is only by correlation with other records that a sound assessment of climatic change becomes possible. The very short period over which careful instrumental records are available (since 1850) does not enable any acceptable assessment of changes in climate to be made. Statistical records indicate certain fluctuations, but there is no reason to suppose that these variations are any different now from what occurred in late prehistoric times. It appears that fluctuations of some magnitude do develop, but, as far as it is possible to judge, these variations do not appear to fit into any obvious cycle.

However, the close correlations of historical descriptions with records of crop yields, failures, natural disasters, knowledge of migrations of people, and other archaeological material allow a chronological pattern of climatic change since the beginning of the Christian era to be created. Nevertheless care must be taken even here because fluctuations in Western Europe need not necessarily be comparable with those in North America. For example, American climatologists produce evidence which suggests that the eleventh century was warm and dry in North America, whereas certain British climatologists consider that Western Europe was at that time having a wetter period than usual. The accompanying table (p. 250) illustrates those climatic changes which are obtained from documentary evidence during historic times.

FORECASTING CLIMATE

It would seem logical that the extension of any proved cyclical trend in past climates is a forecast of future conditions. Unfortunately, so far no acceptable climatic cycle has been established. Certain years provide weather which departs from the normal (for example, the winters of 1946–47 and 1962–63 in Britain), and there is some slight evidence that the summer months tend to be cooler and wetter than those

248 METEOROLOGY AND CLIMATOLOGY

TABLE 20.—THE CORRELATION OF CLIMATES AND THE CULTURES OF MAN FROM PLEISTOCENE TIMES

Date and Glacial Sequence B.C.	Climate and Conditions	Flora and Fauna	Human Cultural Stage	Period	Geological Evidence
500	SUB-ATLANTIC: deterioration of climate: cooler and wetter with cloudy summers; more wind	Mixed forest	150. Belgae. Celtic agriculture. 300. La Tène. 500. Hallstatt	Roman. Iron Age	Surface soil, alluvium
	SUB-BOREAL: dry, frosty winters; warmer summers (continental type of climate)	Birch, alder, willow. Rapid growth of peat. Tree-line 300 metres. Birch and pine. Tree-line 1000 metres	Nomadic pastoralism. Upland settlement. 1800. Beaker folk	Bronze Age — Late, Middle, Early	
3000			Agriculture. Domestication of animals. 2500. Windmill Hill. Hunting and food-gathering	Neolithic— New Stone Age	
5500	ATLANTIC: warm, moist summers, mild winters. General cloudiness and windy	Oak, alder, lime replace pine and birch—mixed forest	3500. Azilian	Mesolithic— Middle Stone Age	
6500	LATE BOREAL: summers become steadily warmer	Birches, pine, hazel, more alder; oak and elm increase			
7500	EARLY BOREAL: continental climate; severe winters, becoming milder later	Pine dominant	7500. Maglemosian		
8500	PRE-BOREAL: gradual rise in temperature, followed by more rapid increase	Birch dominant; much grassland	8300. Sauveterrian		
9000	ARCTIC: (Late Dryas)—deterioration to very cold conditions; extension of Scottish mountain ice	Pine and willow			
10 000	SUB-ARCTIC: climate becomes warmer—associated with the Allerod oscillation	Birch forests			
POST-GLACIAL / 14 000	ARCTIC: (Early Dryas) named after plant of that name; ice sheet slowly retreating with brief halts and small re-advances; climate cloudy, damp, cold; with minor oscillations	Tundra and heath; some pine	12 000. Cresswellian (Modern Man) blade and burin culture		

Period	Climate	Fauna	Culture / Homo	Palaeolithic	Deposits
GLACIAL WURM III 25 000	Arctic conditions; southern England experiences peri-glacial tundra climate	Sub-arctic fauna: cave bear, fox, aurochs, mammoth, horse		Upper Palaeolithic	Coombe Rock in S.E. Hunstanton boulder clay Hessle boulder clay York Moraine Infilling of Thames deep channel Flood Plain Gravels
INTERSTADIAL 50 000	Sub-arctic or tundra climate; becoming colder towards end of the period	Tundra and steppe; fauna of cold variety; reindeer, woolly mammoth, woolly rhinoceros, arctic fox and hare, bison and horse			
GLACIAL WURM II 70 000	Arctic climate; loess steppe on south periphery of ice	Cave bear, cave lion, mammoth, reindeer, woolly rhinoceros, hyena	True *Homo sapiens*		
INTERSTADIAL 100 000	Temperate climate with minor cold oscillations	Sub-arctic forest fauna; lemming, musk ox	75 000. Mousterian—blade and burin culture 100 000. Aurignacian—blade and burin culture		
GLACIAL WURM I 120 000	Arctic conditions	Fauna which have adapted themselves to extreme cold: arctic bear, fox, woolly rhinoceros, great deer	*Homo neanderthalensis*	Middle Palaeolithic	Little Eastern Glaciation
INTERGLACIAL (Last) 180 000	Mild, temperate climate	Walnut, parkland; deer, caballine horse, mammoth	170 000. Acheulian VI—mixed core and flake culture		5 m raised beach Loams 15 m Thames Flood Plain terrace Taplow Terrace
GLACIAL RISS 230 000	Arctic conditions with one interstadial amelioration	Arctic fauna	230 000. Levalloisian—flake culture		Upper Chalky Boulder Clay in E. Anglia Coombe Rock in S.E. Great Eastern Glaciation
INTERGLACIAL (Penultimate) 400 000	Temperate and even warm temperate conditions; evidence indicates some cooler fluctuations	Monkey, mammoth, cave lion, bear, caballine horse, great deer, hippopotamus, bison	275 000. Acheulian I–V core culture *Homo sapiens* (Swanscombe) Clactonian		30 m raised beach in S.E. England Boyn Hill terrace in Thames Valley Brickearths of E. Anglia
GLACIAL MINDEL 475 000	2nd advance of Pleistocene ice and consequent arctic conditions	Arctic fauna: bear, hyena, horse, etc.	*Homo heidelbergensis*	Early Palaeolithic	Contorted Drift Kimmeridge Boulder Clay North Sea Drift
INTERGLACIAL (Antepenultimate) 500 000	Warm temperature with cooler interstades	Monkey, first woolly mammoth, small bear, hippopotamus, rhino	Abbevillian (Chellean) *Homo pithecanthropus*		Corton and Mundesley Sands Ambersham Terrace
GLACIAL GUNZ 600 000 +	Arctic climate which marks the beginning of Pleistocene period in geological history	Straight-tusked elephant gradually developing the curved molar and woolly coat. Many Pliocene fauna disappeared with onset of cold—*e.g.*, various deer, antelope, cheetah	*Homo australopithecus*—used pebble tools		Cromer Till Cromer Forest Bed Norwich Brickearth Sewerby beach

TABLE 21.—CLIMATIC FLUCTUATIONS IN BRITAIN DURING THE HISTORIC PERIOD

CENTURY A.D.	CLIMATIC CONDITIONS BY COMPARISON WITH THE PRESENT
1st	Relatively dry and warm.
1st–3rd	In Roman times the climate of Southern England was damper than at present, and, in general, the winters were colder.
6th and 7th	Drier and less stormy. There is evidence of a greater prevalence of dry, east winds.
8th–12th	Climate gradually became wetter and heavy rainfall is commonly described in the contemporary manuscripts. Marked cold spells occurred during the winters of the 9th and 11th centuries.
13th and 14th	These were centuries of great variability, but there is some evidence of storminess, mild winters, and high rainfall.
15th and 16th	Quieter, warmer conditions commenced the 15th century, but in Elizabethan times the climate as a whole turned colder. The winters became severe. Another period of storms occurred during latter half of 16th century. Glaciers tended to re-advance in the Alps.
18th	Climatic fluctuations were not very different from those of the present century. Winters were exceptionally severe towards the end of this century.
19th	Winters were in the main cooler than at present, whereas the other seasons show little difference from their present-day conditions. Nevertheless, there was an apparent change towards greater dryness in Southern England. From the middle of the century a general recession of the Alpine glaciers commenced.
20th to present	Climate tended to become more maritime at the beginning of this century, with milder, wet winters. Limited evidence suggests a change to more continental influences in the more recent winters.

of the early part of the twentieth century. From May 1975 to the end of August 1976 England and Wales experienced sixteen months when the precipitation was well below average, the southern counties receiving less than 60 per cent of their average rainfall. The drought conditions were the worst on record and then, from mid-June to late August 1976, much of the country was burned brown as, day after remorseless day, the sun shone from a cloudless sky. Finally, to make 1976 a year of extraordinary climatic extremes, the autumn was the wettest since records began in 1727. But these annual cycles do not permit acceptable forecasts for years ahead, and allegations of climatic changes in recent times which are based on yearly variabilities must be refuted. Until more knowledge is available of the variations in solar radiation at the limit of the earth's atmosphere it is unlikely that any direct information can be provided to support theories of climatic change. In any event, it is well to remember that forecasts of climate, like weather forecasts, can be verified only at the *end* of a forecast period.

APPENDICES

Appendix I

SPECIMEN QUESTIONS ON METEOROLOGY AND CLIMATOLOGY

METEOROLOGY

1. Write briefly on FOUR of the following: chinook, tornado, temperature inversion, depression, doldrums.

2. Summarize by means of a sketch-map the data provided by a daily weather report for any selected day and write short notes on the weather conditions illustrated.

3. Give an account of the life-cycle of a frontal low-pressure system.

4. What do you understand by FOUR of the following terms: relative humidity, intertropical front, dew point, condensation trail, hoar frost?

5. How is fog formed? Mention the general conditions and locations and illustrate your answer with diagrams and sketches.

6. Make a classification of clouds. Give a description of cumulonimbus clouds and account briefly for the conditions associated with them.

7. Give an account of the constituents of the atmosphere.

8. Write short notes on FOUR of the following: thunderstorms, mirage, cyclone, troposphere, pressure gradient.

9. What is meant by orographic rain? Illustrate, with reference to any two continents.

10. What meteorological instruments would you expect to find in a weather observation station at school? Briefly describe the workings of any TWO of them.

11. (a) State three ways in which rainfall may be caused.
(b) Describe briefly how rainfall is (i) measured, (ii) shown on rainfall distribution maps.
(c) Name (i) a region where rain is experienced in winter only, (ii) a region where rain is experienced in summer only, (iii) a region where rain is experienced at all seasons.

12. Illustrating your answer with diagrams, describe the following instruments and explain how they are used to obtain weather records: maximum and minimum thermometers, rain-gauge, wind-vane.

13. State clearly what you understand by THREE of the following: anticyclone, warm front, temperature inversion, relative humidity.

14. What are the following: dew, rime, snow-line? Discuss the various factors which influence the position of the snow-line.

15. Compare and contrast the weather conditions associated with the ridge and trough pressure systems.

16. Describe and explain the meaning of not more than SIX of the symbols used on the daily weather map issued by the Meteorological Office.

17. Describe the main types of cloud seen in the British Isles and indicate the weather conditions associated with them.

18. Explain the atmospheric conditions which give rise to each of the following forms of precipitation: rain, fog, snow, hail.

19. Describe the apparatus and methods used at a weather station for the measurement of temperature, humidity, and rainfall.

20. Explain, with the aid of diagrams, what is meant by a cyclone.

21. Describe three different types of cloud.

22. Explain what is meant by THREE of the following: temperature inversion, rime or hoar frost, lapse rate, katabatic wind.

23. Describe the mode of formation of dense fog. Give some account of its occurrence in the British Isles.

24. Describe any THREE of the following cloud types and the weather conditions with which each is associated: cirrus, stratus, cumulus, cirrostratus, cumulonimbus.

25. Comment upon the weather forecasts illustrated in the B.B.C. Television programmes.

26. "The technique of the weather map has changed considerably in recent years." Comment on this statement.

27. What do you understand by THREE of the following: rainfall regime, temperature anomaly, sea breeze, barometric gradient?

28. Write a short account of the observations necessary before the Meteorological Office can issue its daily weather forecasts.

29. Draw specimen isobars to illustrate the following: a trough, a secondary low, an anticyclone. Indicate the wind directions and describe briefly the weather associated with each pressure type.

30. Explain in meteorological terms the following weather sayings:

(a) "When dew is on the grass rain will never come to pass."
(b) "Clear moon, frost soon."

CLIMATOLOGY

31. Compare the characteristics of maritime and continental climates.

32. Describe briefly and account for the Mediterranean climate. Locate on a sketch-map those areas in the Southern Hemisphere which have a similar climate.

33. Some of the climatic records for three stations (A, B, and C) are given below. For each of the stations:

(a) Describe the climate and indicate the type.
(b) Name and locate a part of the world where the type of climate is found.

STATION	MEAN JULY TEMPERATURE (° C)	MEAN JANUARY TEMPERATURE (° C)	TOTAL ANNUAL RAINFALL (MM)	ALTITUDE (M)
A	26·5	26·5	2000	45
B	19·5	4·0	1100	45
C	13·0	13·0	1050	300

34. Explain (a) the differences between the annual temperature ranges at Winnipeg and Vancouver; (b) the differences between the total annual rainfall and seasonal distribution at Winnipeg and Vancouver.

35. (a) Distinguish between isotherm and isobar.

(b) Land-masses heat more quickly in summer, and cool more quickly in winter, than the seas. Discuss the effect of these facts upon the distribution of temperature over the Northern Hemisphere in summer and winter.

36. Discuss the general distribution of pressure and winds over land and sea in summer and winter and illustrate how the monsoons of India are related to the changes in this distribution.

37. Write short notes on the following: doldrums, south-east trade winds, föhn.

38. Discuss the nature and causes of seasonal variation in the distribution of rainfall on any land-mass in the Southern Hemisphere.

39. Define the word 'isotherm.' Account for the position of the winter isotherm for 0° C in the Northern Hemisphere.

40. Give an account of the winds and currents in the Indian Ocean in January and July and discuss the relationship between them.

41. On an outline map of the world show the distribution of areas which have a large mean annual rainfall (of 2000 mm or more) and areas which have a small mean annual rainfall (of 250 mm or less). Account for the distributions.

42. The excellent summer of 1976 has been attributed to the extension and persistence of the Azores high-pressure system over North-west Europe. Discuss this explanation.

43. On an outline map of the world show the distribution of areas which have a marked maximum rainfall in summer. Account for the distribution.

44. Describe the natural vegetation of tundra and equatorial regions and show how it is related to the climate.

45. On an outline map of the world show the distribution of areas which have a seasonal range of temperature of less than 14° C. Account for the distribution.

46. On an outline map show both the tropical and temperate grassland areas of the world. Compare the two types of grassland and show how each is related to the climate.

47. Describe and account for three different types of climate in South America.

48. By reference to the North Atlantic, show how the directions of ocean currents and prevailing winds are related.

49. On a world outline map show the distribution of equatorial forest. Describe the vegetation and show how plant growth is adapted to climate.

50. Compare and contrast the climates of Vancouver, Winnipeg, and Halifax (Nova Scotia).

51. Explain why the water which lies just off the coast of North-west Europe is the warmest for its latitude of any ocean in the world.

52. Give an account of the influence of ocean currents upon the climate of adjacent land-masses.

53. What do you understand by any THREE of the following: taïga, selvas, llanos, mallee. Locate one of these types of vegetation on a map and describe the climate associated with that area.

54. Why is it that the winters in northern Scotland (60° N.) are so much warmer than those in northern Labrador (60° N.)?

55. To what extent are ocean currents dependent upon the planetary winds?

56. Explain what you understand by a 'monsoon climate' and indicate the areas outside South-east Asia where it occurs.

57. Locate and account for the main fog belts of the world.

58. Outline and justify a classification of the climates within the tropical belt (23½° N. to 23½° S.).

59. What are the meteorological observations necessary before a report of the climate of an area can be compiled?

60. Select THREE of the following phenomena and give reasons for their occurrence in those areas in which they are common: hurricane, mirage, chinook, garua.

61. Differentiate between climate and weather.

62. Describe briefly the main rainfall regimes associated with the climates of the world.

63. Make a study of the climatic data for the following stations (A, B, and C). Describe briefly their regimes, state the type of climate which they represent and suggest, with reasons, a possible location for each. (Height may be ignored.)

STATION	—	J.	F.	M.	A.	M.	J.	J.	A.	S.	O.	N.	D.
A	Temperature (° C)	−0·6	−0·6	3·9	9·4	15·6	20·6	23·3	22·2	19·4	13·3	6·7	1·1
	Rainfall (mm)	84	84	86	84	86	86	104	109	86	86	86	84
B	Temperature (° C)	12·8	13·3	13·9	16·1	18·3	21·1	22·8	23·9	22·2	19·4	15·6	13·3
	Rainfall (mm)	130	107	122	69	43	13	0	3	36	84	163	140
C	Temperature (° C)	22·2	21·7	20·6	18·3	15·0	12·2	11·1	12·8	15·0	16·7	19·4	21·1
	Rainfall (mm)	91	112	125	137	130	122	127	76	74	74	71	71

64. What do you understand by the humidity of the atmosphere? In which parts of the world would you expect (a) low humidity, (b) high humidity? Explain why.

65. Explain, with diagrams, the formation of convectional and orographic rain. On an outline map locate regions which experience these types of rain.

66. Describe the climatic regimes of the following European towns and suggest possible locations. (Height may be ignored.)

Town	—	J.	F.	M.	A.	M.	J.	J.	A.	S.	O.	N.	D.
A	Temperature (° C)	1·1	1·1	2·2	5·6	9·4	12·8	14·4	13·9	11·1	7·2	3·9	2·2
	Rainfall (mm)	229	168	157	109	119	104	145	198	234	236	216	226
B	Temperature (° C)	7·2	8·3	10·6	13·9	17·8	21·7	24·4	24·4	21·1	16·7	11·7	7·8
	Rainfall (mm)	81	69	74	66	56	41	18	25	64	127	112	99
C	Temperature (° C)	−11·1	−9·4	−5·0	3·3	11·7	16·7	18·9	17·2	11·1	4·4	−2·2	−8·3
	Rainfall (mm)	28	25	30	38	48	51	71	74	56	36	41	38

67. Where are the hot deserts of the Southern Hemisphere? What factors determine their location and their extent?

68. The climatic statistics below refer to one of the following places: Perth, Dunedin (both at sea-level), and São Paulo (810 m). State, with reasons, to which place they refer, and indicate how the climatic statistics for the other two places would differ from those given.

—	J.	F.	M.	A.	M.	J.	J.	A.	S.	O.	N.	D.
Temperature (° C)	20·6	15·6	20·0	18·3	15·6	15·0	14·4	15·0	16·7	17·2	18·9	20·0
Rainfall (mm)	231	216	157	76	74	56	33	53	86	114	132	183

69. "Britain has no climate, but only weather." Discuss this statement.

70. Study the surface synoptic weather chart (see page 255) for 0600 hours GMT on the 16 December 1974 and answer the following questions:

(a) What types of cloud and present weather are reported at London and Cape Wrath?
(b) What type of air mass is affecting the extreme southwest of England?
(c) Locate by means of latitude and longitude a region on the chart where the pressure gradient is (i) steepest; (ii) most shallow.
(d) Suggest reasons why the surface air temperature at Madrid is below freezing.
(e) What type of front lies through Eire? Assume that this front is moving southeastwards at 25 knots. What will be the approximate time of passage of the front through Liverpool? What kind of weather do you forecast for the remainder of the day once the front has cleared Liverpool?

71. Study the surface synoptic weather chart (see page 256) for 0600 hours GMT on the 8 April 1975 and answer the following questions:

(a) Briefly describe the pressure pattern located over Northwest Europe. What type of air mass covers the British Isles?
(b) Using the synoptic weather information, describe the weather conditions at Lerwick in the Shetland Islands under the headings: surface air temperature, wind speed and direction, low cloud and present weather.
(c) What type of front runs from southern Scandinavia to central Germany?
(d) Is the air flow covering the British Isles stable? Quote all the relevant synoptic chart information on which you base your conclusion.
(e) Which part of the British Isles is likely to have the best weather during the remainder of the day? Give the reasons for your decision.

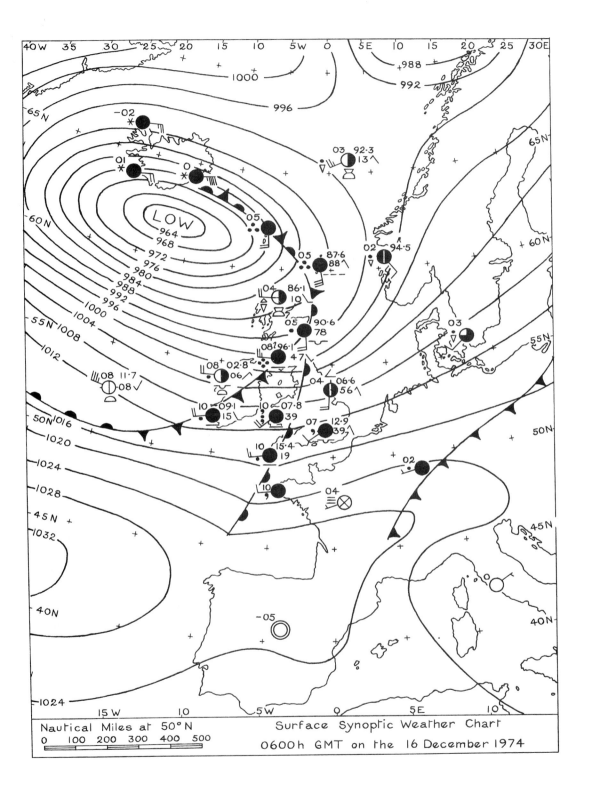

Nautical Miles at 50°N
0   100   200   300   400   500

Surface Synoptic Weather Chart
0600h GMT on the 16 December 1974

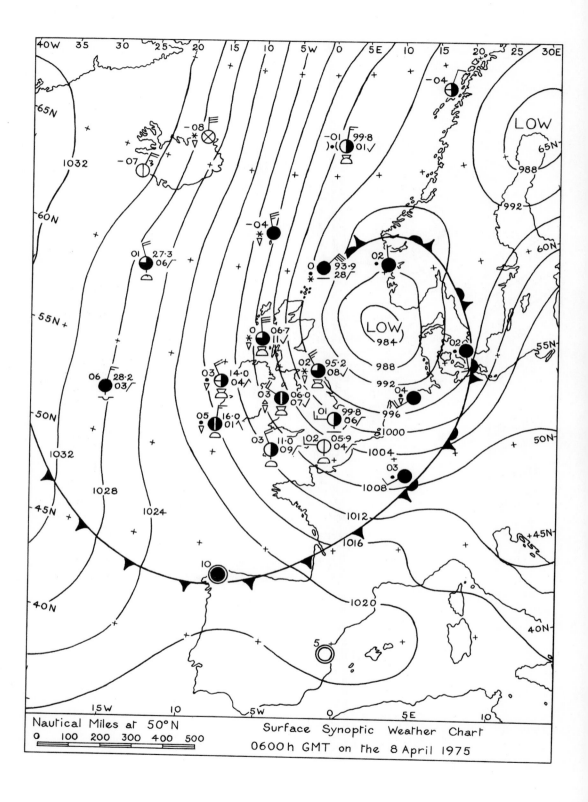

Nautical Miles at 50°N

0   100   200   300   400   500

Surface Synoptic Weather Chart
0600h GMT on the 8 April 1975

Appendix II

METRIC DATA CONVERSION TABLES

Imperial Units to Metric (SI) Units

Quantity	Imperial Unit	SI Equivalent*
Length	1 inch (in)	0·0254 m
	1 foot (ft)	0·3048 m
	1 yard (yd)	0·9144 m
	1 statute mile	1·6093 km

Note: 1 nautical mile = 6080 feet = 1853 metres

Area	1 square inch (in^2)	645·16 mm^2
	1 square foot (ft^2)	0·0929 m^2
	1 square yard (yd^2)	0·8361 m^2
	1 square mile (mile^2)	2·5899 km^2
Volume	1 cubic inch (in^3)	16 387·1 mm^3
	1 cubic foot (ft^3)	0·0283 m^3
	1 UK gallon	0·0045 m^3
Mass	1 ounce (oz)	0·0284 kg
	1 pound (lb)	0·4536 kg
Density	1 lb per cubic inch	2·7679 × 10^4 kg/m^3
	1 lb per cubic foot	16·0185 kg/m^3
Force	1 poundal (pdl)	0·1383 N
Pressure	1 lb per square inch	6894·8 N/m^2
Energy	1 ft pdl	0·0421 J

Note: 1 calorie = 4·1868 joules (J)

Velocity	1 statute mile per hour	0·447 m/s
	1 foot per second	0·3048 m/s

Note: 1 knot = 1 nautical mile per hour = 0·5144 m/s

Temperature	1 degree Fahrenheit (° F)	0·555 degree Celsius(° C)
	$t°$ F = 5/9 (t − 32) ° C	

* To four decimal places.

METRIC DATA CONVERSION TABLES—*contd.*

Metric (SI) Units to Imperial Units

Quantity	SI Unit	Imperial Equivalent
Length	1 centimetre (cm)	0·394 in
	1 metre (m)	3·281 ft
		1·094 yd
	1 kilometre (km)	0·621 miles
		(3280 feet)
Area	1 square metre (m²)	10·764 ft²
	1 hectare (10 000m²)	2·471 acres
	1 square kilometre (km²)	0·386 mile²
Volume	1 cubic metre (m³)	35·315 ft³
	1 litre	0·22 UK gal
Mass	1 kilogramme (kg)	2·205 lb
	1 gramme (g)	0·035 oz
Density	1 kilogramme per cubic metre (kg/m³)	0·062 lb/ft³
	1 gramme per cubic metre (g/m³)	0·036 lb/in³
Pressure	1 newton per square metre (N/m²)	$1{\cdot}4504 \times 10^4$ lb/in²
Temperature	1 degree Celsius (° C)	1·8° Fahrenheit

$$t° C = 9/5\ t + 32° F$$

CLIMATIC DATA FOR SELECTED STATIONS
THROUGHOUT THE WORLD

EUROPE (including MEDITERRANEAN, NORTH ATLANTIC, AND RUSSIA-IN-EUROPE)

STATION	ALTITUDE IN METRES		JAN.	FEB.	MAR.	APR.	MAY	JUN.	JUL.	AUG.	SEP.	OCT.	NOV.	DEC.	MEAN: YEAR
Ajaccio (Corsica) 41° 52′ N. 08° 35′ E.	74	T	8·9	10·0	11·7	13·9	16·7	20·6	23·3	23·3	21·7	17·2	13·3	11·1	16·1
		P	76·2	58·4	66·0	55·9	40·6	22·9	71·1	17·8	43·2	96·5	111·8	78·8	739·1
Archangel (U.S.S.R.) 64° 33′ N. 40° 32′ E.	6·7	T	−15·0	−14·4	−8·9	−1·1	4·4	10·6	13·9	12·2	7·2	0·6	−6·7	−12·2	−0·6
		P	30·5	27·9	27·9	17·8	33·0	48·3	66·0	68·6	55·9	48·3	40·6	33·0	502·9
Astrakhan (U.S.S.R.) 46° 21′ N. 48° 02′ E.	13·7	T	−7·2	−5·0	0·0	8·9	17·2	22·8	25·0	22·8	16·1	8·9	1·7	−3·3	8·9
		P	12·7	12·7	10·2	15·2	15·2	17·8	12·7	10·2	15·2	10·2	15·2	15·2	162·6
Athens (Greece) 37° 58′ N. 23° 43′ E.	107	T	8·9	9·4	11·7	15·0	20·0	24·4	27·2	27·2	23·3	19·4	14·4	11·1	17·8
		P	55·9	40·6	35·6	20·3	20·3	15·2	5·1	10·2	15·2	43·2	71·1	71·1	401·3
Barcelona (Spain) 41° 24′ N. 02° 09′ E.	950	T	8·9	10·0	12·2	13·9	17·8	21·1	23·9	23·9	22·2	17·8	13·3	10·0	16·7
		P	30·5	53·3	48·3	45·7	45·7	33·0	30·5	43·2	66·0	83·6	68·6	45·7	596·9
Belgrade (Yugoslavia) 44° 48′ N. 20° 28′ E.	138	T	0·0	1·1	6·7	12·8	17·2	20·0	22·8	22·2	18·3	13·3	7·2	1·7	11·7
		P	40·6	33·0	40·6	55·9	66·0	71·1	48·3	63·5	43·2	68·6	45·7	48·3	624·8
Bergen (Norway) 60° 24′ N. 05° 19′ E.	43	T	1·7	1·7	2·8	7·2	11·1	14·4	16·7	15·6	12·7	8·3	5·0	2·2	8·3
		P	200·7	152·4	137·2	111·8	99·1	106·7	132·1	185·4	233·7	233·7	203·2	205·7	2001·5
Berlin (Germany) 52° 27′ N. 13° 18′ E.	57	T	−1·1	0·0	3·9	7·8	12·8	15·6	17·8	17·2	13·9	8·9	3·3	0·6	8·3
		P	48·3	33·0	38·1	43·2	48·3	58·4	78·8	55·9	48·3	43·3	43·3	48·3	586·9
Birmingham (U.K.) 52° 29′ N. 01° 56′ W.	163	T	3·3	3·9	6·1	7·8	11·1	14·4	16·7	15·6	13·9	10·0	6·1	4·4	9·4
		P	73·7	53·3	43·2	55·9	63·5	45·7	71·1	68·6	58·4	73·7	81·3	66·0	754·4
Bordeaux (France) 44° 50′ N. 00° 43′ W.	48	T	5·6	6·7	9·4	12·2	15·0	17·8	20·6	20·0	17·8	13·9	8·9	6·1	12·8
		P	68·6	71·1	73·7	66·0	63·5	58·4	50·8	48·3	55·9	76·2	99·1	99·1	830·6
Brest (France) 48° 19′ N. 04° 47′ W.	17	T	6·7	7·2	8·3	9·4	12·8	15·6	17·2	17·8	16·1	12·8	9·4	7·8	11·7
		P	88·9	76·2	63·5	63·5	48·3	50·8	50·8	55·9	58·4	91·4	106·7	111·8	866·1
Brindisi (Italy) 40° 39′ N. 17° 57′ E.	10	T	9·4	10·0	11·7	13·9	18·3	22·2	24·4	25·0	22·2	17·8	13·3	11·1	16·7
		P	83·4	43·2	40·6	25·4	33·0	20·6	20·3	27·9	40·6	88·9	78·7	83·8	576·6
Bucharest (Rumania) 44° 25′ N. 26° 06′ E.	82	T	−2·8	−0·6	5·6	11·1	17·2	20·6	22·8	22·8	17·8	12·8	5·6	0·0	11·1
		P	38·1	27·9	43·2	40·6	63·5	96·5	58·4	45·7	38·1	40·6	48·3	38·1	579·1
Cambridge (U.K.) 52° 12′ N. 00° 08′ E.	12·2	T	3·3	4·4	6·1	8·3	11·7	14·4	17·2	16·1	14·4	10·0	6·7	4·4	10·0
		P	48·3	33·0	30·5	43·2	48·3	38·1	58·4	48·3	50·8	53·3	55·9	40·6	548·6
Copenhagen (Denmark) 55° 41′ N. 12° 33′ E.	13·1	T	0·0	0·0	2·2	6·7	11·1	15·0	17·2	16·7	13·3	8·3	3·9	1·7	7·8
		P	40·6	33·0	30·5	43·2	43·2	53·3	55·9	81·3	48·3	53·3	55·9	53·3	591·8
Corfu (Greece) 39° 37′ N. 19° 55′ E.	26	T	10·0	10·6	12·2	15·0	18·9	22·8	25·0	25·6	22·8	18·9	15·0	11·7	17·2
		P	160·0	139·7	93·9	78·7	48·3	25·4	7·6	17·8	63·5	175·3	160·0	200·7	1170·9

N.B. All temperatures are in ° C and precipitation is in millimetres.

EUROPE (including MEDITERRANEAN, NORTH ATLANTIC, AND RUSSIA-IN-EUROPE)

STATION	ALTITUDE IN METRES		JAN.	FEB.	MAR.	APR.	MAY	JUN.	JUL.	AUG.	SEP.	OCT.	NOV.	DEC.	MEAN: YEAR
CRACOW (Poland) 50° 04′ N. 19° 57′ E.	221	T	−2·8	−1·1	3·3	7·8	13·9	16·7	18·9	17·8	13·9	8·9	3·3	−1·1	8·3
		P	27·9	33·0	35·6	45·7	71·1	101·6	114·3	96·5	68·6	55·9	43·2	33·0	726·4
DIJON (France) 47° 16′ N. 05° 05′ E.	220	T	1·7	2·2	6·7	10·6	14·4	17·2	19·4	18·9	16·1	10·6	5·6	2·8	10·6
		P	48·3	40·6	48·3	50·8	58·4	68·6	63·5	63·5	53·3	73·7	71·1	58·4	698·4
FINISTERRE (Spain) 42° 53′ N. 09° 16′ W.	149	T	10·0	10·0	12·2	13·9	14·4	16·7	18·3	19·4	18·3	15·6	12·8	10·0	14·4
		P	101·6	48·3	86·4	53·3	63·5	33·0	22·9	38·1	53·3	83·8	109·2	127·0	820·4
GÄLLIVARE (Sweden) 67° 08′ N. 20° 40′ E.	315	T	−11·1	−12·2	−7·8	−2·2	5·0	11·1	15·0	12·2	6·1	−1·1	−7·2	−10·0	0·0
		P	43·2	27·9	25·4	30·5	38·1	58·4	76·2	73·7	53·3	58·4	45·7	38·1	568·9
GENEVA (Switzerland) 46° 12′ N. 06° 09′ E.	405	T	1·1	2·2	6·1	10·0	13·9	17·8	19·4	18·9	15·6	10·6	5·6	1·7	10·0
		P	48·3	45·7	55·9	63·5	76·2	78·7	73·7	91·4	91·4	96·5	78·7	60·9	861·1
GIBRALTAR (Spain) 36° 09′ N. 05° 21′ W.	3·4	T	12·8	13·3	15·0	16·7	18·9	22·2	23·9	25·0	22·8	20·0	16·7	13·9	18·3
		P	137·2	114·3	116·8	58·4	20·3	2·5	2·5	2·5	27·9	40·6	127·0	124·5	772·2
GÖTEBORG (Sweden) 57° 42′ N. 11° 58′ E.	16·8	T	−0·6	−0·6	1·1	5·6	11·1	15·0	16·7	15·6	12·8	7·8	3·9	1·1	7·8
		P	63·5	50·8	50·8	43·2	48·3	55·9	71·1	93·9	78·7	78·7	68·6	71·1	774·7
GRONFJORDEN (Spitsbergen) 78° 02′ N. 14° 15′ E.	7	T	−16·1	−17·8	−20·0	−14·4	−5·6	2·2	5·6	4·4	0·0	−6·1	−11·1	−13·9	−7·8
		P	35·6	33·0	27·9	22·9	12·7	10·2	15·2	22·9	25·4	30·5	22·9	38·1	297·2
HAMBURG (Germany) 53° 33′ N. 09° 58′ E.	20	T	0·0	1·1	2·8	7·2	11·7	15·6	17·2	16·1	13·9	8·9	4·4	1·1	8·3
		P	53·3	48·3	50·8	45·7	53·3	68·6	86·4	81·3	63·5	66·0	53·3	63·5	734·1
HELSINKI (Finland) 60° 10′ N. 24° 57′ E.	9·1	T	−5·6	−6·7	−2·8	2·8	8·9	13·3	17·8	15·6	11·1	5·0	0·6	−3·3	4·4
		P	55·9	43·2	43·2	43·2	48·3	50·8	58·4	58·4	71·1	73·7	68·6	60·9	701·0
INNSBRUCK (Austria) 47° 16′ N. 11° 24′ E.	582	T	−2·8	0·0	5·0	10·0	13·9	17·2	18·9	18·3	15·0	9·4	3·9	−1·1	8·9
		P	53·3	45·7	38·1	55·9	73·7	104·1	129·5	114·3	78·7	60·9	55·9	48·3	858·5
INVERNESS (U.K.) 57° 26′ N. 04° 13′ W.	74	T	3·3	3·3	5·0	6·7	8·9	12·2	13·9	13·9	11·7	8·3	5·6	3·9	7·8
		P	68·6	48·3	38·1	45·7	55·9	48·3	78·7	78·7	68·6	76·2	60·9	60·9	728·9
IRAKLION (Crete) 35° 20′ N. 25° 08′ E.	30	T	12·2	12·2	13·9	16·7	20·0	23·3	26·1	25·6	23·9	20·6	17·2	13·9	18·9
		P	93·9	76·2	40·6	22·9	17·8	2·5	2·5	2·5	17·8	43·2	68·6	101·6	487·7
ISTANBUL (Turkey) 40° 58′ N. 28° 50′ E.	18	T	4·4	5·6	7·8	11·7	15·6	20·0	22·8	22·8	20·0	15·6	11·7	7·8	13·9
		P	93·9	58·4	66·0	48·3	35·6	33·0	43·2	38·1	58·4	96·5	104·1	124·5	800·1
JAN MAYEN I. 71° 01′ N. 08° 28′ W.	40	T	−3·3	−5·0	−5·0	−3·3	0·0	2·8	5·6	6·1	3·9	1·1	−1·7	−2·8	0·0
		P	53·3	43·2	40·6	35·6	22·9	22·9	35·6	45·7	63·5	63·5	55·9	55·9	538·5
JUNGFRAU (Switzerland) 46° 33′ N. 07° 59′ E.	3580	T	−15·0	−13·9	−12·2	−9·4	−6·1	−2·8	−1·1	−1·1	−2·2	−6·1	−10·6	−13·9	−7·8
		P						Not available							238·8

N.B. All temperatures are in ° C and precipitation is in millimetres.

Europe (including Mediterranean, North Atlantic, and Russia-in-Europe)

Station	Altitude in Metres		Jan.	Feb.	Mar.	Apr.	May	Jun.	Jul.	Aug.	Sep.	Oct.	Nov.	Dec.	Mean: Year
Kaliningrad (U.S.S.R.) 54° 43' N. 20° 30' E.	7	T	−2·8	−2·2	1·1	6·7	12·2	15·6	17·8	17·2	13·3	7·8	2·2	−1·1	7·2
		P	43·2	33·0	35·6	35·6	48·3	60·9	76·2	88·9	78·7	66·0	55·9	50·8	673·1
Kharkov (U.S.S.R.) 50° 00' N. 36° 14' E.	144	T	−7·2	−5·6	−1·1	5·0	14·4	17·8	20·0	18·9	13·9	7·2	0·0	−5·6	6·7
		P	27·9	27·9	27·9	38·1	48·3	68·6	60·9	50·8	30·5	50·8	35·6	33·0	500·4
Kiev (U.S.S.R.) 50° 27' N. 30° 30' E.	183	T	−5·6	−4·4	0·0	6·7	15·0	18·9	20·0	18·9	13·9	7·8	1·1	−3·9	7·2
		P	33·0	25·4	40·6	43·2	48·3	66·0	78·7	58·4	45·7	45·7	38·1	38·1	561·3
Leningrad (U.S.S.R.) 59° 56' N. 30° 16' E.	4·9	T	−8·3	−7·8	−3·9	3·3	10·0	14·4	17·8	15·0	10·6	5·0	−1·1	−5·6	4·4
		P	25·4	22·9	22·9	25·4	40·6	50·8	63·5	71·1	53·3	45·7	35·6	30·5	487·7
Lisbon (Portugal) 38° 43' N. 09° 08' W.	95	T	10·6	11·1	12·8	14·4	16·7	19·4	21·7	22·2	20·6	17·2	13·9	11·1	16·1
		P	83·8	81·3	78·7	60·9	43·2	17·8	5·1	5·1	35·6	78·7	106·7	91·4	685·8
London (U.K.) 51° 29' N. 00° 00'	45·5	T	3·9	4·4	6·7	8·9	12·2	15·6	17·8	17·2	15·0	10·6	6·7	4·4	10·3
		P	50·8	38·1	35·6	45·7	45·7	40·6	50·8	55·9	45·7	58·4	63·5	50·8	581·7
Madrid (Spain) 40° 25' N. 03° 41' W.	668	T	4·4	6·1	8·9	12·2	15·6	20·0	23·3	23·3	19·4	13·9	8·3	5·6	13·3
		P	27·9	43·2	43·2	43·2	38·1	30·5	10·2	7·6	30·5	48·3	55·9	40·6	419·1
Majorca (Spain) 39° 34' N. 02° 49' E.	23	T	10·0	10·6	11·7	13·9	17·8	21·1	23·9	24·4	22·2	18·3	13·9	11·1	16·7
		P	35·6	40·6	38·1	33·0	33·0	25·4	5·1	20·3	63·5	58·4	71·1	55·9	492·8
Malin Head (Eire) 55° 23' N. 07° 24' W.	15·5	T	5·6	5·6	6·7	7·8	9·4	11·7	13·9	13·9	12·8	10·0	7·8	6·1	9·4
		P	101·6	63·5	60·9	58·4	53·3	68·6	93·9	81·3	96·5	106·7	99·1	99·1	1236·9
Marseilles (France) 43° 18' N. 05° 23' E.	75	T	7·2	6·7	7·8	10·0	13·3	16·1	20·0	22·2	21·7	18·9	14·4	10·6	12·8
		P	48·3	38·1	45·7	50·8	48·3	25·4	15·2	22·9	66·0	93·9	78·7	55·9	589·3
Matochkin Shar (Novaya Zemlya) 73° 16' N. 56° 24' E.	19	T	−17·2	−16·1	−20·0	−14·4	−6·1	0·6	5·6	5·6	1·7	−3·9	−9·4	−16·1	−7·2
		P	15·2	15·2	15·2	10·2	7·6	10·2	35·6	38·1	38·1	15·2	15·2	10·2	226·1
Milan (Italy) 45° 27' N. 09° 17' E.	104	T	1·1	4·4	8·3	13·3	17·2	21·1	23·3	22·8	19·4	13·3	7·2	2·8	12·8
		P	55·9	50·8	53·3	60·9	86·4	66·0	58·4	55·9	71·1	99·1	83·8	60·9	802·6
Moscow (U.S.S.R.) 55° 46' N. 37° 40' E.	154	T	−9·4	−8·9	−4·4	3·9	12·2	16·7	18·3	16·7	11·1	4·4	−2·8	−7·8	3·9
		P	38·1	35·6	27·9	30·6	55·9	73·7	76·2	73·7	48·3	68·6	43·2	40·6	629·9
Munich (Germany) 48° 09' N. 11° 34' E.	530	T	−2·2	−0·6	3·3	7·2	12·2	15·6	17·2	16·7	13·3	7·8	2·2	−0·6	7·8
		P	43·2	35·6	48·3	68·6	93·9	116·8	119·4	106·7	81·3	55·9	48·3	48·3	866·1
Naples (Italy) 40° 53' N. 14° 18' E.	67	T	8·9	9·4	11·7	14·4	17·8	21·7	24·4	24·4	22·2	17·8	13·3	10·6	16·7
		P	121·9	88·9	43·2	45·7	55·9	17·8	15·2	33·0	109·2	116·8	104·1	119·4	871·2
Nice (France) 43° 42' N. 07° 16' E.	12	T	8·9	8·9	11·1	13·3	16·7	20·6	22·8	22·8	21·1	16·7	12·8	10·0	15·6
		P	60·9	60·9	81·3	48·3	71·1	25·4	17·8	33·0	76·2	114·3	142·2	88·9	820·4

N.B. All temperatures are in ° C and precipitation is in millimetres.

EUROPE (including MEDITERRANEAN, NORTH ATLANTIC, AND RUSSIA-IN-EUROPE)

STATION	ALTITUDE IN METRES		JAN.	FEB.	MAR.	APR.	MAY	JUN.	JUL.	AUG.	SEP.	OCT.	NOV.	DEC.	MEAN: YEAR
NICOSIA (Cyprus) 35° 09′ N. 33° 17′ E.	218	T	10.0	10.6	12.8	16.7	21.7	25.6	28.3	28.3	25.6	20.6	16.1	12.2	18.9
		P	73.7	50.8	33.0	20.3	27.9	10.2	Tr	Tr	5.1	22.9	43.2	76.2	370.8
NUREMBERG (Germany) 49° 27′ N. 11° 03′ E.	320	T	−1.1	0.6	4.4	8.3	12.8	16.1	17.8	17.2	13.9	8.9	3.9	0.6	8.9
		P	38.1	30.5	33.0	43.2	55.9	63.5	78.7	78.7	53.3	53.3	48.3	43.2	619.8
OSLO (Norway) 59° 56′ N. 10° 44′ E.	94	T	−3.9	−3.3	0.0	5.6	11.7	15.6	17.8	16.1	11.1	6.1	0.6	−2.8	6.1
		P	43.2	33.0	35.6	40.6	45.7	60.9	73.7	96.5	63.5	73.7	58.4	58.4	683.3
PALERMO (Italy) 38° 07′ N. 13° 19′ E.	108	T	11.1	11.7	12.8	15.6	21.7	23.3	25.6	26.1	24.4	20.0	16.1	12.8	18.3
		P	127.0	91.4	66.0	43.2	20.3	5.1	2.5	40.6	30.5	93.9	99.1	88.9	708.7
PARIS (France) 48° 49′ N. 02° 29′ E.	50	T	2.8	3.9	6.7	10.0	13.9	16.7	18.3	18.3	15.0	11.1	6.7	3.3	10.6
		P	38.1	33.0	38.1	43.2	50.8	53.3	53.3	50.8	50.8	55.9	50.8	48.3	566.4
PRAGUE (Czechoslovakia) 50° 05′ N. 14° 25′ E.	202	T	−1.7	0.6	6.7	8.3	13.9	17.2	18.9	18.3	14.4	9.4	3.3	0.0	8.9
		P	22.9	20.3	27.9	38.1	60.9	71.1	66.0	55.9	43.2	30.5	30.5	22.9	490.2
REYKJAVIK (Iceland) 64° 09′ N. 21° 56′ W.	28	T	0.0	0.0	1.1	3.3	6.7	10.0	11.7	11.1	7.8	4.4	1.7	1.1	5.6
		P	101.6	78.7	76.2	53.3	40.6	43.2	50.8	66.0	78.7	86.4	91.4	93.9	861.1
ROME (Italy) 41° 48′ N. 12° 36′ E.	115	T	7.8	8.3	11.1	13.9	17.8	21.7	24.4	24.4	22.2	17.2	12.2	8.9	16.1
		P	68.6	58.4	38.1	43.2	50.8	25.4	15.2	22.9	68.6	93.9	96.5	71.1	652.8
SCILLY IS. (U.K.) 49° 56′ N. 06° 18′ W.	50	T	7.8	7.8	8.3	9.4	11.1	13.9	15.6	16.1	15.0	12.2	10.0	8.3	11.1
		P	91.4	68.6	60.9	55.9	55.9	43.2	55.9	60.9	60.9	88.9	93.9	88.9	825.5
SEVASTOPOL (U.S.S.R.) 44° 37′ N. 33° 31′ E.	23	T	1.1	2.8	4.4	8.9	14.4	19.4	22.2	21.7	17.8	13.3	6.7	6.7	11.7
		P	27.9	27.9	27.9	22.9	15.2	27.9	20.3	15.2	27.9	38.1	30.5	27.9	309.9
SMOLENSK (U.S.S.R.) 54° 47′ N. 32° 04′ E.	248	T	−9.4	−7.8	−3.3	3.9	11.7	15.0	17.2	15.6	10.0	7.2	−2.2	−7.8	3.9
		P	45.7	40.6	40.6	35.6	53.3	68.6	96.5	76.2	50.8	53.3	50.8	48.3	660.4
SOFIA (Bulgaria) 42° 42′ N. 23° 20′ E.	550	T	−2.2	0.0	5.6	11.1	15.0	18.3	20.6	20.6	16.7	11.7	5.6	0.0	10.0
		P	33.0	27.9	43.2	58.4	83.8	81.3	60.9	50.8	58.4	53.3	48.3	35.6	635.0
SOUTHAMPTON (U.K.) 50° 55′ N. 01° 24′ W.	20	T	5.0	5.0	6.7	9.4	12.2	15.0	17.2	17.2	14.4	11.1	7.2	5.6	10.6
		P	88.9	58.4	48.3	53.3	53.3	45.7	58.4	63.5	63.5	83.8	96.5	86.4	800.1
SPLIT (Yugoslavia) 43° 31′ N. 16° 26′ E.	128	T	7.2	7.8	10.6	13.9	17.8	22.2	25.0	25.0	22.2	16.7	12.2	7.8	15.6
		P	78.7	63.5	81.3	76.2	63.5	53.3	30.5	40.6	73.7	111.8	106.7	111.8	891.4
STAVANGER (Norway) 58° 57′ N. 05° 44′ E.	67	T	1.1	1.1	2.8	6.1	10.6	12.8	15.0	15.0	12.2	8.9	5.6	3.3	7.8
		P	104.1	73.7	60.9	60.9	48.3	63.5	81.3	116.8	119.4	129.5	116.8	109.2	1084.6
STOCKHOLM (Sweden) 59° 21′ N. 18° 04′ E.	46	T	−2.8	−3.3	0.0	3.3	9.4	13.9	17.2	15.0	11.1	6.1	1.1	−1.1	6.1
		P	38.1	27.9	27.9	38.1	40.6	48.3	71.1	78.7	53.3	53.3	48.3	48.3	568.9

N.B. All temperatures are in ° C and precipitation is in millimetres.

EUROPE (including MEDITERRANEAN, NORTH ATLANTIC, AND RUSSIA-IN-EUROPE)

Station	Altitude in Metres		Jan.	Feb.	Mar.	Apr.	May	Jun.	Jul.	Aug.	Sep.	Oct.	Nov.	Dec.	Mean: Year
STRASBOURG (France) 48° 35' N. 07° 46' E.	142	T	2.2	2.2	6.1	10.0	15.0	17.8	19.4	18.9	16.1	10.0	5.0	2.2	10.6
		P	40.6	35.6	43.2	66.0	66.0	78.7	86.4	86.4	78.7	68.6	50.8	48.3	749.3
THORSHAVN (Faeroes) 62° 02' N. 06° 45' W.	25	T	2.8	2.8	2.8	4.4	6.7	8.9	11.1	10.6	8.9	6.7	4.4	3.3	6.7
		P	167.6	132.1	121.9	91.4	86.4	63.5	78.7	88.9	119.4	149.8	160.0	167.6	1427.5
TOULOUSE (France) 43° 33' N. 01° 23' E.	164	T	5.0	6.7	8.9	11.7	15.0	18.9	21.1	21.1	18.3	13.9	8.9	6.1	12.8
		P	48.3	43.2	58.4	68.6	73.7	60.9	38.1	53.3	58.4	55.9	60.9	58.4	678.2
TROMSO (Norway) 69° 39' N. 18° 57' E.	102	T	-3.3	-3.9	-3.3	0.0	3.3	8.3	11.7	11.1	6.7	2.2	-1.1	-2.8	2.2
		P	104.1	96.5	83.8	60.9	53.3	53.3	58.4	73.7	119.4	114.3	101.6	99.1	1018.5
TRONDHEIM (Norway) 63° 25' N. 10° 27' E.	127	T	-3.3	-2.8	0.0	3.3	7.8	11.7	14.4	13.3	9.4	5.0	0.6	-2.2	5.0
		P	78.7	68.6	66.0	50.8	43.2	48.3	60.9	76.2	86.4	93.9	71.1	71.1	815.3
UPPSALA (Sweden) 59° 51' N. 17° 37' E.	24	T	-3.3	-5.0	-0.6	3.3	9.4	12.8	17.2	15.0	11.1	5.0	0.0	-2.8	6.7
		P	43.2	22.9	22.9	33.0	43.2	58.4	66.0	60.9	48.3	48.3	35.6	40.6	556.3
VALENCIA (Spain) 39° 28' N. 00° 23' W.	24	T	10.0	11.1	12.8	15.0	17.8	21.1	23.9	24.4	22.2	18.3	13.3	7.8	16.7
		P	22.9	11.1	22.9	15.0	17.8	33.0	10.2	12.7	55.9	40.6	63.5	33.0	391.2
VALENTIA (Eire) 51° 56' N. 10° 15' W.	9	T	7.2	7.2	7.8	8.9	11.7	13.9	15.0	15.0	13.9	11.7	8.9	7.8	10.6
		P	177.8	119.4	96.5	78.7	81.3	81.3	109.2	116.8	109.2	129.5	160.0	160.0	1419.9
VALLETTA (Malta) 35° 54' N. 14° 31' E.	71	T	12.8	12.8	13.9	16.1	18.9	22.8	25.6	26.1	24.4	21.7	17.2	14.4	18.9
		P	83.8	58.4	38.1	20.3	10.2	2.5	Tr	5.1	33.0	68.6	91.4	99.1	515.6
VAYGACH (U.S.S.R.) 70° 34' N. 58° 48' E.	11	T	-16.1	-16.7	-18.3	-12.8	-5.6	1.1	5.6	6.7	3.3	-1.7	-7.2	-13.3	-6.1
		P	7.6	5.1	5.1	5.1	7.6	17.8	27.9	33.0	33.0	20.3	10.2	10.2	182.9
VIENNA (Austria) 48° 15' N. 16° 22' E.	202	T	-1.1	0.6	4.4	9.4	14.4	17.2	19.4	18.3	15.0	10.0	4.4	0.6	9.4
		P	38.1	35.6	45.7	50.8	71.1	68.6	76.2	68.6	50.8	50.8	48.3	45.7	650.2
WARSAW (Poland) 52° 13' N. 21° 02' E.	120	T	-3.9	-2.8	1.1	7.8	11.1	16.7	18.3	17.8	11.1	8.3	2.2	-2.2	7.8
		P	30.5	27.9	33.0	38.1	48.3	66.0	76.2	76.2	48.3	43.2	35.6	35.6	558.8

N.B. All temperatures are in ° C and precipitation is in millimetres.

Asia (including Asia Minor)

Station	Altitude in Metres		Jan.	Feb.	Mar.	Apr.	May	Jun.	Jul.	Aug.	Sep.	Oct.	Nov.	Dec.	Mean: Year
ADANA (Turkey) 36°59'N. 35°18'E.	25	T	8·9	10·0	12·8	17·2	21·7	25·0	27·8	28·3	25·6	21·7	16·7	11·1	18·9
		P	109·2	101·6	63·5	40·6	50·8	17·8	5·1	5·1	17·8	48·3	60·9	96·5	617·2
AKYAB (Burma) 20°08'N. 92°55'E.	9	T	21·1	22·8	25·6	28·3	28·9	27·8	27·2	27·2	27·8	27·8	25·6	22·2	26·1
		P	2·5	5·1	10·2	50·8	391·2	1150·6	1399·5	1132·8	576·6	287·0	129·5	17·8	5153·7
ALMA ATA (U.S.S.R.) 43°16'N. 76°53'E.	776	T	−9·4	−8·3	−1·1	8·3	15·0	18·9	21·1	20·0	15·0	7·2	−0·6	−5·6	7·2
		P	33·0	22·9	55·9	101·6	93·9	66·0	35·6	30·5	25·4	50·8	48·3	33·0	596·9
AMBOINA (Indonesia) 03°42'S. 128°10'E.	4	T	27·8	27·8	27·8	27·2	26·1	25·6	25·0	25·0	25·6	26·1	27·8	27·8	26·7
		P	127·0	119·4	134·6	279·4	515·6	637·5	601·9	401·3	241·3	154·9	114·3	132·1	3459·5
ANKARA (Turkey) 39°57'N. 32°53'E.	862	T	0·0	1·1	5·0	11·1	16·1	18·3	22·8	22·8	18·3	13·3	8·3	2·2	11·7
		P	33·0	30·5	33·0	33·0	48·3	25·4	12·7	10·2	17·8	22·9	30·5	48·3	345·4
ASHKHABAD (U.S.S.R.) 37°57'N. 58°23'E.	226	T	0·0	3·9	8·3	15·0	18·9	26·1	28·9	24·4	22·2	15·0	8·9	4·4	15·0
		P	25·4	20·3	48·3	35·6	30·5	7·6	2·5	2·5	2·5	12·7	20·3	17·8	226·1
AS SULMAN (Iraq) 30°28'N. 44°43'E.	202	T	10·0	12·8	15·0	21·1	27·8	30·6	33·3	33·3	30·0	25·6	19·4	12·8	22·8
		P	2·5	10·2	2·5	17·8	Tr	0·0	0·0	0·0	0·0	5·1	Tr	15·2	58·4
BAGHDAD (Iraq) 33°20'N. 44°24'E.	34	T	10·0	11·7	15·0	21·7	27·8	31·7	33·9	33·9	30·6	24·4	17·8	11·7	22·8
		P	22·9	25·4	27·9	12·7	2·5	Tr	Tr	0·0	0·0	2·5	20·3	25·4	139·7
BAHREIN (Arabia) 26°12'N. 50°30'E.	5·5	T	19·4	18·3	20·6	25·0	29·4	31·7	33·3	33·9	31·7	27·8	23·9	18·3	25·6
		P	7·6	17·8	12·7	7·6	Tr	0·0	0·0	0·0	Tr	0·0	17·8	17·8	81·3
BANGKOK (Thailand) 13°45'N. 100°28'E.	2	T	25·6	27·8	28·9	30·0	29·4	28·3	28·3	28·3	27·8	27·2	26·1	25·0	27·8
		P	7·6	20·3	35·6	58·4	198·1	160·0	160·0	175·3	304·8	205·7	66·0	5·1	1397·0
BEIRUT (Lebanon) 33°54'N. 35°28'E.	34	T	13·3	13·9	15·6	18·3	21·7	24·4	26·7	27·8	26·1	23·9	19·4	15·6	20·6
		P	190·5	157·8	93·9	55·9	17·8	2·5	Tr	Tr	5·1	50·8	132·1	185·4	891·5
BOMBAY (India) 18°54'N. 72°49'E.	11	T	23·9	23·9	26·1	28·3	30·0	28·3	27·2	26·7	26·7	28·3	27·2	25·6	26·7
		P	2·5	2·5	2·5	Tr	17·8	485·1	617·2	337·8	264·2	63·5	12·7	2·5	1808·5
CALCUTTA (India) 22°32'N. 88°20'E.	6	T	19·4	22·2	27·2	30·0	30·0	29·4	28·9	28·3	28·9	27·8	23·3	19·4	26·1
		P	10·2	30·5	35·6	43·2	139·7	297·2	325·1	327·7	251·5	114·3	20·3	5·1	1600·2
CAR NICOBAR I. (Indian Ocean) 09°15'N. 92°48'E.	8	T	27·8	27·8	28·3	28·3	27·8	27·8	27·8	27·8	27·2	26·7	26·7	27·2	27·8
		P	99·1	30·5	53·3	88·9	317·5	314·9	236·2	259·1	327·7	294·6	289·6	198·1	2509·5
CHERRAPUNJI (India) 25°15'N. 91°44'E.	1320	T	11·7	12·8	16·7	18·3	18·9	20·0	20·0	20·6	20·6	18·9	15·6	12·8	17·2
		P	17·8	53·4	185·4	665·5	1280·2	2694·9	2446·0	1780·5	1099·8	492·8	68·6	12·7	10797·5
CHUNGKING (China) 29°33'N. 106°33'E.	230	T	7·2	10·0	14·4	18·9	22·8	25·6	28·9	30·0	24·4	18·9	13·9	10·0	18·9
		P	15·2	20·3	38·1	99·1	142·2	180·3	142·2	121·9	149·9	111·8	48·3	20·3	1092·2

N.B. All temperatures are in ° C and precipitation is in millimetres.

Asia (including Asia Minor)

Station	Altitude in Metres		Jan.	Feb.	Mar.	Apr.	May	Jun.	Jul.	Aug.	Sep.	Oct.	Nov.	Dec.	Mean: Year
Cochin (India) 09° 58' N. 76° 14' E.	3	T	26.7	27.8	28.9	29.4	28.9	26.7	26.1	26.1	26.7	27.2	27.8	27.2	27.8
		P	22.9	20.3	50.8	124.5	297.2	723.9	591.8	353.1	195.6	340.4	170.2	40.6	2928.6
Colombo (Ceylon) 06° 54' N. 79° 52' E.	7	T	26.1	26.1	27.2	27.8	28.3	27.2	27.2	27.2	27.2	26.7	26.1	25.6	27.2
		P	88.9	68.6	147.3	231.1	370.8	223.5	134.6	109.2	160.0	347.9	314.9	147.3	2364.7
Darjeeling (India) 27° 03' N. 88° 16' E.	2260	T	5.0	5.6	10.0	12.8	14.4	15.6	16.7	16.1	15.6	12.8	8.9	8.9	11.7
		P	12.7	27.9	43.2	104.1	215.9	589.3	797.6	637.5	447.0	127.0	22.9	7.6	3035.3
Delhi (India) 28° 35' N. 77° 12' E.	218	T	13.9	16.7	22.2	27.8	33.3	33.9	31.1	30.0	28.9	26.1	20.0	15.0	25.0
		P	22.9	17.8	12.7	7.6	12.7	73.7	180.3	172.7	116.8	10.2	2.5	10.2	640.1
Hankow (China) 30° 35' N. 114° 17' E.	37	T	4.4	5.6	10.0	16.7	22.2	26.7	30.0	30.0	24.4	18.9	12.8	6.7	17.2
		P	45.7	48.3	96.5	152.4	165.1	243.8	180.3	96.5	71.1	81.3	48.3	27.9	1257.3
Hiroshima (Japan) 34° 22' N. 132° 26' E.	30	T	3.3	4.4	7.8	12.8	17.2	21.1	25.6	27.2	23.3	17.2	11.7	6.7	14.4
		P	45.7	63.5	106.7	160.0	144.8	243.8	220.9	111.8	198.1	114.3	66.0	50.8	1526.5
Hongkong (China) 22° 18' N. 114° 10' E.	33	T	15.6	15.0	17.2	21.7	25.6	27.8	28.3	28.3	27.2	25.0	20.0	17.2	22.8
		P	33.0	45.7	73.7	137.2	292.1	393.7	381.0	360.7	256.5	114.3	43.2	30.5	2161.5
Hualienkang (Taiwan) 23° 58' N. 121° 36' E.	19	T	17.8	17.8	18.9	22.2	24.4	26.7	27.8	27.2	26.7	23.9	21.7	19.4	22.8
		P	50.8	91.4	129.5	129.5	281.9	165.1	302.3	185.4	276.9	215.9	86.4	53.3	1968.5
Hyderabad (India) 17° 26' N. 78° 27' E.	542	T	22.2	24.4	28.3	31.1	33.3	29.4	26.7	26.7	26.7	25.6	22.8	21.7	26.7
		P	7.6	10.2	12.7	30.5	27.9	111.8	152.4	134.6	165.1	63.5	27.9	7.6	751.8
Irkutsk (U.S.S.R.) 52° 16' N. 104° 19' E.	467	T	-21.1	-18.3	-10.6	-0.6	7.2	13.3	15.6	14.4	7.8	-0.6	-11.7	-15.6	-2.2
		P	12.7	10.2	7.6	15.2	33.0	55.9	78.7	71.1	43.2	17.8	15.2	15.2	378.5
Izmir (Turkey) 38° 27' N. 27° 15' E.	28	T	8.3	8.9	11.7	15.0	19.4	23.9	26.7	26.7	22.8	18.3	14.4	10.0	17.2
		P	111.8	83.8	76.2	43.2	33.0	15.2	5.1	5.1	20.3	53.3	83.8	121.9	647.7
Jerusalem (Israel) 31° 47' N. 35° 13' E.	758	T	8.9	9.4	12.8	16.7	20.6	22.2	23.9	23.9	22.8	21.1	16.7	11.1	17.2
		P	132.1	132.1	63.5	27.9	2.5	Tr	0.0	0.0	Tr	12.7	71.1	86.4	528.3
Kabul (Afghanistan) 34° 30' N. 69° 13' E.	1820	T	-2.8	-0.6	6.7	12.8	17.8	21.7	24.4	23.9	20.0	19.4	8.9	2.8	12.2
		P	30.5	35.6	93.9	101.6	20.3	5.1	2.5	2.5	Tr	15.2	20.3	10.2	337.8
Karachi (Pakistan) 24° 48' N. 66° 59' E.	3-4	T	16.1	20.0	24.4	27.8	30.0	30.6	30.0	28.3	28.3	27.8	23.9	20.0	25.6
		P	12.7	10.2	7.6	2.5	2.5	17.8	81.3	40.6	12.7	Tr	2.5	5.1	195.6
Katmandu (Nepal) 27° 42' N. 85° 12' E.	1334	T	10.0	11.7	16.1	20.0	22.8	24.4	24.4	23.9	23.3	20.0	15.0	11.1	18.9
		P	15.2	40.6	22.9	58.4	121.9	246.4	373.4	345.4	154.9	38.1	7.6	2.5	1427.5
Khormaksar (Yemen) 12° 50' N. 45° 01' E.	7	T	25.0	25.6	27.2	28.3	30.6	32.8	32.2	31.7	32.2	28.3	26.1	25.6	28.9
		P	5.1	Tr	5.1	Tr	Tr	Tr	5.1	2.5	Tr	Tr	Tr	5.1	22.9

N.B. All temperatures are in ° C and precipitation is in millimetres.

Asia (including Asia Minor)

Station	Altitude in Metres		Jan.	Feb.	Mar.	Apr.	May	Jun.	Jul.	Aug.	Sep.	Oct.	Nov.	Dec.	Mean: Year
Krasnoyarsk (U.S.S.R.) 56° 01′ N. 92° 52′ E.	152	T	−20·0	−17·8	−10·6	2·2	6·1	13·3	16·1	13·9	7·2	−1·1	−11·1	−17·8	−2·2
		P	2·5	5·1	2·5	5·1	25·4	35·6	30·5	53·3	43·2	22·9	12·7	10·2	248·9
Kuala Lumpur (Malaya) 03° 07′ N. 101° 42′ E.	38	T	27·2	27·8	27·8	27·8	27·8	27·8	27·2	27·2	27·2	27·2	27·2	26·7	27·2
		P	157·5	200·7	259·1	292·1	223·5	129·5	99·1	162·6	218·4	248·9	259·1	190·5	2440·9
Kuwait (Arabia) 29° 21′ N. 48° 00′ E.	5	T	12·8	14·4	18·3	23·9	29·4	32·2	35·0	35·0	32·2	27·8	20·6	15·0	25·0
		P	22·9	22·9	27·9	5·1	Tr	0·0	0·0	0·0	0·0	2·5	15·2	27·9	129·5
Labuan (Borneo) 05° 17′ N. 115° 16′ E.	18	T	27·2	27·2	27·2	27·8	27·8	27·8	27·8	27·8	27·8	27·8	27·8	27·2	27·8
		P	111·8	116·8	149·9	297·2	345·4	350·5	317·5	297·2	416·6	464·8	419·1	284·5	3571·4
Lhasa (Tibet) 29° 40′ N. 91° 07′ E.	3685	T	−1·7	1·1	1·7	7·8	12·2	16·7	16·1	15·6	13·9	8·9	3·9	2·8	8·3
		P	Tr	12·7	7·6	5·1	25·4	63·5	121·9	88·9	66·0	12·7	2·5	0·0	406·4
Madras (India) 13° 04′ N. 80° 15′ E.	15·5	T	24·4	25·6	27·8	30·0	33·3	32·2	30·6	30·0	29·4	27·8	25·6	24·4	28·3
		P	35·6	10·2	7·6	15·2	25·4	48·3	91·4	116·8	119·4	304·8	355·6	139·7	1270·0
Makassar (Celebes) 05° 08′ S. 119° 28′ E.	1·8	T	26·1	26·1	26·1	26·7	26·7	26·1	25·6	25·6	25·6	26·1	26·7	26·1	26·1
		P	685·8	535·9	424·2	149·9	88·9	73·7	35·6	10·2	15·2	43·2	177·8	609·6	2849·9
Mandalay (Burma) 21° 59′ N. 96° 06′ E.	77	T	20·0	22·8	27·8	31·7	31·1	29·4	29·4	28·9	28·3	27·2	23·9	20·0	26·7
		P	2·5	2·5	5·1	30·5	147·3	160·0	68·6	104·1	137·2	109·2	50·8	10·2	828·0
Manila (Philippines) 14° 35′ N. 120° 59′ E.	14	T	25·0	25·6	27·2	28·3	28·9	28·3	27·8	27·2	27·8	27·2	26·1	25·6	27·2
		P	22·9	12·7	17·8	33·0	129·5	254·0	431·8	421·6	355·6	193·0	144·8	66·0	2082·8
Medan (Sumatra) 03° 35′ N. 98° 41′ E.	23	T	25·6	26·1	26·7	27·2	27·2	26·7	26·7	26·7	26·7	26·1	26·1	25·6	26·1
		P	137·2	91·4	104·1	132·1	175·3	132·1	134·6	177·8	210·8	259·1	246·4	228·6	2029·5
Mosul (Iraq) 36° 19′ N. 43° 09′ E.	242	T	6·7	8·9	12·2	17·2	23·3	28·9	32·2	32·2	27·8	20·6	15·0	8·9	19·4
		P	71·1	78·7	53·3	48·3	17·8	Tr	Tr	Tr	Tr	5·1	48·3	60·9	383·5
Muscat (Oman) 23° 37′ N. 58° 35′ E.	4·6	T	22·2	22·2	25·0	28·9	33·3	34·4	33·3	31·1	31·1	30·0	26·1	22·8	28·3
		P	27·9	17·8	10·2	10·2	Tr	2·5	Tr	Tr	0·0	2·5	10·2	17·8	99·1
Nagasaki (Japan) 32° 44′ N. 129° 53′ E.	133	T	5·6	6·1	9·4	14·4	18·3	22·2	26·1	27·2	23·3	18·3	13·3	7·8	16·1
		P	71·1	83·8	124·5	185·4	170·2	312·4	256·5	175·3	248·9	114·3	93·1	81·3	1917·7
Omsk (U.S.S.R.) 54° 58′ N. 73° 20′ E.	85	T	−21·7	−18·9	−12·8	−1·1	10·0	15·6	18·3	16·1	10·0	0·6	−10·6	−18·3	−1·1
		P	15·2	7·6	7·6	12·7	30·5	50·8	50·8	50·8	27·9	25·4	17·8	20·3	317·5
Osaka (Japan) 34° 39′ N. 135° 26′ E.	3	T	3·9	4·4	7·2	13·3	17·8	22·2	26·7	27·8	23·9	17·2	11·7	6·7	15·0
		P	43·2	58·4	96·5	132·1	124·5	187·9	149·8	111·8	177·8	129·5	76·2	48·3	1336·0
Padang (Sumatra) 00° 56′ S. 100° 22′ E.	7	T	26·7	26·7	26·7	27·2	27·8	26·7	26·7	26·7	26·7	26·7	26·7	26·7	26·7
		P	350·2	259·1	307·3	363·2	314·9	307·3	276·9	347·9	152·4	495·3	518·2	480·1	4427·2

N.B. All temperatures are in ° C and precipitation is in millimetres.

Asia (including Asia Minor)

Station	Altitude in Metres		Jan.	Feb.	Mar.	Apr.	May	Jun.	Jul.	Aug.	Sep.	Oct.	Nov.	Dec.	Mean: Year
Penang (Malaya) 05° 25' N. 100° 19' E.	5	T	27.8	27.8	28.3	28.3	27.8	27.8	27.8	27.2	26.7	27.2	26.7	27.2	27.8
		P	93.9	78.7	142.2	187.9	271.8	195.6	190.5	294.6	401.3	429.3	302.3	147.3	2735.6
Petropavlovsk (U.S.S.R.) 52° 53' N. 158° 42' E.	87	T	−8.3	−8.9	−6.1	−1.1	2.8	7.2	11.1	12.8	10.0	4.4	−2.2	−6.1	1.1
		P	76.2	55.9	86.4	63.5	55.9	50.8	78.7	81.3	96.5	99.1	91.4	76.2	911.9
Pontianak (Borneo) 00° 01' S. 109° 20' E.	2.7	T	26.7	27.8	27.8	27.8	27.8	27.8	27.2	27.8	27.8	27.8	27.2	27.2	27.8
		P	274.3	208.3	241.3	276.9	281.9	220.9	165.1	203.2	228.6	365.8	388.6	322.6	3175.0
Quetta (Pakistan) 30° 10' N. 67° 01' E.	1672	T	3.3	5.6	10.6	15.0	20.0	24.4	26.7	25.0	20.0	14.4	8.9	5.0	15.0
		P	48.3	50.8	43.2	25.4	10.2	5.1	12.7	7.6	Tr	2.5	7.6	25.4	238.8
Rangoon (Burma) 16° 46' N. 96° 11' E.	5.5	T	25.0	26.1	28.3	30.0	28.9	27.2	26.7	26.8	27.2	27.8	26.7	25.0	27.2
		P	2.5	5.1	7.6	50.8	307.3	480.1	581.7	528.3	393.7	180.3	68.6	10.2	2616.2
Riyadh (Saudi Arabia) 24° 39' N. 46° 42' E.	592	T	14.4	15.6	20.6	24.4	30.0	33.3	33.9	32.8	30.6	25.0	20.6	15.0	24.4
		P	2.5	20.3	22.9	25.4	10.2	Tr	0.0	Tr	0.0	0.0	Tr	Tr	81.3
Saigon (Vietnam) 10° 47' N. 106° 42' E.	9	T	26.1	26.7	28.3	29.4	28.9	27.8	27.8	27.8	27.2	27.2	26.7	26.1	27.8
		P	15.2	2.5	12.7	43.2	220.9	330.2	314.9	269.2	335.3	269.2	114.3	55.9	1983.7
Salalah (Oman) 17° 03' N. 54° 06' E.	17	T	22.2	23.3	25.0	26.7	28.3	28.9	25.6	25.0	26.1	25.6	25.0	23.9	25.6
		P	Tr	Tr	Tr	Tr	Tr	5.1	2.5	25.4	2.5	12.7	Tr	Tr	81.3
Samsun (Turkey) 41° 17' N. 36° 19' E.	40	T	6.7	6.7	8.3	11.1	15.6	19.4	22.2	22.2	20.0	16.7	12.8	9.4	14.4
		P	73.7	66.0	68.6	58.4	45.7	38.1	38.1	33.0	60.9	81.3	88.9	86.4	739.1
Shaibah (Iraq) 30° 25' N. 47° 39' E.	18	T	11.7	13.9	18.3	23.9	30.0	33.3	35.6	35.6	32.2	26.7	19.4	13.3	24.4
		P	27.9	25.4	15.4	12.7	7.6	Tr	Tr	Tr	Tr	Tr	19.4	27.9	144.8
Shanghai (China) 31° 12' N. 121° 26' E.	7	T	3.9	4.4	8.3	14.4	20.0	23.3	27.8	27.8	23.3	18.3	12.2	6.7	16.1
		P	48.3	58.4	83.8	93.9	93.9	180.3	147.3	142.2	129.5	71.1	50.8	35.6	1135.4
Sharjah (Oman) 25° 20' N. 55° 24' E.	5.5	T	17.8	18.9	21.1	23.9	27.8	30.6	32.8	33.3	31.1	27.2	26.7	20.0	25.6
		P	22.9	22.9	10.2	5.1	0.0	0.0	0.0	0.0	0.0	0.0	10.2	35.6	106.7
Shenyang (China) 41° 48' N. 123° 23' E.	43	T	−11.7	−8.3	0.0	9.4	16.7	22.2	25.6	24.4	17.2	9.4	−0.6	−9.4	7.8
		P	7.6	7.6	17.8	27.9	68.6	83.8	182.9	170.2	63.5	35.6	27.9	15.2	708.7
Singapore (Malaya) 01° 18' N. 103° 50' E.	10	T	26.1	26.7	27.2	27.2	27.8	27.2	27.2	27.2	27.2	26.7	26.7	26.7	26.7
		P	251.5	172.7	193.0	187.9	172.7	172.7	170.2	195.6	177.8	208.3	254.0	256.5	2413.0
Srinagar (Kashmir) 34° 05' N. 74° 50' E.	1587	T	1.1	2.8	8.3	12.8	17.8	21.7	24.4	18.3	20.0	13.3	7.2	3.3	13.3
		P	73.7	71.1	91.4	93.9	60.9	35.6	58.4	60.9	38.1	30.5	10.2	33.0	657.9
Surabaya (Java) 07° 38' N. 112° 55' E.	5	T	27.2	27.2	27.2	27.2	26.7	26.1	25.6	25.6	26.7	27.2	27.8	27.2	26.7
		P	226.1	279.4	213.4	137.2	93.9	55.9	25.4	5.1	5.1	17.8	60.9	165.1	1285.2

N.B. All temperatures are in °C and precipitation is in millimetres.

Asia (including Asia Minor)

Station	Altitude in Metres		Jan.	Feb.	Mar.	Apr.	May	Jun.	Jul.	Aug.	Sep.	Oct.	Nov.	Dec.	Mean: Year
Sverdlovsk (U.S.S.R.) 56° 49' N. 60° 38' E.	272	T	-17.8	-13.9	-8.3	1.1	8.9	13.9	16.7	13.9	8.3	0.0	-9.4	-15.0	0.0
		P	12.7	10.2	12.7	17.8	48.3	68.6	66.0	68.6	40.6	30.5	27.9	20.3	424.2
Tashkent (U.S.S.R.) 41° 20' N. 69° 18' E.	478	T	-1.7	1.7	7.2	13.3	19.4	23.3	25.6	23.3	18.9	11.7	6.7	2.2	12.8
		P	53.3	27.9	66.0	58.4	35.6	12.7	5.1	2.5	2.5	30.5	38.1	40.6	373.4
Tbilisi (U.S.S.R.) 41° 43' N. 44° 48' E.	404	T	0.0	3.3	5.6	11.1	16.1	20.6	23.3	23.3	18.3	13.3	6.7	2.8	12.2
		P	17.8	20.3	33.0	40.6	91.4	78.7	55.9	43.2	48.3	33.0	50.8	30.5	543.6
Tehran (Iran) 35° 41' N. 51° 25' E.	1240	T	2.2	5.0	9.4	15.6	21.1	26.1	29.4	28.9	25.0	17.8	11.7	5.6	16.7
		P	45.7	38.1	45.7	35.6	12.7	2.5	2.5	2.5	2.5	7.6	20.3	30.5	246.4
Tientsin (China) 39° 10' N. 117° 10' E.	4	T	-4.4	-1.1	5.0	13.3	20.0	25.0	27.2	26.1	21.1	14.4	5.0	-2.2	12.2
		P	5.1	2.5	10.2	12.7	27.9	60.9	187.9	152.4	43.2	15.2	10.2	5.1	533.4
Tokyo (Japan) 35° 41' N. 139° 46' E.	5.8	T	3.3	3.9	7.2	12.2	16.7	20.6	24.4	26.1	22.2	16.7	10.6	5.6	14.4
		P	48.3	73.7	106.7	134.6	147.3	165.1	142.2	152.4	233.7	208.3	96.5	55.9	1564.6
Tomsk (U.S.S.R.) 56° 30' N. 84° 58' E.	123	T	-21.1	-17.8	-11.1	-1.7	7.2	13.9	17.2	15.0	14.4	0.0	-12.2	-18.9	-1.7
		P	27.9	17.8	20.3	22.9	40.6	68.6	66.0	66.0	40.6	50.8	45.7	38.1	505.5
Trincomalee (Ceylon) 08° 35' N. 81° 15' E.	7	T	25.0	26.1	26.7	28.3	29.4	29.4	29.4	28.9	28.9	27.8	26.1	25.6	27.8
		P	172.7	66.0	48.3	58.4	68.6	27.9	50.8	106.7	106.7	220.9	358.1	363.2	1648.5
Ulan Bator (Mongolia) 47° 55' N. 106° 50' E.	1322	T	-25.6	-21.1	-12.8	-1.1	5.6	13.3	16.1	13.9	7.8	-1.1	-12.8	-22.2	-3.3
		P	Tr	Tr	2.5	5.1	10.2	27.9	76.2	50.8	22.9	5.1	2.5	2.5	208.3
Urumchi (China) 43° 45' N. 87° 40' E.	908	T	-16.1	-13.9	-6.1	8.9	15.0	18.9	21.1	20.0	14.4	4.4	-6.1	-11.1	4.4
		P	15.2	7.6	12.7	38.1	27.9	38.1	17.8	25.4	15.2	43.2	40.6	10.2	292.1
Verkhoyansk (U.S.S.R.) 67° 34' N. 133° 51' E.	100	T	-50.6	-44.4	-32.2	-15.0	0.0	12.2	13.3	9.4	1.7	-15.6	-37.2	-47.8	-17.2
		P	5.1	5.1	2.5	5.1	7.6	22.9	27.9	25.4	12.7	7.6	7.6	5.1	134.6
Vientiane (Laos) 17° 58' N. 102° 36' E.	162	T	21.1	23.3	26.1	28.3	27.2	27.8	27.2	27.2	27.2	25.6	23.9	21.7	25.6
		P	5.1	15.2	38.1	99.1	266.7	302.3	266.7	292.1	302.3	109.2	15.2	2.5	1714.5
Vladivostok (U.S.S.R.) 43° 07' N. 131° 55' E.	29	T	-14.4	-10.0	-3.3	4.4	9.4	13.9	18.3	20.6	16.1	8.9	-1.1	-10.0	4.4
		P	7.6	10.2	17.8	30.5	53.3	73.7	83.8	119.4	109.2	48.3	30.5	15.2	599.4
Yakutsk (U.S.S.R.) 62° 01' N. 129° 43' E.	163	T	-45.0	-36.0	-23.3	-8.9	4.4	13.9	17.2	13.9	5.6	-8.3	-28.9	-41.1	-11.7
		P	7.6	5.1	2.5	7.6	10.2	27.9	40.6	33.0	25.4	12.7	10.2	7.6	187.9

N.B. All temperatures are in ° C and precipitation is in millimetres.

Africa (including South Atlantic and South Indian Ocean)

Station	Altitude in Metres		Jan.	Feb.	Mar.	Apr.	May	Jun.	Jul.	Aug.	Sep.	Oct.	Nov.	Dec.	Mean: Year
Accra (Ghana) 05° 33' N. 00° 12' W.	27	T	26·7	27·8	27·8	27·8	27·2	26·1	25·0	23·9	25·0	26·1	27·2	27·8	26·7
		P	15·2	33·0	55·9	81·3	142·2	177·8	45·7	15·2	35·6	63·5	35·6	22·9	723·9
Addis Ababa (Ethiopia) 09° 20' N. 38° 45' E.	2480	T	15·0	16·7	17·2	17·2	17·2	16·7	15·0	15·0	15·6	15·6	14·4	13·9	15·6
		P	12·7	38·1	66·0	86·4	86·4	137·2	279·4	299·7	190·5	20·3	15·2	5·1	1236·9
Agadir (Morocco) 30° 23' N. 09° 34' W.	50	T	13·9	15·0	16·7	18·3	19·4	21·1	22·2	22·8	22·2	20·6	17·8	14·4	18·9
		P	43·2	27·9	25·4	17·8	2·5	Tr	Tr	Tr	5·1	22·9	35·6	43·2	223·5
Alexandria (Egypt) 31° 12' N. 29° 53' E.	32	T	14·4	15·0	16·7	18·9	22·2	24·4	26·1	26·7	26·1	23·9	20·6	16·7	21·1
		P	48·3	22·9	10·2	2·5	Tr	Tr	Tr	Tr	Tr	5·1	33·0	55·9	177·8
Algiers (Algeria) 36° 46' N. 03° 03' E.	59	T	12·2	12·8	13·9	16·7	18·9	21·7	24·4	25·6	23·9	20·0	16·1	12·8	18·3
		P	111·8	83·8	73·7	40·6	45·7	15·2	Tr	5·1	40·6	78·7	129·5	137·2	762·0
Aswan (Egypt) 24° 02' N. 32° 53' E.	113	T	16·7	18·3	22·2	27·2	31·1	33·3	33·3	33·3	31·7	28·9	23·3	18·3	26·7
		P	Tr	Tr	Tr	Tr	Tr	Tr	0·0	0·0	0·0	Tr	Tr	Tr	Tr
Bamako (Mali) 12° 39' N. 07° 58' W.	340	T	24·4	27·8	30·0	31·7	31·7	28·3	26·7	26·1	26·7	27·8	26·1	25·0	27·8
		P	Tr	Tr	2·5	15·2	73·7	137·2	279·4	347·9	205·7	43·2	15·2	Tr	1120·1
Banana (Zaïre) 06° 00' S. 12° 25' E.	2	T	27·2	27·2	27·8	27·2	26·1	23·9	22·2	22·2	23·9	25·6	26·7	26·7	25·6
		P	27·9	167·6	152·4	139·7	106·7	Tr	Tr	Tr	2·5	10·2	93·9	68·6	769·6
Bathurst (Gambia) 13° 21' N. 16° 40' W.	27	T	22·8	23·9	25·6	25·6	25·6	27·2	26·7	26·1	26·7	26·7	25·0	23·3	25·6
		P	2·5	2·5	Tr	Tr	10·2	58·3	281·9	500·4	309·9	109·2	17·8	2·5	1295·4
Beira (Mozambique) 19° 50' S. 34° 51' E.	9	T	27·8	27·8	26·7	25·6	22·8	21·1	20·6	21·1	22·8	26·1	26·1	26·7	24·4
		P	276·9	213·4	256·4	106·7	55·9	33·0	30·5	27·9	20·3	132·1	134·6	233·7	1521·5
Benghazi (Libya) 32° 06' N. 20° 04' E.	25	T	13·3	13·9	16·7	18·9	21·7	23·9	25·0	25·6	24·4	22·8	19·4	20·6	20·0
		P	66·0	40·6	20·3	5·1	2·5	Tr	Tr	Tr	2·5	17·8	45·7	66·0	266·7
Berbera (Somalia) 10° 26' N. 45° 02' E.	14	T	24·4	25·0	26·1	28·3	31·1	35·6	36·1	35·6	33·9	28·9	26·1	24·4	29·4
		P	7·6	2·5	5·1	12·7	7·6	Tr	2·5	2·5	Tr	2·5	5·1	5·1	50·8
Biskra (Algeria) 34° 51' N. 05° 44' E.	124	T	11·1	12·8	16·7	20·0	24·4	30·0	33·9	33·3	28·3	22·2	16·1	11·7	21·7
		P	17·8	10·2	17·8	10·2	15·2	7·6	2·5	2·5	17·8	15·2	22·9	17·8	157·5
Bizerta (Tunisia) 37° 14' N. 09° 49' E.	2	T	11·1	11·7	13·3	15·0	18·3	22·8	25·0	25·6	24·4	20·6	16·7	12·2	17·8
		P	106·7	76·2	50·8	40·6	20·3	12·7	5·1	5·1	30·5	68·6	86·4	119·4	622·3
Bloemfontein (S. Africa) 29° 07' S. 26° 11' E.	1420	T	22·8	21·7	19·4	15·6	11·1	8·3	8·3	11·1	14·4	17·8	19·4	22·2	16·1
		P	91·4	78·7	76·2	55·9	25·4	7·6	10·2	20·3	20·3	50·8	66·0	60·9	563·9
Brazzaville (Rep. of Congo) 04° 15' S. 15° 15' E.	318	T	25·6	26·1	26·7	27·2	26·1	23·3	22·8	23·9	25·6	26·1	26·1	25·6	25·6
		P	160·0	124·5	187·9	177·8	109·2	15·2	Tr	Tr	55·9	137·2	292·1	213·4	1473·2

N.B. All temperatures are in ° C and precipitation is in millimetres.

AFRICA (including SOUTH ATLANTIC AND SOUTH INDIAN OCEAN)

STATION	ALTITUDE IN METRES		JAN.	FEB.	MAR.	APR.	MAY	JUN.	JUL.	AUG.	SEP.	OCT.	NOV.	DEC.	MEAN: YEAR
BULAWAYO (Rhodesia) 20° 09′ S. 28° 37′ E.	1342	T	21·7	21·1	20·6	19·4	16·7	13·9	13·9	16·1	19·4	22·2	22·2	21·7	18·9
		P	142·2	109·2	83·8	17·8	10·2	2·5	Tr	Tr	5·1	20·3	81·3	121·9	594·4
CAIRO (Egypt) 29° 51′ N. 31° 20′ E.	116	T	13·3	14·4	17·2	21·1	25·0	27·8	28·3	28·3	26·1	23·9	20·0	15·0	22·2
		P	5·1	5·1	5·1	2·5	2·5	Tr	0·0	0·0	Tr	Tr	2·5	5·1	27·9
CAPE TOWN (S. Africa) 33° 54′ S. 18° 32′ E.	17	T	20·6	20·6	19·4	16·7	14·4	12·8	12·2	12·8	13·9	16·1	17·8	19·4	16·7
		P	15·2	7·6	17·8	48·3	78·7	83·8	88·9	66·0	43·2	30·5	17·8	10·2	508·0
CASABLANCA (Morocco) 33° 35′ N. 07° 39′ W.	50	T	12·2	12·8	14·4	15·6	17·8	20·0	22·2	22·8	21·7	19·4	15·6	13·3	17·2
		P	53·3	48·3	55·9	35·6	17·8	5·1	0·0	Tr	7·6	38·1	66·0	71·1	403·9
COLOMB-BECHAR (Algeria) 31° 36′ N. 02° 10′ W.	770	T	8·3	11·7	15·0	19·4	23·3	28·3	32·8	31·7	27·2	17·8	13·9	9·4	20·0
		P	5·1	5·1	7·6	2·5	2·5	5·1	0·0	2·5	5·1	15·2	17·8	10·2	78·7
CONAKRY (Guinea) 09° 31′ N. 13° 43′ W.	7	T	26·7	26·7	27·2	27·8	27·8	26·1	25·0	25·0	26·1	26·7	27·2	27·2	26·7
		P	2·5	2·5	10·2	22·9	157·5	558·8	1297·9	1054·1	683·3	370·8	121·9	10·2	4292·6
DAKAR (Senegal) 14° 42′ N. 17° 29′ W.	40	T	22·2	22·2	22·2	22·8	24·4	26·7	27·8	27·8	28·3	28·3	26·1	23·3	25·0
		P	Tr	Tr	Tr	Tr	Tr	17·8	88·9	254·0	132·1	38·1	2·5	7·6	541·0
DAR-ES-SALAAM (Tanganyika) 06° 50′ S. 39° 18′ E.	14	T	27·8	27·8	27·2	26·1	25·6	24·4	23·3	23·3	23·9	25·0	26·1	27·2	25·6
		P	66·0	66·0	129·5	289·6	187·9	33·0	30·5	25·4	30·5	40·6	73·7	91·4	1064·3
DJIBOUTI (French Somali) 11° 36′ N. 43° 09′ E.	7	T	25·6	26·1	27·8	28·9	30·6	33·9	35·6	34·4	32·2	30·0	27·8	26·1	30·0
		P	10·2	12·7	25·4	12·7	5·1	Tr	2·5	7·6	7·6	10·2	27·8	12·7	30·0
DODOMA (Tanganyika) 06° 10′ S. 35° 46′ E.	1120	T	23·9	23·3	22·8	22·8	22·2	20·6	19·4	20·0	22·2	23·3	22·9	22·7	22·8
		P	152·4	109·2	137·2	48·3	5·1	Tr	0·0	0·0	Tr	5·1	24·4	24·4	571·5
DONGOLA (Sudan) 19° 08′ N. 30° 29′ E.	236	T	18·9	21·1	23·9	29·4	31·7	33·9	33·9	33·9	33·3	29·4	25·6	20·0	27·8
		P	0·0	0·0	Tr	Tr	Tr	0·0	7·6	7·6	Tr	Tr	Tr	Tr	15·2
DOUALA (Cameroun) 04° 03′ N. 09° 41′ E.	8	T	26·1	26·7	26·1	26·1	26·1	25·0	23·9	23·9	24·4	24·4	25·6	26·1	25·6
		P	45·7	93·9	203·2	231·4	299·7	538·5	741·7	693·4	530·9	429·3	154·9	63·5	4025·9
EAST LONDON (S. Africa) 33° 02′ S. 27° 50′ E.	125	T	21·1	22·2	21·1	18·9	17·8	15·6	15·6	16·1	17·2	17·8	18·9	20·0	18·3
		P	73·7	76·2	96·5	68·6	55·9	35·6	35·6	43·2	68·6	91·4	86·4	76·2	807·7
EL ADEM (Libya) 31° 51′ N. 23° 55′ E.	160	T	11·7	12·2	14·4	17·8	21·7	24·4	25·6	25·6	23·9	20·6	16·7	12·8	18·9
		P	20·3	10·2	15·2	Tr	5·1	Tr	Tr	Tr	Tr	20·6	27·9	12·7	101·6
EL FASHER (Sudan) 13° 38′ N. 25° 21′ E.	730	T	20·6	22·2	25·0	28·3	30·0	30·0	28·3	26·7	27·8	27·2	23·9	23·3	26·1
		P	Tr	0·0	Tr	Tr	7·6	17·8	114·3	134·6	30·5	5·1	0·0	0·0	309·9

N.B. All temperatures are in ° C and precipitation is in millimetres.

Africa (including South Atlantic and South Indian Ocean)

Station	Altitude in Metres		Jan.	Feb.	Mar.	Apr.	May	Jun.	Jul.	Aug.	Sep.	Oct.	Nov.	Dec.	Mean: Year
Entebbe (Uganda) 00° 04' N. 32° 29' E.	1179	T	22.2	22.2	22.2	22.2	21.7	21.1	20.6	20.6	21.1	21.7	21.7	21.7	21.1
		P	66.0	91.4	160.0	256.0	243.8	121.9	76.2	73.7	73.7	93.9	132.1	116.8	1506.2
Enugu (Nigeria) 06° 27' N. 07° 29' E.	232	T	27.2	28.3	28.9	28.3	26.7	25.6	25.0	23.9	25.6	26.1	26.7	26.7	26.7
		P	17.8	27.9	66.0	149.9	264.2	289.6	193.0	170.2	325.1	248.9	53.3	12.7	1816.1
Fort Lamy (Chad) 12° 07' N. 15° 02' E.	296	T	23.9	26.1	30.6	32.2	32.2	31.1	27.8	26.1	27.2	28.3	26.7	23.3	27.8
		P	0.0	0.0	0.0	2.5	30.5	66.0	170.2	320.0	119.4	35.6	0.0	0.0	744.2
Freetown (Sierra Leone) 08° 30' N. 13° 14' W.	11	T	26.7	27.2	27.2	27.8	27.2	26.7	25.6	25.0	25.6	26.1	26.7	26.7	26.7
		P	12.7	2.5	12.7	55.9	160.0	302.3	894.1	901.7	609.6	309.9	132.1	40.6	3434.1
Gaza (Egypt) 31° 31' N. 34° 27' E.	71	T	12.8	13.3	15.6	18.3	21.1	23.9	25.6	26.1	25.0	22.8	19.4	15.0	20.0
		P	104.1	76.2	30.5	12.7	2.5	Tr	0.0	Tr	Tr	17.8	63.5	81.3	388.6
Ibadan (Nigeria) 07° 26' N. 03° 54' E.	200	T	26.7	27.8	28.3	27.8	26.7	25.6	24.4	23.9	25.6	26.1	26.7	26.7	26.1
		P	7.6	22.9	76.2	124.5	144.8	162.6	132.1	73.7	170.2	152.4	43.2	10.2	1120.1
Idris (Libya) 32° 41' N. 13° 10' E.	80	T	11.7	12.8	15.0	19.4	22.2	26.1	27.8	27.8	26.1	23.3	17.8	12.8	22.0
		P	63.5	50.8	27.9	12.7	5.1	2.5	Tr	Tr	10.2	25.4	35.6	76.2	309.9
In Salah (Algeria) 27° 12' N. 02° 28' E.	280	T	13.3	15.6	20.0	25.0	26.1	35.0	36.7	35.6	32.8	26.7	18.9	14.4	25.0
		P	2.5	2.5	Tr	Tr	Tr	Tr	0.0	2.5	Tr	Tr	5.1	2.5	15.2
Ismailia (Egypt) 30° 37' N. 32° 15' E.	12	T	13.3	14.4	16.7	20.6	24.4	27.2	28.9	28.9	26.7	23.3	19.4	15.0	21.7
		P	7.6	5.1	7.6	2.5	2.5	Tr	Tr	Tr	Tr	2.5	2.5	7.6	38.1
Juba (Sudan) 04° 51' N. 31° 37' E.	460	T	28.3	29.4	29.4	28.9	27.8	26.7	25.6	25.6	26.1	27.2	27.8	28.3	27.8
		P	5.1	15.2	33.0	121.9	149.9	134.6	121.9	132.1	106.7	93.9	35.6	17.8	967.7
Kabwe (Zambia) 14° 24' S. 28° 24' E.	1180	T	21.7	21.7	21.1	20.6	18.3	16.1	15.6	18.3	22.2	24.4	23.9	22.2	20.6
		P	269.4	200.7	127.0	20.3	Tr	Tr	Tr	0.0	2.5	17.8	93.9	208.3	939.8
Kano (Nigeria) 12° 02' N. 08° 32' E.	464	T	21.1	23.9	27.8	31.1	30.6	28.3	26.1	25.0	26.1	26.7	24.4	22.2	26.1
		P	Tr	Tr	2.5	10.2	68.6	116.8	205.7	309.9	142.2	12.7	Tr	0.0	868.7
Khartoum (Sudan) 15° 37' N. 32° 33' E.	390	T	23.3	25.0	28.3	31.1	33.3	33.3	31.7	30.6	31.7	31.7	28.3	22.2	29.4
		P	Tr	Tr	Tr	Tr	2.5	7.6	53.3	71.1	17.8	5.1	Tr	0.0	157.5
Kigoma (Tanganyika) 04° 53' S. 29° 38' E.	887	T	22.8	23.3	23.3	23.3	23.9	22.8	22.8	23.3	24.4	24.4	23.3	25.6	23.3
		P	121.9	127.0	149.9	129.5	43.2	5.1	2.5	5.1	17.8	48.3	142.2	134.6	927.1
Kimberley (S. Africa) 28° 48' S. 24° 46' E.	1197	T	25.6	23.9	21.7	17.8	13.3	10.6	10.0	13.3	16.1	20.0	22.2	23.9	18.3
		P	60.9	63.5	78.7	38.1	17.8	5.1	5.1	7.6	15.2	20.0	40.6	50.8	408.9
Kisangani (Zaïre) 00° 26' N. 25° 14' E.	418	T	25.6	25.6	25.6	26.1	25.6	25.0	23.9	23.9	24.4	25.0	25.0	25.0	25.0
		P	53.3	83.8	177.8	157.5	137.2	114.3	132.1	165.1	182.9	218.4	198.1	83.8	1704.3

N.B. All temperatures are in ° C and precipitation is in millimetres.

Africa (including South Atlantic and South Indian Ocean)

Station	Altitude in Metres		Jan.	Feb.	Mar.	Apr.	May	Jun.	Jul.	Aug.	Sep.	Oct.	Nov.	Dec.	Mean: Year
Kumasi (Ghana) 06° 40′ N. 01° 37′ W.	287	T	25·0	26·7	27·2	26·7	26·7	25·6	24·4	23·9	24·4	25·6	25·6	25·0	25·6
		P	20·3	58·4	144·8	129·5	190·5	200·7	109·2	78·7	172·7	180·3	93·9	20·3	1402·1
Lagos (Nigeria) 06° 27′ N. 03° 24′ E.	3	T	27·2	28·3	28·3	28·3	27·8	26·1	25·6	23·3	25·6	26·1	27·8	27·8	26·7
		P	27·9	45·7	101·6	149·9	269·2	459·7	279·4	63·5	139·7	205·7	68·6	25·4	1836·4
Las Palmas (Canary Is.) 28° 11′ N. 15° 28′ W.	6	T	17·8	17·8	18·3	18·9	19·4	21·1	22·2	23·3	23·3	22·8	21·1	18·9	20·0
		P	35·6	22·9	22·9	12·7	5·1	Tr	Tr	Tr	5·1	27·9	53·3	40·6	218·4
Libreville (Gabon) 00° 23′ N. 09° 26′ E.	35	T	26·7	26·7	27·2	27·2	26·7	25·0	23·9	24·4	25·6	25·6	25·6	26·1	25·6
		P	248·9	236·2	335·3	340·4	243·8	12·7	2·5	17·8	104·1	345·4	373·4	248·9	2509·5
Lindi (Tanganyika) 10° 00′ S. 39° 42′ E.	8	T	27·8	27·2	27·2	26·7	25·6	25·0	24·4	24·4	24·4	25·0	26·7	27·2	26·1
		P	144·8	116·8	170·2	172·7	38·1	10·2	7·6	5·1	12·7	15·2	53·3	149·9	896·6
Livingstone (Zambia) 17° 50′ S. 25° 49′ E.	965	T	23·9	23·9	23·3	22·2	18·9	16·1	16·1	18·9	23·3	26·7	26·1	24·4	22·2
		P	144·8	152·4	109·2	25·4	7·6	2·5	0·0	Tr	2·5	22·9	73·7	132·1	673·1
Lobito (Angola) 12° 22′ S. 13° 32′ E.	1	T	25·0	26·1	27·2	26·7	25·0	22·2	20·0	20·0	21·1	23·3	25·0	25·0	23·9
		P	20·3	38·1	119·4	53·3	2·5	0·0	0·0	Tr	2·5	30·5	25·4	60·9	353·1
Lourenço Marques (Mozambique) 25° 58′ S. 32° 36′ E.	59	T	25·6	26·1	25·0	23·3	21·1	18·9	18·3	19·4	21·1	22·8	23·9	25·0	22·8
		P	129·5	124·5	124·5	53·3	27·9	20·3	12·7	12·7	27·9	48·3	81·3	96·5	759·5
Luanda (Angola) 08° 49′ S. 13° 13′ E.	59	T	25·6	26·7	26·7	26·7	25·0	22·2	20·6	20·6	22·2	23·9	25·0	25·6	24·4
		P	25·4	35·6	76·2	116·8	12·7	Tr	Tr	Tr	2·5	5·1	27·9	20·3	322·6
Lubumbashi (Zaïre) 11° 39′ S. 27° 28′ E.	1229	T	22·2	22·2	22·2	20·6	18·3	16·7	16·1	17·8	21·1	23·3	23·3	22·2	20·6
		P	266·7	243·8	213·4	55·9	5·1	0·0	0·0	Tr	2·5	30·5	149·9	269·2	1236·9
Luluaborg (Zaïre) 05° 54′ S. 22° 25′ E.	670	T	24·4	24·4	25·0	25·0	25·0	24·4	23·3	24·4	24·4	24·4	24·4	24·4	24·4
		P	137·2	142·2	195·6	193·0	83·8	20·3	12·7	58·4	116·8	165·1	231·1	226·1	1584·4
Lusaka (Zambia) 15° 25′ S. 28° 19′ E.	1278	T	21·1	21·7	21·1	20·6	18·3	16·7	16·1	18·3	22·2	24·4	23·3	22·2	20·6
		P	231·1	190·5	142·2	17·8	2·5	Tr	Tr	0·0	Tr	10·2	91·4	149·9	835·7
Mali (Guinea) 12° 08′ N. 12° 18′ W.	1467	T	18·9	21·1	22·8	23·3	22·8	20·0	18·9	18·3	18·9	19·4	19·4	19·4	20·0
		P	Tr	Tr	7·6	20·3	121·9	236·2	386·1	474·9	327·7	190·5	22·9	2·5	1790·7
Marrakesh (Morocco) 31° 36′ N. 08° 01′ W.	460	T	11·1	12·8	16·1	18·3	21·1	25·0	28·9	28·9	25·0	21·1	16·1	12·2	19·4
		P	25·4	27·9	33·0	30·5	15·2	7·6	2·5	2·5	10·2	22·9	30·5	30·5	238·7
Massawa (Ethiopia) 15° 37′ N. 39° 27′ E.	19	T	25·6	25·0	26·7	28·3	30·6	33·3	34·4	34·4	33·3	31·1	27·8	26·1	29·4
		P	27·9	35·6	15·2	20·3	2·5	Tr	7·6	Tr	2·5	17·8	20·3	43·2	193·0
Mauritius (Indian Ocean) 20° 06′ S. 57° 32′ E.	55	T	26·1	26·1	25·6	24·4	22·2	20·6	20·0	20·0	21·1	22·2	23·9	25·6	23·3
		P	215·9	198·1	220·9	127·0	96·5	66·0	58·4	63·5	35·6	40·6	45·7	116·8	1285·2
Mbabane (Swaziland) 26° 19′ S. 31° 08′ E.	1162	T	20·0	20·0	18·9	17·2	14·4	12·2	12·2	13·9	16·1	17·8	18·9	19·4	16·7
		P	254·0	213·4	193·0	71·1	33·0	20·3	22·9	27·9	60·9	127·0	170·2	208·3	1402·1

N.B. All temperatures are in ° C and precipitation is in millimetres.

Africa (including South Atlantic and South Indian Ocean)

Station	Altitude in Metres		Jan.	Feb.	Mar.	Apr.	May	Jun.	Jul.	Aug.	Sep.	Oct.	Nov.	Dec.	Mean: Year
Mindelo (Cape Verde Is.) 16° 54′ N. 25° 04′ W.	15	T	21·1	20·6	21·1	21·1	21·7	23·3	24·4	25·0	24·4	23·9	23·9	22·2	22·8
		P	2·5	2·5	Tr	0·0	0·0	Tr	0·0	22·9	45·7	20·3	5·1	Tr	99·1
Mogadishu (Somalia) 02° 02′ N. 45° 21′ E.	12	T	26·1	26·7	27·8	28·9	28·3	26·1	25·6	25·6	26·1	27·2	27·2	26·7	26·7
		P	Tr	Tr	Tr	58·4	58·4	96·5	63·5	48·3	25·4	22·9	40·6	12·7	429·3
Mombasa (Kenya) 04° 03′ S. 39° 39′ E.	16	T	27·2	27·8	28·3	27·2	25·6	25·0	24·4	24·4	25·0	26·1	26·7	26·7	26·1
		P	25·4	17·8	63·5	195·6	320·0	119·4	88·9	63·5	63·5	86·4	96·5	60·9	1201·4
Monrovia (Liberia) 06° 18′ N. 10° 48′ W.	23	T	26·1	26·1	26·7	26·7	26·1	25·0	24·4	24·4	24·4	25·0	26·1	26·1	25·6
		P	30·5	55·9	96·5	215·9	515·6	972·8	995·7	373·4	744·2	772·2	236·2	129·5	5138·4
Morondava (Malagasy) 10° 17′ S. 44° 17′ E.	5	T	27·8	27·8	27·2	26·7	23·9	22·2	21·1	22·2	23·3	25·6	26·7	27·8	25·0
		P	220·9	198·1	86·4	12·7	7·6	7·6	2·5	2·5	7·6	10·2	17·8	134·6	708·7
Moyale (Kenya) 03° 32′ N. 39° 03′ E.	1120	T	24·4	25·0	24·4	22·8	21·1	20·0	19·4	20·0	21·1	22·2	22·2	22·8	22·2
		P	12·7	17·8	50·8	165·1	116·8	20·3	17·8	15·2	27·9	88·9	81·3	40·6	655·3
Nairobi (Kenya) 01° 16′ S. 36° 48′ E.	1830	T	18·3	19·4	19·4	18·9	17·8	16·7	15·6	16·1	17·2	18·3	18·3	18·3	18·3
		P	38·1	63·5	124·5	210·8	157·5	45·7	15·2	22·9	30·5	53·3	109·2	86·4	957·6
Nara (Mali) 15° 10′ N. 07° 18′ W.	?	T	22·2	25·0	28·3	30·6	33·3	31·1	27·8	26·7	27·2	28·9	27·8	23·3	27·8
		P	2·5	Tr	Tr	2·5	25·4	73·7	160·0	210·8	99·1	20·3	2·5	0·0	594·4
N'délé (Central African Republic) 08° 24′ N. 20° 39′ E.	600	T	28·3	28·9	30·6	30·6	27·2	26·1	25·0	25·0	25·0	26·1	26·1	26·7	27·2
		P	5·1	33·0	15·2	43·2	213·4	154·9	210·8	256·5	271·8	198·1	15·2	0·0	1417·3
Ndola (Zambia) 12° 59′ S. 28° 37′ E.	1265	T	21·1	21·1	21·1	20·0	17·8	14·4	15·0	16·7	20·6	23·3	22·8	21·7	19·4
		P	350·5	264·2	233·7	33·0	2·5	0·0	0·0	0·0	Tr	17·8	139·7	251·5	1292·9
Niamey (Niger) 13° 31′ N. 02° 06′ E.	216	T	23·9	26·7	31·1	33·9	33·9	31·7	28·9	27·2	28·3	30·6	28·3	24·4	28·9
		P	Tr	Tr	5·1	7·6	33·0	81·3	132·1	187·9	93·9	12·7	Tr	0·0	548·6
Nouakchott (Mauritania) 18° 07′ N. 15° 36′ W.	21	T	21·7	22·8	24·4	25·0	27·2	28·3	27·8	28·3	28·9	27·2	27·8	20·6	25·6
		P	Tr	2·5	Tr	Tr	Tr	2·5	12·7	104·1	22·9	10·2	2·5	Tr	157·5
Nova Lisboa (Angola) 12° 48′ S. 15° 45′ E.	1697	T	20·0	20·0	20·0	20·0	17·8	16·1	16·7	18·9	20·6	20·6	20·0	20·0	19·4
		P	220·9	198·1	248·9	144·8	10·2	0·0	Tr	Tr	15·2	139·7	243·8	226·1	1447·8
Oran (Algeria) 35° 44′ N. 00° 39′ W.	11	T	12·2	13·3	14·4	16·7	18·9	21·7	24·4	25·6	23·3	19·4	16·1	12·8	18·3
		P	71·1	48·3	50·8	30·5	20·3	5·1	Tr	2·5	12·7	33·0	50·8	50·8	375·9
Ouagadougou (Upper Volta) 12° 22′ N. 01° 31′ W.	302	T	24·4	28·3	31·1	32·8	31·7	30·0	28·3	26·1	27·2	28·9	28·3	25·6	28·9
		P	Tr	2·5	12·7	15·2	83·8	121·9	203·2	276·9	144·8	33·0	Tr	0·0	894·1
Oudtshoorn (S. Africa) 33° 35′ S. 22° 12′ E.	334	T	23·9	23·9	22·2	18·3	14·4	11·7	11·1	12·8	15·0	17·8	20·0	22·2	17·8
		P	10·2	12·7	25·4	20·3	20·3	10·2	17·8	15·2	22·9	20·3	30·5	20·3	226·1

N.B. All temperatures are in ° C and precipitation is in millimetres.

AFRICA (including SOUTH ATLANTIC AND SOUTH INDIAN OCEAN)

STATION	ALTITUDE IN METRES		JAN.	FEB.	MAR.	APR.	MAY	JUN.	JUL.	AUG.	SEP.	OCT.	NOV.	DEC.	MEAN: YEAR
PEBANE (Mozambique) 17° 16′ S. 38° 08′ E.	25	T	27·2	27·2	26·7	26·1	23·9	22·2	21·7	21·7	23·9	26·1	27·2	27·2	25·0
		P	210·8	246·4	203·2	93·9	50·8	91·4	53·3	25·4	12·7	5·1	58·4	170·2	1221·7
PORT ELIZABETH (S. Africa) 33° 59′ S. 25° 36′ E.	58	T	20·6	21·1	20·0	17·8	15·6	13·3	13·3	13·9	15·0	16·7	17·8	19·4	17·2
		P	30·5	33·0	48·3	45·7	60·9	45·7	48·3	50·8	58·4	55·9	55·9	43·2	576·6
PORT HARCOURT (Nigeria) 04° 46′ N. 07° 01′ E.	15	T	26·1	27·8	26·7	27·2	26·7	25·6	25·0	25·0	25·6	25·6	26·1	26·1	26·1
		P	33·0	60·9	127·0	180·3	251·5	335·3	322·6	335·3	383·5	271·8	147·3	48·3	2496·8
PORT NOLLOTH (S. Africa) 29° 14′ S. 16° 52′ E.	7	T	15·6	15·6	15·6	14·4	13·9	12·8	11·7	12·2	12·8	13·3	14·4	15·0	13·9
		P	2·5	2·5	5·1	5·1	7·6	7·6	7·6	7·6	5·1	2·5	2·5	2·5	58·4
PORT SAID (Egypt) 31° 16′ N. 32° 19′ E.	4	T	14·4	15·6	17·2	19·4	22·8	25·6	27·2	27·8	26·7	25·0	21·1	16·7	21·7
		P	17·8	12·7	10·2	5·1	2·5	Tr	0·0	0·0	Tr	2·5	10·2	15·2	76·2
PORT SUDAN (Sudan) 19° 37′ N. 37° 13′ E.	5·5	T	23·3	22·8	23·9	26·7	29·4	32·2	34·4	34·4	31·7	28·9	27·2	25·0	28·3
		P	5·1	2·5	Tr	Tr	Tr	Tr	7·6	2·5	Tr	2·5	27·2	25·0	93·9
PORT VICTORIA (Seychelles) 04° 37′ S. 55° 27′ E.	4·6	T	26·1	26·7	27·2	27·2	27·2	26·7	25·6	25·6	26·1	26·1	26·1	26·1	26·1
		P	386·1	266·7	233·7	182·9	170·2	101·6	83·8	68·6	129·5	154·9	231·1	340·4	2349·5
PRETORIA (S. Africa) 25° 45′ S. 28° 14′ E.	1367	T	21·1	21·1	19·4	16·7	13·3	11·1	11·1	13·3	17·2	19·4	20·0	21·1	17·2
		P	127·0	109·2	114·3	43·2	22·9	15·2	7·6	5·1	17·2	55·9	132·1	132·1	784·9
RAGA (Sudan) 08° 28′ N. 25° 41′ E.	460	T	23·9	26·1	27·8	28·9	28·3	26·1	25·6	25·0	25·6	26·7	25·6	23·9	26·1
		P	Tr	Tr	15·2	55·9	149·9	165·1	223·5	254·0	193·0	78·7	10·2	Tr	1145·5
SALISBURY (Rhodesia) 17° 50′ S. 31° 08′ E.	1470	T	20·6	20·6	20·0	18·9	16·7	13·9	13·9	15·6	18·9	21·1	21·1	20·6	18·3
		P	195·6	177·8	116·8	27·9	12·7	2·5	Tr	2·5	5·1	27·9	96·5	162·6	828·0
SFAX (Tunisia) 34° 43′ N. 10° 41′ E.	21	T	11·1	12·2	14·4	16·7	19·4	23·3	25·6	26·1	25·0	22·2	16·7	15·6	18·9
		P	25·4	17·8	25·4	12·7	10·2	5·1	Tr	2·5	5·1	27·9	16·7	15·6	195·6
SIWA (Egypt) 29° 12′ N. 25° 29′ E.	−15	T	11·7	13·3	16·7	20·6	25·0	28·3	29·4	28·9	26·1	23·3	18·3	12·8	21·1
		P	Tr	Tr	Tr	Tr	2·5	Tr	0·0	0·0	0·0	Tr	Tr	2·5	10·2
SOCOTRA (Indian Ocean) 12° 38′ N. 53° 53′ E.	43	T	24·4	24·4	25·6	27·8	30·6	30·0	28·3	28·9	28·3	26·1	25·6	25·0	26·7
		P	2·5	2·5	10·2	0·0	2·5	30·0	28·3	0·0	2·5	10·2	50·8	81·3	193·0
SOKOTO (Nigeria) 13° 01′ N. 05° 16′ E.	351	T	23·9	26·1	30·6	33·3	32·8	30·0	27·8	26·1	27·2	28·9	27·8	24·4	28·3
		P	Tr	Tr	2·5	10·2	43·2	93·9	152·4	243·8	132·1	12·7	Tr	0·0	690·9
SOLLUM (Egypt) 31° 33′ N. 25° 11′ E.	154	T	12·2	13·3	15·0	17·8	20·0	22·8	25·0	24·4	23·3	22·2	18·3	14·4	19·4
		P	20·3	15·2	7·6	Tr	5·1	Tr	Tr	0·0	Tr	Tr	18·3	17·8	91·4
SONGEA (Tanganyika) 10° 41′ S. 35° 40′ E.	1153	T	22·2	22·8	22·2	21·1	19·4	17·8	17·2	18·3	20·6	22·2	22·8	22·8	20·6
		P	274·3	220·9	266·7	111·8	12·7	Tr	Tr	Tr	2·5	10·2	43·2	182·9	1125·2

N.B. All temperatures are in ° C and precipitation is in millimetres.

AFRICA (including SOUTH ATLANTIC AND SOUTH INDIAN OCEAN)

Station	Altitude in Metres		Jan.	Feb.	Mar.	Apr.	May	Jun.	Jul.	Aug.	Sep.	Oct.	Nov.	Dec.	Mean: Year
Takoradi (Ghana) 04°53′ N. 01°46′ W.	9	T	26·1	26·7	27·8	27·2	26·7	25·6	24·4	23·9	24·4	25·6	26·1	26·1	25·6
		P	33·0	25·4	78·7	109·2	276·9	248·9	83·8	40·6	48·3	127·0	63·5	45·7	1181·1
Tamale (Ghana) 09°24′ N. 00°50′ W.	193	T	27·8	30·0	30·6	30·0	28·3	26·7	25·6	25·0	25·6	26·7	27·8	27·8	27·8
		P	2·5	2·5	53·3	68·6	104·1	142·2	134·6	195·6	226·1	99·1	10·2	5·1	1041·4
Tamanrasset (Algeria) 22°42′ N. 05°31′ E.	1399	T	11·7	13·3	17·2	21·7	25·0	27·8	28·3	27·8	25·6	22·2	20·6	13·3	20·6
		P	5·1	Tr	Tr	5·1	10·2	2·5	2·5	10·2	2·5	Tr	Tr	Tr	38·1
Tamatave (Malagassy) 18°07′ S. 49°24′ E.	6	T	26·7	26·7	26·1	25·0	23·3	22·2	21·1	21·1	22·2	23·3	25·0	26·1	23·9
		P	365·8	375·9	452·1	398·8	264·2	281·9	302·3	203·2	132·1	99·1	116·8	261·6	3256·3
Tangier (Morocco) 35°48′ N. 05°49′ W.	73	T	11·7	12·2	13·3	14·4	17·2	20·0	22·2	22·8	21·1	18·3	14·4	12·2	16·7
		P	114·3	106·7	121·9	88·9	43·2	15·2	Tr	Tr	22·9	99·1	147·3	137·2	896·6
Tegéérhi (Libya) 24°21′ N. 14°28′ E.	502	T	12·2	15·0	18·9	23·9	30·6	33·3	31·7	31·7	29·4	25·0	18·3	11·7	23·3
		P	0·0	Tr	0·0	0·0	Tr	0·0	0·0	0·0	Tr	Tr	Tr	Tr	5·1
Timbuktu (Mali) 16°46′ N. 03°01′ E.	302	T	21·7	23·9	28·3	31·7	34·4	34·4	32·2	30·0	31·7	31·1	27·8	22·2	28·9
		P	Tr	Tr	2·5	Tr	5·1	22·9	78·7	81·3	38·1	2·5	Tr	Tr	231·1
Tristan da Cunha (Atlantic) 37°03′ S. 12°19′ W.	23	T	16·7	17·8	16·7	15·6	13·3	12·2	11·7	11·1	11·1	12·8	13·9	15·6	13·9
		P	88·9	88·9	162·6	119·4	180·3	149·9	154·9	175·3	200·7	147·3	109·2	101·6	1678·9
Villa Cisneros (Spanish Sahara) 23°42′ N. 15°52′ W.	11	T	17·2	18·3	18·9	19·4	20·0	21·1	22·2	22·8	22·8	22·2	21·1	18·3	20·6
		P	Tr	Tr	Tr	Tr	2·5	0·0	Tr	5·1	2·5	2·5	5·1	25·4	76·2
Wadi Halfa (Sudan) 21°55′ N. 31°20′ E.	125	T	15·6	17·2	21·7	26·7	30·6	32·2	32·2	32·2	30·0	27·8	22·2	17·2	25·6
		P	Tr	Tr	Tr	Tr	Tr	0·0	Tr	5·1	Tr	2·5	Tr	Tr	2·5
Walvis Bay (S.W. Africa) 22°56′ S. 14°30′ E.	7	T	18·9	19·4	18·9	18·3	17·2	16·1	14·4	13·9	13·9	17·8	16·7	17·8	17·2
		P	Tr	5·1	7·6	2·5	2·5	Tr	2·5	2·5	Tr	Tr	Tr	Tr	22·9
Wankie (Rhodesia) 18°22′ S. 26°29′ E.	784	T	26·1	26·1	25·6	25·0	22·2	18·9	18·9	21·7	26·1	29·4	28·3	26·7	24·4
		P	147·3	147·3	78·7	17·8	5·1	Tr	0·0	Tr	Tr	17·8	58·4	119·4	591·8
Windhoek (S.W. Africa) 22°34′ S. 17°06′ E.	1730	T	23·3	22·2	20·6	18·9	15·6	13·3	12·8	15·6	18·3	22·2	22·2	23·3	18·9
		P	76·2	73·7	78·7	40·6	7·6	Tr	Tr	Tr	2·5	10·2	22·9	48·3	363·2
Yaoundé (Cameroun) 03°53′ N. 11°32′ E.	770	T	24·4	24·4	24·4	23·9	23·9	22·8	22·8	22·2	22·8	22·8	23·3	23·3	23·3
		P	22·9	66·0	147·3	170·2	195·6	152·4	73·7	78·7	213·4	294·6	116·8	22·9	1554·5
Zomba (Malawi) 15°23′ S. 35°19′ E.	960	T	22·8	22·8	22·2	21·1	19·4	17·2	17·2	18·3	21·1	23·3	23·9	22·8	21·1
		P	307·3	251·5	256·5	68·6	17·8	10·2	7·6	7·6	5·1	25·4	109·2	276·9	1343·7

N.B. All temperatures are in ° C and precipitation is in millimetres.

NORTH AMERICA. (including GREENLAND and NORTH PACIFIC)

STATION	ALTITUDE IN METRES		JAN.	FEB.	MAR.	APR.	MAY	JUN.	JUL.	AUG.	SEP.	OCT.	NOV.	DEC.	MEAN: YEAR
AKLAVIK (N.W. Territories) 68° 14' N. 134° 50' W.	9	T	−27·8	−26·7	−22·2	−12·8	−0·6	9·4	13·3	10·0	3·3	−6·7	−19·4	−26·7	−8·9
		P	12·7	12·7	10·2	12·7	12·7	20·3	35·6	35·6	22·9	22·9	20·3	10·2	228·6
ANCHORAGE (Alaska) 61° 14' N. 149° 49' W.	40	T	−11·1	−7·8	−5·0	1·7	7·2	11·7	13·9	12·8	8·9	2·2	−5·6	−10·6	1·7
		P	20·3	17·8	15·2	10·2	12·7	17·8	40·6	66·0	66·0	55·9	25·4	22·9	370·8
ANGMAGSSALIK (Greenland) 65° 37' N. 37° 34' W.	29	T	−8·9	−10·0	−7·8	−3·9	1·7	5·6	7·2	6·7	3·3	−1·1	−5·6	−7·2	−1·7
		P	73·7	60·9	66·0	53·3	50·8	45·7	38·1	53·3	83·8	119·4	76·2	68·6	789·9
ALERT (N.W. Territories) 82° 30' N. 62° 20' W.	62	T	−33·9	−33·9	−32·8	−21·7	−9·4	0·0	3·9	0·0	−9·4	−20·6	−25·6	−30·0	−17·8
		P	5·1	7·6	7·6	7·6	12·7	15·2	12·7	27·9	25·4	22·9	5·1	10·2	160·0
ATKA (Aleutian Is.) 52° 10' N. 174° 12' W.	8	T	0·6	0·6	0·6	2·8	4·4	7·2	10·0	10·6	10·0	5·6	2·8	0·6	4·4
		P	162·6	119·4	127·0	124·5	121·9	99·1	134·6	137·2	180·3	187·9	210·8	154·9	1760·2
ATLANTA (Georgia) 33° 45' N. 84° 23' W.	372	T	6·1	7·2	11·1	16·1	20·6	24·4	25·6	25·0	22·8	17·2	11·1	6·7	16·1
		P	124·5	121·9	139·7	93·9	91·4	93·9	119·4	109·2	81·3	66·0	78·7	114·3	1234·4
BAKER LAKE (N.W. Territories) 64° 18' N. 96° 05' W.	9	T	−35·0	−32·2	−25·0	−16·7	−5·6	2·2	10·0	10·9	2·2	−8·9	−19·4	−27·2	−12·2
		P	5·1	5·1	7·6	7·6	5·1	17·8	22·9	27·9	20·3	12·7	7·6	7·6	147·3
BELLE I. (Newfoundland) 51° 53' N. 55° 22' W.	130	T	−11·7	−11·1	−7·8	−2·8	1·1	5·0	8·9	10·0	7·2	2·8	−2·2	−8·3	−1·1
		P	35·6	50·8	53·3	53·3	71·1	88·9	73·7	78·7	83·8	88·9	68·6	68·6	815·3
BIRMINGHAM (Alabama) 33° 34' N. 86° 45' W.	186	T	7·8	8·3	13·3	17·2	21·7	25·6	26·7	26·7	24·4	18·3	12·2	7·8	17·2
		P	137·2	121·9	149·9	127·0	109·2	111·8	132·1	106·7	78·7	60·9	88·9	121·9	1346·2
BOSTON (Mass.) 42° 22' N. 71° 04' W.	38	T	−2·2	−1·7	1·7	7·8	13·9	18·9	21·7	21·1	17·2	12·2	5·6	0·6	10·0
		P	91·4	83·8	96·5	88·9	78·7	81·3	83·8	91·4	81·3	83·8	91·4	86·4	1036·3
CALGARY (Alberta) 51° 06' N. 114° 01' W.	1078	T	−10·6	−8·3	−3·9	4·4	10·0	13·3	16·1	15·0	10·0	4·4	−2·8	−7·2	3·3
		P	12·7	12·7	20·3	25·4	58·4	78·7	63·5	58·4	38·1	17·8	17·8	15·2	424·2
CHARLESTON (S. Carolina) 32° 47' N. 79° 56' W.	2·7	T	10·0	10·6	14·4	18·3	22·8	26·1	27·2	27·2	25·0	20·0	14·4	10·6	18·9
		P	73·7	83·8	86·4	71·1	81·3	119·4	185·4	167·6	129·5	81·3	58·4	71·1	1209·0
CHEYENNE (Wyoming) 41° 09' N. 104° 49' W.	1870	T	−3·9	−2·8	0·6	5·0	10·0	15·6	18·9	18·3	13·9	7·2	1·1	−2·2	6·7
		P	10·2	15·2	25·4	48·3	60·9	40·6	53·3	40·6	30·5	25·4	12·7	12·7	375·9
CHICAGO (Illinois) 41° 53' N. 87° 38' W.	251	T	−3·9	−2·8	2·2	8·3	13·9	19·4	22·8	22·2	18·3	12·2	4·4	−1·1	10·0
		P	50·8	50·8	66·0	71·1	86·4	88·9	83·8	81·3	78·7	66·0	60·9	50·8	835·7
CHURCHILL (Manitoba) 58° 47' N. 94° 11' W.	13	T	−28·3	−26·7	−21·1	−10·0	−1·1	6·1	11·7	11·1	5·0	−2·8	−14·4	−23·9	−8·3
		P	12·7	15·2	22·9	22·9	22·9	48·3	55·9	68·6	58·4	35·6	25·4	17·8	406·4
COPPERMINE (N.W. Territories) 67° 49' N. 115° 10' W.	4	T	−28·3	−28·3	−26·1	−17·8	−5·6	3·3	10·0	7·8	2·2	−8·3	−21·1	−26·1	−11·7
		P	15·2	10·2	15·2	20·3	12·7	20·3	33·0	48·3	25·4	30·5	20·3	15·2	266·7

N.B. All temperatures are in ° C and precipitation is in millimetres.

North America (including Greenland and North Pacific)

Station	Altitude in Metres		Jan.	Feb.	Mar.	Apr.	May	Jun.	Jul.	Aug.	Sep.	Oct.	Nov.	Dec.	Mean: Year
Dallas (Texas) 32° 46′ N. 96° 47′ W.	156	T	7·2	10·0	13·3	18·3	22·2	26·7	28·9	28·9	25·6	19·4	13·3	8·3	18·3
		P	63·5	60·9	83·8	106·7	114·3	96·5	71·1	76·2	68·6	71·1	68·6	63·5	944·9
Detroit (Michigan) 42° 24′ N. 83° 00′ W.	189	T	−3·9	−3·9	1·1	7·8	13·9	19·4	22·2	21·7	17·8	11·1	3·9	−1·1	9·4
		P	53·3	53·3	63·5	63·5	83·8	91·4	83·4	68·6	71·1	60·9	60·9	58·4	812·8
Dodge City (Kansas) 37° 46′ N. 99° 58′ W.	790	T	−1·7	0·6	5·6	12·2	17·2	22·8	25·6	24·4	20·6	13·3	6·1	0·0	12·2
		P	10·2	17·8	22·9	48·3	73·7	81·3	78·7	66·0	48·3	35·6	20·3	15·2	518·2
Duluth (Minnesota) 46° 47′ N. 92° 06′ W.	344	T	−13·3	−11·1	−4·4	2·8	8·3	13·9	17·2	16·7	12·8	6·7	−1·1	−9·4	3·3
		P	25·4	25·4	38·1	50·8	81·3	104·1	96·5	81·3	88·9	60·9	38·1	27·9	718·8
Edmonton (Alberta) 53° 35′ N. 113° 30′ W.	676	T	−15·0	−11·1	−5·0	4·4	10·6	13·9	16·1	15·0	10·0	5·0	−3·9	−10·6	2·2
		P	22·9	15·2	20·3	22·9	48·3	78·7	83·8	58·4	33·0	17·8	17·8	20·3	439·4
*Eismitte (Greenland) 70° 53′ N. 40° 42′ W.	3000	T	−41·7	−47·2	−40·0	−32·2	−21·1	−16·7	−12·2	−18·3	−22·2	−35·6	−42·8	−38·3	−30·6
		P	15·2	5·1	7·6	5·1	2·5	2·5	2·5	10·2	7·6	12·7	12·7	25·4	109·2
El Paso (Texas) 31° 48′ N. 106° 24′ W.	1194	T	6·7	10·0	12·8	17·2	22·2	26·7	27·2	26·1	23·3	17·8	11·7	7·2	17·2
		P	10·2	12·7	7·6	5·1	7·6	15·2	45·7	40·6	33·0	17·8	12·7	7·2	220·9
Fairbanks (Alaska) 64° 51′ N. 147° 43′ W.	134	T	−23·9	−17·8	−12·2	−1·1	8·3	14·4	15·6	12·8	6·1	3·3	−15·6	−21·7	−3·3
		P	22·9	12·7	17·8	7·6	15·2	33·0	48·3	53·3	33·0	20·3	17·8	15·2	297·2
Godthaab (Greenland) 64° 11′ N. 51° 43′ W.	20	T	−10·0	−10·0	−7·8	−3·9	1·1	4·4	7·2	6·7	3·3	−1·1	−5·0	−7·8	−1·7
		P	35·6	43·2	40·6	30·5	43·2	35·6	55·9	78·7	83·8	63·5	48·3	38·1	596·9
Goose Bay (Labrador) 53° 20′ N. 60° 25′ W.	44	T	−17·8	−15·0	−9·4	−2·2	4·4	10·6	16·1	14·4	10·0	3·3	−4·4	−12·8	−0·6
		P	58·4	58·4	60·9	48·3	53·3	60·9	81·3	71·1	58·4	60·9	63·5	63·5	739·1
Halifax (Nova Scotia) 44° 39′ N. 63° 36′ W.	30	T	−5·0	−5·0	−1·1	3·9	10·0	14·4	17·8	18·3	14·4	9·4	3·9	−2·2	6·7
		P	137·2	109·2	124·5	114·3	104·1	101·6	96·5	111·8	104·1	137·2	134·6	137·2	1412·2
Honolulu (Hawaii) 21° 19′ N. 157° 52′ W.	12	T	22·2	21·7	22·2	22·8	23·9	24·4	25·0	25·6	25·6	25·0	23·9	22·8	23·9
		P	104·1	66·0	78·7	48·3	25·4	17·8	22·9	27·9	35·6	48·3	63·5	104·1	642·6
Indianapolis (Indiana) 39° 46′ N. 86° 10′ W.	219	T	−1·7	−0·6	4·4	11·1	17·2	22·2	24·4	23·3	19·4	13·3	5·6	0·0	11·7
		P	76·2	68·6	101·6	91·4	99·1	101·6	99·1	83·8	81·3	71·1	83·8	76·2	1033·8
Kansas City (Missouri) 39° 07′ N. 94° 35′ W.	226	T	−1·1	0·0	6·1	12·8	18·3	23·3	26·1	25·0	21·1	14·4	6·7	0·6	12·8
		P	33·0	43·2	66·0	81·3	124·5	121·9	104·1	104·1	116·8	71·1	48·3	33·0	947·4
Key West (Florida) 24° 33′ N. 81° 48′ W.	7	T	21·1	21·7	22·8	24·4	26·1	27·8	28·3	28·3	28·3	26·1	23·3	21·1	25·6
		P	50·8	33·0	35·6	33·0	88·9	106·7	83·8	114·3	170·2	152·4	55·9	43·2	967·7
Kotzebue (Alaska) 66° 52′ N. 162° 38′ W.	3	T	−21·1	−19·4	−18·3	−11·1	−1·7	6·1	11·7	10·0	4·4	−3·3	−12·8	−18·9	−6·7
		P	7·6	10·2	7·6	7·6	7·6	12·7	45·7	68·6	30·5	15·2	15·2	10·2	241·3

N.B. All temperatures are in ° C and precipitation is in millimetres.

* One-year record only.

North America (including Greenland and North Pacific)

Station	Altitude in Metres		Jan.	Feb.	Mar.	Apr.	May	Jun.	Jul.	Aug.	Sep.	Oct.	Nov.	Dec.	Mean: Year
La Paz (Mexico) 24° 10′ N. 110° 18′ W.	13	T	17·8	18·3	20·0	21·7	24·4	26·7	29·4	28·9	28·9	26·7	22·8	18·9	23·3
		P	5·1	2·5	0·0	0·0	0·0	5·1	10·2	30·5	35·6	15·2	12·7	27·9	144·8
Las Vegas (Nevada) 36° 12′ N. 115° 07′ W.	?	T	6·7	10·0	12·8	17·2	21·1	26·7	29·4	28·9	24·4	18·3	11·7	7·2	17·8
		P	17·8	12·7	7·6	7·6	5·1	5·1	12·7	12·7	7·6	7·6	5·1	10·2	111·8
Little Rock (Arkansas) 34° 45′ N. 92° 16′ W.	109	T	5·6	7·2	11·7	16·7	21·1	25·6	27·2	26·7	23·3	17·8	11·1	6·7	16·7
		P	121·9	96·5	114·3	129·4	124·5	96·5	86·4	93·9	78·7	71·1	104·1	104·1	1221·7
Los Angeles (California) 34° 03′ N. 118° 15′ W.	95	T	12·8	13·3	13·9	15·6	16·7	18·9	21·1	21·7	20·6	18·3	16·1	13·9	16·7
		P	78·7	76·2	71·1	25·4	10·2	2·5	Tr	Tr	5·1	15·2	30·5	66·0	381·0
Mexico City (Mexico) 19° 24′ N. 99° 12′ W.	2305	T	12·2	13·3	16·1	17·8	18·9	18·3	17·2	17·2	17·2	15·6	13·9	12·2	15·6
		P	12·7	5·1	10·2	20·3	53·3	119·4	170·2	152·4	129·5	50·8	17·8	7·6	746·8
Miami (Florida) 25° 48′ N. 80° 12′ W.	8	T	19·4	20·0	21·7	22·8	25·0	26·7	27·8	27·8	27·2	25·0	22·2	20·6	23·9
		P	71·1	53·3	63·5	81·3	172·7	177·8	154·9	160·0	203·2	233·7	71·1	50·8	1516·4
Mobile (Alabama) 30° 42′ N. 88° 02′ W.	3	T	11·1	12·2	15·0	18·9	23·3	26·7	27·8	27·2	25·6	20·6	15·0	11·7	19·4
		P	121·9	134·6	165·1	119·4	109·2	139·7	170·2	172·7	132·1	88·9	99·1	124·5	1577·3
Montgomery (Alabama) 32° 23′ N. 86° 18′ W.	61	T	9·4	10·6	14·4	18·3	22·8	26·7	27·2	27·2	24·4	18·9	13·3	10·0	18·3
		P	129·5	139·7	160·0	119·4	99·1	104·1	119·4	101·6	78·7	60·9	88·9	119·4	1320·8
Monterrey (Mexico) 25° 40′ N. 100° 18′ W.	528	T	14·4	16·7	18·9	22·8	25·0	27·2	26·7	27·8	25·6	22·2	17·2	13·9	21·7
		P	15·2	17·8	20·3	33·0	33·0	76·2	58·4	60·9	132·1	76·2	38·1	20·3	579·1
Mount Wilson (California) 34° 14′ N. 118° 04′ W.	1780	T	5·6	6·1	7·2	10·0	13·3	19·4	22·8	22·2	18·9	13·9	10·0	7·2	12·8
		P	160·0	170·2	154·9	66·0	30·5	5·1	Tr	2·5	12·7	27·9	48·3	111·8	789·9
Nashville (Tennessee) 36° 10′ N. 87° 47′ W.	166	T	3·9	5·0	10·0	15·0	20·0	24·4	26·1	25·6	22·2	16·1	9·4	5·0	15·0
		P	116·8	104·1	129·5	109·2	96·5	104·1	101·6	91·4	86·4	66·0	88·9	101·6	1196·3
New Orleans (Louisiana) 29° 57′ N. 90° 04′ W.	2·5	T	12·2	13·9	17·2	20·6	23·9	27·2	28·3	28·3	26·1	21·7	16·7	13·3	20·6
		P	116·8	106·7	119·4	121·9	114·3	139·7	167·6	147·3	121·9	88·9	96·5	116·8	1457·6
New York (New York) 40° 43′ N. 74° 00′ W.	96	T	−1·1	−0·6	2·8	10·0	15·6	20·0	23·3	22·8	20·6	15·0	9·4	1·7	11·4
		P	93·9	96·5	91·4	81·3	81·3	83·8	106·7	109·2	86·4	88·9	76·2	91·4	1087·0
Norfolk (Virginia) 36° 51′ N. 76° 12′ W.	3·3	T	5·0	5·6	9·4	13·9	19·4	23·3	26·1	25·0	22·2	16·7	11·1	6·1	15·6
		P	81·3	86·4	96·5	83·8	93·9	106·7	147·3	132·1	96·5	76·2	63·5	81·3	1145·5
Oklahoma (Oklahoma) 35° 29′ N. 97° 32′ W.	382	T	2·8	4·4	10·0	15·6	22·8	25·0	27·2	27·2	23·3	16·7	10·0	3·9	15·6
		P	33·0	25·4	55·9	83·8	129·5	88·9	73·7	68·6	76·2	76·2	50·8	40·6	802·6
Ottawa (Ontario) 45° 20′ N. 75° 41′ W.	103	T	−11·1	−11·1	−4·4	5·0	12·8	18·3	20·6	18·9	14·4	7·2	0·0	−8·9	5·0
		P	73·7	55·9	71·1	68·6	63·5	88·9	86·4	66·0	81·3	73·7	76·2	66·0	871·2

N.B. All temperatures are in ° C and precipitation is in millimetres.

NORTH AMERICA (including GREENLAND AND NORTH PACIFIC)

STATION	ALTITUDE IN METRES		JAN.	FEB.	MAR.	APR.	MAY	JUN.	JUL.	AUG.	SEP.	OCT.	NOV.	DEC.	MEAN: YEAR
PHOENIX (Arizona) 33° 28′ N. 112° 04′ W.	330	T	11·1	13·3	16·1	19·4	23·9	29·4	32·2	31·1	28·3	21·7	15·6	11·7	21·1
		P	20·3	20·3	17·8	10·2	2·5	2·5	25·4	25·4	17·8	10·2	15·2	22·9	190·5
PITTSBURGH (Penn.) 40° 06′ N. 80° 00′ W.	228	T	−0·6	−0·6	4·4	10·6	16·7	21·1	23·3	22·2	18·9	12·8	6·1	1·1	11·7
		P	76·2	66·0	76·2	76·2	78·7	93·9	106·7	81·3	63·5	66·0	58·4	71·1	914·4
PRINCE RUPERT (Brit. Columbia) 54° 17′ N. 130° 23′ W.	52	T	1·1	2·2	3·9	6·1	8·9	11·7	12·8	13·9	11·7	8·3	5·0	2·2	7·8
		P	248·9	193·0	213·4	170·2	134·6	104·1	121·9	129·5	195·6	309·9	312·4	287·0	2420·6
PUEBLO (Colorado) 38° 14′ N. 104° 38′ W.	1460	T	−1·1	0·6	5·0	10·0	15·0	20·6	23·3	22·8	18·3	11·7	4·4	0·0	10·6
		P	7·6	15·2	17·8	40·6	40·6	33·0	50·8	45·7	22·9	15·2	10·2	12·7	312·4
QUEBEC (Quebec) 46° 48′ N. 71° 13′ W.	90	T	−12·2	−11·1	−5·0	2·8	10·6	16·7	18·9	17·2	12·8	6·7	−1·1	−9·4	3·9
		P	88·9	68·6	76·2	58·4	78·7	93·9	101·6	101·6	91·4	86·4	81·3	81·3	1008·4
REGINA (Saskatchewan) 50° 26′ N. 104° 39′ W.	575	T	−17·8	−16·7	−8·9	3·3	10·6	15·6	18·3	16·7	10·6	3·9	−6·1	−13·3	1·1
		P	12·7	7·6	17·8	17·8	45·7	83·8	60·9	45·7	33·0	22·9	15·2	10·2	373·4
ST JOHN'S (Newfoundland) 47° 34′ N. 52° 42′ W.	74	T	−5·0	−5·6	−2·8	1·7	5·6	11·1	15·0	16·1	12·2	7·8	2·8	−1·7	4·4
		P	134·6	124·5	116·8	106·7	91·4	88·9	88·9	93·9	96·5	134·6	149·9	139·7	1366·5
ST LOUIS (Missouri) 38° 38′ N. 90° 12′ W.	173	T	0·0	1·1	7·2	13·3	18·9	23·9	26·1	25·6	21·7	15·0	7·8	1·7	13·3
		P	58·4	63·5	88·9	96·5	114·3	114·3	88·9	86·4	81·3	73·7	71·1	63·5	1000·8
SACRAMENTO (California) 38° 35′ N. 121° 30′ W.	21	T	7·2	10·0	12·8	14·4	17·8	21·1	23·3	22·8	21·1	16·7	12·2	7·8	15·6
		P	96·5	71·1	71·1	38·1	20·3	2·5	Tr	Tr	7·6	20·3	48·3	96·5	472·4
SEATTLE (Washington) 47° 36′ N. 122° 20′ W.	38	T	4·4	5·6	7·2	10·0	12·8	15·6	17·2	17·8	15·0	11·7	7·8	5·6	11·1
		P	121·9	93·9	78·7	58·4	45·7	35·6	15·2	17·8	43·2	73·7	121·9	142·2	848·4
SALINA CRUZ (Mexico) 16° 12′ N. 95° 12′ W.	56	T	25·6	25·6	26·7	27·8	28·9	27·8	27·8	28·3	27·2	27·2	26·7	25·6	27·2
		P	2·5	5·1	Tr	Tr	50·8	241·3	165·1	187·9	297·2	60·9	12·7	2·5	1026·2
SAN FRANCISCO (California) 37° 47′ N. 122° 25′ W.	16	T	10·0	11·7	12·2	12·8	13·9	15·0	15·0	15·0	16·7	16·1	13·9	11·1	13·3
		P	119·4	96·5	78·7	38·1	17·8	2·5	Tr	Tr	7·6	25·4	63·5	111·8	561·3
SANTE FÉ (New Mexico) 35° 41′ N. 105° 57′ W.	2135	T	−1·7	0·6	4·4	8·3	12·8	18·3	20·0	19·4	16·1	10·0	3·9	−1·1	9·4
		P	17·8	20·3	20·3	25·4	33·0	27·9	60·9	58·4	35·6	30·5	17·8	17·8	365·8
THULE (Greenland) 76° 33′ N. 68° 49′ W.	38	T	−21·7	−26·7	−23·3	−17·8	−3·6	1·7	5·0	3·3	−2·8	−9·4	−15·0	−22·8	−11·1
		P	2·5	2·5	2·5	2·5	2·5	5·1	12·7	12·7	10·2	2·5	2·5	5·1	63·5
TORONTO (Ontario) 43° 40′ N. 79° 24′ W.	116	T	−5·0	−5·6	−1·1	5·6	11·7	17·8	20·6	19·4	15·6	8·9	2·8	2·8	7·2
		P	68·6	60·9	66·0	63·5	73·7	68·6	73·7	68·6	73·7	60·9	71·1	66·0	815·3
VANCOUVER (Brit. Columbia) 49° 17′ N. 123° 05′ W.	14	T	2·2	3·9	6·1	9·4	12·8	15·6	17·8	17·2	13·9	10·0	6·1	3·9	10·0
		P	218·4	147·3	127·0	83·8	71·1	63·5	30·5	43·2	91·4	147·3	210·8	223·5	1457·9

N.B. All temperatures are in ° C and precipitation is in millimetres.

NORTH AMERICA (including GREENLAND AND NORTH PACIFIC)

STATION	ALTITUDE IN METRES		JAN.	FEB.	MAR.	APR.	MAY	JUN.	JUL.	AUG.	SEP.	OCT.	NOV.	DEC.	MEAN: YEAR
VERA CRUZ (Mexico) 19° 12′ N. 96° 08′ W.	16	T	21·7	22·2	22·8	25·0	26·7	27·2	26·7	26·7	26·7	26·1	23·3	22·2	25·0
		P	22·9	15·2	7·6	20·3	53·3	243·8	246·4	299·7	345·4	152·4	88·9	25·4	1521·5
VICTORIA (Brit. Columbia) 48° 25′ N. 123° 20′ W.	70	T	3·9	5·0	6·7	9·4	11·7	13·9	15·6	15·6	13·9	10·6	7·2	5·0	10·0
		P	114·3	76·2	58·4	30·5	25·4	22·9	10·2	15·2	38·1	71·1	109·3	119·4	690·9
WASHINGTON (D.C.) 38° 54′ N. 77° 03′ W.	22	T	1·1	2·2	6·7	12·2	17·8	22·8	25·0	23·9	20·0	13·9	7·8	2·8	13·3
		P	86·4	76·2	91·4	83·8	93·9	99·1	111·8	109·2	93·9	73·7	66·0	78·7	1064·3
WHITEHORSE (Yukon) 60° 43′ N. 135° 05′ W.	700	T	−15·0	−13·9	−6·1	−0·6	7·2	12·2	13·3	11·7	7·8	1·1	−10·0	−15·6	−0·6
		P	15·2	12·7	15·2	10·2	15·2	25·4	40·6	38·1	33·0	17·8	25·4	17·8	266·7
WINNIPEG (Manitoba) 49° 54′ N. 97° 14′ W.	240	T	−19·4	−16·7	−8·9	2·8	11·1	16·7	19·4	17·2	12·2	5·0	−6·1	−14·4	1·7
		P	22·9	22·9	30·5	35·6	58·4	78·7	78·7	63·5	58·4	38·1	27·9	22·9	538·5
YELLOW KNIFE (N.W. Territories) 62° 28′ N. 114° 20′ W.	202	T	−27·8	−26·1	−17·8	−7·8	3·9	11·1	15·6	13·9	7·2	−0·6	−13·9	−25·0	−5·6
		P	12·7	12·7	10·2	10·2	15·2	17·8	27·9	25·4	22·9	25·4	17·8	15·2	213·4
YELLOWSTONE PARK (Wyoming) 44° 58′ N. 110° 42′ W.	1900	T	−7·8	−7·2	−3·3	2·8	7·8	12·2	16·1	15·6	10·6	4·4	−1·7	−6·7	3·3
		P	40·6	33·0	43·2	33·0	50·8	43·2	33·0	30·5	30·5	35·6	35·6	35·6	444·5

N.B. All temperatures are in ° C and precipitation is in millimetres.

South and Central America

Station	Altitude in Metres		Jan.	Feb.	Mar.	Apr.	May	Jun.	Jul.	Aug.	Sep.	Oct.	Nov.	Dec.	Mean: Year
ANCUD (Chile) 41° 47′ S. 73° 52′ W.	56	T	13·3	13·3	12·2	11·1	9·4	8·3	7·8	7·8	8·3	10·0	10·6	12·2	10·6
		P	78·7	93·9	134·6	187·9	251·5	279·4	261·6	238·8	165·1	106·7	119·4	116·8	2034·5
ANTOFAGASTA (Chile) 23° 42′ S. 70° 24′ W.	94	T	20·6	20·6	19·4	17·8	16·1	14·4	13·9	13·9	14·4	15·6	17·2	18·9	17·2
		P	0·0	0·0	0·0	Tr	Tr	2·5	5·1	2·5	Tr	2·5	Tr	0·0	12·7
ARICA (Chile) 18° 28′ S. 70° 20′ W.	29	T	21·7	22·2	21·1	19·4	17·8	16·7	15·6	15·6	16·1	17·2	18·9	20·0	18·3
		P	Tr	0·0	0·0	0·0	0·0	0·0	0·0	Tr	0·0	0·0	0·0	Tr	Tr
ASUNCION (Paraguay) 25° 17′ S. 57° 30′ W.	139	T	28·3	27·8	26·7	23·3	19·4	16·7	17·2	19·4	21·7	23·3	25·0	27·8	23·3
		P	139·7	129·5	109·2	132·1	116·8	68·6	55·9	38·1	78·7	139·7	149·9	157·5	1315·7
BAHIA (Brazil) 13° 00′ S. 38° 30′ W.	47	T	26·7	26·7	26·7	26·1	25·0	23·9	23·3	23·3	23·9	25·0	25·6	25·6	25·0
		P	66·0	134·6	154·9	284·5	274·3	238·8	182·9	121·9	83·8	101·6	114·3	142·2	1899·9
BAHIA BLANCA (Argentina) 38° 43′ S. 62° 16′ W.	29	T	23·9	22·2	20·0	16·1	12·2	8·9	8·9	10·0	12·2	15·0	18·9	22·2	16·1
		P	43·2	55·9	63·5	58·4	30·5	22·9	25·4	25·4	40·6	55·9	53·3	48·3	523·2
BELEM (Brazil) 01° 27′ S. 49° 29′ W.	13	T	26·1	26·1	26·7	26·7	26·7	26·7	26·1	26·1	26·7	26·7	26·7	26·7	26·7
		P	317·5	358·1	358·1	320·0	259·1	170·2	149·9	111·8	88·9	83·8	66·0	154·9	2438·4
BELIZE (Brit. Honduras) 17° 31′ N. 88° 11′ W.	5	T	23·3	23·9	25·0	26·7	27·2	27·2	27·2	27·2	26·7	26·1	23·9	23·3	25·0
		P	137·2	60·9	38·1	55·9	109·2	195·6	162·6	170·2	243·8	304·8	226·1	185·4	1889·8
BERMUDA (Atlantic) 32° 17′ N. 64° 46′ W.	46	T	17·2	16·7	16·7	18·3	21·1	23·9	26·1	26·7	25·6	23·3	20·0	18·3	21·1
		P	111·8	119·4	121·9	104·1	116·8	111·8	114·3	137·2	132·1	147·3	127·0	119·4	1463·0
BOGOTA (Colombia) 04° 36′ N. 74° 05′ W.	2645	T	13·9	14·4	14·4	15·0	14·4	14·4	13·9	13·9	13·9	14·4	14·4	13·9	14·4
		P	58·4	66·0	101·6	147·3	114·3	60·9	50·8	55·9	60·9	160·0	119·4	66·0	1059·2
BRIDGETOWN (Barbados) 13° 08′ N. 59° 36′ W.	55	T	24·4	24·4	25·0	26·1	26·7	26·7	26·7	26·7	26·7	26·1	26·1	25·0	25·6
		P	66·0	27·9	33·0	35·6	58·4	111·8	147·3	147·3	170·2	177·8	205·7	96·5	1275·1
BUENOS AIRES (Argentina) 34° 35′ S. 58° 29′ W.	27	T	23·3	22·8	20·6	16·7	12·8	9·4	10·0	10·6	12·8	15·0	18·9	21·7	16·1
		P	78·7	71·1	109·2	88·9	76·2	60·9	55·9	60·9	78·7	86·4	83·8	99·1	949·9
CARACAS (Venezuela) 10° 30′ N. 66° 56′ W.	1040	T	18·3	18·9	20·0	21·1	21·7	21·1	20·6	21·1	21·1	21·1	20·0	20·0	20·6
		P	22·9	10·2	15·2	33·0	78·7	101·6	109·2	109·2	106·7	109·2	93·9	45·7	833·1
CATALAO (Brazil) 18° 10′ S. 47° 52′ W.	853	T	22·8	22·8	22·8	22·2	20·6	19·4	20·0	21·1	22·8	23·3	22·8	22·2	21·7
		P	299·7	259·1	223·5	96·5	27·9	7·6	12·7	7·6	58·4	154·9	210·8	378·5	1729·7
CAYENNE (French Guiana) 04° 56′ N. 52° 27′ W.	6	T	26·1	26·1	26·1	26·7	26·1	26·7	26·7	27·2	27·8	27·8	27·2	26·7	26·7
		P	365·8	312·4	401·3	480·1	551·2	393·7	175·3	71·1	30·5	33·0	116·8	271·8	3210·6
CIUDAD TRUJILLO (Dominica) 18° 29′ N. 69° 54′ W.	17	T	23·9	23·9	23·9	25·0	25·6	26·1	26·7	26·7	26·7	26·1	25·6	24·4	25·6
		P	60·9	35·6	48·3	99·1	172·7	157·5	162·6	160·0	185·4	152·4	121·9	60·9	1417·3

N.B. All temperatures are in ° C and precipitation is in millimetres.

SOUTH AND CENTRAL AMERICA

STATION	ALTITUDE IN METRES		JAN.	FEB.	MAR.	APR.	MAY	JUN.	JUL.	AUG.	SEP.	OCT.	NOV.	DEC.	MEAN: YEAR
CONCEPTION (Bolivia) 16° 15′ S. 62° 03′ W.	490	T	23·9	24·4	23·9	23·3	21·7	20·0	19·4	21·7	24·4	23·9	25·0	23·9	23·9
		P	193·0	154·9	116·8	60·9	76·2	22·9	27·9	15·2	58·4	76·2	205·7	132·1	1143·0
CRISTOBAL (Panama) 09° 21′ N. 79° 54′ W.	11	T	26·7	26·7	27·2	27·2	27·2	27·2	26·7	26·7	26·7	26·7	26·1	26·7	26·7
		P	86·4	38·1	38·1	104·1	317·5	353·1	396·2	388·6	322·6	401·3	566·4	297·2	3309·6
CUMBERLAND BAY (S. Georgia) 54° 16′ S. 36° 30′ W.	2·4	T	5·0	5·6	4·4	1·7	0·0	−2·2	−2·2	−2·2	0·0	1·1	3·3	3·9	1·7
		P	83·8	109·2	134·6	137·2	132·1	124·5	139·7	134·6	88·9	66·0	86·4	76·2	1313·2
CUZCO (Peru) 13° 33′ S. 71° 55′ W.	3300	T	13·3	13·9	13·9	12·8	11·1	10·6	10·0	11·1	12·8	13·9	14·4	13·9	12·8
		P	162·6	149·9	109·2	50·8	15·2	5·1	5·1	10·2	25·4	66·0	76·2	137·2	812·8
EASTER I. (Pacific) 27° 10′ S. 109° 26′ W.	30	T	23·9	23·3	22·8	21·1	20·6	18·3	17·8	17·8	17·8	18·3	19·4	21·7	20·0
		P	132·1	40·6	228·6	129·5	99·1	241·3	81·3	66·0	88·9	55·9	127·0	73·7	1363·9
GALAPAGOS Is. (Pacific) 00° 28′ S. 90° 18′ W.	11	T	26·1	26·7	27·9	27·2	26·1	25·0	23·9	23·3	22·8	23·3	23·3	24·4	25·0
		P	20·3	35·6	17·8	17·8	Tr	Tr	Tr	Tr	Tr	Tr	Tr	Tr	101·6
GEORGETOWN (Guyana) 06° 50′ N. 58° 12′ W.	1·8	T	26·1	26·1	26·1	26·7	26·7	26·7	26·7	26·7	27·2	27·2	27·2	26·1	26·7
		P	203·2	114·3	175·3	139·7	289·6	302·3	254·0	175·3	81·3	76·2	154·9	287·0	2252·9
GUATEMALA CITY (Guatemala) 14° 37′ N. 90° 31′ W.	1480	T	17·2	18·3	20·6	21·1	22·2	21·7	20·6	20·6	20·6	20·0	18·3	17·2	20·0
		P	7·6	2·5	12·7	30·5	152·4	274·3	203·2	198·1	231·1	172·7	22·9	7·6	1315·7
GUAYAQUIL (Ecuador) 02° 10′ S. 79° 53′ W.	6	T	26·1	26·1	26·7	26·7	25·6	25·0	23·9	23·9	24·4	25·0	25·6	26·1	25·6
		P	238·8	248·9	276·9	116·8	27·9	7·6	5·1	0·0	2·5	7·6	25·6	50·8	985·5
HAVANA (Cuba) 23° 08′ N. 82° 21′ W.	24	T	22·2	22·2	23·3	24·4	26·1	27·2	27·8	27·8	27·2	26·1	23·9	22·8	25·0
		P	71·1	45·7	45·7	58·4	119·4	165·1	124·5	134·6	149·9	172·7	78·7	58·4	1124·3
JUAN FERNANDEZ I. (Pacific) 33° 37′ S. 78° 52′ W.	6	T	18·9	18·9	18·3	16·7	15·6	13·3	12·8	12·2	12·8	13·3	15·0	17·2	15·6
		P	20·3	30·5	40·6	86·4	149·9	162·6	147·3	111·8	73·7	48·3	40·6	25·4	937·3
KINGSTON (Jamaica) 17° 58′ N. 76° 48′ W.	33	T	24·4	24·4	25·0	25·6	26·1	27·2	27·2	27·2	27·2	26·7	26·1	25·6	26·1
		P	22·9	15·2	22·9	30·5	101·6	88·9	38·1	91·4	99·1	180·3	73·7	35·6	800·1
LA GUÉRITE (St Kitts) 17° 20′ N. 62° 45′ W.	48	T	23·9	23·9	24·4	25·6	26·1	26·7	27·2	27·2	27·2	26·1	26·1	25·0	26·1
		P	104·1	50·8	58·4	58·4	96·5	91·4	111·8	132·1	152·4	137·2	185·4	114·3	1292·9
LA PAZ (Bolivia) 16° 30′ S. 68° 08′ W.	3670	T	11·7	11·7	11·7	11·1	10·0	8·9	8·3	9·4	10·6	11·7	12·2	11·7	10·6
		P	114·3	106·7	66·0	33·0	12·7	7·6	10·2	12·7	27·9	40·6	48·3	93·9	574·0
LIMA (Peru) 12° 05′ S. 77° 03′ W.	120	T	23·3	23·9	23·3	21·7	19·4	17·2	16·7	16·1	16·7	17·8	19·4	21·1	20·0
		P	2·5	Tr	Tr	Tr	5·1	5·1	7·6	7·6	7·6	2·5	2·5	Tr	40·6
LOS EVANGELISTOS (Chile) 52° 24′ S. 75° 06′ W.	55	T	8·3	8·3	7·8	6·7	5·6	4·4	3·9	3·9	5·0	5·6	6·1	7·2	6·1
		P	297·2	254·0	287·0	289·6	243·8	238·8	238·8	218·4	233·7	223·5	251·5	256·5	3032·8

N.B. All temperatures are in ° C and precipitation is in millimetres.

SOUTH AND CENTRAL AMERICA

STATION	ALTITUDE IN METRES		JAN.	FEB.	MAR.	APR.	MAY	JUN.	JUL.	AUG.	SEP.	OCT.	NOV.	DEC.	MEAN: YEAR
MANAUS (Brazil) 03° 08′ S. 60° 01′ W.	44	T	27·2	27·2	27·2	27·2	27·2	27·2	27·8	28·3	28·3	28·9	28·3	27·8	27·8
		P	248·9	231·1	261·6	220·9	170·2	83·8	58·4	38·1	45·7	106·7	142·2	203·2	1811·0
MARACAIBO (Venezuela) 10° 39′ N. 71° 36′ W.	6	T	27·2	27·2	27·8	28·9	28·9	29·4	29·4	29·4	29·4	28·9	28·3	28·3	28·9
		P	2·5	Tr	7·6	20·3	68·6	55·9	45·7	55·9	71·1	149·9	83·8	15·2	576·6
MENDOZA (Argentina) 32° 53′ S. 68° 49′ W.	800	T	23·9	22·8	20·0	15·6	11·7	8·3	8·3	10·0	12·7	17·2	20·0	22·8	16·1
		P	22·9	30·5	27·9	12·7	10·2	7·6	5·1	7·6	12·7	17·8	17·8	17·8	190·5
MONTEVIDEO (Uruguay) 34° 52′ S. 56° 12′ W.	22	T	22·2	21·7	20·0	16·7	13·3	10·6	10·0	10·6	12·2	14·4	17·8	20·6	16·1
		P	73·7	66·0	99·1	99·1	83·8	81·3	73·7	78·7	76·2	66·0	73·7	78·7	949·9
NASSAU (Bahamas) 25° 05′ N. 77° 21′ W.	3·7	T	21·7	21·1	22·2	23·9	25·0	26·7	27·2	27·8	27·2	26·1	23·9	22·8	24·4
		P	35·6	38·1	35·6	63·5	116·8	162·6	147·3	134·6	175·3	165·1	71·1	33·0	1178·6
NATAL (Brazil) 05° 46′ S. 35° 12′ W.	16	T	27·2	27·2	26·7	26·1	26·1	25·0	23·9	23·9	25·6	26·7	27·2	27·2	26·1
		P	48·3	121·9	177·8	233·7	180·3	220·9	195·6	96·5	35·6	20·3	17·8	27·9	1376·7
PARANA (Brazil) 12° 26′ S. 48° 06′ W.	260	T	23·3	23·3	23·3	23·3	22·2	21·1	20·6	21·7	23·9	24·4	23·3	23·3	22·8
		P	287·0	236·2	238·8	101·6	12·7	Tr	2·5	5·1	27·9	127·0	231·1	309·9	1582·4
PORT OF SPAIN (Trinidad) 10° 40′ N. 61° 31′ W.	20	T	25·6	25·6	25·6	26·1	26·7	26·7	26·1	26·1	26·7	26·7	26·7	25·6	26·1
		P	68·6	40·6	45·7	53·3	93·9	193·0	218·4	246·4	193·0	170·2	182·9	124·5	1630·7
QUITO (Ecuador) 00° 13′ S. 78° 32′ W.	2880	T	15·0	15·0	15·0	14·4	14·4	14·4	14·4	15·0	15·0	15·0	14·4	15·0	15·0
		P	99·1	111·8	142·2	175·3	137·2	43·2	20·3	30·5	68·6	111·8	96·5	78·7	1115·1
RECIFE (Brazil) 08° 04′ S. 34° 53′ W.	30	T	27·2	27·2	27·2	26·7	26·7	25·6	25·0	24·4	25·0	26·1	26·7	27·2	26·1
		P	53·3	83·8	160·0	220·9	266·7	276·9	254·0	152·4	63·5	25·4	25·4	27·9	1610·4
RIO DE JANEIRO (Brazil) 22° 55′ S. 43° 12′ W.	61	T	25·6	26·1	25·0	23·3	21·7	21·1	20·6	21·1	21·1	21·7	22·8	24·4	22·8
		P	124·5	121·9	129·5	106·7	78·7	53·3	40·6	43·2	66·0	78·7	104·1	137·2	1082·0
ROSARIO (Argentina) 32° 58′ S. 60° 40′ W.	30	T	24·4	24·4	21·7	17·8	13·9	10·0	11·1	11·7	13·9	16·7	20·6	23·3	17·2
		P	83·8	83·8	109·2	91·4	48·3	33·0	33·0	40·6	53·3	86·4	91·4	114·3	868·7
SAN JOSÉ (Costa Rica) 09° 56′ N. 84° 08′ W.	1145	T	18·9	19·4	20·6	21·1	21·7	21·7	20·6	20·6	21·1	20·0	20·0	18·9	20·0
		P	15·2	5·1	20·3	45·7	228·6	241·3	210·8	241·3	304·8	299·7	144·8	40·6	1793·3
SANTA CRUZ (Argentina) 50° 01′ S. 68° 32′ W.	12	T	15·0	15·0	12·2	8·9	6·7	1·7	1·1	3·9	6·1	8·9	11·1	12·8	8·9
		P	15·2	7·6	7·6	15·2	10·2	12·7	10·2	12·7	7·6	7·6	10·2	17·8	134·6
SENA MADUREIRA (Brazil) 09° 04′ S. 68° 39′ W.	134	T	26·7	26·7	26·7	26·1	25·6	25·0	25·0	26·1	26·7	27·2	27·2	27·2	26·7
		P	284·5	287·0	259·1	238·8	104·1	55·9	27·9	38·1	101·6	177·8	190·5	297·2	2062·5
STANLEY (Falkland Is.) 51° 42′ S. 57° 51′ W.	1·8	T	9·4	8·9	7·8	6·1	3·9	2·2	1·7	2·2	3·9	5·0	6·7	7·8	5·6
		P	71·1	58·4	63·5	66·0	66·0	53·3	50·8	50·8	38·1	40·6	50·8	71·1	680·7

N.B. All temperatures are in ° C and precipitation is in millimetres.

SOUTH AND CENTRAL AMERICA

STATION	ALTITUDE IN METRES		JAN.	FEB.	MAR.	APR.	MAY	JUN.	JUL.	AUG.	SEP.	OCT.	NOV.	DEC.	MEAN: YEAR
TEOFILO OTONI (Brazil) 17° 45′ S. 41° 26′ W.	305	T	25·6	25·6	25·0	23·9	21·7	21·1	19·4	20·6	22·2	23·9	23·9	24·4	23·3
		P	190·5	124·5	154·9	114·3	76·2	27·9	30·5	20·3	33·0	101·6	200·7	238·8	1315·7
UAUPÉS (Brazil) 00° 08′ S. 67° 05′ W.	83	T	26·7	26·7	26·7	26·7	26·1	25·6	25·0	26·1	26·7	26·7	27·2	26·7	26·1
		P	261·6	195·6	254·0	269·2	304·8	233·7	223·5	182·9	129·5	175·3	182·9	264·2	2677·2
VALDIVIA (Chile) 39° 48′ S. 73° 14′ W.	4·9	T	16·7	16·7	15·0	12·2	10·0	8·3	7·8	8·3	10·0	11·7	12·8	15·0	11·7
		P	66·0	73·7	132·1	233·7	360·7	449·6	393·7	327·7	208·3	127·0	124·5	104·1	2600·9
VALPARAISO (Chile) 33° 01′ S. 71° 38′ W.	41	T	17·8	17·8	16·7	15·0	13·3	12·2	11·7	12·2	12·8	13·9	15·6	16·7	14·4
		P	2·5	Tr	7·6	15·2	104·1	149·8	99·1	73·7	33·0	10·2	5·1	5·1	505·5
WILLEMSTAD (Curaçao) 12° 06′ N. 68° 56′ W.	23	T	26·1	26·1	26·1	27·2	27·2	27·8	27·8	28·3	28·3	28·3	27·2	26·1	27·2
		P	53·3	25·4	20·3	27·9	20·3	25·4	38·1	30·5	27·9	106·7	111·8	99·1	581·7

N.B. All temperatures are in ° C and precipitation is in millimetres.

AUSTRALASIA (including ANTARCTICA AND SOUTH PACIFIC)

STATION	ALTITUDE IN METRES		JAN.	FEB.	MAR.	APR.	MAY	JUN.	JUL.	AUG.	SEP.	OCT.	NOV.	DEC.	MEAN: YEAR
ADELAIDE (S. Australia) 34° 56′ S. 138° 35′ E.	43	T	22·8	23·3	21·1	17·8	14·4	12·2	11·1	12·2	13·9	16·7	19·4	21·7	17·2
		P	20·3	17·8	25·4	45·7	68·6	76·2	66·0	66·0	53·3	43·2	27·9	25·4	535·9
AITUTAKI (Cook Is.) 18° 55′ S. 159° 45′ W.	3	T	27·2	27·2	27·2	26·1	25·6	23·9	24·4	23·9	24·4	25·0	26·1	26·1	25·6
		P	236·2	279·4	256·4	175·3	129·5	106·7	76·2	81·3	81·3	144·8	182·9	223·5	1973·6
ALBANY (W. Australia) 35° 02′ S. 117° 50′ E.	12·5	T	18·9	18·9	17·8	16·7	14·4	12·8	11·7	12·2	12·8	14·4	16·1	17·8	15·6
		P	35·6	25·4	45·7	73·7	134·6	137·2	152·4	137·2	109·2	83·8	25·0	30·5	1008·4
ALICE SPRINGS (N. Australia) 23° 28′ S. 133° 35′ E.	580	T	28·3	27·8	24·4	19·4	15·0	12·2	11·7	14·4	18·3	22·8	25·0	27·8	20·6
		P	43·2	33·0	27·9	10·2	15·2	12·7	7·6	7·6	7·6	17·8	30·5	38·1	251·5
AUCKLAND (New Zealand) 36° 47′ S. 174° 39′ E.	26	T	18·9	18·9	18·3	16·1	13·3	11·7	10·6	11·1	12·2	13·9	15·6	17·2	15·0
		P	78·7	93·9	81·3	96·5	127·0	137·2	144·8	116·8	101·6	101·6	88·9	78·7	1247·1
BRISBANE (Queensland) 27° 28′ S. 153° 02′ E.	42	T	25·0	24·4	23·3	21·1	18·3	15·6	14·4	15·6	18·3	21·1	22·8	24·4	20·6
		P	162·6	160·0	144·8	93·9	71·1	66·0	55·9	48·3	48·3	63·5	93·9	127·0	1135·4
BROOME (W. Australia) 17° 57′ S. 122° 15′ E.	19	T	29·4	29·4	29·4	27·8	24·4	21·7	21·1	22·2	25·0	27·2	28·9	30·0	26·1
		P	160·0	147·3	99·1	30·5	15·2	22·9	5·1	2·5	Tr	Tr	15·2	83·8	581·7
CAIRNS (Queensland) 16° 55′ S. 145° 47′ E.	5	T	27·8	27·2	26·7	25·0	22·8	22·2	20·6	21·7	22·8	25·0	26·1	27·8	24·4
		P	421·6	398·8	459·7	287·0	111·8	73·7	40·6	43·2	43·2	53·3	99·1	220·9	2252·9
CAMPBELL I. (S. Pacific) 52° 33′ S. 169° 08′ E.	23	T	9·4	10·0	8·9	7·2	5·0	4·4	4·4	4·4	5·0	5·6	7·2	8·9	6·7
		P	83·8	63·5	93·9	144·8	119·4	96·5	157·5	111·8	121·9	124·5	121·9	142·2	1381·8
CANBERRA (New South Wales) 35° 20′ S. 149° 15′ E.	561	T	20·0	20·0	17·2	12·8	8·9	6·1	5·6	7·2	10·0	12·8	16·7	18·9	13·3
		P	48·3	43·2	55·9	40·6	45·7	53·3	45·7	55·9	40·6	55·9	48·3	50·8	584·2
CAPE DENISON (Antarctica) 67° 00′ S. 142° 40′ E.	6·5	T	-1·1	-5·0	-11·1	-16·7	-17·8	-20·0	-20·0	-18·3	-18·3	-15·6	-7·8	-3·3	-13·3
		P								Not available					
CARNARVON (W. Australia) 24° 54′ S. 113° 39′ E.	4·5	T	26·7	26·7	26·7	23·9	20·0	17·2	16·1	17·2	18·9	20·6	22·8	25·0	21·7
		P	10·2	17·8	17·8	15·2	38·1	60·9	40·6	17·8	5·1	2·5	Tr	5·1	231·1
CHARLEVILLE (Queensland) 26° 25′ S. 146° 13′ E.	294	T	28·9	28·3	25·6	21·1	16·7	12·8	12·2	13·9	17·8	22·8	25·6	27·8	21·1
		P	63·5	66·0	58·4	33·0	30·5	33·0	30·5	17·8	20·3	30·5	43·2	60·9	487·7
CHRISTCHURCH (New Zealand) 43° 32′ S. 172° 37′ E.	10	T	16·1	16·1	14·4	11·7	8·9	6·1	5·6	6·7	8·9	11·7	13·3	15·6	11·1
		P	55·9	43·2	48·3	48·3	66·0	66·0	68·6	48·3	45·7	43·2	48·3	55·9	637·5
CLONCURRY (Queensland) 20° 43′ S. 140° 30′ E.	193	T	31·1	29·4	28·9	25·6	22·2	18·3	17·8	20·0	23·3	27·8	29·4	31·1	25·6
		P	111·8	106·7	60·9	17·8	12·7	15·2	7·6	2·5	7·6	12·7	33·0	68·6	457·2
CURRIE (Tasmania) 39° 58′ S. 143° 53′ E.	19·5	T	16·1	16·7	16·7	13·9	12·2	11·1	10·0	10·6	11·1	12·2	13·3	15·0	13·3
		P	38·1	38·1	43·2	60·9	88·9	107·6	114·3	109·2	88·9	68·6	50·8	55·9	858·5

N.B. All temperatures are in ° C. and precipitation is in millimetres.

AUSTRALASIA (including ANTARCTICA AND SOUTH PACIFIC)

STATION	ALTITUDE IN METRES		JAN.	FEB.	MAR.	APR.	MAY	JUN.	JUL.	AUG.	SEP.	OCT.	NOV.	DEC.	MEAN: YEAR
DALY WATERS (N. Australia) 16° 16′ S. 133° 23′ E.	210	T	30·0	29·4	28·3	26·7	23·3	21·1	20·6	22·2	26·7	30·0	31·1	31·1	26·7
		P	165·1	152·4	121·9	22·9	5·1	7·6	2·5	2·5	5·1	20·3	55·9	101·6	662·9
DECEPTION I. (S. Shetlands) 62° 59′ S. 60° 34′ W.	8	T	1·1	1·1	0·0	−2·8	−5·0	−7·8	−8·9	−8·3	−6·1	−2·8	−2·2	0·6	−3·3
		P	58·4	53·3	68·6	50·8	5·1	7·6	15·2	25·4	22·9	109·2	96·5	50·8	563·9
DUNEDIN (New Zealand) 45° 52′ S. 170° 32′ E.	73	T	14·4	14·4	12·8	11·1	8·3	6·7	5·6	6·7	8·9	10·0	11·7	13·3	10·6
		P	86·4	71·1	76·2	71·1	81·3	81·3	78·7	76·2	68·6	76·2	81·3	88·9	937·3
EYRE (W. Australia) 32° 14′ S. 126° 22′ E.	4·6	T	20·6	21·1	20·0	17·8	15·0	12·8	11·7	12·8	13·9	16·1	17·8	19·4	16·7
		P	15·2	12·7	22·9	22·9	40·6	40·6	30·5	33·0	22·9	20·3	17·8	15·2	294·6
FANNING I. (Line Is.) 03° 54′ N. 159° 23′ W.	5·2	T	27·2	27·2	27·8	27·8	27·8	27·8	27·8	28·3	27·8	28·3	28·3	27·8	27·8
		P	274·3	266·7	271·8	358·1	320·0	254·0	208·3	111·8	81·3	91·4	73·7	203·2	2514·6
FUNAFUTI (Ellice Is.) 08° 30′ S. 179° 13′ E.	2·4	T	28·9	28·3	28·3	28·3	28·3	27·8	27·2	27·8	28·3	28·9	29·4	28·9	28·3
		P	406·4	449·6	403·9	279·4	185·4	274·3	259·1	292·1	345·4	358·1	312·4	436·9	4003·0
GABO I. (Victoria) 37° 34′ S. 149° 55′ E.	15	T	18·3	18·9	18·3	16·1	13·9	11·7	11·1	8·9	12·8	13·9	15·6	17·2	15·0
		P	71·1	68·6	73·7	83·8	99·1	106·7	86·4	71·1	76·2	78·7	66·0	60·9	942·3
HOBART (Tasmania) 42° 53′ S. 147° 20′ E.	54	T	16·7	16·7	15·0	12·8	10·6	8·3	7·8	8·9	10·6	12·2	13·9	15·6	12·2
		P	48·3	38·1	45·7	48·3	45·7	55·9	53·3	48·3	53·3	58·4	60·9	53·3	609·6
HOKITIKA (New Zealand) 42° 43′ S. 170° 58′ E.	3·7	T	15·0	15·6	14·4	12·2	10·0	7·2	7·2	7·8	9·4	11·1	12·2	13·9	11·7
		P	261·6	190·5	238·8	236·2	243·8	231·1	218·4	238·8	226·1	292·1	266·7	261·6	2905·8
INVERCARGILL (New Zealand) 46° 26′ S. 168° 21′ E.	3·7	T	13·8	13·8	12·8	10·6	7·2	6·1	5·0	6·7	8·3	10·6	11·1	12·8	10·0
		P	106·7	83·8	101·6	104·1	111·8	91·4	81·3	81·3	81·3	104·1	106·7	101·6	1155·7
JALUIT (Marshall Is.) 05° 55′ N. 169° 38′ E.	6	T	27·2	27·8	28·3	27·8	27·8	27·8	27·8	27·8	27·8	28·3	27·8	27·8	27·8
		P	259·1	215·9	360·7	401·3	421·6	388·6	391·2	304·8	332·7	309·9	302·3	345·4	4033·5
KALGOORLIE (W. Australia) 30° 45′ S. 121° 30′ E.	380	T	25·6	25·6	22·8	18·9	15·0	12·2	11·1	12·2	15·6	18·3	22·2	25·0	18·9
		P	10·2	20·3	22·9	22·9	30·5	30·5	22·9	22·9	12·7	17·8	15·2	17·8	246·4
LITTLE AMERICA (Antarctica) 78° 34′ S. 163° 56′ W.	9	T	−6·7	−16·1	−21·1	−28·9	−31·1	−26·7	−37·8	−36·1	−40·0	−26·1	−18·9	−7·8	−24·4
		P						Not available							
LORD HOWE I. (S. Pacific) 31° 31′ S. 159° 07′ E.	4·6	T	22·2	22·2	21·7	20·0	18·3	16·7	15·6	15·6	16·7	17·8	19·4	21·1	18·9
		P	124·5	106·7	127·0	170·2	157·5	195·6	195·6	134·6	134·6	132·1	114·3	124·5	1717·0
MACMURDO SOUND (Antarctica) 77° 40′ S. 166° 30′ E.	0	T	−5·0	−10·0	−15·6	−22·2	−25·0	−25·0	−26·1	−26·1	−25·6	−20·6	−10·6	−5·0	−17·8
		P						Not available							
MADANG (New Guinea) 05° 14′ S. 145° 45′ E.	6	T	27·2	27·2	27·2	27·2	27·2	27·2	27·2	27·2	27·2	27·2	27·2	27·2	27·2
		P	307·3	302·3	378·5	429·3	383·5	274·3	193·0	121·9	134·6	254·0	337·8	368·3	3484·9

N.B. All temperatures are in ° C and precipitation is in millimetres.

AUSTRALASIA (including ANTARCTICA AND SOUTH PACIFIC)

STATION	ALTITUDE IN METRES		JAN.	FEB.	MAR.	APR.	MAY	JUN.	JUL.	AUG.	SEP.	OCT.	NOV.	DEC.	MEAN: YEAR
MAPOON (Queensland) 12° 04′ S. 141° 55′ E.	6	T	28·9	28·9	28·9	28·3	27·2	25·6	25·0	25·6	27·2	28·3	29·4	29·4	27·8
		P	457·2	391·2	307·3	96·5	17·8	5·1	2·5	Tr	5·1	10·2	60·9	228·6	1582·4
MELBOURNE (Victoria) 37° 49′ S. 144° 58′ E.	35	T	19·4	19·4	18·3	15·0	12·2	10·0	9·4	9·4	12·2	13·9	16·1	17·8	17·2
		P	48·3	45·7	55·9	58·4	53·3	53·3	48·3	48·3	58·4	66·0	58·4	58·4	652·8
MUNDIWINDI (W. Australia) 23° 52′ S. 120° 10′ E.	562	T	27·8	30·0	27·2	23·3	17·8	13·9	12·8	15·6	19·4	22·8	27·8	29·4	22·8
		P	25·4	48·3	50·8	20·3	15·2	22·9	2·5	7·6	7·6	12·7	12·7	30·5	256·5
NAPIER (New Zealand) 39° 29′ S. 176° 55′ E.	1·5	T	18·9	18·3	17·2	14·4	12·2	9·4	8·9	10·0	11·7	13·9	15·6	17·8	13·9
		P	73·7	76·2	73·7	76·2	88·9	86·4	101·6	83·8	55·9	55·9	60·9	58·4	891·5
NEW PLYMOUTH (New Zealand) 39° 04′ S. 174° 05′ E.	18	T	16·7	17·2	16·1	15·0	12·2	10·0	9·4	10·0	11·1	12·8	13·9	16·1	13·3
		P	111·8	104·1	91·4	119·4	152·4	154·9	160·0	142·2	127·0	139·7	121·9	111·8	1536·7
NIUE (Tonga) 19° 02′ S. 169° 55′ W.	20	T	26·7	26·7	26·7	25·6	24·4	23·3	22·8	22·8	23·3	24·4	25·0	25·6	24·4
		P	266·7	261·6	312·4	185·4	132·1	76·2	88·9	114·3	93·9	119·4	147·3	210·8	2009·1
NORFOLK I. (Pacific) 29° 04′ S. 167° 59′ E.	99	T	22·2	22·2	21·7	20·6	18·3	17·2	16·1	15·6	16·7	17·8	19·4	21·1	18·9
		P	83·8	109·2	93·9	127·0	144·8	139·7	154·9	137·2	93·9	93·9	66·0	86·4	1330·5
NOUMEA (New Caledonia) 22° 16′ S. 166° 27′ E.	9	T	26·1	26·1	25·6	24·4	22·2	21·1	20·6	20·0	21·1	22·2	23·9	25·6	23·3
		P	93·9	129·5	144·8	132·1	111·8	93·9	91·4	66·0	63·5	50·8	60·9	66·0	1104·9
OCEAN I. (Gilbert Is.) 00° 52′ S. 169° 35′ E.	40	T	27·8	27·8	27·8	27·8	27·8	27·8	27·8	27·8	28·3	28·3	28·3	27·8	27·8
		P	309·9	223·5	193·0	149·9	111·8	109·2	147·3	106·7	93·9	99·1	142·2	205·7	1892·3
PALAU (Caroline Is.) 07° 19′ N. 134° 28′ E.	32	T	26·7	26·7	27·2	27·2	27·2	27·2	26·7	26·7	27·2	27·2	27·2	26·7	27·2
		P	388·6	238·8	172·7	193·0	393·7	314·9	505·5	355·6	398·8	375·9	299·7	322·6	3959·9
PAPEETE (Tahiti) 17° 32′ S. 149° 34′ W.	92	T	26·7	26·7	26·7	26·7	25·6	25·0	25·0	25·0	25·0	25·6	25·6	26·7	26·1
		P	251·5	243·8	429·3	142·2	101·6	76·2	53·3	43·2	53·3	88·9	149·9	248·9	1628·1
PERTH (W. Australia) 31° 57′ S. 115° 51′ E.	60	T	23·3	23·3	21·7	18·9	16·1	13·9	12·8	13·3	14·4	16·1	18·9	21·7	17·8
		P	7·6	10·2	20·3	43·2	129·5	180·3	170·2	144·8	86·4	55·9	20·3	12·7	881·4
PITCAIRN I. (Pacific) 25° 04′ S. 130° 04′ W.	73	T	24·4	25·6	25·0	23·3	22·2	23·9	20·0	20·0	20·0	21·1	22·2	23·9	22·2
		P	91·4	114·3	83·8	208·3	177·8	129·5	271·8	185·4	68·6	106·7	68·6	193·0	1699·3
PONAPE (Caroline Is.) 07° 00′ N. 158° 14′ E.	39	T	26·7	26·7	26·7	26·7	26·7	26·1	26·1	26·1	26·1	26·1	26·1	26·1	26·1
		P	312·4	231·1	330·2	441·9	523·2	454·7	426·7	396·2	408·9	408·9	403·9	520·7	4859·0
PORT DARWIN (N. Australia) 12° 28′ S. 130° 51′ E.	30	T	28·3	28·3	28·9	28·9	27·8	25·6	25·0	26·1	27·8	29·4	30·0	29·4	27·8
		P	386·1	312·4	254·0	96·5	15·2	2·5	Tr	2·5	12·7	50·8	119·4	238·8	1490·9
PORT MORESBY (New Guinea) 09° 29′ S. 147° 09′ E.	38	T	27·8	27·2	27·8	27·2	26·7	26·1	25·6	25·0	26·1	26·7	27·8	28·3	26·7
		P	177·8	193·0	170·2	106·7	63·5	33·0	27·9	17·8	25·4	35·6	48·3	111·8	1010·9

N.B. All temperatures are in ° C and precipitation is in millimetres.

AUSTRALASIA (including ANTARCTICA AND SOUTH PACIFIC)

STATION	ALTITUDE IN METRES		JAN.	FEB.	MAR.	APR.	MAY	JUN.	JUL.	AUG.	SEP.	OCT.	NOV.	DEC.	MEAN: YEAR
PUKAPUKA (Danger Is.) 10° 53′ S. 165° 54′ W.	2	T	27·8	27·8	27·8	28·3	28·3	27·8	27·2	27·8	27·8	27·8	27·8	27·8	27·8
		P	347·9	408·9	256·5	210·8	205·7	160·0	154·9	157·5	144·8	223·5	322·6	391·2	2984·5
RABAUL (New Britain) 04° 13′ S. 152° 15′ E.	12·5	T	27·2	27·2	27·2	27·2	27·2	27·2	27·2	26·7	27·8	27·8	27·8	27·2	27·2
		P	375·9	264·2	259·1	254·0	132·1	83·8	137·2	93·9	88·9	129·5	180·3	256·5	2280·9
RAOUL (Kermadec Is.) 29° 15′ S. 177° 55′ W.	38	T	21·1	22·2	21·7	20·0	18·3	16·1	15·6	15·6	16·1	17·2	18·3	20·6	18·3
		P	111·8	114·3	101·6	114·3	175·3	154·9	152·4	154·9	111·8	93·9	50·8	116·8	1452·9
ROCKHAMPTON (Queensland) 23° 24′ S. 150° 30′ E.	11	T	26·7	26·7	25·6	23·3	20·0	17·2	16·1	18·3	21·1	23·9	25·6	26·7	22·8
		P	190·5	193·0	111·8	66·0	40·6	66·0	45·7	20·3	33·0	45·7	60·9	119·4	993·1
ROTORUA (New Zealand) 38° 10′ S. 176° 16′ E.	298	T	17·8	17·2	16·1	13·3	10·6	8·3	7·2	8·3	10·0	12·2	13·9	16·1	12·8
		P	111·8	104·1	88·9	116·8	139·7	134·6	124·5	127·0	121·9	124·5	109·2	93·9	1397·0
SUVA (Fiji Is.) 18° 08′ S. 178° 26′ E.	6	T	26·7	26·7	26·7	25·6	24·4	23·3	22·8	22·8	23·3	23·9	25·0	26·1	25·0
		P	289·6	271·8	368·3	309·9	256·5	170·2	124·5	210·8	195·6	210·8	248·9	317·5	2974·3
SYDNEY (New South Wales) 33° 52′ S. 151° 12′ E.	42	T	21·7	21·7	20·6	17·8	15·0	12·2	11·7	12·8	15·0	17·2	19·4	21·1	17·2
		P	88·9	101·6	127·0	134·6	127·0	116·8	116·8	76·2	73·7	71·1	73·7	73·7	1181·1
TARCOOLA (S. Australia) 30° 42′ S. 134° 33′ E.	120	T	25·6	25·6	23·3	18·3	14·4	11·1	10·6	12·2	15·6	18·9	22·2	24·4	18·3
		P	10·2	17·8	12·7	7·6	12·7	17·8	12·7	17·8	12·7	17·8	12·7	12·7	167·6
TONGAREVA (Cook Is.) 09° 01′ S. 158° 03′ W.	1·5	T	27·8	27·8	28·3	28·9	28·3	28·3	27·8	27·8	27·8	28·3	28·3	27·8	28·3
		P	325·1	266·7	210·8	162·6	121·9	129·5	175·3	203·2	83·8	193·0	193·0	231·1	2296·2
VILA (New Hebrides) 17° 44′ S. 168° 19′ E.	57	T	26·7	27·2	26·7	25·6	24·4	23·3	22·2	22·2	23·3	24·4	25·0	26·7	25·0
		P	259·1	284·5	297·2	243·8	142·2	124·5	96·5	88·9	96·5	121·9	167·6	180·3	2103·1
WELLINGTON (New Zealand) 41° 16′ S. 174° 46′ E.	126	T	16·7	16·7	15·6	13·9	11·1	10·0	8·3	8·9	10·6	12·2	13·3	15·6	12·8
		P	81·3	81·3	81·3	96·5	116·8	116·8	137·2	116·8	96·5	101·6	88·9	88·9	1203·9
WYNDHAM (W. Australia) 15° 27′ S. 128° 07′ E.	7	T	31·1	31·1	30·6	30·0	27·2	25·0	23·9	26·1	28·9	31·1	31·7	31·7	28·9
		P	185·4	152·4	116·8	20·3	5·1	5·1	5·1	Tr	2·5	10·2	50·8	104·1	657·9

N.B. All temperatures are in ° C and precipitation is in millimetres.

BIBLIOGRAPHY

AUSTIN MILLER, A.:   *Climatology* (Methuen, 1962)
BARRY, R. G. and   *Atmosphere, Weather and Climate* (Methuen 1976)
   CHORLEY, R.J.:
BERRY, F. A., BOLLAY, E.,   *Handbook of Meteorology* (McGraw-Hill, 1945)
   and BEERS, N. R.:
BILHAM, E. G.:   *The Climate of the British Isles* (London, 1938)
——:   *'Here is the Weather Forecast'* (Galley Press, 1947)
BRUNT, SIR D.:   *Physical and Dynamical Meteorology* (Cambridge, 1939)
——:   *Weather Study* (Nelson, 1954)
BYERS, H. R.:   *General Meteorology* (McGraw-Hill, 1959)
CHALMERS, J. A.:   *Atmospheric Electricity* (Pergamon, 1968)
CRITCHFIELD, H. J.:   *General Climatology* (Prentice-Hall, 1960)
GARBELL, M. A.:   *Tropical and Equatorial Meteorology* (Pitman, 1947)
GEORGE, J. J.:   *Weather Forecasting for Aeronautics* (Academic Press, 1960)
GOODY, R. M.:   *The Physics of the Stratosphere* (Cambridge, 1954)
HARE, F. K.:   *The Restless Atmosphere* (Hutchinson, 1966)
HAURWITZ, B.:   *Dynamic Meteorology* (McGraw-Hill, 1941)
HEWSON, E. W., and   *Meteorology, Theoretical and Applied* (Wiley; Chapman and Hall, 1944)
   LONGLEY, R. W.:
HUMPHREYS, W. J.:   *Physics of the Air* (McGraw-Hill, 1940)
KENDREW, W. G.:   *Climatology* (Oxford, 1957)
——:   *The Climates of the Continents* (Oxford, 1953)
LESTER, R. M.:   *Observer's Book of Weather* (Warne, 1955)
LUDLAM, F. H., and   *Further Outlook* (Wingate, 1954)
   SCORER, R. S.:
——:   *Cloud Study* (Murray, 1957)
MANLEY, G.:   *Climate and the British Scene* (Collins, 1955)
MASON, B. J.:   *The Physics of Clouds* (Oxford, 1957)
MEETHAM, A. R.:   *Atmospheric Pollution* (Pergamon Press, 1963)
NIEUWOLT, S.:   *Tropical Climatology* (John Wiley 1977)
PACK, S. W. C.:   *Weather Forecasting* (Longmans, 1948)
PERRIE, D. W.:   *Cloud Physics* (Toronto Press; Oxford, 1950)
PETTERSSEN, S.:   *Weather Analysis and Forecasting* (McGraw-Hill, 1956)
SAWYER, J. S.:   *The Ways of the Weather* (Black, 1957)
SHAW, SIR N.:   *Manual of Meteorology* (Cambridge, 1930)
——:   *Forecasting Weather* (London, 1940)
SUTTON, O. G.:   *Understanding Weather* (Penguin, 1960)
TANNEHILL, I. R.:   *Hurricanes* (Princeton Press; Oxford, 1952)
TAYLOR, J. A., and   *British Weather in Maps* (Macmillan, 1968)
   YATES, R. A.:
TREWARTHA, G. T.:   *An Introduction to Climate* (McGraw-Hill, 1968)
WATTS, I. E. M.:   *Equatorial Weather* (London, 1955)
H.M.S.O. PUBLICATIONS: *Elementary Meteorology for Aircrew* A.P. 3307
   Handbook of Aviation Meteorology M.O. 818 (1971)
   Handbook of Meteorological Instruments M.O. 577 (1956)
   Memorandum on the Intertropical Front (1952)
   Meteorology for Aviators M.O. 432 or A.P. 1699 (1969)
   Meteorological Glossary M.O. 842 (1971)
   Observer's Handbook M.O. 554 (1952)
   Tables of Temperature, Relative Humidity and Precipitation for the World M.O. 617 (1965–71)
   The Weather Map M.O. 595 (1956)
ROYAL METEOROLOGICAL   *Weather:* monthly periodical
   SOCIETY: *Journal:* quarterly periodical
UNITED STATES DEPART-
   MENT OF AGRICULTURE: *Climate and Man* (1941)

Most of the questions listed at the end of the book are based upon examples set by the Oxford and Cambridge Joint Board in their Geography Papers for the General Certificate of Education Examination.

INDEX

Absolute humidity, 68, 169

Adiabatic change, 169; cooling, 76, 79–81; lapse rates, 41

Advection, 169

Agriculture and climate, 235

Air masses, 108–122, 166, 169; Arctic, 109; Polar, 109–111, 166; tropical, 111–113, 166

Albedo, 36, 169, 220

Altimeter, 32

Altocumulus, 89

Altostratus, 89

Anemometer, 22, 169

Anticyclone, 33, 169

Astrakhan, 210

Atmosphere: circulation, 176; constituents, 26; pressure distribution, 31, 32, 53–59; temperature, 34–50

ATS satellites, 153

Backing, 169

Bar, 18, 169

Barometer, 17, 169; aneroid, 18; mercury, 17

Bathurst, 202

Beaufort wind scale, 22, 169

Bombay, 204

Boston (Mass.), 217

Buys–Ballot's Law, 54, 169

Campbell–Stokes sunshine recorder, 24

Campos, 201

Castellatus, 90

Chernozem, 227, 233, 234

Chinook, 85

Cirrocumulus, 89

Cirrostratus, 89

Cirrus, 89

Clean Air Bill (1956), 94

Climates: cold forest, 193; cold temperate, 194, 215; continental, 194, 218; cool east-coast, 194, 216; dry, 193, 194, 207–211; equatorial, 194, 196; Köppen's classification of, 191–193; Laurentian, 216; marine West European, 193, 213; mountain, 194, 223; Polar, 193, 194, 220; Savanna, 193, 199; temperate, 212–219; temperate-mountain, 225; tropical-mountain, 225; tropical rainy, 191, 196, 199; warm east-coast, 194, 205; warm-temperature rainy, 193; world, 191, 194

Climatic change, 241–250

Climatic fluctuations in Britain, 250

Climatology, 176

Cloud: amounts and heights, 89, 90; classification, 86; convection, 75, 85; formation, 74–85, 169; fracto, 90; frontal, 76, 85; lenticular, 90; orographic, 75, 84; turbulence, 74, 83; types, 89–90, 165

Codes for weather maps, 137

Col, 34, 35, 169

Cold sector, 116

Commerce and climate, 238

Communications and climate, 239

Compass points, 22

Condensation, 70; trails, 134

Conduction, 38, 169

Congo, the, 199

Coniferous forest, 228

Contour charts, 131

Convection, 38, 169

Cumulonimbus, 90

Cumulus, 90

Cyclone, 33, 114, 116, 123, 169

Darwin (Australia), 202

Dawson (Yukon), 217

Deciduous forest, 228

Depression, 33, 115, 116

Dew point, 68, 170

Disease and climate, 237

Doldrums, 177, 183, 184, 201

Douala, 198

Dry adiabatic lapse rate (D.A.L.R.), 41, 76

Dyne, 18

East Indies, 199

Eccentricity of the earth's orbit, 244

Edmonton (Alberta), 218

Environmental lapse rate (E.L.R.), 40, 41, 77–79

Epiphytes, 228

ESSA satellites, 153

Ferrel's Law, 54

Fog, 72; advection, 92–94, 168; mixing, 94; movement, 92, 93; radiation, 91, 92, 168; sea, 93, 168; steaming, 94; thaw, 93

Frontology, 114

Fronts, 108, 109, 112, 167; cold, 108, 117, 119, 121, 167, 169; intertropical, 112, 113, 122, 124, 170; Polar, 112, 114, 170, 178; warm, 108, 117, 118, 121, 167, 171

Frost-free days, 182

Garua, 210

Gases, general law of, 30
Geochronology, 241, 246
Geological Time Scale and climate, 242
Geostrophic force, 54
Glazed frost, 105
Gradient, 170
GOES satellites, 160

HAIL, 106
Haloes, 104
Heterosphere, 28
High-pressure area, 33
Hoar frost, 105
Homosphere, 28
Horse latitudes, 177, 183, 184
Housing and climate, 239
Humidity, 68
Hurricane, 124
Hygrometer, 21, 170
Hygrophytes, 227
Hygroscopic nuclei, 72

ICE IN THE ATMOSPHERE, 105–107
In Salah, 209
Insolation, 36, 170, 221
Instability, 41, 42, 77, 82, 170
International Standard Atmosphere, 31
Isobar, 33, 170
Isohyet, 170
Isotherm, 43, 170
ITOS satellites, 155

JET STREAMS, 66, 131–134

KÖPPEN W., 191, 192

LAND BREEZES, 60, 61
Lapse rate, 170
Lightning, 97
Llanos, 201
Low-pressure area, 33, 34

McMURDO SOUND, 222
Mallee, 229
Man and climate, 235, 248
Manaus, 198
Maquis, 229
Measurement of: atmospheric pressure, 16; humidity, 21; rainfall, 23; sunshine, 23; temperature, 19; wind velocity, 21
Mediterranean: climate, 194, 212; rainfall, 187, 213; vegetation, 229
Microclimatology, 195
Millibar, 18, 170

Mirage, 102
Monsoon, 63, 194, 196, 201

NASA, 146
NEW ORLEANS, 205
Nimbostratus, 90
NIMBUS satellites, 149
North-east monsoon, 203
North-west Europe, 213

OBLIQUITY OF THE ECLIPTIC, 244
Observation stations, 137
Occlusion, 120, 121, 170
Ocean currents, 187–190
Optical effects, 102–104
Orographic rain, 170

PALAEOCLIMATOLOGY, 241
Pedalfer, 233
Pedocal, 233
Peru, 188
Pleistocene Ice Age, 246
Podsol, 233, 234
Points of the compass, 22
Pontianak (Java), 200
Port Nolloth, 209
Prairies, 229
Precession of the equinox, 245
Precipitation, 23, 70
Pressure gradient, 53, 170
Psychrometer, 21

RADIATION, 38, 170; solar, 36
Radio-sonde, 170
Rain gauge, 23
Rainbows, 102
Rainfall: continental, 187; east-coast, 187; equatorial, 187; Polar, 187; regimes, 187; Savanna, 187; tropical desert, 187; West European, 187, 213
Relative humidity, 69, 170
Ridge, 35, 170
Rime, 107
Rome, 214

SAIGON, 200
Saprophytes, 228
Satellites, 146
Saturated adiabatic lapse rate (S.A.L.R.), 42
Saturation water vapour content, 68
Sea breezes, 60, 61
Secondary depression, 34, 122, 170
Selvas, 199
Sleet, 106
Smog, 72, 95, 167
Snow, 23, 106
Soils, 227, 231; world distribution, 234
Solar constant, 220

Solar wind, 30
South-west monsoon, 203
Specific heat, 39
Spitsbergen, 222
Stability, 41, 42, 77, 82, 170
Station model, 143
Steppes, 229
Stratocumulus, 90
Stratosphere, 28, 170
Stratus, 90
Structure of a hurricane, 129
Sudan, 201
Synoptic chart, 137, 138, 170

Taïga, 215
Temperature: anomalies, 52, 169; conversion, 20; diurnal variation, 39; horizontal distribution, 43; inversion, 43, 170; observations, 20; scales, 20; vertical distribution, 40; world distribution, 44–47
Tephigram, 81, 83, 171
Thermal anomaly, 52
Thermal equator, 178
Thermometers: maximum, 19; minimum, 20; wet-and-dry, 21
Thunderstorms, 96–102
TIROS satellites, 147
Tokyo, 204
Tropical revolving storms, 123
Tropopause, 28, 130, 170
Tropophilous plants, 227
Troposphere, 28, 171
Trough, 33, 171
Tundra, 223, 230
Turbulence, 60, 74, 83, 171
Typhoon, 124

Units of pressure, 18

Unstable air, 41, 42, 82
Upper atmosphere, 130–135

Vancouver, 214
Varves, 246
Veering, 171
Vegetation: Alpine, 230; and climate, 226; desert, 229; forest, 228, 232; grassland, 229, 232
Veld, 201

Wadi Halfa, 208
Warm sector, 114, 116
Water droplets, 72
Water vapour, 68
Weather: codes and symbols, 137, 140, 142, 143, 172; definition of, 15; elements of, 16; forecasting, 136–145; plotting information on, 142
Weather satellites, 146
Weather satellites and Forecasting, 163
Wedge, 35
Willy-willy, 124
Wind: definition, 21; diurnal variations, 60
Winds: anabatic, 62, 63, 169; Föhn, 63, 84, 85, 170; isobaric, 65; katabatic, 62, 63, 169; thermal, 65; upper, 23, 64, 131; world distribution of, 56–59, 177
World distribution of: climates, 194; frost-free days, 182; precipitation, 184, 186; pressure and winds, 56–59, 177, 183; temperature, 44–47, 181; temperature anomalies, 48–51
World Meteorological Organization, 159
World Weather Watch, 159

Xerophytes, 227